GWR DOCKS & MA

THE BIGGEST DOCK OWNER IN THE WORLD

Tony Atkins

Noodle *N.B.* Books

© Tony Atkins & Noodle Books (Kevin Robertson) 2014

ISBN 978-1-909328-20-4

First published in 2014 by Kevin Robertson under the Noodle Books imprint

NOODLE BOOKS, PO Box 279, Corhampton, SOUTHAMPTON. SO32 3ZX

www.noodlebooks.co.uk

Printed in England by Berforts Information Press.

DEDICATION

To Thomas Pill (1882-1938) Engineer of the tugboat *The Earl(II)*, GWR tug at Cardiff Docks.

Front cover - *Flowers from the Scilly isles being unloaded from the 2.00pm ferry boat SS Lyonesse on to a GW one-horse lorry to be taken to Penzance station in the spring of 1899. [F E Gibson]*

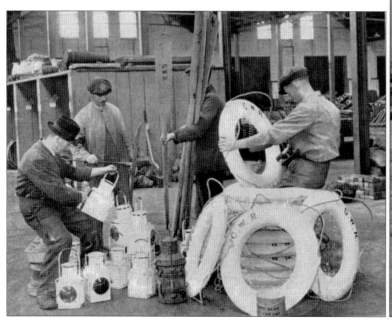

CONTENTS

Preface   4

Introduction   5
   Docks Owned or served by the GWR   5
   Roads, River Navigations/Canals and   7
   Habours/Docks before the Railways
   The Arrival of Railways   8
   Railways and Coastal Shipping   10
   Fishing Ports   12
   Earnings at Ports   13
   Cargoes at the docks   14
   Engineering at the docks   19
   Tides, Pilots and Dredging   20
   Locks and Lock Gates, Divers   22
   Ship Repairs   23
   Power for Quayside Equipment   24
   Cranes   26
   Coal Tips and Hoists   28
   Anti-Breakage Devices   34
   Coal Conveyors   38
   Coal Blending & 'Patent Fuel Briquettes' 40
   Shunting in Docks   41
   GW Ports in Wartime   41
   GW Vessels   43

The Docks: Brentford to Manchester   47
   Brentford   47
   Chelsea Basin   52
   London   53
   Southampton   58
   Weymouth & The Channel Islands   62
   Portland Dockyard   74
   Exeter City (Canal) Basin   75
   Teignmouth   77
   Kingswear / Dartmouth   78
   Totnes Quay   80
   Plymouth Millbay Dock /
         Sutton Harbour   81
   Devonport Dockyard   91
   Looe   92

Fowey   93
Par   99
Truro Newham Quay   101
Falmouth   101
Penzance and Newlyn   103
Lelant Quay (St Ives branch)   106
Hayle   107
Portreath   110
Newquay   111
Watchet   111
Bridgwater and Dunball Wharf   112
Bristol City Docks   118
Portishead and Avonmouth   123
Sharpness and Gloucester   129
The Forest of Dean:
     Bullo Pill and Lydney   134
Chepstow   137
Newport   139
Cardiff   143
Penarth   158
Barry   165
Pothcawl   172
Port Talbot and Aberavon   172
Briton Ferry   173
Swansea   175
Llanelly, Burry Port, Kidwelly,
Pembrey and Carmarthen   181
Pembroke Dock   186
New Milford (Neyland)   187
Milford Haven   192
Fishguard   195
Aberdovey   207
Saltney   208
Birkenhead / Liverpool   209
Ellesmere Port   221
Warrington   222
Manchester (Ship Canal Docks)   222

Bibliography   223

Title page - *No 1370 on Weymouth Quay, 19 August 1955. [G F Bannister]*

Rear cover - *Victoria harbour, St Helier, Jersey.[STEAM Swindon]*

Opposite page - *Marine equipment in the GWR stores at Barry. [GWR Magazine]*

PREFACE

Why were ports, which the Great Western came to own or to serve, there in the first place? What was the staple traffic, and did it change after the railway was connected? Did some ports run down, or were new ports built, as a consequence of the railway arriving in an area? What effect had railways on coastal shipping? These questions have been investigated not only for the comparatively few docks owned, developed and operated by the GWR before the Grouping, but also for the South Wales coal shipping docks that were already 'fully mature' when the Great Western absorbed them, after which the GW became the largest dock owner in the world.

Many of the Great Western docks had common equipment, activities and similar ways of operating. To avoid repetition, these features are described separately in an Introduction where opportunity has also been taken to explain various dock/nautical/shipping terms that recur through the book.

It is impossible to discuss the activities of some ports without reference to the GW vessels that sailed from them, so details will be found of the GWR fleet and its history.

Anglicised spelling of Welsh name places, rivers and so on (e.g. Llanelly rather than Llanelli, Aberdovey rather than Aberdyfi) is used throughout, since it was in use for most of the period covered by this volume; similarly, the old names of the Welsh counties have been used.

Thanks are due to those knowledgeable in railway matters who have generously supplied information. The comprehensive coverage of GW docks could not have been achieved without the generosity of David Hyde who made his collection of documents and photographs available for my use. The late Mr and Mrs Leslie King gave me numerous GW documents. Tremendous thanks must also go to the many 'local studies' librarians around those parts of the country served by the GWR, too numerous to mention individually, who have looked things up and advised on sources and references to dock material. David Jenkins, Mark Etheridge and their colleagues at Amgueddfa Cymru/ National Museum Wales, and staff of the National Maritime Museum have been of great help over GW ships. Elaine Arthurs, Chris Turner and volunteers at *Steam* in Swindon have likewise been very helpful. Track layouts at docks have been kindly clarified by Tony Cooke. Gordon Nash has been very informative about GW timber importation through Poplar docks; John Dixon and Geoff Pickard about Saltney; Geoff Body and Roy Gallop about Bridgwater/ Dunball; Mike Barnsley on Southampton; and Gerry Nichols on Bristol (Gerry is also thanked for details of the SLS photographic collection). The bibliography lists the many books that have been consulted.

Needless to say, any errors in the book are down to me. I should be glad to be corrected.

Tony Atkins

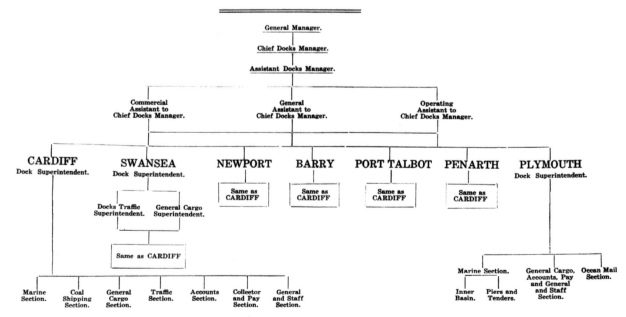

ORGANISATION OF DOCKS DEPARTMENT

INTRODUCTION
Docks Owned or Served by the GWR

Before the Grouping, the GWR's dock interests were relatively small, but when the coal-exporting docks in South Wales (the Bute Docks in Cardiff; Penarth Docks; Barry Docks; Newport Docks; Port Talbot Docks; and the dock at Burry Port) came into the GW in 1922, the Great Western became the largest dock owner in the world, even before the Swansea Harbour Trust was taken over in 1923. At that time, dock properties represented about £18 million of capital, or about 12% of the whole GWR undertaking, and after the railway proper, the docks formed the major part of the enlarged company's property. Out of a total of 50 million tons of goods dealt with annually by the railway between the two world wars, no less than 40 million tons passed through its docks, i.e. four out of every five tons handled.

In addition to owning docks, the GWR served many others - both before and after the Grouping - which were owned and operated by independent organisations. 'Serving' meant different things at different locations. On the one hand, it could mean rail connexion to an extensive dock railway system (Bristol/Avonmouth/Portishead, Birkenhead, the Port of London), and on the other it could indicate merely joining up with one or two tracks along the quayside at a small harbour (as at Newquay and Watchet). Perversely, it could also refer to any town on the GW where there was a commercial harbour, even though no quays were connected with the railway, and where the nearest tracks might be some distance away from the water (as at Torquay). Even so, in one or two such places where there were large fishing fleets, the harbour might provide regular traffic for the railway (as at Brixham).

At the bigger independent docks, the Great Western leased its own offices, depots and warehouses, and shipping appliances right through to nationalisation. Even in broad gauge days the South Wales Rly operated its own coal hoists within the independent Bute East Dock at Cardiff and rented two other coal tips at the basin, reached by a branch from its mainline at Long Dyke Jct. In those days a great deal of coal was shipped from these tips to the GW coking plant at Bristol; (the invention of the firebox brick arch in the 1860s by which 'locos could consume their own smoke' made it possible thereafter to use coal instead of coke on locos).

Before the Grouping of 1922, the company owned only one major dock, namely Plymouth Millbay (44 acres of water), building of which commenced in 1846 jointly by the South Devon, Bristol & Exeter and Great Western Railways; it came to the GW in 1878. The large jetty at New Milford (Neyland), dating from 1856, came into the GW on the absorption of the South Wales Railway in 1863, and was the port for services to Ireland until 1906. In acquiring the SWR, the GW then also took over - or soon afterwards -

25

General Conditions of Service of Grades not included in Conciliation Boards—*continued.*

98.—SUPERNUMERARIES AND CASUAL LABOURERS.

These men are to be paid for the time actually worked at hourly rates on a basis not lower than the minimum rates of wages and hours of duty of permanent men working in similar positions.

Rates of wages.

99.—RATES OF PAYMENT, ETC., OF CASUALS AT G.W. PORTS.

FISHGUARD - 4/3 per day.
WEYMOUTH - 5½d. per hour.
JERSEY - 6d. per hour during Potato and Fruit Season.
5d. per hour during Winter Season.

GUERNSEY.

GRADE.	Rate of Wages per man per day.			
	One inwards or outwards boat.	Two boats.	Three boats.	Four boats.
Boatmen Checkers Gangers	2/6	3/6	4/6	5/-
Regular Dockers and Holders	2/-	3/-	4/-	4/9
Other Dockers	1/9	2/6	3/6	—
Casuals	1/- to 1/6	—	—	—

NOTE—
6d. extra when working beyond noon.
6d. „ „ „ „ 6.0 p.m.
6d. „ „ „ „ 9.0 „

FOWEY.
3½d. per ton, with the following minima for a full week's work :
"Old Pair" men . . . 50/-
Capstanmen 21/-
Ordinary Top Labourers . . 21/-
Jetty Gangers and Silo Workers.. . 23/6
Trimmers 28/-
Leading Trimmers 30/-
Head Trimmers 31/-
The labourers at Fowey are in the employ of a Contractor, Mr. Harris, who is paid 75/- per week, out of which he has to provide planks and bars for the stowing of casks, also lamps and wicks.

Hours of duty at Fowey.

HOURS OF DUTY.
Day Work :—
7.0 a.m. to 5.30 p.m. . 10½ overall. } Monday
Breakfast, 8.0 to 8.30 .. } 1½ } to
Dinner, 12.0 to 1. 0 .. } } Saturday.
9 net, or 54 hours per week.
Night Work :—
6.0 p.m. to 6.0 a.m. .. .. 12 overall. } Monday
2 meals, 10.0 to 11.0 .. } 2 } to
and 2.0 to 3.0 .. } } Friday.
10 net.
6.0 p.m. to 10.0 p.m. = 4 net Saturday = 54 hours per week.

ports belonging to mineral lines worked in conjunction with the SWR, such as Briton Ferry Docks (1873), Llanelly (1873), and Porthcawl (1884). Fishguard Harbour, and Rosslare Harbour in Ireland, both opened in 1906, were the joint property of the GWR and the Great Southern & Western Railway of Ireland. The GWR also jointly owned the small dock at Lydney (Severn & Wye Jt Rly) and rented the harbour at Chelsea Basin (West London Railway). Furthermore, the GW owned wharves on canals and rivers, such as Bear Wharf on the Kennet & Avon Canal at Reading Central Goods (Coley Bridge), and another on the Dart at Kingswear. A branch to serve the privately-owned Totnes Quay was opened in 1873.

Smaller docks or wharves which the Great Western owned before the Grouping included Saltney (1854, ex-

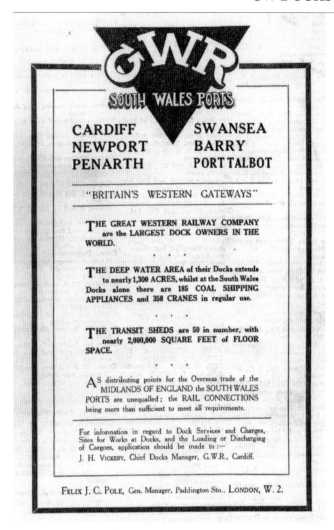

quays. In a single year, the combined docks typically dealt with over 38 million tons of coal (the GW operated a total of 190 coal shipping hoists) and 12 million tons of other traffic.

In all, the Great Western owned around twenty docks and harbours after the Grouping, and additionally served forty or so, including:

Owned by the GWR (rail-connected)

Aberdovey, Barry, Brentford, Bridgwater/Dunball Wharf, Briton Ferry, Bullo Pill, Burry Port, Cardiff, Fowey, Llanelly, Lydney, Newport, Newquay (Cornwall), Neyland (New Milford), Penarth, Plymouth, Port Talbot, Saltney, Swansea, and Truro (Newham Quay).

Served by the GWR (rail-connected)

Avonmouth, Birkenhead, Bristol, Chelsea Basin, Chepstow, Dartmouth, Ellesmere Port, Exeter City Basin, Falmouth, Gloucester, Hayle, Kidwelly, Lelant Quay (off the St. Ives branch), Liverpool, Looe, Manchester Ship Canal Docks, Milford Haven, Neath, Par, Pembroke Dock, Penzance, Porthcawl, Portishead, Port of London (Poplar, Victoria & Albert, etc), Portreath (near Redruth), Sharpness, Southampton, Teignmouth, Totnes Quay, Warrington, Watchet, Weymouth.

Served by the GWR (but not rail-connected)

Aberayron, Aberystwyth (there was a line to the quay in Victorian times and a short-lived Vale of Rheidol line in 1902), Barnstaple (GW broad gauge goods trains ran to Bideford until 1877), Bridport, Brixham, Cardigan, Kingsbridge, Minehead, Portmadoc, Pwllheli, St. Ives, Tenby, Torquay. These ports not connected by rail are not covered in any detail in this book.

When the GWR's dock interests were relatively small, they were administered by the Chief Marine & Dock Superintendent, who resided at Paddington. At the end of the C19[th] Mr J Dunster occupied that post, assisted by Capt Hemmings at Weymouth and Capt Sharp at New Milford. The headquarters of the GW Marine Department, and where the ships were at first registered, was at New Milford (Neyland), then Fishguard up to the Grouping. Following the Grouping, it was decided to form an entirely new Docks Department housed in the former Bute Docks (Cardiff Railway) headquarters building of 1896 at the Pier Head in Cardiff. The first Chief Docks Manager was J. H. Vickery, who had been General Manager of the Alexandra Docks Co. at Newport at the Grouping. Sir Henry Mather Jackson, who had been Chairman of the ADR, became a Great Western director, and was appointed chairman of the GWR Board's Docks and Steamships Committee. E. Lowther, former General Manager of the Port Talbot Railway, became GWR Chief Goods Manager at the Grouping, and later Chief Docks Manager, followed by C S Page and W J Thomas and finally L E Ford into nationalisation. The Marine Department remained separate until 1927 when it, too, was brought under the Chief Docks Manager's control. When a Federation of Port Employers in South Wales was

Shrewsbury & Chester Railway) and Brentford (dating from 1859, and owned by the independent Great Western & Brentford Railway until 1872, when taken over). Bridgwater (canal) docks passed to the GWR by amalgamation with the B & E in 1876. Newquay Harbour came into the Great Western fold by the absorption of the Cornwall Minerals Rly in 1896, the same year that Fowey Harbour became GWR property.

Prior to the Grouping, the Great Western had also, in effect, acquired the Port Talbot Railway and the Rhondda & Swansea Bay Railway, both in 1906 to prevent the Barry Rly from spreading westwards. The GW took over working of the PTR (but *not* the Port Talbot docks) in 1908, at which time the trade of the port was some half-a-million tons. The bankrupt South Wales Mineral Rly also came under the control of the PTR and hence GWR.

At the Grouping, the small harbour at Aberdovey, dating originally from the 1860s, was brought into GWR ownership through the Cambrian Railways. But it was the amalgamations with the coal-carrying lines in South Wales in 1922 that put the GWR in the league of big dock owners. The enlarged Great Western dock system comprised a number of large and small ports that had collectively a deep water area of about 1,300 acres and over 33 miles length of constituted in 1923 to coordinate terms and conditions of dock labour, the Great Western's Chief Docks Manager was appointed its first chairman.

A book entitled *The Docks of the GWR* published in 1924 described the South Wales ports and thirteen other ports, harbours or docks that the Great Western owned, or was closely connected with. The author was H. N. Appleby, who had written a similar book for the Swansea Harbour Trust just before the Grouping. The book, of which there were subsequent editions up to the Second World War, contained dimensions of all locks, docks, dry docks, craneage, transit sheds, and cold storage facilities etc at the various ports. The various editions of *GWR Docks* (and other pamphlets and brochures such as *Trade, Travel and the Great Western Railway* of 1923; *New Works & Facilities at the South Wales Ports & Plymouth* of 1928; and *Dock Sites for Works* of 1927), acquainted shippers and traders of the facilities offered by the enlarged railway, and kept the information up to date. The shorter distance between the South Wales ports and the Midlands when compared with all other ports around the country was driven home in these publications, reflecting the need to find alternative traffic as the coal trade declined. (A distance of about 120 miles was an economic radius for the distribution of goods through a port: in the 1930's, there was a population of 4 millions within 50 miles radius of the South Wales docks, 10 million in 100 miles and 30 million in 150 miles). Plymouth served a similar distributive role for the West of England. To encourage flagging business, dock dues in all South Wales ports were reduced after 1929. Even so, imports (at least in tonnage terms) remained fairly constant at 5 million tons collectively for all the South Wales ports up to the beginning of World War II. In WWII, however, GW docks proved their mettle as general cargo ports.

Roads, River Navigations/Canals and Harbours/Docks before the Railways

The main towns in Britain were connected by surfaced roads, following the Turnpike Act of 1663, but roads elsewhere remained quagmires, impassable for wheeled traffic except in fine weather. In bad weather, few people or goods moved at all, and only then on foot or on horse, with pack-horses, rather than road waggons, being employed for the transport of goods.

In this environment, 'navigations' (rivers that were navigable by boats) and later canals, were important. Not only did they provide a route for goods between inland towns, but at their mouths they connected with coastal and overseas shipping. Compared with the same rivers today, small craft could reach quite far inland. For example, the name 'Langport' indicates that the River Yeo in Somerset was navigable that far, and even beyond. Some estuary-going vessels were specially designed with shallow drafts in order to get far up rivers and up the numerous creeks ('pills') to reach isolated hamlets and farms. One of the most famous of such designs was the Severn Trow (rhymes with 'crow'); others were the Thames Barge and the Mersey Flat.

Goods carried by river/estuary/coastal boats ranged from 'market goods' (corn, cider, fish, bacon, salt, butter and general groceries, pots and pans, earthenware, wool and cloth etc.) to commercial loads of coal, timber, fertilizer, fish, flour, hides and skins, iron, bricks and tiles, sand and gravel, stone, cattle and sheep. Regular shipping routes were operating long before canals and railways appeared on the scene. There was a considerable trade in coal across the Bristol Channel from South Wales. So-called 'sea coal' had been utilised for years throughout the south-west of England for domestic purposes, and for firing furnaces in brick and tile making. Coal and 'culm' (a naturally-occurring shale/limestone mix containing thin veins of coal), was used to make lime for agricultural use by burning at local sites (lime deteriorated with prolonged exposure to moisture and could not be transported over long distances). Culm was also used a s household fuel in Wales and the West Country.

In the C17[th], the cost of transportation was high: after coming across from Lydney and being transhipped at Bridgwater, two bushels of coal (the load of a pack-horse) cost 1s 6d at Ham Mills, but 2 shillings by the time it had been taken to Taunton. By the 1830s, coal cost 8s a ton at Newport; sea transport to Bridgwater added 4s; and it cost another 2s to get it up to Creech St Michael, together with 1s 8d in canal and shipping dues. The railways would bring those costs down significantly, as it would for all goods, whether brought by sea or not.

Ships grounded as water level fell, and it was common practice to load or unload them on beaches where there were no quays. Coal, for example, was taken out of the hold in baskets, using just a hand winch, and then taken ashore by horse and cart. If possible, vessels sought the safety and convenience of a harbour. But even when river quays or harbour walls had been built, boats would settle for periods between tides. Whilst settling was acceptable for small ships, regular grounding was structurally undesirable for larger vessels, particularly when iron and steel replaced wood in construction. Further, as ships became more expensive to construct and operate, it was financially sensible that cargo ships should have quick turn-rounds. In the coal trade, too, a rapid turn-round was important in reducing the costs of large numbers of railway wagons awaiting attention.

At a limited number of locations, there were natural deep-water harbours where quays could be built (Plymouth), and sometimes it was possible to construct deep-water jetties in sheltered locations at which ships could berth without being too much affected by the tides (New Milford/Neyland). Where changes in tide levels were significant, the solution to the grounding problem took the form of 'wet docks' (or 'floating harbours'), which were walled-in areas of water, the level of which was maintained by access and egress being made through basins with locks, whose massive gates kept in the water. Dry (graving) docks for ship repair were, of course, wet docks from which the water was drained or pumped. There was a dry dock at Bridgwater dating from 1790, and Bristol's 'Floating

Harbour' was opened in 1809, with the tidal Avon flowing along the 'New Cut'.

London was already the greatest port in the world by the end of the C18th, but conditions were congested and chaotic. All unloading and loading took place at tidal quays and wharves on the banks of the Thames. These were run privately under jealously-guarded historical royal charters and monopolies (mediaeval 'legal and sufferance quays'), that restricted where goods could be landed and by whom. Only small craft berthed at wharves; larger vessels remained in mid-river, and nearly 3,500 barges, lighters, canal boats etc. conveyed goods from mid-stream to the quays. River crime existed on a vast scale. It was estimated that the annual plunder at the port was worth £500,000------an astronomic sum in today's figures. The solution was wet docks enclosed by 30ft high walls with limited entrance and exit, patrolled by armed guards (the forerunners of the dock police). Hence a number of commercial wet docks were built in quick succession on the north side of the Thames. These included the West India Dock, 1799; the London Dock, 1800; and the East India Dock, 1806.

A number of wet docks started life as exits of canals into estuaries, rather than harbours for ships. Along canals there were lock systems to regulate water levels, but locks were also required when joining tidal waters. At such junctions where goods may have been transhipped, the canal might have been widened out to form a basin, or a fully-fledged dock. The Surrey dock system and Regent's Canal Dock, both in London, and the dock at Bridgwater came about in this way.

Before the age of steamers, traffic conveyed by ocean-going sailing ships was seasonal, depending upon favourable winds, so goods of all sorts often had to be stockpiled to last the year round. After the widespread introduction of the condenser for feedwater, and of compound steam marine engines in the 1860s (and triple expansion engines in the 1880s), steamers could sail economically to a timetable at all times of the year regardless of the wind direction. Furthermore, since goods could now be quickly distributed round the country by railway, the need for stockpiling was reduced considerably. (Local lime burning died out with the coming of railways as lime could be delivered quickly from kilns established at inland quarries). The invention of the submarine telegraph meant that buying and selling abroad could be carried out in an instant, and this, too, gave great impetus to international trade in Victorian times and the prosperity of docks around the country.

As all ships increased in size throughout the C19th, many existing docks could no longer accommodate the larger vessels. Improvements and new dock building took place as rival ports competed to attract trade, leapfrogging over one another in terms of what size of lock they could offer, what facilities, what inducements in terms of dock dues they charged, and so on.

The Arrival of Railways

Apart perhaps from low value goods in bulk, where time in transit was not too important, railways eventually took most of the traffic from river navigations and canals, and also made some of them completely redundant by altering local trading routes and patterns, as shown by the reduction of traffic on the River Parrett after the opening of the Durston to Yeovil branch railway in 1853. The Parrett Navigation Committee as early as 1855 noted that the coming of railways had made the price of Somerset coal from Radstock cheaper than Welsh sea coal.

The building of railways sometimes caused obstruction to navigations: the Axe was dammed by the B & E in 1841, so that Bleadon/Lympsham became the furthest direct navigable place from the sea (just two miles away by water). Many creeks in West Wales were stopped off by the South Wales Railway, whose main line was built close to the coast around Llanelly. Problems also arose over the siting of railway bridges, and Admiralty objections to supposed obstruction to shipping thwarted many railway proposals in Victorian times. But for the Admiralty, the GW might have joined the SWR by a bridge across the Severn to Lydney; (later the Severn & Wye Joint Rly did construct a bridge at Lydney). Again, Swansea came to be served by a branch from the main SWR main line at Landore because the Neath Harbour Commissioners objected to Brunel's proposal to construct a bridge across the river to allow the main line to follow the coast westwards; (eventually a bridge was installed below Neath by the Rhondda & Swansea Bay Rly, in this case the only swing bridge in Britain both on the skew and on a curve).

It is not generally known that Brunel's bridge on the B & E over the Parrett near Bridgwater was a stone elliptical arch bridge which was 'twice as flat' as the already-world-beating Maidenhead bridge. During construction in the early 1840s, coastal shipping brought in materials for the new railway which were taken upriver to the line by lighters. The timber centring over the Parrett caused some obstruction to navigation, particularly with the increased boat traffic, and it led to a fatal boating accident, following which the B & E was instructed to remove the obstruction. Because Brunel had come to realise that the bridge was not safe (the abutments were moving apart) he designed a replacement laminated timber structure, which was built around the arch without interruption to traffic. It was not replaced until 1904.

The effects of the arrival of railways in towns with ports varied considerably from place to place, and also depended on whether the ports handled overseas, or just local, trade. Some minor seaports became important, and once-important harbours declined. Harbours in coastal towns through which a railway did not pass tended to fall into decay. Exeter had grown as an up-river trading port exporting woollen goods from the West Country cottage industry, but it was in decline at the turn of the C18th/19th, after wool manufacture became concentrated in the more efficient mills of northern industrial England. Nevertheless, coal brought in by coastal vessels continued to be an important traffic until the railway arrived.

At Aberdovey and Barmouth, river traffic on the

Dovey and on the Mawddach practically ceased after the railway arrived. However, the coastal railway was initially a boon to the slate trade: the Talyllyn Railway was built to link up with the Cambrian company, bringing slates to Aberdovey for export and the Cambrian set up interchange sidings with the Festiniog Rly in 1872 at Minffordd. Lead, zinc and copper ores from Mid and North Wales continued to be shipped out from local harbours. The major part of the slate export traffic continued to be taken by boat until turn of the C19th/20th, as coastal shipping rates were so low, but afterwards the tonnage of slate leaving North Wales by rail exceeded the amount taken by shipping. Thus, Portmadoc (served by the FR and the Croesor & Port Madoc Rly long before the Cambrian Rlys arrived in 1867) declined after the arrival of the railway as it was found easier to distribute slate by rail to ports having ocean-going cargo lines.

The arrival of the railway at Bridport brought the commercial days of the harbour to an end, even though there was no line to the quay. If trading patterns changed or a source of supply ran out, a harbour might decline whether a railway was present or not. Long before the arrival of railways, the harbour at Lostwithiel declined because tin 'streaming' on the upper reaches of the River Fowey deposited large quantities of rubble, sand and soil into the river, which silted up on meeting the tidal waters at the sea and choked the navigable channel; it was the exhaustion of the lead ore deposits at the East Wheal Rose mine that led to the demise of the harbour at Portreath. Similarly the exhaustion of easily-won local anthracite coal caused the harbours at Tenby and Saundersfoot to stop coal exports. In some of those towns with very small harbours supporting a limited seaborne trade, what little business remained was slowly killed off by the arrival of the railway. Clevedon and Weston-super-Mare are examples, but they were really resorts, and never significant ports. Even so, coal was regularly brought into Knightstone harbour at Weston up to the Great War, and the loading only petered out in the 1930s.

In South Wales, where the broad-gauge SWR and GWR initially paid little attention to mineral traffic, coal brought down to the coast by the 'isolated' standard gauge lines, such as the Taff Vale and Rhymney companies was sent on by sea. It was said that rail transhipment between the gauges added perhaps 1s 6d per ton to the price of coal. Townsend Kirkwood (a coal owner and director of the Llanelly Railway & Dock Co.), when giving evidence to a Parliamentary Committee in 1861, exclaimed: 'Defend us from the broad gauge in collieries.' It was, of course, the double-wagon transit in bringing Staffordshire coal to Southampton that sounded the death knell of the broad gauge.

One effect of an integrated rail network was that ports in the same general area began to compete with each other. Beforehand, the expense of transporting bulky goods overland meant that each port had its own local 'sphere of influence', but later, when goods could be moved inland by rail, ports were able to supply wider hinterlands than before. But if those hinterlands themselves became rail-connected -

particularly by railways serving larger, more efficient, ports - then the smaller port would decline. Alternatively, the hinterlands might become connected to rail by road. The first, embryonic, GWR 'Country Lorry Service' was started in 1907 between Llandyssul and New Quay (Cardiganshire). Such routes were considered by the GW as feeder services bringing traffic to the railway rather than road services in their own right. Nevertheless, if the nearest railway was far off, a harbour which had traded for centuries would remain in business. Hence, Aberayron survived as a busy port bringing in market goods, because it was not until 1911 that the railway arrived.

The increased size of iron and steel steamers in the latter half of the C19th caused trade to gravitate to those major ports with large entrance locks and docks. This, in turn, caused the bigger docks to become better equipped, so that loading and discharge of cargoes proceeded more swiftly. Thus activity at Plymouth grew while that at neighbouring Dartmouth and Exeter fell, and the hinterland of the smaller ports came to be served from the larger ports, at first by rail, and later by road; Porthcawl dock could not compete with the new dock at Port Talbot; activity at Llanelly and Burry Port docks dwindled after WW I because it made economic sense to send manufactured goods to Swansea, which had regular cargo services to places all over the world.

The ability to distribute imported goods from a port throughout the country by rail, and to take manufactured goods for export, was a great asset for any traffic, but particularly so for trade in perishable goods. Thus, the fishing ports of Cornwall and Devon received a great boost when the railway arrived, and made fresh fish available cheaply at inland towns. Milford Haven became a major fishing port out of virtually nothing, owing to the GWR. Rapid transport by rail also led to entirely new traffics (e.g. bananas in bulk at Avonmouth Docks), and led to the growth and development of entirely new or previously-insignificant ports specialising in certain commodities. Obvious examples were the South East Wales coal ports. The West Wales ports - Swansea in particular - had not grown up entirely to handle coal, but rather because of the smelting of copper ores brought in from Cornwall and overseas. Later, tinplate traffic and the export of anthracite coal became very important, the deposits in the valleys above Swansea being the largest in Europe. Later still, the oil refinery at Llandarcy brought a heavy traffic to Swansea docks.

Some ports became specialised in certain imports and exports: Birkenhead was a centre for importing cattle and grain; Cardiff docks not only was a major coal exporting port, but later became the principal UK port for importing potatoes and, like a number of other ports had large flour mills.

When the railways began to operate their own shipping services, they tended to take the shortest practicable sea route, with the maximum possible journey by rail, and the ports for embarkation were chosen by that maxim, e.g. Fishguard for Ireland. Passengers and goods

Busy times at Neyland - the former New Milford. Although posed for the camera, there is nevertheless a hive of activity recorded here. Railway staff are visible amongst the fish porters and buyers whilst fish boxes attributable to John Gibson and E. Davies can be seen together with those belonging to a merchant from Fleetwood in Lancashire. In 1909 nine boats were sailing from Neyland and weekly catches could exceed £1,000. Thirty-one men and ten boys were employed by the 'Neyland Steam Trawling and Fishing Co.' in 1912. (A superb rendition of life in both the railway and fishing industries at Neyland around the late 19th and early 20th century will be found in 'Behind the Steam' and 'Behind the Light' - respectively by Bill Morgan and Bette Meyrick, and Bette Meyrick.).[NRM GWR A1386]

were taken quickly by train from the densely-populated areas to the ports, thus minimising the overall journey time. Similarly, journey times on ocean-going services (particularly inbound) were shortened when ships called at Plymouth, for example, and transferred passengers and mails to the railway at Millbay for a very fast run to London. In contrast, those shipping routes predating railways tended to serve existing cities in tidal waters and the journey times by sea were longer.

Railways and Coastal Shipping

The effects of the spread of railways in early Victorian times on coastal shipping was not so clear cut as their almost-immediate effect on river navigations and canals. Railway-connected ports would be more attractive to shippers and so prospered over those that were not rail-connected. Some port authorities were reluctant to allow rail connections to their harbours, in an attempt to keep coastal shipping going: Exeter Basin was not provided with a rail link until 1867,

and Totnes Quay until 1873. In contrast, the Harbour Commissioners at Teignmouth quickly strengthened a quay and put in railway tracks during 1851.

Sea and rail vied for coal transport into London. Coastal shipping was dealt a blow in 1851 when the Great Northern Railway began to bring coal into King's Cross from the North East for onward transport by the Regent's Canal at cheaper rates than sea colliers into London. But soon afterwards, the North London Railway began to distribute sea-borne coal around its part of London in competition, from its dock at Poplar.

Although it was not possible for C19[th] road hauliers to mount any significant competition to the railways except, perhaps, at local level (and even then they often became cartage agents for the railways), the long-established coastal shipping industry did continue to provide a cheap, though slow, alternative means of goods transportation. Boats plying between Glasgow, Liverpool, Dublin, Bristol, Plymouth and London traditionally called at many of the coastal towns which later came to be served by the Great Western or its constituent companies. Indeed, these coastal services were often the means of bringing construction materials and equipment to the isolated building sites of the new railways. The registered tonnage of coastal shipping entering British ports grew steadily at about 2% per annum from 1830 to 1914 and demonstrates that a healthy and competitive coastal shipping business co-existed with the growth of railways.

Coastal shipping was most competitive to the railways on longer hauls of over 100 miles, such as South Wales to the Thames, or Cornwall to the North West, where the fixed costs at the beginning and end of a voyage were a smaller proportion of the total costs. In contrast, railway costs were more-or-less proportional to the length of journey. In the C20th, petrol would be added to the list of commodities for which coastal shipping was competitive with rail.

Four different types of cargo service existed in coastal shipping:

Coastal Liners: these were the most expensive, running to a timetable whether full or not; in Victorian times, when goods trains were slow and being frequently sidelined to give passenger trains priority, coastal liners could compete in terms of speed and reliability, particularly when sailing vessels were replaced by steamers.

Regular Traders: these either specialised in a particular route or in a particular trade; they suited customers such as riverside gas works, power stations, potteries etc. who wanted large, regular deliveries.

Coastal Tramp Steamers: these picked up loads as and when available. Preferring to sail with full holds, they tended to carry bulky goods; though slow, they were reliable.

Sailing Coasters: journey times were unpredictable owing to wind and tide, but they were cheap for bulky, low-value cargoes like stone, sand, gravel, coal, china clay, grain, salt, timber etc.

Ease of navigation into and out of harbours was affected by sandbars at river mouths (the location of which could change over the years), and by silting-up. All of this became more troublesome as boats became larger. Thus, the port of Carmarthen (10 miles from the sea, and the reason for Brunel's 1853 swing bridge over the River Towy, replaced by a drawbridge in 1908) gradually became defunct owing to the difficulties of getting larger vessels up to the quay. A number of ports (including Gloucester and Exeter) suffered from being situated on shallow, difficult-to-navigate estuaries, and trade inevitably fell off as ships became bigger, and simply could not get up to berth.

Despite these changes of detail, coastal shipping continued in much the same way after the country's network of railways was established, and was competitive with the railway for goods traffic. In 1910, coastal shipping and the railways carried the same tonnage of goods. At meetings of senior GWR goods staff in the 1890s, the various district officers would often report that coastal shipping rates were considerably lower than could possibly be quoted by the company for rail-throughout transit.

It is not generally realised that, in the development of Birkenhead as a port, a significant factor in its success was its ability to provide *South* Wales bunker coal brought up by train for all the ships docking on the Mersey. At the turn of the C20th century, however, Rea's (a lighterage firm on the Mersey) was able to bring steam coal by coaster from the Bristol Channel cheaper than the railway, and the rail traffic dropped significantly. Sully's, the big firm of coal factors based in Bridgwater, continued to employ their own and other firm's coasters to bring coal to Bridgwater long after there was a rail route from South Wales. Given that onward distribution of the coal from Bridgwater would have been by rail, it is presumed that all the double handling made economic sense at the time. There again, the Weston, Clevedon & Portishead Railway for its whole existence unloaded its South Wales loco coal from its own trows at the Wick St. Lawrence wharf at the mouth of the Congresbury Yeo, even though there was a rail connection with the Great Western after 1907/8 through Portishead Dock.

WWI was a turning point in the history of coastal shipping. There were two important factors that curtailed traffic: firstly, the threat from enemy submarine and surface vessels, and secondly that shipping costs rose 200%, whereas railway rates were government-controlled at 1913 values. Of course, real costs of everything went up considerably (for example, after WWI some sizes of Baltic telegraph poles had increased in price as much as nine times over pre-war figures), the railways were out of pocket, and adjustments to railway goods rates had eventually to be made in the 1920's. After the First World War, much of the traffic formerly taken by coastal shipping remained with the railways, but both modes of goods transport thereafter came under increasing threat from road hauliers.

Another change in coastal shipping practice that gained momentum after the First Word War was the replacement of sailing vessels by steam, and later by motor-engined, ships. Other things being equal, wooden sailing ships were cheaper to build than steamers, and an appropriate choice of rigging could make them inexpensive to crew and operate. However, the weather was always uncertain around the coasts of Great Britain and Ireland, making journey times variable, which is one of the reasons why sail cargo boats eventually died out. Even with auxiliary motors, they could not compete with steam. For example, before the First World War, the 66-ton schooner *New Design* out of Bridgwater once ran the 210 nautical miles to Dublin before a gale in 10 hours, yet the same vessel on another voyage took 100 days from Clonakilty (west of Cork in Ireland) to Plymouth, a direct journey of around 220 nautical miles. By the 1930s, it was also increasingly difficult to get experienced crews, and the last of the sailing coasters to dock at Bristol were ketches from Bideford and Braunton, which brought gravel dredged from the Taw and the Torridge.

During the WWII, coastwise shipping was much

A rare photograph of two 4-wheeled GW open bar-sided Tadpole fish wagons on the centre road at Torquay recorded sometime after 1905 when large lettering came in. These vehicles were rebuilt from 6-wheeled BG wagons in 1892 (S7 in the wagon diagram index). There is a 5-digit running number under the 'G' (425?3) on the end of the nearer vehicle. At that time the vehicles would have been painted wagon grey with white lettering and numbering (they did not become brown vehicles with van numbers until WWI). On the extreme right is a short-wheelbase horse-box. Postcard stamped December 1908]

used to relieve the over-stretched railway system, rather than the other way round as in WWI. Thus, Portishead docks (a petrol distributing port in WWI), in addition to handling a lot of coal, stored a great deal of foodstuffs and cattle feed, all of which was constantly being turned over and carried in and out by steam and motor coasters. Many smaller ports, such as Highbridge, saw much increased activity for that reason in the second war.

Fishing Ports

Long before the coming of railways a fishing industry existed in the West Country. Herring off North Devon and pilchards (called sardines when tinned) off South Devon and around Cornwall used to be the principal catches. Since both could be preserved by salting, smoking and drying, quantities beyond local needs could be transported over a wide area inland, be used for victualling ships and even exported abroad. Pressing of salted pilchards in barrels produced fish oil that, in good years, was shipped to Italy. Cod and hake could be preserved by salting and before the middle of the C18th, West Country boats fished off Newfoundland. In contrast to surface-shoaling herring and pilchard, fish that lay on or near the seabed included cod, plaice, sole and turbot, and these were caught by trawling a large net along the bottom of the sea, a method of fishing invented at Brixham. Some types of trawled fish were highly sought after and were transported to London and other large centres by coastal shipping and roads from early times.

When railways arrived, rapid expansion in the size of fishing fleets occurred because the rail system made distribution so much easier, cheaper and quicker. At the same time, the population of Victorian Britain was rising quite rapidly, and so did the demand for fresh food. At Brixham and Plymouth, there were a total of 15 sail trawlers in 1830, and 190 in 1860, all locally built. The South Devon Railway carried 940 tons of fish in 1854, but 3,000 tons in 1864. By the end of the C19th, some 12,000 tons of trawled fish was being landed annually at Brixham and Plymouth. Of the fish landed at Brixham, 99% was taken on by the GWR. While there were local and export markets for fish landed at Plymouth, nearly 7,000 tons was still taken away by the GWR and LSWR.

Milford Haven, where the private dock was opened in 1888, soon became the principal fishing port on the GWR system with a fleet of 100 steam trawlers: 10,000 tons of fish were landed in 1890; 40,000 tons/year by WWI; 50,000 tons/year between the wars; and 60,000 tons/year after WWII. Commercial fishing fleets were also established at the South Wales coal ports during the tail-end of the C19th, and Swansea become the second most important fishing port on the GW.

Before WWI, because of its perishable nature, a great deal of fish was carried by passenger trains at passenger train rates. At the end of the C19[th] fish from the West Country, packed in ice or salt, was carried in barrels or boxes for which the GW provided specially-built BG open 'Tadpole' trucks. Owing to the need for speed in transit the 4- and 6-wheeled, and bogie, Tadpoles were built with coach fittings, Mansell wheels and vacuum brake (some were conversions of coaching stock). Some had a central guard's cabin. A number were built 'convertible' and these, together with many of the BG Tadpoles became NG after 1892. Siphon milk churn wagons were also sometimes employed on fish traffic, often marked for 'Fish and Poultry'. Fish vans did not appear until 1909. The success of the C-headcode vacuum-fitted fast goods trains at the beginning of the C20[th] had demonstrated that carriage fittings were not necessary for fast running, so three versions of standard GW goods vans were subsequently produced for fish traffic, viz: (i) in 1909, a 16 foot over headstocks 4-wheeled van (originally in the wagon diagram index as V13, later re-diagrammed S2), based on the V12 Mink ventilated goods van design; (ii) in 1912, a 21 foot over headstocks 4-wheeled van (S6) based on the contemporary Mink C; and (iii) in 1916, a 28 foot 6 inches van design coded Bloater based on the V11 Mink D. Variations in design of all three sizes led to other diagram numbers being issued (see *GWR Goods Wagons*). Bloaters and S6 vehicles were distinguished by having sliding doors. Many S6-type vans were employed on traffic from Swansea South Dock. Even so, in 1923, 74,000 tons of fish were still being carried by passenger train but this had dropped to rather less than 50,000 tons by WWII.

In 1947, the weekly loading of fish wagons averaged 250 at Milford Haven, and 120 at Swansea. In the West Country, 12 fish wagons per week were required at Penzance (for fish from Newlyn), and more wagons for traffic from St. Ives (meeting the main line services at St Erth); from Looe (at Liskeard); from Kingsbridge (at Brent); and from Brixham (at Churston). During 1947, a new type of fish van (coded 'Insixfish') was developed from the insulated Palethorpe's sausage vans of 1936 (see *GWR Goods Wagons*). Fifty eventually came into service just after nationalisation on the Penzance & London, Milford Haven & Birmingham, and Milford Haven & London routes.

Some examples of telegraph code words relating to fish traffic by rail were:
Fish: 'fish expected to leave here today about following time. Will wire particulars on departure of train'
Lobster: 'following packages of London fish today approximate weight … tons'
Magpie: 'fish particular today approximately … tons trawl … herrings … mackerel …'

In the late C19[th], pilchard fishing declined in west Cornwall and was replaced by mackerel fishing that was a spring and summer activity. Many Cornish boats went to the North Sea and to Ireland in search of herring in the summer. There were often complaints from Penzance fishermen that railway charges were too high in relation to the prices

> **Private and not for publication.**

GREAT WESTERN RAILWAY

———

RULES

AND

REGULATIONS ·

FOR

OBSERVANCE BY EMPLOYEES.

DOCKS DEPARTMENT.

———

1937.   **James Milne**
General Manager

received at market. Commercial shipping in the South West reached a peak about 1880, after which it went into relative decline when Brixham trawlers failed to adapt to steam propulsion. Brixham and Plymouth's annual combined total of 12,000-odd tons of fish (about one-third of all fish landed at south coast ports) compared unfavourably with Hull and Grimsby's 150,000-odd tons (about one-half of all east coast fish). Even though the steam trawlers at Milford Haven and Swansea landed far greater catches than the West Country fishing ports, they, too, were not in the same league as Hull and Grimsby.

Earnings at Ports

The strict definition of a 'port' is one that is authorised to collect customs dues, and is responsible for navigation aids. It is an administrative unit, rather than a particular place. When trade waxed, new ports were created; when trade waned, old ports lost that status. Thus, it was not until 1861 that Cardiff, Newport and Gloucester became independent ports; before that, Bristol was the major port of the Bristol Channel. The Cardiff customs port embraced Penarth, and later Barry. Chepstow lost its port status in 1881 owing to lack of trade.

Dock owners derived their revenues principally

Docks Department.
COAL TIPPERS, ETC.

GRADE.	C.D.M.O.	Newport.	Cardiff.	Penarth.	Barry.	Port Talbot.	Swansea.	Plymouth.	Pembrey & Burry Port.	TOTAL.
Belt Conveyormen	—	—	—	—	—	10	—	—	—	10
Boxmen	—	—	31	—	—	—	—	—	—	31
Capstanmen	—	4	87	8	80	20	34	—	—	233
Cradlemen, Turntablemen, etc.	—	88	137	56	80	39	67	—	—	467
Hoistmen	—	40	83	26	80	18	34	—	—	281
Retarers	—	—	—	—	—	—	18	—	—	18
Reweighers	—	32	—	—	—	—	—	—	—	32
Signallers	—	4	—	—	—	—	—	—	—	4
Tippers	—	—	—	—	—	—	—	—	6	6
Traversermen	—	8	—	—	—	—	—	—	—	8
Weighers	—	40	87	28	79	18	30	—	—	282
TOTAL	—	216	425	118	319	105	183	—	6	1,372

Coal Shipping and General Cargo work at Llanelly and Briton Ferry dealt with by contractors.

from (i) tonnage rates on vessels ('dock dues'), and (ii) import or export rates on goods ('wharfage'). Dock dues were levied on the net registered tonnage of the vessel, but dues were dependent on the length of the voyage (the longer the voyage, the higher the freight charge received by the shipowner, so the more he was able to afford for dock accommodation). Such revenues were used by the dock owner for the provision and maintenance of quays, dredging, working of lock gates, lighting, buoyage etc., pumping costs for replacement of water lost by locking and by occasional sluicing to remove silt, and the wages of company staff. Other sources of income included charges for craneage, charges for weighing and tipping coal, charges for mixing coal, towage, labour charges for movement of traffic within the dock, rentals from businesses on the dock estate and so on.

Under the Chief Docks Manager and Assistant Docks Manager of the new GWR Docks Department at Cardiff, there were three departments. The *Commercial* department dealt with rates, dock dues and other charges; development of traffic; docks advertising and publicity; commercial statistics; and the encouragement of new industries on the dock estates. There was a great deal of rationalisation and normalisation of charges after the Grouping, as the former independent companies had different scales for essentially similar tasks. The *Operating* department had charge of all matters affecting the working of traffic at the docks (often including a separate 'Control' organisation for docks trains), and collaborated with the Superintendent of the Line's Department to ensure the free flow of trains from and to the docks. The goods discharged from a vessel of 20,000 tons, say, might represent 20 train loads, and should things go wrong, there could be operating repercussions across the system. The *Staff* department had charge of all staff questions relating not only to the numerous grades employed directly by the GW at the docks,

but also to those many other people working at the docks who were not employed by the railway, such as some general cargo stevedores, coal trimmers, riggers, boatmen, dock pilots, channel pilots and so on. It was the policy of the GW to provide some stevedores and a few tugs of its own, so that the railway had some influence on costs and quality of service that would otherwise be in the hands of independent firms. Every individual GW dock had its own Superintendent, under whom were sections dealing with Traffic, Marine, Coal Shipping, General Cargo, Accounts, etc.

Various editions of the GWR *Rules and Regulations for Observance by Employees of the Docks Department* had, in addition to the sort of general instructions found in other rule books, special sections for those who worked coal shipping appliances including coaling crane drivers, hoist cradlemen and belt conveyor operators, as well as comprehensive instructions for employees engaged in general cargo handling.

Cargoes at the docks

Some export cargoes at the GW docks, notably coal, were transported in bulk; a similar import cargo was iron ore. Like mileage traffic in goods yards, these cargoes arrived and departed by the wagon load, and could be dealt with in the open. In contrast general cargo was packed in a variety of ways, with great differences in weight, dimension and shape, and could be conveyed by the box, the bag, the bale and the barrel, each of which required different handling facilities and vehicles. Up to WWII, and for some time after until the 'container revolution', thousands of articles would have been conveyed loose, or in bundles in a cargo, and a consignment might have consisted of anything from a carton weighing a few pounds to a tierce (large barrel) of tobacco weighing half-a-ton, or from a motor-car to a locomotive weighing a hundred tons or more.

In those days, manpower was comparatively cheap: men humped around jute sacks weighing 156 lb (and more) and it took many years to reduce sack weights to 1cwt or less. The unloading of sawn timber was very labour-intensive. While some planks of wood might be rope-slung by crane, a great deal of timber was shouldered from shipside to wagon or to storage area. Even so, labour-saving devices were gradually introduced from WWI onwards both for loading and unloading vessels, and within warehouses and transit sheds.

Transit sheds at docks should not be confused with warehouses. The former were for goods in transit between ship and shore: export cargo would be sorted and marshalled in readiness for appropriate loading into an expected vessel;

Exports in December 1946. Hillman cars loaded by quayside crane into the ship's hold. The crates on the GW twin flat Mite wagons contain Commer lorries, also from the Rootes group. The white crosses on the wagons indicate that they are restricted to run on docks lines only. [D J Hyde collection]

or, goods from a ship would be received, passed through customs and then loaded on to rail or road transport for onward delivery. In warehouses, goods were stored over lengthy periods, and during that storage, may have been bought and sold. Licensed 'bonded warehouses' (introduced in 1803) were secure, and contained particular categories of goods that paid no excise duty until they were removed for home use. Goods re-exported paid no duty (so-called *entrepôt* trade). The type of goods subject to bonded treatment varied over the years, depending upon government policy: at different times this included - in addition to wines and spirits - copper ore, timber, hemp, linseed, tallow, tar, and iron.

In the coal-exporting ports, vessels arriving with pitwood, say, would, after unloading, be moved across the dock to a coal hoist for loading. Operations such as this involved a dock pilot, boatmen, riggers and tugs. The job of dock boatmen was to move mooring lines from point to point when vessels were on the move in the docks. Riggers were sailors employed by the owners of vessels while in

dock. They formed a skeleton crew to perform the duties of the sea-going crew, who were usually were paid off on arrival at the port. The term rigger went back to sailing ship days, when vessels were fitted out in dock.

Pit props and pitwood were often taken back to collieries in private-owner wagons after shipment of coal at the docks. The difference between the two categories was that pit props had the bark removed abroad before shipment to Great Britain. It was sorted into sizes dependent on the diameter of the smaller end. Pitwood, on the other hand, was imported in 6-9 ft lengths with the bark still on. Spacious areas with siding connections were often set apart at docks to deal with the import and distribution of pit props and mining timber. The import of such timber was related to the output of the mines; the rise or fall in the one was reflected in the other.

In sailing ship days, large, long pieces of timber were loaded and unloaded into sailing ships by means of a 'timber bow port', which was a square hole about 2 ft by 2 ft cut into the bow below deck level, through which long

Statement showing Exports of Coal and Coke at the principal South Wales and Monmouthshire Ports for the past 30 years.
(INCLUDING EXPORTS, COASTWISE SHIPMENTS, AND BUNKERS).

Year	Cardiff.	Penarth	Barry	Total for the Port of Cardiff	Newport	Port Talbot	Swansea	Llanelly	Year
1884	6,773,189	2,445,501	..	9,218,690	2,501,086		1,289,145	..	1884
1885	6,678,133	2,795,025	..	9,473,158	2,684,111		1,239,338	.	1885
1886	6,521,956	2,522,177		9,044,073	2,872,315	.	1,240,344	..	1886
1887	6,858,299	3,130,480	.	9,988,779	3,260,565		1,331,838	..	1887
1888	7,604,856	3,390,252		10,995,108	3,050,803		1,334,019	..	1888
*1889	7,735,536	2,776,712	1,073,575	11,585,823	2,835,892	.	1,387,052	..	*1889
1890	7,420,080	1,566,599	3,129,691	12,179,370	2,643,022	..	1,488,242	..	1890
1891	6,949,424	1,940,117	3,959,621	12,849,162	2,617,233	..	1,415,058	..	1891
1892	7,323,095	2,079,483	4,192,691	13,593,652	2,798,912	..	1,456,842	..	1892
1893	6,725,320	2,133,284	4,211,822	13,070,426	2,818,128		1,459,475	..	1893
1894	7,668,606	2,429,408	4,896,822	14,994,836	3,619,799	..	1,652,414	.	1894
1895	7,542,220	2,507,913	5,051,832	15,010,965	3,359,829	.	1,721,079	..	1895
1896	7,690,205	2,818,368	5,279,232	15,787,805	3,661,217	.	1,756,490	..	1896
1897	7,722,995	3,051,743	5,854,920	16,629,658	3,807,734	..	1,961,158	..	1897
†1898	5,652,666	1,953,263	4,369,448	11,975,377	2,348,025	..	2,022,272	..	†1898
1899	8,279,005	3,368,209	7,223,369	18,870,583	3,989,537	..	2,275,402	..	1899
1900	7,549,312	3,253,257	7,225,599	18,028,168	3,657,997	315,530	2,404,793	..	1900
1901	7,216,311	3,467,846	7,844,464	18,528,621	3,508,394	431,161	2,294,939	..	1901
1902	7,090,291	3,599,382	8,675,475	19,365,148	3,769,187	574,969	2,514,943	202,911	1902
1903	7,169,912	3,800,230	8,840,891	19,811,033	4,104,638	731,822	2,495,016	311,352	1903
1904	7,490,481	3,871,226	9,113,762	20,475,469	4,400,032	936,169	2,452,967	363,362	1904
1905	7,294,020	3,740,061	8,651,511	19,685,592	4,186,430	1,072,676	2,653,447	376,565	1905
1906	7,935,490	4,229,594	9,730,588	21,895,672	4,986,008	1,400,491	3,323,644	398,974	1906
1907	8,909,823	4,569,989	9,883,096	23,362,908	5,229,773	1,662,502	3,655,050	287,579	1907
1908	9,017,603	4,267,585	9,731,110	23,016,298	5,419,612	1,533,286	3,773,406	287,683	1908
1909	9,614,950	3,916,760	10,047,370	23,579,070	5,321,617	1,633,924	3,712,086	262,207	1909
1910	9,501,960	3,966,096	9,673,499	23,141,555	5,208,424	1,971,682	3,532,542	276,551	1910
1911	9,320,656	3,979,401	9,145,788	22,445,845	5,650,910	2,016,254	3,777,713	236,076	1911
†1912	9,601,648	4,179,506	9,728,319	23,509,473	5,302,713	2,031,901	3,819,319	209,825	†1912
1913	10,576,506	4,513,117	11,049,711	26,139,334	6,147,701	2,385,495	4,515,491	326,130	1913

* Barry Dock Opened.   † Colliers' Strike.

COAL EXPORTS, 1913.
SUMMARY OF TOTALS.

Geographical Division.	Cardiff.	Newport.	Port Talbot.	Neath.	Swansea.	Llanelly.	Total from S. Wales & Mon. Ports. 1913	1912
	Tons.	Tons.	Tons.	Tons.	Tons.	Tons.	Tons.	Tons.
Arctic, Baltic and North Sea	609,731	10,549	47,200	..	342,133	32,174	1,041,797	996,213
Coasting Limits, Hamburg to Brest ..	1,559,761	395,752	280,161	124,740	1,380,028	189,276	3,929,718	3,127,085
North French Limits ..	1,115,331	302,380	827,485	17,122	621,084	7,699	2,891,101	2,489,904
North Spanish and Portuguese Limits ..	973,249	502,989	80,891	1,325	37,332	3,989	1,599,775	1,368,560
Near Mediterranean Limits ..	5,469,707	1,730,891	212,101	1,126	821,152	2,574	8,237,551	7,726,485
Upper Mediterranean Limits ..	1,903,721	136,594	20,932		59,457	..	2,120,704	1,851,491
North African, etc., Limits ..	812,307	495,504	99,303		101,426	..	1,508,540	1,252,975
West African Limits ..	1,280,098	6,683	20,804		28,933	257	1,336,775	1,323,829
East African Limits ..	251,863	37,798	9,529		5,483	..	304,673	230,921
Red Sea, Persian Gulf, Indian, etc., Limits ..	501,530	67,621	10,188	..	13,303	..	592,642	483,090
Far East Limits ..	87,792	20,920	..	..	314	..	109,026	97,905
Australasian and Pacific Island Limits ..	7,003	..	..	..	..	..	7,003	..
North and South America, Pacific Ports Limits ..	237,162	2,211	209,125	..	10,896	..	159,394	465,985
North and South America, Atlantic Ports Limits ..	4,537,563	843,212	27,038	..	104,221	483	5,512,517	5,002,099
Total Exports to foreign Countries	19,346,828	4,553,104	1,844,757	144,313	3,525,762	236,452	29,651,216	26,416,542
Shipped as Bunkers for the use of Foreign-going Steamers	3,292,076	712,972	192,246	..	502,862	14,800	4,714,956	3,916,633

Timber unloaded from ship about to enter local timber yards on the dock estate at Cardiff in 1932. John Bland & Co Ltd's timber seasoning shed in far distance. Most wagons are marked with an 'X' indicating that they were for use within the dock precincts only and were not travel more than a limited distance on the mainline [GWR].

Pitprops stored at the Bute Roath dock in July 1932. Quayside cranes in the background and the jib of Simson III, the GW floating crane, at the right [GWR]

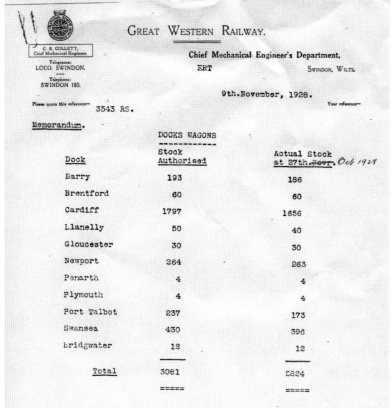

GREAT WESTERN RAILWAY.

C. B. COLLETT,
Chief Mechanical Engineer.
Telegrams:
LOCO. SWINDON.
Telephone:
SWINDON 185.

Chief Mechanical Engineer's Department,
ERT   SWINDON, WILTS.

9th. November, 1928.

Please quote this reference—   3543 RS.   Your reference—

Memorandum.

	DOCKS WAGONS	
Dock	Stock Authorised	Actual Stock at 27th. Novr. *Oct 1928*
Barry	193	186
Brentford	60	60
Cardiff	1797	1656
Llanelly	50	40
Gloucester	30	30
Newport	264	263
Penarth	4	4
Plymouth	4	4
Port Talbot	237	173
Swansea	430	396
Bridgwater	12	12
Total	3081	2824

Above - *An iron Mink van 'For use at Cardiff Docks only'. Painting is in post-1936 style. Numbering of wagon is in the series for docks vehicles. [GWR]*

Left - *Letter from CME's department in 1928 regarding authorised and actual numbers of docks wagons across all GWR docks.*

Opposite *- Potato traffic at Weymouth in June 1933. A joint scheme between the GW and Weymouth Corporation increased and improved harbour facilities (new Customs shed; platforms for 36 coaches and 6 electric cranes on a 100 ft wide new pier capable of handling 6 steamers simultaneously).*

baulks could be slid in or out; this timber port was caulked for the voyage, and uncaulked at the quayside. In many docks, large areas of water (called timber floats or timber ponds) were employed for storing large timber in log or sawn baulk form. Part of the reason for doing so was that it was difficult to handle bulky pieces of timber, perhaps 2 ft square by up to 30 ft long, on crowded quaysides; also, by remaining wet before being required, the timber did not dry out and crack. Bute Docks at Cardiff, for example, had 22 acres of timber floats, and there were 44 acres at Plymouth. Mechanisation of quaysides after railway nationalisation saw the use of timber floats decline. Much of the GW's timber for railway use was imported through its depot at the Poplar docks in London.

Stevedores loaded general cargo, working in the holds of ships releasing the slings of goods craned over from railway wagons, and stowing cargo appropriately. Stowing of general cargo was a skilled job: not only did the cargo have to be kept in the order of the ship's loading plan for subsequent removal at different destinations, but it had to be stowed so that one type of goods did not damage another; it had to be loaded in such a way that there was no danger of cargo shifting during the voyage, and arranged in such a way that the ship was in trim. This distinguished the stevedore from the 'docker' who merely unloaded vessels.

The GW dock foreman was in charge of all loading/unloading of general goods including cattle, fruit and vegetables etc. Given the number of docked ships and their cargoes, experience enabled him to estimate the number of casual workers to recruit every day and the number of railway wagons required. In the case of fruit, a cargo would be unloaded and stored, and samples sent to market for auction. Consignment orders from the purchasers would be relayed back to the docks, after which wagons were loaded and sent off to arrive at the destination of the wholesaler/retailer as soon as possible.

For moving cargo within a dock from ship to warehouse or transit shed and vice versa, old down graded mainline open wagons and vans were employed. They were identified by a large white cross, painted on their sides and legends such as *For Use at Plymouth Docks Only* and *Not to Travel more than 3 miles on the Mainline*.

Engineering at the docks

Matters dealing with cargoes and operation resided with the Docks Department, but installation and maintenance of heavy dock equipment such as hydraulic mains and pumps, electricity supplies etc was the responsibility of the GWR's Chief Mechanical Engineer's department at Swindon. In 1911, when new hydraulic coal hoists were constructed by

Left - The bucket dredger David Davies(II) was delivered to Barry docks in 1925. Buckets are attached to an endless chain as shown and scoop up mud from a predetermined depth as the ship slowly goes ahead. The mud was discharged overside down shoots into mud hopper barges that were later taken out into the Bristol Channel for dumping. [STEAM Swindon]

Bottom - The Mudeford grab dredger built for the GW in the Netherlands in 1924. Used for dredging close up to quay walls and in corners. [Amgueddfa Cymru National Museum of Wales]

the GWR on land rented from the Swansea Harbour Trust at the King's Dock, the layout around the dock, permanent way etc were designed by Mr. W. Armstrong the GW's new works (civil) engineer, and the tips were erected under the supervision of Mr. F. G. Wright (Principal Assistant to the CME) of Wright-Marillier cattle wagon tamper-proof partition design fame (see *GWR Goods Wagons*). At the grouping, John Auld, the last Barry Rly CME, became personal assistant to Charles Collett for docks. On the civil engineering side, Edward Waddell from the Barry Rly became docks assistant to the GW civil engineer.

Tides, Pilots and Dredging

There is a tide every 12½ hours. Low tides are 'neap' tides and high tides are 'spring' tides. Spring tides occur at, or soon after, new or full moons, whilst neap tides occur mid-way between spring tides. A ship that enters a harbour on a spring tide, but cannot get out owing to low tides, is said to be 'beneaped'. Few places around the coast of Britain are unaffected by tides, but the Bristol Channel experiences one of the largest rises and falls of tide in the world, at over 40 ft (the Bay of Fundy in Canada, at 50 ft, is the world's largest). The large tidal differences affected not only ports directly on the Bristol Channel, but also rivers discharging into it. At low water, the banks of the Avon and Parrett on the English side, and the Wye, Ebbw, Usk, Rumney, Taff and Ely rivers in South Wales, are deeply mud-lined. The silt deposited at high and low water in approach channels

GREAT WESTERN RAILWAY.

ENGINEERING DEPARTMENT.

RULES

AND

SPECIAL INSTRUCTIONS

FOR

OBSERVANCE BY MASTERS AND ENGINEERS EMPLOYED ON DREDGING CRAFT.

1st January, 1934.

and docks has to be removed regularly (30,000 tons of mud was dredged each week from the main channels approaching Cardiff). Dredging was a constant battle against nature and was one of the costliest items of maintenance in the South Wales docks: £100,000 per annum in the early 1920s to remove about 4 million cubic yards of material annually. Dredging was necessary in small docks as well as large, so dredgers were in operation at Bridgwater, Gloucester, and so on.

Some of the silt was removed by sluicing, which involved letting a large volume of water (from a reservoir or river stream) run over the bottom of a dock at very low tide to scour away deposits. Notices of 'scouring days', which had legal authority, were issued to warn boat owners that it would not be possible to use a dock on such occasions. Upstream sources of water also topped-up the losses in water in docks from locking and from evaporation. At Cardiff there were feeders from the Glamorganshire Canal, but at Newport, there was no suitable

A diver at Barry No 3 dock (the basin) in June 1933. Aboard the diver's cot are two air-pump handle drivers and man with telephone. According to the GW register of photographs, this was "among pictures taken for work for Mr Quartermain" (the chief [civil] engineer at the time). [GWR]

The 125-ton floating crane Simson III purchased from Holland by the GW in 1925 being used to discharge heavy machinery at Newport Alexandra docks. The crane required the attendance of tugs to manoeuvre and maintain station. [STEAM Swindon]

upstream source of water for scouring, and since the high tide attained the level of water kept in the Alexandra Docks on only seven days in the year, topping up had to be done by pumping. The original steam-driven dock pumps were capable of lifting 13 million gallons of water per hour, and about 50 million gallons were pumped into the dock every day from the River Usk. The culverts carrying this water were as large as London Tube tunnels. In 1936, a new set of pumps rated at 50,000 gallons per minute was installed at Swansea, but the 248 acre water surface of the Prince of Wales, King's and Queen's docks was such that an hour's pumping could raise the water level by one inch only!

There were different types of dredger, of which the Great Western and the constituent companies had various examples. The bucket dredger scooped up mud at a prearranged depth as the vessel went slowly ahead, collecting it by means of a series of buckets fitted to an endless chain passing through the bottom of the boat. The sludge was discharged into the dredger's own hoppers and/ or into barges alongside, thence taken out to sea and dumped through bottom hopper doors (the vessel did not sink owing to buoyancy chambers). Steam-driven barges were self-propelling, whilst so-called 'dumb' barges had to be taken out to sea by tug. For dredging close up to quayside walls, and in the corners of docks, where bucket dredgers could not work, small 'grab' (crane) dredgers were employed. In conjunction with the Engineering Department, the GW Docks Department unified the dredging programme at all the South Wales ports after the Grouping, resulting in savings and greater efficiency. By the late 1920s the Great Western's dredging fleet consisted of 14 dredgers, 14 steam hopper barges and 16 dumb hopper barges. The vessels included new ships built to replace some of the aged vessels inherited from the pre-Grouping companies. A booklet issued by the GW's Engineering Department entitled *Rules*

& Special Instructions for Observance by Masters and Engineers Employed on Dredging Craft was regularly updated.

Owing to conditions in the Bristol Channel, seamanship of high quality is required, as there are many sandbanks and swift currents as well as the big tides. While it is not compulsory at the S Wales ports that ships entering and leaving should employ sea pilots, it was customary for larger vessels to take pilots, who were familiar with the dredged channels. Up until about the WWI, pilots would go out in their own sailing cutters to seek incoming vessels, but subsequently steam cutters occupied fixed stations in the Bristol Channel, the pilots taking turns and pooling their earnings. In South Wales, vessels were docked from three or four hours before high tide to three or four hours after, and ships presented themselves accordingly. The Channel pilot usually handed over to the Dock pilot at the entrance lock. Dock pilots were employed in the movement of vessels within the docks, and were organised like the Channel pilots. All pilots came under the control of Pilotage Boards, none being employed by the GWR.

Locks and Lock Gates, Divers

The immense range of tides in the Bristol Channel meant that there had to be lock gates to retain water in the docks, and since high water did not always reach the level of water in the dock, two sets of lock gates were necessary, often with a third outermost set (flood gates) that were only closed during abnormally high tides or in storms. Depths of water in locks 'over the cill' are given for OST (ordinary spring tides) and ONT (ordinary neap tides). The cill is the floor of the lock (strictly, that part of the floor on which the lock gates rest). To minimise the loss of water on docking, a gated 'basin' was often built between the lock and the dock proper. When a large number of vessels was to be locked in and out on the same tide, the outgoing ships were assembled in the basin and as many as possible were passed through in one go; after each such transit incoming vessels were admitted. When there were barges, as well as ships, regularly passing in and out, different-sized locks were sometimes provided to minimise loss of water (e.g. at Bridgwater and at Sharpness). When water in a dock was kept at about the high-tide level, the number of hours during which locking could take place was limited. To extend the period of locking, so-called 'half-tide basins' were sometimes built. Here, the gates were opened when the tide reached half its maximum level and shut halfway through the falling tide to retain enough water to keep afloat those vessels within. Sometimes, coal loading appliances were erected along the sides of basins so that colliers could enter, be loaded, and sail on the same tide (e.g. Penarth).

Dock gates were initially of wood (hard Australian jarrah or karri), later of steel. Maintenance and repair of lock gates featured prominently in dock work. Steel gates were hollow plate structures and each, at about 50 ft square in the widest locks, could weigh up to 100 tons per leaf. They were flooded in their lowest chambers with ballast water in normal use. To remove a gate, the ballast was pumped out - the gate then began to float upwards, and lift off its pintles (hinge pins). Progressive pumping eventually caused the gate to tip over onto the surface, after which it could be towed to a dry dock or slipway, and taken out of the water for repair. Re-installation was carried out in reverse. The GWR's 125-ton floating crane *Simson III* purchased after the Grouping was often used in such work. When new inner lock gates were provided at Barry in 1936, the gates were constructed on the quayside and launched into the dock. Spare gates were kept on slipways at some ports.

Diving was necessary for the inspection and maintenance of all underwater structures and equipment at docks, such as quay walls, jetties, lock gates, maintenance of mooring chains, buoys etc. Divers were also used by the GW civil engineers for similar work on canals, and to inspect foundations of river bridges and so on. The GW had a number of broad-beamed diver's boats with a ladder over the stern, called 'cots', some of which are listed in Duckworth & Langmuir's book '*Railway & Other Steamers*', e.g. one built for Fishguard in 1901 and others (replacements) for Cardiff and Newport in WWII. In addition to the diver himself, a diving crew consisted of four or more men: two worked the air pump, and one was the attendant who had charge of the air-pipe and a life-line. The diver's equipment, manufactured by Siebe-Gorman, consisted of a waterproof corselet on which the brass helmet was screwed, along with lead weights over the body and on his 'clogs'. The weight of about 1½ cwt was necessary to prevent the diver becoming buoyant, and to enable him to descend rapidly to the workplace, clutching in murky waters the shot line that had been dropped from the cot to where he was to work. When submerged, he could move around quite easily, and might stay down for as long as four hours. Divers were very skilled workmen, and their underwater activities embraced carpenter's, fitter's and mason's work.

Palmer's dry dock at Swansea in the 1920s. [GWR]

Ship Repairs

Among services offered to shipping at GW docks was repair work. Ships' bottoms had occasionally to be cleaned, repaired and painted, and historically with small vessels this was done with the ship pulled over on its side at low water ('careening'). When a rising tide could float a vessel on to a 'hard standing', repairs could be performed between tides. If the hard standing were cut into rising ground, or otherwise surrounded by walls, and gates be provided to keep out the water at high tide, a 'dry dock' or 'graving dock' resulted. These were known in the C18th, one at Bridgwater dating from 1790. Another development of the hard-standing was the building of 'grid-irons', which were wooden, open platforms supported by piles driven into the river bottom, on which were placed wooden keel blocks. They were below water at high tide, and a ship floating above would come down onto the grid-iron as the tide fell. With moveable bilge blocks to keep the vessel upright, plenty of clear space for work above water was given. There were grid-irons at Great Western docks such as the Penarth Tidal Harbour, and at Bridgwater, whilst a massive grid-iron was built at New Milford for the *SS Great Britain*.

Steamships required frequent examination and painting, and it paid cargo docks to provide facilities where ships could be put on an even keel for work to be carried out. The sides of dry docks were often stepped to aid the shoring-up of the ship, keeping it vertical. Floating docks (confusingly sometimes given the name 'pontoons' in the sense of open-topped boxes) were less common, but there was one in the Roath Dock at Cardiff in the 1920s, and the Southern Railway constructed a monster floating dock at Southampton with a lifting capacity of 60,000 tons, sufficient for the largest liners at that time. Curiously, despite the importance of the docks of South Wales and their numerous shipping companies, the amount of shipbuilding was negligible. Ship repairing, on the other hand, was strong in South Wales: in its heyday, it was not uncommon for a million tons of shipping to be undergoing

Left - Hydraulic power house at Newport. [STEAM Swindon]

Opposite top - Fixed jib (non-luffing) hydraulic crane unloading pitwood at Swansea South dock in 1924. Method of carrying such timber in 5-plank open wagons is to use some pieces as vertical bolsters to enable a taller load to be taken as shown on right. Counter-balance weight for crane behind vertical post. [Amgueddfa Cymru National Museum of Wales]

repair in Cardiff docks alone. At one time there were 20 dry docks and three floating docks at the South Wales ports, most of which were owned by private ship repairers, but the GW inherited two graving docks at Cardiff, one at Newport and one at Barry, while the GW already ran the dry docks at Plymouth Millbay and Bridgwater. Some of these docks were entered from the tideway, but most were entered from GW wet docks (and some lock entrances were later converted into dry docks by damming the entrance gates with concrete, as in the 1930's at Newport after traffic dropped to a level that did not justify keeping all locks in operation).

Power for Quayside Equipment

The earliest power source for cranes, lock gates, coal tips, capstans and so on was hand power. The introduction of hydraulic power, with a network of high pressure water mains around the dock area, revolutionised old methods of working at docks (and indeed also at large railway goods depots), where the loading and discharging of cargoes proceeded much more quickly. Hydraulic power on a large scale for dockside equipment was pioneered by Sir W. G. Armstrong Whitworth & Co. in the 1850's. The typical working pressure would have been about 750lbs sq in, with 8in diameter delivery and 12in return mains, delivered by steam-driven pumping engines situated in the dock 'engine house' or 'power house'. The boilers of the system required regular coal deliveries by rail. To prevent the pressure from dropping too much when hydraulic equipment was in use,

there were high-pressure water accumulators connected to the mains system, the pressure in which was maintained by the pumps working against dead-weights on the accumulators. Power was obtained from cylinders and rams giving movement to work machinery.

The first hydraulically-driven equipment was in fixed locations, but in later years cranes and coal hoists could be moved small distances along tracks with the use of flexible connections ('walking legs'). Large distances were covered by coupling the connections to a series of hydrants alongside the crane or hoist tracks.

Electric power was more flexible than hydraulic power: wiring required less maintenance than high pressure mains, and the capital cost of electrical equipment was less, other things being equal. Nevertheless, heavy duty electric motors were not really reliable until WWI and afterwards, which explains the preponderance of hydraulic equipment in docks well into the C20th, particularly for the operation of lock gates and swing bridges. In addition to electric quayside cranes that appeared after the Grouping, some later coal hoists had part electric drive.

Modernisation of dock facilities by the GW after the Grouping involved replacing steam or oil/gas engines by electric drives for the hydraulic pumps, connection of dock estates to local electricity (and gas) supplies, and so forth. There was also the wider use of electric power for equipment such as electric platform trucks (in use since 1922 at Fishguard and Jersey), and portable electromechanical cranes were introduced at ports and

Opposite bottom - The new general cargo berth on the east side of the Bute East dock, installed by the GWR as part of its modernisation programme soon after the Grouping. Re-arranged layout and large hydraulic cranes with modern lattice jibs that can be luffed. Buffer stops on right are those of the Cardiff Rly. [GWR]

goods depots in great numbers during the 1930s, particularly in transit sheds and warehouses at docks. These developments were followed by the introduction of electric 'elevating platform trucks' (fork lift trucks) for use with 'stillages' ('tables with very short legs', the forerunners of pallets). Electrically-driven conveyor belts had been in use in transit sheds and warehouses at docks from even before WWI.

Cranes

Cargoes brought in by sailing vessels that had no power aboard were often unloaded by means of 'winch boats', sometimes called 'gadgets'. They were small, redundant vessels (the hulls of old pilot cutters or yachts) fitted up with a steam boiler and winch in a hut amidships. A winch line was run up to a sailing ship's rigging, enabling material to be unloaded. A model of one of these devices may be found in the Kirkaldy Testing Machine Museum in Southwark, London.

The first dock cranes were fixed in position, had fixed jibs, but could *slue* (swing the jib to one side or the other). The first craneage installed in the older commercial docks consisted of hydraulic cranes fixed in the transepts of transit sheds. Vessels had to be moored to suit the fixed positions, and moved ('warped') by rope if necessary to complete loading or unloading. This process became inconvenient as ships became larger, and led to the employment on the quays of self-propelled travelling portal -type cranes, with a superstructure situated above a four-legged frame. These cranes ran on their own tracks, parallel with dock copings, on a wide gauge (sometimes 21 ft or more) and permitted more than one crane to plumb the hatches of vessels and work into the same hold. The wide

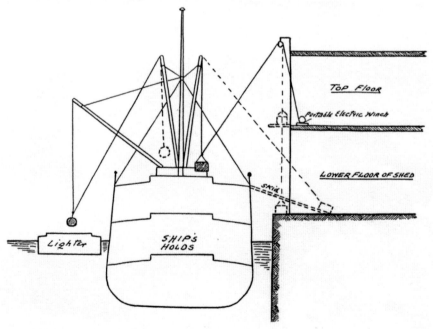

Top - Three 3-ton electric level-luffing cranes newly installed in 1929 at King's dock, Swansea., loading tinplates in special device to avoid damage. New warehouse under construction on left. A wagon still marked LSWR under crane and open wagon with large 'G' and 'W' (1905-1922 period) at far end of rake of wagons [GWR]

Left - Various methods of handling cargo by a steamship's derricks in combination with Shore Gear and Lighters.

Opposite bottom - SS Maltese Prince at the Queen Alexandra dock in Cardiff in October 1948. General cargo being unloaded into barge, railway wagon and warehouse. [STEAM Swindon]

Top - The 125-ton floating crane Simson III being used to move No 3 coal hoist formerly at Newport Town dock to the ADR South dock in 1929. Newport's transporter bridge over the River Usk is in the left distance. [GWR]

gauge and height of the travelling frame provided sufficient space for lines of railway to pass underneath the cranes.

The earliest such cranes had, nevertheless, immoveable jibs, i.e. they could slue but not *luff* (move the jib up and down). While moving a jib up or down enabled loads to be shifted closer to, or further away from, the crane, the load was concomitantly moved higher or lower. In *level-luffing* cranes, gearing maintained the load at a fixed height as the jib was moved, and this helped to avoid collisions with a ship's superstructure when taking cargo from quayside to ship, and vice-versa. Some designs of level-luffing cranes had a small hinged jib at the top end of the main jib, which drooped downwards; its movement, as the main jib luffed, kept loads at a fixed height.

Hydraulic cranes often had metal 'turrets' above the superstructure, in the tower of which were the cylinders and rams for hoisting or lowering the hook, sluing and luffing (if so equipped), the three motions capable of being performed at the same time if necessary and controlled by one operator. By WWI, some electric cranes had been installed at GW docks and, after the Grouping, the Great Western embarked on a programme of modernisation at its docks in which about a hundred of the old type fixed-jib hydraulic cranes were replaced with level-luffing electric cranes.

With the exception of those quays where loading and unloading usually took place by manual labour, cranes were provided at all commercial wharfs, transit sheds and warehouses, and at points in the open where significant storage of goods took

Gravity and winch tips at Brentford used to load Thames barges with coal. Three tracks for each tip converge to wagon turntables to bring in full wagons and take away empties, moved by capstan and reel equipment. Covered shipping shed in background and 40-ton crane on far quay. In the 1930 reconstruction, the tips were removed and the site became a covered wharf for export motor traffic from Morris Cowley. [GWR]

place. Not all cranes at Great Western docks were owned and operated by the railway: it is perhaps surprising that there were privately-owned cranes at some locations. Most quayside cranes were typically of 10-15 ton capacity, with some up to 30 tons, though larger capacity cranes up to 60 or 100 tons (goliath cranes, shear legs etc.) were provided at those ports whose traffic required heavy lifting power. For goods stored in the open, standard-gauge rail-mounted steam cranes of about 2 tons capacity, travelling at up to10 mph, were provided.

Floating cranes were often used at docks, and the Great Western purchased a 125-ton lift Dutch-built floating crane (*Simson III*) in 1925 for the South Wales ports. In addition to performing lifts out on the water that were not possible from the quayside, the floating crane was often used when quayside cranes were incapable of extending across moored ships and, of course, when quayside cranes did not have the requisite capacity. In WWII, the running of all docks was taken over by the Ministry of War Transport, and derrick barges MoWT Nos. 30 and 31, both capable of a 50-ton lift, were supplied for the South Wales ports and were managed by the GWR, who bought them in 1946

(GWR Nos. 30 and 31). In anticipation of the build-up for D -Day, some GW ports were equipped with additional new cranes after 1943.

Coal Tips and Hoists

In the heyday of coal, there were 700 working collieries in the South Wales coalfield, with 200,000 employees. Shipment coal was that taken from mine to docks for export or for bunkering coal-burning ships. Of the 57 million tons output of coal in South Wales in 1913 (which was 20% of all UK production), 42 million tons were exported, of which 33 million tons was cargo, 5 million was steamer bunker coal, and 4 million tons 'other'. By the late 1930s, of the 35 million tons output of coal, 20 million tons was exported: 15 million tons as cargo, 3 million tons as bunker, and 2 million tons as 'other'.

While railway-owned wagons were used for some shipment and landsale coal traffic, and for most loco coal, the majority of shipment coal traffic was carried in wagons privately-owned by the collieries. Similar vehicles were owned and used by coal factors, coal merchants, and other coal-using firms such as gasworks, electricity companies

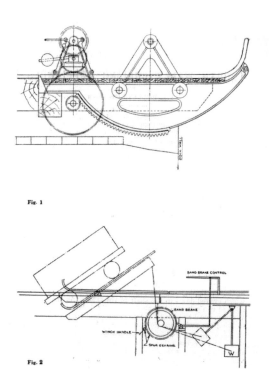

Fig. 1

Fig. 2

1. *Diagram of mechanism of a gravity-and-winch coal tip.*
2. *Diagram of mechanism of a counter-balance tip.*

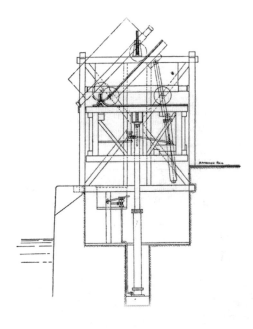

Diagram of early type of hoist to raise wagons above the level of the quay. Driven by hydraulic power, the ram to elevate the cradle on which the wagon stands is in a pit, but tipping ram is hinged to the cradle.

and, for many years, those firms with extensive steam-driven machinery. Nationally, there were some half-million private owner coal wagons (mostly of 10-ton capacity) employed in shipment and landsale coal traffic

In the early days of shipping coal, the contents of tramroad or railway wagons were tipped from the quayside down to the vessels that lay below the level of the wharf; in some cases wagons even had to be lowered below the level of the quay before tipping to prevent undue breakage of lumps of coal. The bunkering of small vessels such as steam trawlers and tugs was as simple: their decks were below quay level, and coal from rail wagons on the quay was shovelled into a sloping chute from ground level down into the ship.

The earliest tipping devices were designed to balance the weight of the wagon during tipping so as to minimise the effort required to actuate the device. In such 'counter-balance' tips, the weight of the laden wagon forced the cradle down at one end, and so tipped the contents of the wagon into a chute, and thence to the hold of the vessel; then, the counterbalance weights brought the empty wagon back to a horizontal position, ready to be run away, the whole process being regulated by powerful brakes. The rail tracks at the front end of the tipping table rose slightly, and were curved upwards at the very end to stop the wagon running off. That provision was carried through to the last types of coal hoist cradle, the slope helping the empty

wagon to run back off the table. At Brentford Dock, 'gravity and winch' coal tips were employed with the capacity to tip 15 wagons per hour, or 2,500 tons per day. Other quay-level coal-shipping devices involved portal frames with ropes and winches to tilt up wagons. At Sharpness, there was a coal-tipping cradle worked by a 30-ton crane.

Later, as ships (particularly steamers) became bigger, the wagons had to be raised up into the air above the quay before tipping in order to get over the side of the ship. To attain greater heights, the same type of tip used at quay level might simply be built on a timber frame above the quay, and wagons be brought in on raised embankments. In other cases, wagons were lifted up within a framework (a 'hoist') before tipping. Later, wagons coming in a higher level than the quay might also be hoisted in the air for tipping. In this way, elevated coal lines did not interfere with general cargo lines at quay level. So all hoists were tips, but not all tips were hoists. While all the operations could be done by ropes and winches, it was usually performed hydraulically.

The SWR erected one of the earliest hydraulic wagon hoists for the shipment of coal at Gloucester docks in 1854. A wagon was placed on a platform that was lifted into the air by a hydraulic ram situated in a pit beneath the hoist, and then tilted by chains to allow the coal fall into the hold of a vessel. In hydraulic hoists, there was a limit to the length of cylinders and rams that could be employed, due to

Elevated tip at the Prince of Wales dock at Swansea loading Glyncorrwg (Briton Ferry) 'smokeless steam coals' into the Norwegian SS Gyda. [GWR]

of the depth of pit required, and problems of the ram buckling ('whipping') under load. The problems were overcome by placing the hydraulic cylinder (usually a number of cylinders) on the sides of the coal hoist framework, and suspending the cradle from above by means of wire ropes or chains. This was the basis for most subsequent designs, and was called a 'suspended cradle hoist'.

Heights to which wagons had to be elevated depended, of course, on the size of ship, and its height in the water. At first, perhaps 20 ft was sufficient. At Penarth, the original hydraulic hoists installed in the 1860s could lift a loaded 8-ton wagon above the quay, tip the contents, return the wagon to quay level and run it off the cradle, all within 30 seconds. In later designs, particularly those for 20-ton loaded wagons, more than one cylinder had to be used for lifting. The speed of lifting was some 180ft per minute. Bunker hatches were much higher than deck level, and the last types of big coal-burning ships when unladen were so high that some hoists installed in the 1920s had to be able to raise 20-ton wagons 75ft in the air (Nos 18 and 20 hoists at Newport, for example). The role of dock water level in the operation of tips is illustrated by the case of the *SS*

Campania at Birkenhead in 1894: the level of the 'Great Float' dock was increased to allow this large ship to enter the graving dock and this brought the hoists to a standstill as they could not get high enough!

In the Port of London, some bunkering was done from floating elevator devices, the coal for which had to be transferred from barges alongside; that coal sometimes came on lighters from the GW dock at Brentford. Before oil-fired ships, the GWR had a fleet of over one hundred 12-ton coal wagons to supply its own steamers at New Milford, Fishguard, Plymouth, Weymouth and elsewhere

The designs of hoists, and details of operation, depended on which contractor had built and installed them: these included Sir W. G. Armstrong Whitworth & Co. of Newcastle, the Hydraulic Engineering Co, Taunatt Walker & Co, of Leeds and Fielding & Platt of Gloucester. Depending on the layout and confines of the dock, each hoist road had three or four parallel tracks feeding it with loaded wagons. Shunting engines were employed only to place incoming trains into the reception sidings, and to draw out trains of empty wagons. At docks like Penarth - which was long and narrow, hemmed in by a hill on one side and the River Ely on the other - the feeding tracks were almost

A fixed hoist at Barry No 1 dock in January 1926. Such hoists were newly installed for the Pole 20-ton coal wagons. The shoot at the side of the hoist was for recycling screenings (in this case spilled coal) that was loaded into the open wagon at the bottom left. Grounded coach body on right marked 'Engineering' [STEAM Swindon]

Reconstruction of ex-Barry Rly wagon storage sidings at Cadoxton North, 1925. Old tracks at the right bottom. Constructors tracks on the far left. [GWR]

parallel to the dockside, and turntables had to be employed to swing both incoming and outgoing wagons. In contrast, the extensive space available at Barry for sidings enabled the tracks to arc around and come in perpendicular to the quayside. Other places had both systems, depending on the age of the particular dock and installation. There were turntables even at places where the feeding lines were at right angles to the quay, in case some wagons had not arrived tip-end first. The feeding lines sloped gently downwards, converging to a wagon brake situated between the running lines, just before a weighbridge. Often there was a mechanical 'wagon kicker' to move the wagon off and on its way. There was a corresponding set of lines sloping away from the hoist on to which the emptied wagons ran over another weighbridge. Originally both full and empty wagons went to, and came away from, the hoist at quay level, but in later designs empty wagons were run off the cradle at a higher level. All wagon movements could be accomplished without locomotives, using capstans and gravity.

The operation of a 1920's coal hoist is described in Chapman's *Twixt Rail and Sea*:

'...the weighman releases the brakes of two or three wagons and lets them gravitate down under control until the leading wagon is on the weighing machine. Now he weighs the truck and its contents and records the weight on a tipping note. The man who now attaches a chain to the wagon has the distinction of being known as a 'jiggerman'. He operates a lever, the chain is wound round a drum, and the wagon is pulled off the weighing machine, across the roadway, and on to the cradle of the hoist.

'Watch the cradle-man. You see he fixes stops so that the wagon cannot run backwards, and signals to the hoistman, who is in that little cabin high up on the side of the hoist. The hoistman, or topman, as he is more frequently called, works his hydraulic levers and the cradle with its truck containing 20 tons of coal is lifted swiftly and smoothly upwards to the required height, carrying the cradle-man with it. You see the cradle-man release the pin which holds the end door of the wagon, and signal to the topman that he has done so. Now the topman brings other machinery into motion, which tilts that part of the cradle on which the wagon is standing. With a roar and a rattle out tumbles the coal from the truck into the great wide chute, which directs it into the hold of the ship.

'As we watch the coal sliding into the hold, the empty wagon is already brought back to horizontal position and lowered, not to ground level, but to an overhead bridge on to which it passes from the cradle of the hoist, and then to another weighing machine where the wagon is again weighed, and the weight inserted on the tipping note. This empty weight, deducted from that of the full wagon, gives, of course, the weight of the coal actually shipped.

'As soon as the empty wagon passes on to the overhead bridge the cradle resumes its journey to the ground, and the process is rapidly repeated with the next loaded wagon, and so on, until the full quantity of coal has been shipped.

'As you can see, tipping coal in this manner is carried out much more expeditiously than it can be

No. 8 moveable hoist in the Alexandra North dock at Newport. In this arrangement, the loaded wagons arrive at high level and are traversed at high level to the position of the hoist. Empty wagons return to ground level and are traversed to the fixed exit road. SS Grangewood being loaded from 'PD' (Powell Duffryn) wagons. [GWR]

described, and although you are struck with the speed with which all these processes are performed, you will probably be surprised to hear that 60 wagons of coal can be weighed, hoisted, tipped, re-weighed, and passed off on to the empty roads in an hour, or an average of a wagon a minute!

'The system of weighing in South Wales is regarded by sellers and buyers of the coal, as well as by the ship-owners, as the best in existence. The coal is bought and sold on the weight thus ascertained, and the ship-owner is paid his freight charges in shipment coal on the same figures. The method does away with all disputes as to whether the coal has been correctly weighed at the colliery, or whether the tare weight as painted on the wagon is correct ...'

In the early 1900s, most South Wales hoists were capable of loading up to 400 tons per hour. But there were inevitable delays: ships had to be moved into and out of berth; there were fluctuations in the supply of coal and ships; coal had to be loaded through more than one hatch; and coal had to be trimmed (levelled out and shovelled by hand into the unfilled corners of holds). All this reduced the practical loading rate to less than 100 tons per hour per hoist. By 1890, at Birkenhead, vessels using hoists were required to load minimum amounts of coal in 24 hours: steamers, 900 tons shipment coal or 300 tons bunkers; and sailing ships 600 tons of shipment coal. The different amounts reflected the size of, and ease of access to, holds: bunker coal hatches were smaller and had to feed the coal down to storage areas close to the boilers.

As colliers became bigger, they had more and bigger hatches and, with the need for quicker turn-rounds, devices that enabled a ship to be loaded simultaneously by more than one hoist became important. Thus, at the tail-end of the C19th, moveable hydraulic tips were introduced, running on wide tracks along the quayside, like cranes. One of the earliest was installed in 1884 at the Bute Docks in Cardiff. At Penarth, a Fielding & Platt four-hoist berth, erected in 1900 for the TVR on the northern side of the outer lock basin, consisted of two fixed and two moveable hoists, all four of which could work simultaneously into one ship. The cradles were lifted directly by the rams to a height of 45ft. When the fast Atlantic liners burned coal, great feats of loading were achieved by this berth, feeding bunker coal into colliers proceeding coastwise to supply the liners with fuel. It was not uncommon for colliers to arrive on a tide, load with 3,000 or even 4,000 tons of coal in a few hours at this special berth, and sail on the same tide.

Moveable coal hoists obviously presented track alignment difficulties in getting the wagons to the cradles. In the 1907 installation at the Queen Alexandra Dock, Cardiff, a series of wagon turntables was provided alongside the hoist tracks, from each of which ran five roads, so that wagons could be presented to the hoist cradle every 12ft or so. The moveable hoist was moved in line with the appropriate hatchway on the ship, with its final position determined by the nearest convenient wagon road. An improvement of this arrangement was to employ traversers instead of turntables.

The traversers at the 1910/11 Taunatt-Walker installation at King's dock Swansea could run at the fast speed of 300ft per minute. With a suitable ship and an

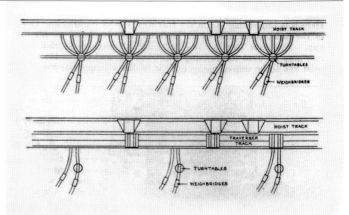

Top - Track approaches for the group of five moveable hoists at Queen Alexandra dock in Cardiff. Upper diagram shows the arrangement as originally installed by the Bute Trustees in which each of the five sets of approach roads led to a turntable from which five tracks radiated. All hoists were self-propelled by a hydraulic engine mounted on the hoist, power being supplied by connecting with 'walking leg pipes' to a series of hydrants situated along the quay. Each hoist would be moved opposite the most convenient curved track that permitted loading into a required hold of a ship. Lower diagram shows the more-rapid replacement scheme for moving hoists and wagons, installed as part of the GW post-Grouping modernisation to all eleven hoists along the south side of the QA dock. An electric motor drove endless wire ropes that passed through brackets in the lower frameworks of all hoists. The brackets had dogging jaws that could grip the rope to move the hoists as required. Each hoist was provided with an electrically-driven traversing table carrying two tracks that lined up with the roads of full and empty wagons. The portion of track carrying full trucks could be tilted towards the hoist, and the other away from the hoist, so that full and empty wagons could be run on and off simultaneously. The turntables could also be tilted towards the hoists. [A G Atkins collection]

Bottom - Coal wagon weighbridges on the entry and exit lines of a coal hoist at Cardiff in August 1945. The entry road on the left is higher than the track for empties on the right thus permitting them to run away from the hoist. [D J Hyde collection]

adequate supply of coal, four hoists together were capable of loading at the rate of 2,000 tons an hour, until the need for trimming slowed down the process. Pre-grouping competing dock companies installed moveable hoists to encourage coal shipment at their ports, but the practice of utilising four hoists for tipping simultaneously into one ship was probably uneconomic for the railway, with all the advantages accruing to the shipowner. Furthermore, moveable hoists served fewer actual ship *berths* than single hoists.

At Cardiff, the track layout for the 1907 moveable hoists at the Queen Alexandra Dock was reconstructed with electrically-driven traversers after the Grouping. Electric motors were also used on the 25 new hoists, and improvements to existing coal hoists, installed in the South Wales coal ports for the Pole 20-ton coal wagons (see *GWR Goods Wagons*). Later, more were built under the 1929 Development Act, so that in 1930 there were over 150 new or refurbished coaling appliances in the Great Western docks (including 50 hoists at Cardiff, 41 at Barry, 30 at Swansea, and 25 at Newport). Additional sidings for coal shipment were also installed in the South Wales docks after the Grouping.

There used to be no coal shipping operations at Cardiff between 10.0 p.m. and 6.0 a.m. In 1923, negotiations were started to get the coal tippers and trimmers to work an additional night shift, to minimise delays to departing colliers. After a trial period of six months, the idea was abandoned, but in 1927 a split shift system (separate night and day shifts with an interval in between) was introduced. The gaps in tipping gave more time for wagons to be marshalled, and to be shunted to and from the tips.

Anti-Breakage Devices

The chutes down which coal was discharged into the ship from hoists might be about 24ft long (extendable to 30ft), and were adjustable to any height or angle. The speed of descent of the coal from the hoist could be controlled by gates at the ends of the chutes, operated by men on the vessel. To assist in trimming the coal, many chutes had double wings that could swing 5ft in either direction from the centre of the chute. Later, there were 'self-trimming' colliers ('turret and 'truck-decked' vessels).

There could still be an appreciable fall for the coal into the ship, especially at the commencement of loading when the hold was empty. Because large coal commanded a premium in price, colliery owners and coal shippers were concerned about the excessive breakage of the rather friable Welsh coal that occurred when efforts were made to speed up loading of ships. Indeed, breakage of coal in transhipment between railway wagons was a factor in broad gauge/standard gauge days.

Anti-breakage bucket on a tip at Swansea at the end of the C19th. Wagons brought in above quay level to the heavy timber framework of tip (no subsequent hoisting of wagons). Goods wagon in bottom right of picture (enlargement) has 5-link couplings. [STEAM Swindon]

One of the first remedial solutions against breakage was tried by the Vale of Neath Rly in the 1850s at Swansea. Anti-breakage boxes (rather like small coal containers) were employed, and these were hauled from the collieries on flat railway wagons ('platforms for boxes'), each of which took four containers. At the dockside, 'coaling cranes' lowered them down into the holds of ships, and the hinged bottom of the box was released, depositing the coal with a minimum drop.

The problem of coal breakage on conventional tips was to employ an 'anti-breakage' bucket or box that was put into position at the nose of the chute by a 6-ton crane attached to the side of the tip framework. The box received a load of coal, and was then lowered right down into the hold of the collier and opened. This operation was repeated until a heap of coal had been built up reaching almost to the bottom of the chute, after which normal tipping took place. There were various designs of anti-breakage box: for example, the 'Dispatch' design was used by the TVR at Penarth. The final type of anti-breakage device involved coal being fed from the end of the coal hoist shoot into an escalator having slats or buckets that had been lowered vertically into the empty hold. When a sufficient pile of coal had been built up, tipping by ordinary means started. Designs by different makers (Handcock, Head-Wrightson etc) were tried out between 1929-1933 at Barry, Cardiff and Swansea.

There was also a 3-ton crane on the other side of most tips which handled buckets of small coal 'screenings'. Many shoots had floors with screening bars that, for special cargoes, sieved out small coal into a bucket below. The practice of screening in the shoot was dying out by the

Left - A Lewis-Hunter box in its pit being loaded from a private-owner end-tip wagon. Photograph taken in April 1933 when Lewis-Hunter coaling cranes at Cardiff were being replaced by conventional hoists. [GWR]
Right - SS Carrigan Head at No. 9 coaling belt at Port Talbot in October 1930. The shoot is high up and delivering coal behind the ship's bridge, so she is being bunkered. No. 10 conveyor is in background; its shoot is low and is discharging coal into the hold of a collier. There were only two belt conveyors at this location; numbers 9 and 10 refer to old hoists formerly at these sites. [STEAM Swindon]

1920's however. 'Screenings' was also the word used for coal spilled on to the decks of ships around the hatches. Depending on the design and layout of the tip, screened coal was collected up and loaded into one or two wagons stabled on the quay or on gantries attached to the hoist when tracks came in at high level.

Breakage of coal might still take place during normal tipping on to coal already piled up in the hold by anti-breakage buckets. To minimise breakage of coal shipped at the new Cardiff Roath dock (1887), a special coaling crane was designed by W. T. Lewis (dock manager) and C. L. Hunter (dock engineer). Here the idea was to use Lewis-Hunter coaling cranes to load a ship *throughout,* not only to build up a pile of coal in an empty hold.

Two of these cranes were constructed and erected

by Taunatt, Walker and Co. and, after exhaustive trials, nine more were provided, making a total of eleven coaling-cranes on the south side of the Roath Dock. Four similar, but more powerful, hydraulic coaling cranes were later erected at the south-east corner of the new South (Queen Alexandra) Dock in 1907. The wide gauge of the cranes provided sufficient space and height for two lines of railway to pass underneath, and thus the quay could be utilised for imports as well as exports.

The device was a development of the VofN's concept at Swansea, but using normal coal wagons to convey the load to the docks. After a loaded wagon had been weighed at quay level, it ran on to a tip-up cradle. The cradle was tilted, and the coal discharged from the wagon into one of the Lewis-Hunter coaling-boxes, which was

Vale of Neath Rly coal containers on standard gauge flat wagons at the South dock Swansea in the late1860's (mixed gauge track; loco is BG). The containers (four to a wagon) were craned into the holds of ships and their bottoms opened to discharge the coal. Various covered-in tips in the background. Standard gauge wagons in foreground belong to "Rhys & Richards, Merthyr Dare, Smokeless Steam Coal, Shippers Noad & Thomas Swansea" [Amgueddfa Cymru National Museum of Wales]

suspended from the crane and had been previously lowered into a special pit below quay level to receive the 10 or 12-ton wagon-load of coal. The box was then lifted, and swung into position over the hatchway of the vessel. It was lowered to within a few feet of the bottom of the hold, and when its conical bottom was released hydraulically and dropped 2ft 6ins (the box itself being held by two side chains), the coal was deposited with only a small fall. The basic idea was that two short falls (one from the wagon to the box, and the second from the box to the hold) were substituted for one large fall. At Bute Roath Dock, the first two cranes worked with a special pit arranged so that a 20-ton wagon of coal could be tipped at one operation (although there were few 20-ton coal wagons in use at that time). The coal was delivered through a double-chute into two boxes, each capable of taking 10 to 12 tons, which were then dealt with in the usual way.

The L-H cranes were of the ordinary turret-top type, controlled by one man, and were self-propelling on lines running parallel with the dock coping, movement being effected by separate hydraulic engines, suitably geared (the VofN coaling cranes at Swansea were fixed). The hoisting cylinder and ram were placed in the tower, as well as the ram for lifting and closing the cone of the coal-box. Coaling cranes could also lift light loads not exceeding 2 tons by means of a small cylinder and ram outside the centre tower, the chain passing through a special sheave on the jib head. Ships' stores were loaded this way.

Being moveable, two or more of the L-H coaling cranes were frequently employed on the same steamer. They loaded into adjoining ship hatches alternately, so that while trimming was proceeding in one hatch, it was possible to load at the adjacent hatch. Considerable sums of money were expended by the Bute Estate in providing such appliances, in order that coal should be delivered to the consumer abroad in as near as possible the same condition as when hewn from the coal face. Soon after their introduction it was said that coal shipped by the Lewis-Hunter coal cranes had an increased value of one shilling per ton to the purchaser. However, in time, Lewis-Hunter and other designs of coaling cranes were found to be slow in action and awkward to handle, and they were replaced by conventional hoists in the modernisation programme for the South Wales docks carried out by the GWR under the 1929 Development Act to boost the economy.

Coal Conveyors

At Port Talbot, there were electrically-driven belt conveyor shipping appliances in addition to the usual type of coal hoist. Belt conveyors had been installed by the GWR at Fowey in 1909 for bulk loading of china clay. Two coal conveyors had been erected at Port Talbot in 1911 (one by Spencers & Co of Melksham), and a new, third appliance was introduced in 1925. Here, the coal wagon was not hoisted to a high level, but was tilted at ground level into a hopper on the quay which fed a 3ft 6in-wide endless belt. Wagons could be tipped at either end of the bunker, so no wagon turntable was required. Furthermore, the wagons ran forward onto the empties tracks, and did not impede following loaded wagons. The belt conveyed the coal to the

Above - Manual scraping out of 'duff' (wet sticky small coal left in wagons after tipping) **from coal wagons.** *[STEAM Swindon]*

Opposite page - Removal of 'duff' using the Norfolk hydraulic pusher. The upper picture shows a loaded wagon at the beginning of tipping with the blade of the device above the wagon; the lower shows the wagon being scraped clean before lowering on the hoist. Norfolk pushers were installed at most South Wales ports after 1931. [GWR]

necessary height (up to 60 ft) above the hatchway of the ship, where it dropped off the belt into a chute, and into the hold. A belt conveyor was installed at Newport in 1926 and two at the Roath Dock in Cardiff in 1932/36 all capable of receiving Pole 20-ton wagons. Even so, conveyors were not suitable for all types of Welsh coal owing to the wide range in lump size. Belts were best with free-running, small coal. Since not all Welsh coal was graded, and could arrive as 'through coal' in a variety of sizes, the door from the bunker, which controlled the flow of coal onto the belt, could sometimes get jammed by very large lumps (lumps weighing one cwt were not unknown in the 'good old days').

Belt conveyors were used a lot by the North

Eastern Railway, and questions were sometimes asked about the different practices for shipping coal as between the North-East of England (particularly on the Tyne) and South Wales. In South Wales, the land was generally flat, and only a few feet above level of dock water. It was the same at Hull, Middlesborough and other places on the North East coast, so hoists or belts were used there too. On the Tyne, it so happened that the surrounding land formed a plateau some 50 feet above the dock water; this enabled hopper wagons with bottom doors to be run out on to high level jetties where the coal fell out and through a hole between the rails into a box, whence it gravitated down a spout into the ship. For end-tip wagons, the framing on the jetty dropped at one end to release the coal.

Coal Blending & 'Patent Fuel Briquettes'

In South Wales, coal was graded at the collieries by means of screens and washeries into many varieties (far more than anywhere else in the UK) such as Large, Through, Nuts, Grains, Peas, Beans, Small, Duff etc. Anthracite coal from the West Wales coalfields was also graded into some fifteen different sizes. Duff was the sticky mess of wet, small coal which often remained in wagons after tipping, and had to be dug out by men with picks and shovels. The quantity of this duff ran to about a million tons a year. In order to speed up shipments, the Vickers-Armstrong 'Norfolk' pusher appliance (which was a hydraulic spade fitted into the tipped -up rail wagon while still on the hoist) was installed at the principal S Wales docks from 1931 onwards.

So-called 'through' coal was coal direct from mine to ship but, starting in the 1890s, the practice of mixing different coals to make up a shipment began. Not only were different sizes of similar coal mixed to produce a certain blend for export, but also different coals from separate collieries were mixed in the process of shipment. For example, Monmouthshire coals contained a higher proportion of volatiles than Rhondda coals, and a mixture of both was good for quick steam raising. The aim of mixing was to produce a blend to serve the particular needs of the buyer abroad, at a required price/ton. Just before WWI, about 30% of all shipment coal was in mixed form. To mix coal, the various grades had to be collected together by shunting in the docks' reception sidings. If there were only three or four sorts of coal to be mixed, the process was comparatively simple at the later design of hoist where there were three or four sidings for full wagons, but when mixing was more complex and had to be performed at old hoists with only one or two roads for full wagons, the vehicles had to be placed in the order required before they were taken to the hoist. Mixing was uneconomic for the railway. Both Sir James Inglis in 1907, and Sir Felix Pole after the Grouping, averred to the Swansea Chamber of Commerce that mixing was the cause of considerable delay in turning collier ships round quickly. In one instance given by Inglis, 17 parcels of coal were required to make up a load of 1,500 tons. Instead of loading at about 200 tons per hour, it could only be loaded at the rate of 40 tons per hour because the 17 parcels consisted of six different descriptions of coal from different collieries, and that required the shunting-out of trucks from various sidings all over the docks. Not only that, but further orders were given by the shippers that different tonnages had to be allocated to different parts of the ship because delivery was required at different times! Orders from the shippers to the dockside for mixing could be quite fantastic, so much so that dock owners reserved the right to decline to perform complex mixing.

Finely-broken coal and coal dust was converted into so-called 'Patent Fuel' by combining with tar and binders to form large blocks or briquettes in cube or ovoid shapes, which could then be used as a coal substitute. The process started in mid-Victorian days. There were sometimes factories for the production of patent fuel in the mining valleys (e.g. Middle Duffryn Fuel Works at Mountain Ash), but owing to the need to bring together the ingredients from across the whole coalfield, and also due to the lack of flat land near the pits, many works were to be found in all the South Wales dock estates (there was also a factory at Bristol). Much of the production was, in any case, exported. .

Between 1901 and 1906, a levy of 1s per ton was charged by the Government on export coal to pay for the Boer War. This affected business at all coal exporting ports. Small coal was, however, duty free, and Newport exported a great tonnage to France and Italy where briquettes were manufactured for railway use. The tonnages of briquettes that were exported fluctuated quite a lot: a peak was reached in the late 1920s of nearly one million tons, but thereafter it slipped to only 250,000 tons in 1938. The figures followed the fortunes of the lump coal industry.

An interesting statistic in an address by Sir Felix Pole to the Cardiff Business Club in 1924, discussing the GW's reductions in shipment coal rates in order to help the depressed coal industry, revealed that had railway and dock charges remained at the higher levels of 1920, nearly £7,700,000 would have been received by the company instead of about £4,700,000 actually charged for the 37 million tons of coal shipped in the year. Significantly, the GWR purchased about 2,250,000 tons of locomotive coal annually, the cost at the pit being about £3 million, so the railway returned to the coal industry a large part of the money it received for carriage of shipment coal!

Another attack on making coal exporting more efficient was the introduction of the 20-ton Pole mineral wagon from the mid-1920's onwards. The cost of constructing two 10-ton ordinary wagons was roughly 50 per cent more than the cost of one 20-ton wagon, and as the number of private owners' 10-ton coal wagons in South Wales was about 116,000, there were many advantages to be gained by use of the bigger capacity wagons, e.g. smaller train tare load, reduced running resistance, shortened lengths of trains, and increase of load within practical limits of length and engine capacity. The GWR offered a rebate of 5% off the rates charged on coal traffic conveyed wholly over the Great Western system in fully-loaded 20-ton wagons. The rebate also applied to coal forwarded to SR stations, and to the Great Western mileage of coal sent to LMS and LNE stations. The first 20-ton Pole wagons were tipped by hoist at Port Talbot in August 1924 and by 1930, a total of 974,562 tons of coal were shipped at South Wales ports from these 20-ton wagons.

Much of the traffic carried by the GW during both world wars would have been classified as 'special'. This train, photographed at Newport on 31 March 1915, has a single consignment of 'two sets of ground platforms and timber loading structures for 6-pounder guns'. The components are carried in O9 5-plank open wagons having Dean-Churchward brakes. The eight-wagon train is hauled by Metro tank No 3565 and carries an express passenger 'A' headcode. To the right of the loco is a 3-planker with wooden end stanchions No 9917 labelled 'Return empty to Loco Dept Pontypool Rd' (partially obscured by loco headlamp). [GWR]

Shunting in docks

The track layouts in docks depended on whether the railway had to adapt itself to an existing dock (as at Bridgwater), or whether the dock was built new along with the railway (as at Barry).

Tracks often had to thread their way along existing narrow quays and around constrictions of existing waterways, warehouses and so on. In Victorian times, wagon turntables were often used to join up lines and avoid sharp curves so as to make the best use of the available space. In the C20th, turntables were gradually removed, but the curves that were substituted were often still very sharp. Shunting locomotives for dock work were therefore short-wheelbase tank engines. At Weymouth, where the notorious bend at Ferry Corner on the line to the quay caused great problems until relieved in 1938, the GWR employed small, lightweight engines that had come from various absorbed companies; similarly at Plymouth Great Western Dock, Bridgwater Dock and elsewhere. Some GWR locos were provided new for dock shunting, such as the six 0-4-0T engines of the '1101' class, specially designed and built by the Avonside Co. for Swansea docks. When a dock was built to accommodate railways as at Barry and Birkenhead, the layout could be integrated to the benefit of dock owner, importer and exporter.

In docks where the traffic was intense, capstans driven by hydraulic or electric power were installed to avoid the use of horses or locomotives for shunting. Hydraulic capstans had initially been developed to move large sailing ships through locks. Their operation was the same as that in railway goods depots: after the rope hook had been attached to the wagon, the rope was wound two or three times round the drum of the capstan, which was made to revolve by the depression of a pedal lever. When it was required to move a wagon away from a capstan, the rope was firstly passed through a fairlead (called a 'reel' in GWR installations), that was a grooved wheel fixed in a horizontal position at a location beyond the wagon, and then brought back around the capstan. Reels were positioned strategically along sidings throughout dock estates.

GW Ports in Wartime

During the Boer and First World Wars, Southampton was the principal military port for troop embarkations, and the L & SWR took the brunt of that traffic. The surface ship and submarine threat drastically reduced coastal shipping in the Great War, and it is well-known that all the Admiralty coal for the Grand Fleet at Scapa Flow had to be moved from South Wales to Scotland by train instead of by sea, with most of the GWR's '28XX' class heavy freight locos being involved.

The first German ship to be captured in WWI was taken into Newport Docks. She was the *Belgia*, of the Hamburg-Amerika Line, that had left the United States in a hurry but had not managed to reach her home port before the outbreak of war on 4th August 1914; so, she came up the Bristol Channel and virtually offered herself as a prize. Belgian fishing boats were laid up at Newport for the duration and captured goods from Turkish campaigns were stored there.

From 1st September 1939, the operation of all

docks was taken over by the Ministry of War Transport (MoWT), and the trade in meat and foodstuffs was controlled by the Food (Defence Plans) department of the Ministry of Agriculture. In 1940, the Admiralty took over control of merchant shipping repairs from the Ministry of Shipping.

During WWII, attack from the air was an additional factor to the danger from enemy ships, submarines and mines. In defence planning before war broke out, it was envisaged that all the eastern ports, from Aberdeen to Portsmouth, might be closed to shipping, and that all exports and imports would have to pass through the western docks. Ports were prime targets for bombing, and in one of the early air attacks on Great Britain, some of the first civilian casualties occurred at the King's Dock, Swansea: in July 1940, a single plane, probing the air defences, strafed the quay, killed a number of workers and damaged the railway tracks. Of all the South Wales ports, Swansea suffered most severely from bombing, particularly in the heavy raids of February 1941.

Lessons learnt from the convoy system of shipping, introduced towards the end of WWI, were applied from the outset in WWII. During peacetime, ships arrived at ports all over the country in a fairly even flow, but convoys of large numbers of cargo vessels arrived spasmodically (depending on enough warships being available for escort). The time and place of arrival was difficult to predict, owing to enemy activity. When the ships did arrive, they had to be emptied, and some reloaded. They had to be turned round as quickly as possible, often at the same time that military transports were being loaded up. This resulted in periods of intense activity at the docks, which worked around the clock. Quayage was insufficient for the temporary heavy demand, and warehouses were crammed to overfilling.

In the build-up to 'D-Day', men and materials had to be moved south to marshalling areas within easy reach of the embarkation ports scattered along the coast between Cornwall and the Thames estuary. As the invasion of the Continent advanced, and fighting spread further afield, ports in the east became safer locations, and progressively more were involved in military transportation. Those ports in GW territory such as Falmouth, Plymouth, and Torquay that had been involved before the invasion therefore saw less and less of the general military traffic as the war progressed towards its end.

The record of the South Wales docks during WWII proved their capabilities as general cargo ports. Ninety-seven million tons of traffic were handled in and out of 100,000 vessels – of which export coal was now only a small fraction. These figures included 78% of the whole tonnage of equipment and stores of the US Army on the Continent, and about one-third of the total cargo tonnage of all British ports. The amount of shipping grew after 1943, with increasing imports while still supplying the armed forces overseas. Arrival of meat boats, in particular, necessitated strict control on the movement of insulated rolling stock.

From 3rd September 1939 to 14th August 1945,

The Lord Glanely tug newly delivered to Cardiff in 1927 and named after W J Tatem the Cardiff shipowner.

some 459,028 officers and men, and 7,891,423 tons of stores, ammunition and petrol and had been loaded or discharged. Of the overall total of military traffic, 2,730 vessels conveyed 260,393 officers and men, and 4,993,421 tons of US Government traffic. Activity at this level continued for some time after cessation of hostilities, as British, Empire and US troops returned home with all their equipment.

GWR Vessels

This book does not attempt at a full history of GW ships. Details of the GW and pre-grouping company fleets, liveries and so on, will be found in *Railway and Other Steamers* by C.L.D.Duckworth and G.E.Langmuir (Prescot, Lancs: T.Stephenson & Sons Ltd, 1948 and 1968) and *'Merchant Fleets: Britain's Railway Steamers'* by D.Haws (Hereford: TCL Publications, 1993). Most of the vessels are listed in the sections on the various ports from which they usually operated.

The quoted *tonnage* or *burthen* of ships is confusing because it does not relate to the actual weight of a ship but rather to its cargo-carrying capacity, originally measured in 'tuns' (barrels) of wine! Furthermore there are various definitions, depending on how much of the hull volume is counted as cargo space. *Net register tonnage* is the revenue-earning tonnage of the vessel and dock dues are charged on this figure. The requirement to register all British ships and give their tonnage began with an Act of 1786.

Ships sailing or steaming empty between ports had to have ballast low within the vessel in order to maintain stability. This could be in the form of rocks or lumps of

scrap iron and there were 'ballast quays' at some ports with cranes for removing or adding ballast, some of which was brought in by rail. Some ships had to carry a certain amount of ballast even when loaded with cargo. Sometimes heavy 'bottom cargo' could serve the dual purpose of ballast and revenue-earning freight: thus loads of coal were employed as ballast on ships carrying general goods from the Mersey to Ireland, and iron ore or coal was used out of Lydney. Grain from North America was used as bottom cargo on some transatlantic ships.

The word 'packet' used with shipping services

. The GWR marine flag was white with red horizontal bands at top and bottom, the GW arms at the centre encircled by a yellow garter on which 'GREAT WESTERN RAILWAY' was inscribed.

Above - *The Barry Rly tug Clive alongside the SS Walkure that has partially capsized and spilled her load of timber into Barry dock in February 1909. Tug is below the left hoist and in front of the Walkure's funnel.[Amgueddfa Cymru National Museum of Wales]*

Above - St Patrick (I) converted to a hospital ship in World War 1. [STEAM Swindon]

meant a *regular* service. Although it was most often used with mail or passenger services, occasionally one reads of 'coal packets' across the Bristol Channel from South Wales. Falmouth used to be an important packet station for mail sailing ships, since the prevailing winds made progress very slow when proceeding westwards along the English Channel, and road journeys from London were still quicker than by sea. The coming of steamships - which could of course keep up speed into the wind - and railways meant that there was no longer a need for packet ports to be situated in the far west.

The prefix to the name of a steamer indicated whether it was a paddle steamer (PS); paddle tug (PT); or screw steamer (SS). Up until WWI, designations such as TrSS (triple screw steamer) were used to indicate the number of propellers. Marine steam engines were originally reciprocating compound engines; later steam turbines came into the picture. When GW ships were replaced by more modern versions, the names of old GW ships were sometimes used again. The nomenclature employed in this book for such cases is that used by Duckworth & Langmuir: the first use of a name is indicated by the Roman numeral I in brackets after the vessel name; the second by II and so on. Thus in 1880, *PS Sir Francis Drake (I)* was the first vessel to use that name. When *SS Sir Francis Drake (II)* came along in 1908, the older vessel was renamed *PS Helper* for its remaining period in GW service before being sold.

The earliest steamers owned by GWR came not from the well-known Irish or Channel Islands routes but from rather obscure services. When the GW took over the Shrewsbury & Chester Railway in 1854, it inherited two wooden paddle tugs (see Saltney). Other vessels came into GW ownership by acquisitions such as, in 1868, the Bristol & South Wales Union Rly paddle steamers that operated the New Ferry Passage across the Severn before the opening of the Severn Tunnel in 1886 (see Chepstow). Originally, Parliament forbade railway companies to own and run their own passenger vessels in order that existing shipowners should not sufferer unfair competition. At first, therefore, private vessels operated the services between West Wales and Ireland, and between Weymouth and the Channel Islands, even though the boats ran in connexion with timetabled trains. However, that prohibition in the Railway Act was repealed in 1862 and eventually, in 1871, the GW obtained Parliamentary powers to operate steam vessels from Weymouth to the Channel Islands, St Malo and Cherbourg, and also from New Milford to Waterford and Cork in Ireland. Whereas the Channel Islands traffic was left in the hands of an independent shipping company for many years, the GW invested in its own new ships for its Irish traffic.

Smaller ships operated as tenders for ocean liners at both Fishguard and Plymouth; others ran the Kingswear & Dartmouth Ferry; and the GW ran excursion paddle boats, timetabled with the trains, between Kingsbridge and Salcombe in the late 1920's.

Opposite bottom - SS St Julien as converted to a hospital ship (No 29, with red crosses on white hull and on funnel) in Penarth dock in June 1944. Behind her on the other side of the dock is the pontoon dry dock that GW maps show was positioned there. Across the tidal harbour can be seen some of the early covered-in coal tips, while at the top right are travelling hydraulic cranes on the wooden-sided oil wharf [GWR].

The River Dart excursion boat PS Kenwith Castle of 1914 that, with her sister ship PS Ilton Castle, were the last paddle steamers to be owned and operated by the GWR. [L Fairweather]

In addition, there were tugs and 'service' vessels for dredging and other purposes, the number of which grew on the amalgamations with the South Wales docks railways.

Other boats which came to the GW through acquisition (before the Grouping) included:

PS Weston and *PS Clevedon,* tugs employed in the Bristol Channel; and a scraper at Bridgwater (all ex-B&E). The Brunel-designed scraper was officially unnamed but known as *Bertha.*

1880 *PS Sir Francis Drake (I)* (built 1873) and *PS Sir Walter Raleigh (I)* (built 1874) tenders at Plymouth (registered in the name of the West Cornwall Rly which had by then arrived at Plymouth, even though the Plymouth Great Western Docks Co, as such, was jointly owned by the GW, B&E and SDR).

1901 *PS Dolphin* the 61-ton Dartmouth ferry boat (iron paddle steamer built 1860) when the Dartmouth & Torbay Rly, opened in 1864, was absorbed by the GW in 1901.

Ships taken over retained their original liveries at first, but after 1873 the 'standard' GW livery of red funnel with black top, black hull with red waterline, brown masts, white or deep buff brown upper structure and mahogany bridges, became normal. Paddle steamers had white paddle boxes. There were variations, eg between 1889 and 1914 a white band was added to the hull at main deck level in some vessels; some of the tenders had 'GWR' vertically down the funnel. The sterns of vessels, round about where a ship's name was marked, were highly decorated up to the turn of the C19th/20th. The house marine flag was white with red horizontal bands top and bottom, the GWR arms in the centre encircled by yellow garter on which 'GREAT WESTERN RAILWAY' was inscribed. The *Railway Magazine* for 1927 (p.194) gives details of the livery of vessels belonging to pre-Grouping railway companies.

The first boats ever *built* for the GWR as such were the pair of paddle steamers *PS Limerick* and *PS Milford* in 1873 for the Waterford service. The last vessel purchased before the Grouping (in 1920) was the second-hand double-grab hopper dredger named *Basingstoke* bought from Cork; she was sold in 1937 to the Milford Docks Co. The first new

vessel built for the enlarged GWR after the Grouping was the *Viscount Churchill* (named after the company chairman), which was a hopper barge delivered from Holland in 1924. New vessels *St David (III)* and *St Patrick (III)* had been ordered to replace the vessels of the same names lost in WWII. While *St David (III)* was delivered for the Irish services in 1947, *St Patrick (III)* – which, despite its name, was intended for daytime Channel Islands journeys – was not handed over until early 1948. Both these vessels had the GW coat-of-arms at the bow. The final new ship to come into service for the GWR in 1947 was the bucket dredger *Abertawe.*

The Great Western introduced road motors in the South Hams during 1904, which later included a service between Kingsbridge and Salcombe, opened in 1909; this took so much traffic from Dart river boats that in 1927 the two paddle steamers on the run were sold off to the GWR; they were 53-ton, 'sister' excursion boats, but built at different dates: *PS Ilton Castle* (1906) and *PS Kenwith Castle* (1914). They were operated by the GWR between Kingsbridge and Salcombe in the summer months, timetabled with the trains, but the company sold them off in 1932. These two boats have historical significance as they were the last paddle steamers to be owned and operated by the GWR. The last paddle steamer actually *constructed* for the Great Western was the 927-ton steel-hulled *PS Pembroke* in 1880 (see New Milford).

Various railway steamers were requisitioned by the Admiralty in both world wars: their shallow draught, passenger berth accommodation, manoeuvrability and high speed made them ideal as hospital ships and troop ships. Ships not taken over remained to carry on limited services. Which GW vessels were requisitioned and what happened to them, including sinkings, is described in the sections on Weymouth, New Milford and Fishguard. Originally, British hospital ships carried the recognised sign of the Red Cross, illuminated at night, on their sides. Late in 1918, after a number had been sunk, the livery was changed to dazzle type camouflage. This was not intended to make the ship invisible, rather to deceive an attacker about its speed and direction. Even so, in WWII, requisitioned GW hospital ships were painted white with large red crosses.

BRENTFORD
(Owned; ex-Great Western & Brentford Railway)

Brentford riverside dock was located at the junction of the River Brent, the Grand Junction Canal and the Thames, on the north bank of the river just to the west of Kew Bridge. The original dock dated from 1859, having been built by the independent Great Western & Brentford Railway, which was taken over by the Great Western in 1872. The 3-mile long branch line from Southall to Brentford continued for half a mile eastwards beyond the passenger station, over the 242-yard canal viaduct to the riverside.

Local river traffic connected waterside premises all the way between Chiswick and Tilbury, and export traffic was taken by barge and lighter to the London Docks - some 14 miles downriver - for reloading into ocean-going ships. The reason for extensive barge and lighter traffic on the Thames was the 'free water clause' explained in the section on London Docks. Barges and lighters were moved by tug, the major provider being the Thames Steam Tug & Lighterage Co; this company had been featured in the original prospectus for the construction of the Brentford line in 1856. With a 29ft 4 ins-wide dock gate to the Thames, the 400-yard-long dock had nearly four acres of water, the depth of which was kept at about 10ft at low water, and between14 and 18ft at high water. There was room for seventy barges

and small vessels. In the C20th, sea-going vessels up to 300 tons capacity used for near-Continental traffic came to Brentford, being navigated in and out of the dock by their own captains, or by pilots.

Well over 500,000 tons of goods passed annually in and out of the Brentford docks during the 1920's and 1930's. Traffic to and from all parts of the world was handled, the principal imports being grain, motor cars, wood pulp from Newfoundland and Scandinavia, tin and zinc from Malaya and Australia, esparto grass from North Africa, hemp and marble from Italy, and figs from the Middle East. A heavy coal tonnage also was handled, the rail conveyance rates for shipment coal being inclusive of all charges. Furthermore, in the 1930s, the GWR allowed a rebate of 1s per ton on all South Wales coal that was to be tipped into barges for delivery to riverside premises on the Thames, or was for bunkering steam tugs. Later, the allowance became 2s 6d per ton and applied to barge traffic at Poplar and Chelsea docks as well as at Brentford. Exports from the docks included motor cars to Australia, New Zealand, Africa, India, Russia, Germany and Spain; rubber tyres to Spain, Portugal and France; aeroplanes to overseas British Possessions; and iron-work to India and Egypt.

Originally, local goods for Brentford was dealt with within the docks area, the Great Western's depot at

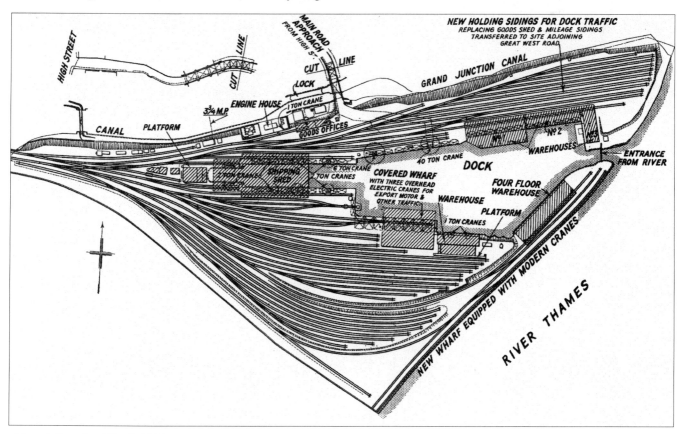

Map of Brentford Dock 1930

Before the rebuilding of the dock at Brentford in the late 1920's, barges could be loaded from wagons tipped at gravity-and-winch tips. Winch is to the left of the man. A covered wharf later was built on the site for Morris Cowley export car traffic. The dock gates to the River Thames may be seen to the right of the distant No 3 warehouse on the left, the trees beyond being in Kew Gardens. [GWR]

Brentford having the distinction of having the first concrete-built railway goods shed and warehouse, in 1899. Following the First World War, shipment traffic through the docks had grown so much that a new (local) goods depot was built in 1930 at the point where the branch line crossed the 'new arterial road' (the Great West Road) on the Southall side of the passenger station (see *GWR Goods Services, Vol 2A*). The new depot provided 'collection and delivery' (C & D) shed and mileage facilities not only for Brentford, but also for Isleworth, Hounslow, Heston, Osterley Park and Twickenham. The space vacated at the docks was included in a rebuilding programme to increase the siding accommodation for shipment traffic. Warehouse accommodation for bulk storage at the riverside depot had already been increased for private firms some years before.

The total area encompassed by the dock, railway sidings, shipping sheds and warehouses was 15 acres, with over 2,000ft of quayage (over 3,000ft after the 1920's rebuilding, with a reconstructed riverside quay on the

Thames and electric floodlighting installed throughout). By WWI, accommodation was provided on some forty sidings for around 860 wagons, the number increasing to nearer 1,000 wagons after the removal of the goods shed and laying down of extra sidings on the site. The western arm of the dock (known locally as the 'shipping shed') was completely under cover, including the surrounding platform, wagon roads and craneage on either side. The original wooden structure covering the area had been designed by Brunel, but was destroyed by fire in June 1920 and was replaced by a new structure in the 1920's redevelopments. Eleven wagons on each side of the covered dock could be dealt with at one time.

On the south side of the dock, three tip lines dating from the C19[th] were used to discharge coal from wagon to barge employing 'gravity and winch' coal tips. No. 1 tip dealt with wagons of 15 tons capacity (25 tons gross weight) whilst Nos. 2 and 3 tips handled 12 ton loads (20 tons gross). All wagons to be tipped had to have a wheelbase of

Top - *Looking out from the inside the shipping shed at Brentford dock in September 1933. On the right, one of the 2-ton cranes unloading cattle cake from a lighter. On the opposite side there is iron-bodied 1908-built CC4 workshop van No 43968 from G-shop Swindon Works with men to perform crane testing and maintenance duties.*

Middle - *A view from outside the dock in 1933, with a barge emerging from the lock gates at right centre. The new 3-ton semi-portal cranes running alongside the riverside wharf are on the left, in front of the four-storey warehouse. 'Great Western' on roof of No 3 warehouse, with No 2 recessed to the left and No1 out over the water further to the left again. One of the 40-ton cranes is visible in the far distance between the gap in the warehouses.*

Bottom - *The riverside wharf outside the dock proper, before rebuilding. The wharf dated from 1918. Timber, barged up river from the Port of London, being unloaded by travelling steam crane and placed on bogie J11 Macaw B No 70815, dating from 1906. 'Wm Cory & Son Ltd London' wagons to left of Macaw B. Barges at quayside aground on mud. Kew Gardens on right. Tower of Kew pumping station in distance below jib of second crane. [GWR]*

no more than 12ft, and fifteen wagons per hour could be dealt with, amounting to some 2,500 tons in a day. Full loads were stabled on two of the tracks serving each tip, empty wagons being returned on the third. Wagon movement was by hydraulic capstan and a turntable. By 1936, one hydraulic coal tip had been installed, the bottom of its moveable shoot being about 14 ft above water level. A conveyor belt, within a horizontal framework, was also installed. The device could reach out over the water and load barges not against the quay wall.

In the warehouses, there were 11 hydraulic hoists with 35ft-high lifts for general traffic purposes. A special feature of the reconstruction, also on the south side, was a covered wharf built in 1927 for export motor traffic from Morris Motors Ltd. at Cowley works (on the Oxford & Princes Risborough branch). It was a steel and galvanised iron erection, with three bays each fitted with a 3-ton overhead electric travelling gantry crane. With a 150ft x 80ft concrete floor, it had standing room for six wagons and a 25 ft awning to cover two barges. Each bay had two tracks. It was one of the few covered berths in London capable of taking sea-going vessels. The depot was also useful for handling timber from Norway or Sweden, much of which went as return traffic for making into crates for exported motor cars.

On the north side of the dock at Brentford were located 40-ton hydraulic cranes which became well known in railway photographs of exceptional loads, such as out-of-gauge railway coaches for export to overseas railways. Special 100ft barges - 75ft clear in the hold - were provided by the tug company, and the coaches were transported downriver for transfer to ocean-going ships.

There was extensive warehouse accommodation within the dock confines: three on the north side and one on the south side of the dock, all overhanging the water, and all equipped with hydraulic hoists and electric cranes. No 4 warehouse on the south side, dating from the 1920's redevelopment, was a typical GW brick and concrete design having 4 floors, with a total floor space of some 4,000 sq yds capable of holding, for example, 32,000 sacks of grain.

On the riverside, outside the dock proper, was a 960ft-long reinforced concrete wharf, which had been built as a war measure in 1918 to deal with coal, timber, scrap and general cargo not requiring cover. All the concrete piles and wall panels were constructed at the GW Concrete Works at Taunton. The riverbed was deepened some 6ft so that the wharf could be used at all states of the tide; it could accommodate ten ordinary barges, or special 1,000 ton

Top - The riverside wharf after rebuilding with new 3-ton semi-portal electric cranes for unloading coal by grab. [GWR]

Bottom - The motor yacht Helen III being loaded on to bogie well trolley (C15 Crocodile E No 41948 built in 1908) by 40-ton crane. White-painted Dean-Churchward brake handle at right end of wagon is in the dropped (brake on) position. Shipping shed in left background. [GWR]

lighters that could not be berthed in the dock itself. The wharf was served originally by three 6-ton travelling steam cranes, using one of the sidings which extended the whole length of the wharf. These cranes were capable of 40 lifts per hour, and when fitted with coal grabs, 500 tons of coal per day could be transferred from railway truck to barge. Later, electric cranes operating on a 'leg and gantry' system along the whole length of the wharf replaced the travelling steam cranes. Separate 'in' and 'out' tracks connected the wharf with the rest of the dock sidings.

. The dock gates were opened approximately two hours before high tide, and closed two hours after. Invoices for incoming goods barged upriver from the London Docks were sent from the GW's city and shipping office at the Minories in London, and gave contents and destination. In the case of private barges, documents were received direct from the senders. From these details, the chief inspector or foreman on duty was able to decide the allocation of craft to the various cranes or berths according to cargo and in order of arrival; any demurrage charges were worked out from details and times of discharge of the barges.

Twenty-six gangs of men, each consisting of a checker and two loaders, were employed throughout the week in two eight hour shifts – 6 a.m. to 2 p.m. and 2 p.m. to 10 p.m. Their method of working was very similar to that of ordinary railway goods sheds: the checker was supplied with a copy of the barge invoice for the barge which the gang was unloading, and also with a checking note upon which he recorded details of the traffic received. After scrutiny by the foreman, the notes formed the basis upon which the gang's weight for the week (and bonus payments) was assessed. Any remarks as to condition of the goods or discrepancies were noted and dealt with, and the documents passed to the invoicing office.

For inwards rail traffic intended for shipment out by river, an entry was made in the shipping book, which showed origin, consignee, goods marks, weight, steamer and dock, and port dues. A loading note was then prepared in duplicate, one copy being used by the checker and the other for obtaining the receipt of the lighterage company. A shipping note was also prepared in duplicate and handed to the tug company for presentation to the ship's officer down river for signature. Barge invoices, corresponding to those received with up-river traffic, were prepared and sent to the GW's Minories office for completion of transit. In the days when Brentford town traffic was dealt with in the dock area, it was dealt with separately, both as regards loading/unloading and clerical work.

All incoming trains destined for Brentford Dock were made up at Southall, and worked over the branch through Brentford passenger station. There were six timetabled inwards trains of mixed traffic (up to 50 wagons per train), and six outwards trains (with up to 45 wagons each). Two shunting engines were kept continually employed moving wagons to and from the various loading and unloading berths at the dock..

On the nights of 3/17 July 1944, bombing of Brentford Dock resulted in warehouse walls collapsing and windows and doors being blown out, but business continued.

This page - *Two shots of GW 'BK' removals container No. 1869 built in 1936 being transferred from lighter to rail at Brentford in February 1937. A second GW container, BK-1872, yet to be unloaded remains in the lighter with the tarpaulin that covered it partially still in place. The containers were loaded with effects from the boys' Training Ship Warspite that was moored down the Thames at Greenhithe. Crane driver in cabin on left. Second heavy-duty crane on right with No 1 warehouse behind, the angled-off end of which is at the extreme right and just out of the picture. Top half of letter 'X' on iron Mink to left of container indicates a 'docks-only' van. Lighters to the right are named Yardhill, Judge and Yarmouth. [GWR]*

Brentford when wagon turntables were being removed prior to the shipping shed for Morris Cowley being constructed on the same site. [David Hyde collection]

CHELSEA BASIN
(Leased Jointly with the LNWR/LMS)

In the early days of railways, some lines were built to link up directly with canals. A notable example was the mixed-gauge Birmingham, Bristol & Thames Junction Railway (the original name of the West London Railway, opened in 1844) which was laid out to connect the London & Birmingham and Great Western Railways with the River Thames by means of the Chelsea (Kensington) Canal that had been constructed under an Act of 1824. Goods were transferred from railway wagons to barges at Warwick Road basin, just to the south of the Hammersmith Road, and taken to and from the Thames at Chelsea Creek.

The Chelsea Canal was subsequently absorbed by the WLR, and a proposal to build a dock at Chelsea was submitted to Parliament by the West London Extension Railway (L&NW, GW, L&SW and LB&SC, joint from Addison Road to Clapham), resulting in an Act of 1861. Subsequently, Chelsea dock was leased to, and worked by, the L&NW and GW Railways. Chelsea dock and basin was reached from Old Oak Common over the WLR to West London Extension Junction (some 750 yards south of Addison Road station) and then the WLER line. Originally, there were broad gauge tracks all the way to Victoria passenger station which were used by the GWR only for one coal train a day each way between West London Jct. and Chelsea Basin, until in 1863 three broad gauge passenger trains worked daily into Victoria. The Kensington

(Warwick Rd) basin later became a normal GWR goods depot, handling station-to-station and mileage traffic (see *GWR Goods Services*).

Chelsea dock was over 500ft long and had a water area of 2½ acres, some 9ft deep, and nearly 1,400ft of quay. Access to the river at high tide was via a lock 80ft long by 19ft 2ins wide, and craft up to 120 tons could be accommodated. Water depths at the outer cill of the lock were 11ft/8 ft at spring/neap tides. In the C20th the contractor for dredging at both Chelsea and Brentford was Messrs H Covington & Sons Ltd, originally at Railway Wharf, Battersea (contract set up by Mr Grierson in 1915), later at Cremorne Wharf, Lots Rd, Chelsea. A record was kept by the railway of the dimensions of all barges using the docks.

The goods shed at the dock had a height restriction of 13ft for wagon loads, but elsewhere around the depot clearances permitted the height above the tracks to be 13ft 6 ins. Local goods was dealt with as well as shipment traffic. In the 1920s, for example, the following firms had premises near the depot and barged or carted their own traffic:

Asiatic Petroleum Co, Fulham; Gas Light & Coal Co, Fulham; Macfarlane, Lang & Co, Fulham; M o r g a n Crucible Co, Battersea; Price's Patent Candle Co, Battersea; Shell-Mex, Fulham; and H. Windsor & Co, Fulham.

Also, the nearby firms of Barrett, Tagant & Gotts of Fulham, and Garton, Sons & Co. of Battersea required their 'returned empties' to be sent to Chelsea basin. Empties for

Aerial photograph of Chelsea Basin including Lots Road power station that generated electricity for London Underground.

these firms were invoiced 'to Paddington for Chelsea Basin', truck loads being labelled direct to Chelsea Basin and small lots sent to Paddington for transfer.

There were around thirty sidings on the site, with storage accommodation for around 850 wagons. Two wagon weighbridges each of 20-ton capacity were provided. Shunting locos were supplied from Old Oak Common depot.

Coal was shipped by means of three end-door wagon tips and two side-door wagon tips, all capable of dealing with loaded wagons of 23 tons gross, and capable of tipping a total of 1,500 tons of coal per day. Depending on the water level in the basin, coal fell between 3 and 5 ft into barges from the balance-type tips. There was one 10-ton hand crane and two rail steam cranes of 2½ ton capacity on the quayside. As at Brentford and Poplar docks, there was a 1s per ton (later 2s 6d) rebate allowed on all coal tipped at Chelsea destined for premises on the River Thames, and a drawback of 1/9d per ton was granted on coal for bunkering steam tugs and shipment coal.

LONDON
(Served)

By 1921, all the London Docks had finally been constructed. There were, from west to east, the St Katherine dock (opened 1828); the London dock (1800); Surrey Commercial dock (origins began in 1807 with the Surrey Canal basin); West India (1799) and South-West India (1870, ex-City Canal) docks; Millwall docks (1868); Poplar Docks (began life as a water-regulating basin for the West India dock, but in 1833 began to be used as a timber float and from 1852 was rented to the North London Railway as a commercial coal dock); East India (1806); Royal Victoria (1855) and Royal Albert (1880); King George V Dock (1921); and Tilbury Docks (1886). All were originally privately owned, and competed with each other for business. Riverside wharves, where all trade had previously been

LONDON.

The Company have first-class accommodation and transport facilities for all descriptions of town, river and dock traffic.

In connection with their numerous Goods Stations and Receiving Offices, which are established in the most important business centres, their carts collect and deliver merchandise daily from and to all parts of London and in many of the principal suburbs; and in such suburban districts as are not reached by the Company's carts the chief Road Carriers are under arrangement to perform those services.

The Company collect and deliver by Barge to and from the Docks and riverside premises and ships in the river and docks, and also have efficient arrangements for dealing with traffic by truck or cart to and from all the Docks in the London district.

The GOODS STATIONS in London are:—

PADDINGTON. Adjoins the Paddington Passenger Station (the two stations covering an area of about 70 acres) and is approached from Praed Street, *via* South Wharf Road or London Street, Bishop's Road and Harrow Road.

It affords ample accommodation for all descriptions of traffic, is provided with hydraulic crane power, and has a high level yard for Coal; and traffic to or from barges on the Regent's Canal can be transferred direct from or to the Railway Wagons.

There is extensive warehouse accommodation for every description of traffic. The Company's teams collect and deliver goods to and from this station.

For the convenience of freighters in the North-Western, West and South-Western Districts, Subsidiary Goods Depôts for dealing with Coal, Building Materials, Hay and Straw and other similar traffics not requiring warehousing or cartage by the Company's teams have been established at:—

Chelsea Basin.	Hammersmith.
Old Oak Common.	Kensington (Warwick Road.)
Westbourne Park (Mileage Yard.)	Shepherd's Bush.

SMITHFIELD. Is situated in the heart of the City, underneath the Central Meat Market, and is the only Goods Station connected with the Market by hydraulic lifts, by means of which Meat, Poultry, etc., is delivered direct from the Railway Trucks to the salesmen's shops without cartage, perishable goods being thus delivered promptly in the best possible condition.

The Station is also convenient for general traffic to or from the City Warehouses and Central London, where the Company's vans collect and deliver. It has warehouse accommodation and hydraulic crane power.

LONDON—*continued.*

BRENTFORD. This Station, which is connected with the Great Western Main Line at Southall, is situated on the River Thames, and has ample Dock accommodation for barged traffic of all descriptions, which is transferred direct to or from the Railway Wagons, and lightered **to or from riverside premises anywhere on the Thames in the London District, and to and from ships in the various docks.**

There is extensive warehouse accommodation at this Station for Grain and similar traffic; also ample sidings for dealing with local Grain and Mineral Traffic, Hay, Straw, etc.; appliances for tipping Coal from truck to barge and for transferring from barge to truck; hydraulic cranes for lifting weights up to 40 tons; provision for Furniture Vans and other vehicles on wheels, and Live Stock.

General Goods for Brentford Town and Market, Kew, Gunnersbury and other places in the neighbourhood are dealt with here, the Company's own teams collecting and delivering in the district.

Information respecting the lighterage arrangements can be obtained from the Company's representatives at 43 and 44, Crutched Friars, London, E.C., at Brentford Station, or from the District Goods Manager, 23, Newgate Street, E.C.

POPLAR. For all descriptions of local traffic and traffic to and from the :—

WEST INDIA DOCK.	**SOUTH WEST INDIA DOCK.**
EAST INDIA DOCK.	**MILLWALL DOCK.**
ROYAL VICTORIA	**ST. KATHERINE DOCK.**
AND ALBERT DOCKS.	**SURREY COMMERCIAL DOCKS.**
LONDON DOCKS.	

This station, situated on the River Thames between the East and West India Docks, affords ample accommodation for all descriptions of traffic.

Traffic is barged between this station and all the Docks named above.

The Company has rail connection with the East India, West India, South West India and Millwall Docks, to and from which their trucks run direct.

The Company's carts collect and deliver traffic in all the Docks.

The station is also conveniently situated for the neighbourhoods of Greenwich, Lewisham, New Cross, Blackheath and Deptford, in which the Company's own teams collect and deliver.

LONDON—*continued.*

POPLAR (*continued*).

There is extensive warehouse accommodation for traffic of all descriptions, also accommodation for Live Stock, Furniture Vans, and other wheeled vehicles, Coal, Hay, Straw, and General Mileage traffic.

Crane power with lifting capacity up to 30 tons is provided, and cranes of greater power, in some cases reaching 50 tons, are available for Shipping traffic to and from the various docks.

VICTORIA AND ALBERT STATION. This Station is close to the Connaught Road Station of the London and India Docks Company's Line, and adjoins the Royal Albert Dock, with which (and the Victoria Dock) it has direct rail communication, the Company's trucks running alongside vessels berthed in the Docks.

Goods are also collected or delivered by cart or barge.

Extensive sidings and warehouse accommodation for all descriptions of traffic enable the Company to store Goods awaiting instructions, where they are available for immediate shipment.

In addition to the facilities for dock traffic, **this station has every convenience for dealing with the trade of the district,** and of the surrounding neighbourhoods of Silvertown, Woolwich, Charlton, Plumstead, Barking, East Ham, Upton Park, Forest Gate, Ilford, Plaistow and Canning Town, in which the Company's teams collect and deliver.

The Station is provided with electric cranes for lifting weights up to 12 tons, lifts, etc., as well as wharfage facilities for Coal, Stone, Timber, Hay and Straw, and other descriptions of heavy traffic.

WATERSIDE DEPÔT (VICTORIA AND ALBERT). The Waterside Depôt, which is actually inside the Docks, affords perfect facilities for dealing with shipping traffic in all conditions of tide and weather, also with traffic of all kinds from or for firms having waterside premises on the Lower Thames about Woolwich, Beckton, Barking Creek, Abbey Wood, Manor Way, Belvedere, Crossness, Erith, Greenhithe, Dartford Creek, Dagenham, Rainham, Purfleet, Grays, Tilbury (not Tilbury Docks) and on the River Medway, no charge being made for the use of the Company's Wharf. The Depôt is in direct rail communication with the whole of the Company's System, and Goods are collected or delivered by cart or barge.

handled, continued in business after the building of the wet docks, and there was much river-borne traffic using barges and lighters between warehouses and businesses situated on the Thames, its tributaries, and along connecting canals.

As explained in the Introduction, the first wet docks on the Thames came about principally because of the 'plundering' of goods. The London docks' success was assured in 1803 when the government introduced the idea of 'bonding', whereby customs duties payable on arrival at a port became excise duties to be paid only when the goods were removed for consumption. This laid the foundations of London's subsequent eminence as an *entrepot* port where goods landed were warehoused and subsequently re-exported.

Before the building of the docks, lighters had taken goods to and from those big ships that could not berth at the quays, and were moored in mid-river. To put their operation within the docks on the same basis as on the open river, lighters entering to deliver or receive goods on board ship were to be exempt from dues. This *free-water clause* in the Acts of Incorporation of the London docks meant that barges and lighters could enter and leave the enclosed docks at will, paying no dues, take freight overside from ships at

berth in the docks and then take the goods to wharves and warehouses on the open river, bypassing the dock warehouses. This hidden subsidy to off-dock firms became a lasting problem and an enduring feature of London dock operation; many attempts to get the clause abolished always failed. Much of the traffic to and from the later GWR riverside docks at Brentford and Chelsea was by barge and lighter to the enclosed docks downriver.

As more and more world trade was carried by ever bigger steamers, dock construction in the late C19th at London became a process of leapfrogging in dock sizes, entrance lock sizes, and facilities. By the end of the century, London was overprovided with docks and dock warehouses, and shipping lines had to be bribed through spiralling-downwards unprofitable rates to transfer their business from one new dock to another. This, in turn, brought on considerable labour problems in the docks. To sort out these difficulties, the Port of London Authority (PLA) was formed in 1909 to take over all the docks, with the exception of Poplar Dock that was owned by the North London Railway. The PLA controlled the 94 miles of both banks of the tidal Thames downstream from Teddington.

The Victoria Dock of 1855 was the first to be built

LONDON—*continued.*

SHIPPING TRAFFIC.

The Company have every facility for dealing with Shipping Traffic in the Port of London, and a specially trained staff give careful and prompt attention to shipping orders.

The Company have rail connection with many of the Docks, and Import and Export Goods can be loaded direct between the Ships and Railway Stations on the G.W.R. and its connections, or can be barged or carted from the Docks or Wharves or from alongside ship in the river to one of the stations before named for further transit.

TILBURY DOCKS. The Company have through rail communication with the Docks at Tilbury, *via* Acton, Bromley and the London, Tilbury and Southend Railway; traffic of all descriptions can be conveyed direct between the docks and all stations on the Great Western Railway and its connections.

MARKET TRAFFIC.

Special arrangements exist for the prompt delivery of traffic to, and collection from the under-mentioned Markets :—

NAME OF MARKET.	PRODUCE DEALT WITH.
†BILLINGSGATE, LOWER THAMES ST., E.C....	Fish.
†BOROUGH, S.E.	Fruit and Vegetables.
BRENTFORD	Fruit and Vegetables.
†CENTRAL MARKETS, SMITHFIELD, E.C. ...	Meat, Poultry and Provisions.
†COVENT GARDEN, W.C.	Fruit, Vegetables and Flowers.
FARRINGDON ROAD, E.C.	Fruit, Vegetables and Fish.
†LEADENHALL, LEADENHALL ST., E.C.	Poultry and Meat.
†SPITALFIELDS, E.	Fruit and Vegetables.
STRATFORD, E.	Fruit and Vegetables.

† The Company's representatives are in regular attendance at these Markets to receive orders and afford information.

LONDON—*continued.*

WAREHOUSE ACCOMMODATION.

The Company have extensive warehouses at :—

PADDINGTON.

SMITHFIELD. Specially constructed for accommodating Meat, Poultry, Butter, Eggs and similar traffic. This warehouse is connected by hydraulic lifts with Central Markets.

BRENTFORD
POPLAR } Most convenient for Shipping Traffic awaiting orders.
VICTORIA & ALBERT

ORDERS FOR THE COLLECTION AND DELIVERY
OF GOODS SHOULD BE ADDRESSED TO—

(The figures shown in brackets indicate the Telephone numbers).

COLLECTION AND DELIVERY BY CART.

Mr. W F WILSON, Paddington Goods Station, W (4880) Paddington.
Mr. P HARPER, Smithfield „ „ E.C. (5960) Holborn.
Mr. F J MEAD, Poplar „ „ E. (1720) Eastern.
Mr. F J MEAD, Victoria and Albert Goods Station, Connaught Road, E. (608) Eastern.

COLLECTION BY BARGE.

Mr. W. SQUIRE, 43, Crutched Friars, E.C. (2429 Avenue).

DELIVERY BY BARGE.

Mr. W ADAMS, Brentford Docks, W (73 Ealing).
Mr. F J MEAD, Poplar Goods Station, E. (1720) Eastern.

LONDON SUBURBAN STATIONS.

The Company have Stations fully equipped for dealing with general traffic in the Western Suburbs at :—

ACTON	WEST EALING (for Ealing and
PARK ROYAL (for Willesden,	Hanwell) (488 P.O. Ealing)
Harlesden, Neasden, Crickle-	SOUTHALL (18)
wood, Alperton, etc.) (393	GREENFORD
Chiswick)	HAYES & HARLINGTON (21 P.O.)

Goods should be addressed and consigned " per Great Western Railway."

integral with railways - the Great Eastern Rly in that instance. For London docks traffic, the GWR had two large goods depots, one at Poplar Dock (depot opened in 1877), and another at the Victoria & Albert Docks (depot opened 1902). Both not only dealt with dock traffic, but also carted local C&D goods traffic; they were large, fully-fledged yards with extensive warehouse accommodation, sidings for mileage, mineral, hay and straw, and livestock traffic. General traffic could be delivered by cart, railway wagon or barge to local premises. In addition, the company had small offices and staff at Millwall Docks (dealing with truck-loads of traffic to or from sidings other than those belonging to the PLA) and at Tilbury Docks (dealing only with shipping traffic).

The GWR's customs agents for the London Docks were Messrs C.S. Lovell & Sons of 38 Eastcheap, EC: bills of lading for delivery of goods to the GWR from ships were to be endorsed on the back by the owner and posted, with instructions for clearing and particulars of value, to the GW District Goods Manager at 23 Newgate St, EC1. Orders for collection of goods were to be forwarded to the relevant GWR Goods Agent as follows:

(i) all general traffic to be collected by barge, to the Agent at 43 Crutched Friars, EC3.

(ii) tea from the docks and bonded warehouses, and general traffic to be carted from the London and the St Katherine Docks, to the Agent at 118 Minories, E1.

(iii) general traffic to be collected by railway wagon or by cart,

a) from the East India, West India, South West India and Millwall docks, to the Agent at Poplar Dock Station, E14 and

(b) from the Royal Albert, Royal Victoria and King George V Docks, to the Agent at V&A Station, E16.

(iv) general traffic to be collected by cart from the Surrey Commercial Docks, to the Agent at South Lambeth Goods Depot, SW8.

The GWR Receiving Office at Crutched Friars also dealt with empty sacks provided by customers to be filled with grain from ships in the docks; they were collected by lighter. Such sacks were to be forwarded by rail from the customers' home stations to Smithfield goods depot in the first instance, thence to be carted to Crutched Friars or to the docks.

The GW depot at Poplar dock as leased from the North London Rly in 1898. The cartage loading bay with glass roof proclaims over its entrance that the Great Western Railway Company are 'carriers to the West and South of England, South and North Wales, South Staffordshire, North Staffordshire, The Channel Islands, & the Principal Towns in Lancashire and Yorkshire'. Carboys in GW 4-plank open wagon in front of outside office near horse lorry tilt, iron Minks on other tracks into warehouse. Wagon turntable to left of 4-planker. GNR saddle tank shunting on adjacent lines.

Poplar Dock, that eventually became NLR property, was in direct water communication with the West India and South West India Docks, and also had rail connections with them and the East India and Millwall Docks, over which GWR wagons ran directly from Acton. Great Western traffic for the other docks had to be taken to and from Poplar by barge.

The GWR depot at Poplar comprised a large warehouse served by five long sidings with wagon turntables at either end; about 240 wagons could be accommodated (see *GW Goods Services Vol. 2A*, pp174-7). Just over 200 staff were employed by the GWR at Poplar Dock for most of its existence, but the numbers dropped to 150-odd by the end of the 1930s. The office staff at Poplar handled copies of all invoices relating to GWR Tilbury Dock traffic, the details of which were included in Poplar's returns. The total tonnage (docks and local) of goods handled at the Poplar depot was some 300,000 tons annually before the WWI, though this fell to 100,000 tons between the wars. Of these totals, Poplar was receiving and forwarding annually about 90,000 tons each of general merchandise before the First World War; in the 1920s these figures dropped to 70,000 tons each per year and fell further to the 50,000 ton level each in the 1930s. Even so, over the same period, the consistent figure of 70,000 tons of goods was carted annually to and from the depot. The annual tonnage of coal and coke forwarded was a few thousand tons every year (hardly any was received), but there was a regular forwarded traffic in 'other minerals' of 10,000-20,000 tons annually: received other minerals fluctuated, usually being around the 5,000 ton level but occasionally rising to 11,000 tons annually. Livestock traffic at Poplar was minimal, normally amounting to only a few wagon loads per year, although in 1938 over 100 wagons passed through. The GWR crane power at Poplar was 15 tons, and there was a 30-ton dock crane. The de Glehn locomotive *La France* arrived in England at Poplar docks in October, 1903. In September 1940, the depot was so badly

damaged by bombing that, for all practical purposes, it closed down for the duration.

A traffic in which Poplar Docks (including the Blackwall Basin) specialised was the importation of large, rough-sawn timber baulks (2ft by 2ft by up to 30ft long) of Baltic and Russian redwood, (substituted by Douglas Fir baulks from Canada and the USA in WWII). The logs were dumped over the sides of ships into the dock and gathered into rafts, each belonging to particular traders. The railways were often customers for such timber, and sent inspectors to check what the merchants were offering against a particular contract. Inspection involved walking the length of the floating baulk; this involved nifty footwork, as the timber went down into the water under the weight of the walker - 'green' timber floated only an inch or two above the water, and logs which had been stored for a long time and taken up water floated with even less 'freeboard'. On approval, a brass number tab was nailed to the timber. To leave the dock, baulks were craned to bogie 'Macaw' rail and timber wagons, if space could be found on the dock sidings. Alternatively, they would be loaded onto barges and (in the case of the GWR) towed to Brentford docks where they would be transferred to rail. Frank Morris was one of the last GWR timber inspectors, as was Gordon Nash, who inspected the very last lot of 'floaters' bought by BR in the mid-1950s. By this time, mechanisation permitted the baulks to be stored on land, and timber floats had been abandoned at most docks around the country. There is the tale of an LMS timber inspector from Derby who was not happy with one of the baulks he saw at Poplar, and so asked that the log be taken ashore for him to look at - this was troublesome for the merchant, involving the cost of a crane and much labour. On his next visit, the LMS inspector was followed by the same merchant's representative as they walked the baulks. As the Derby man got to the far end of a log, it began slowly to sink. For some unaccountable reason, the merchant's representative (in wellies) was unable to

View of GW depot from the dockside showing fixed (wooden) jib crane. Empty lighters alongside and under the covered corrugated iron loading shed. The two tall parts cover two cranes for work in the dry.

retreat quickly enough so that the LMS inspector had a train journey back to Derby wet up to the knees!

The GW's Victoria & Albert depot was reached by rail from Acton over the NLR to Hackney Wick, thence by GER to its North Woolwich/Beckton lines and off to the Gallions line of the V & A dock company (later PLA), see *GW Goods Services Vol. 2A*, pp174-7. There were two GW sites at the V&A docks: one was the 'Victoria and Albert Goods Station' in Connaught Road, E6 which was a road-and-rail connected depot outside the docks proper, and the other the 'Waterside Depot' inside the docks with a covered wharf to deal with barge traffic. The goods station comprised five lines serving the main building, with several more outside, whilst the Dockside premises had four sidings connected by a traverser, and another short siding alongside the PLA lines. The 1924 *'Instructions relating to London Goods Traffic for the Guidance of Agents and Others at Country Stations'* indicates that the V&A Waterside depot was ideal for traffic of all kinds from or for firms having waterside premises on the Lower Thames round about Abbey Wood, Barking Creek, Beckton, Belvedere, Crossness, Dagenham, Dartford Creek, Erith, Grays, Greenhithe, Manor Way, Purfleet, Rainham, Tilbury (but not Tilbury Docks proper), Woolwich, and on the River Medway. The Great Western made no charge for the use of its wharf. Freight to or from ships berthed in the docks was handled by the V&A station.

Transport could be by railway wagons stabled alongside vessels; or by cartage; or by barge. Crane power at the station was 12 tons, and that at the Waterside depot was 7 tons (the maximum load accepted for barging).

About 150 wagons could be stabled at the V&A depot. The total tonnage (docks and local) of goods handled at the V&A depot was some 200,000 tons annually before the First World War, though this fell to 125,000 tons in the 1930s. Throughout its existence, roughly 50,000 tons per year of general merchandise were each forwarded and received, and some 100,000 tons carted annually. Coal and coke traffic contributed only little to the depot's business although 'forwarded other minerals' were over the 5,000-ton level annually between the wars; 'received other minerals' was very small. In 1925, 150 staff were employed by the GW at this depot, and over 70 horse-drawn and 34 motor vehicles were based there. Great play was made of the extensive Great Western warehousing at the V&A docks which was "suitable for all kinds of traffic consigned there to wait orders for ultimate shipment in the Royal Albert, King George V and Victoria Docks, to which it is so close that goods lying there 'To Order' are practically alongside the ships and can be delivered at very short notice". One (and probably more) of the thirteen diagonally-planked ex-South Wales Railway 'Mica A' refrigerated meat vans (wagon diagram X3) was written 'To work between Victoria Dock

Ex-South Wales Rly refrigerator meat van (later X3 in the wagon diagram index), used for carrying chilled meat from Victoria Dock to Cardiff. Newly painted when photographed in March 1903, this was the first time that a telegraph code name had been painted on any GW goods vehicle (Mica A in this case). Screw couplings and safety chains on this through-piped (but not vacuum-braked) van.

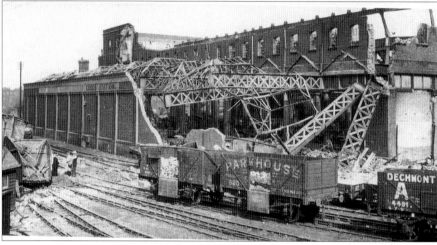

War damage at the GW Polar goods depot after bombing raid of September 1940. [GWR]

London & Cardiff'. The photograph dates from March 1903; the GWR V&A depot was opened in 1902, so clearly this was a 'new' traffic.

The GW collected general merchandise leaving London from docks, wharves, warehouses and factories by cart, barge or railway wagon, depending on the access available to sites and premises, and the volume of traffic. Full wagon loads, or heavy or awkward articles that were difficult to cart, were taken by rail to the GWR depots in the London docks; some of the Great Western's dock cranes could not in fact be approached by road vehicles. But for other goods, there had to be horse cartage routes to and from Poplar Dock, and from the Victoria & Albert Docks to Paddington; at 12 and 15 miles respectively, they were the longest horse-drawn cartage routes on the whole of the GWR. The first Great Western motor lorry used in London (a 5-ton Milnes-Daimler) in 1905 was put on these long cartage routes to the docks, and also to Billingsgate Market (returning with empty fish boxes). The first GWR motor lorry driver was Charles Willis, who had been in charge of a pair-horse team at Paddington. An article in the 1936 *GWR Magazine*, at the time of Mr Willis's retirement, highlighted the 'primitive features' of this first motor lorry - oil lamps, low radiator, and iron-rimmed wheels that 'rattled like thunder over the cobbled streets'. In favourable circumstances ('which were rare') 20 m.p.h. could be

achieved. A second Milnes-Daimler was put on to the Billingsgate/Victoria & Albert roster soon afterwards. Upkeep of these iron-tyred lorries was expensive, but improvements soon enabled new vehicles to be fitted with solid rubber tyres. The GWR seemed to use the Thames docks and Paddington run to try out new designs of motor lorries; for example, two 5-ton Maudslay vehicles were fully-loaded in each direction for long periods in 1913. Eventually horses were removed altogether from the Poplar/V&A run.

In December 1939 the GW issued a circular that barging facilities at the V&A Waterside depot were to be discontinued, and that the London District Goods Manager was to be consulted in case of doubt as to the correct method of dispatching traffic from depots across the system which was labelled to the V&A docks for barging.

SOUTHAMPTON, LSWR
(Served; MSWJ/GWR Running Powers from Andover)

While Southampton had been important in mediaeval times - the British army embarked there for Agincourt in 1415 - it was not commercially significant in the early 1800s. Unlike Liverpool, for example, the port at Southampton did not develop because of river and canal connections to industrial regions. Rather, as at Birkenhead, it was the prospect of what railways integrated with docks

SOUTHAMPTON.

The Great Western Company carry between Southampton and Southampton Docks and nearly all parts of the United Kingdom. Their route to **BIRMINGHAM** and the **MIDLAND COUNTIES, LIVERPOOL, MANCHESTER** and the **NORTH OF ENGLAND** and the **NORTH OF IRELAND** is the shortest and most convenient.

To **BRISTOL, SOUTH WALES** and **SOUTH OF IRELAND** the route *via* Salisbury and G.W.R. is a most convenient and expeditious one.

The Company have access to all parts of the Southampton Docks, and traffic consigned by the Great Western route has the advantage of all the modern appliances at that place for rapidly shipping all descriptions of merchandise.

The Company's representative in Southampton is Mr. A. Blackwell, 18, Bridge Street ; and Messrs. White & Co., 71, High Street, are the Company's Agents.

SALISBURY PLAIN AND CAMPS.

The Company's Station at **Lavington** on the new main line between London and the West of England, is conveniently situated for dealing with traffic for the camps in the west end of Salisbury Plain, with which it is connected by first-class roads.

By an arrangement entered into between the Great Western Railway and the Midland and South Western Junction Railway Companies, the Great Western Company have facilities for sending merchandise traffic of every description over the Midland and South Western Junction Railway Company's line to **LUDGERSHALL,** and thence over the Military Railway to **TIDWORTH,** for the numerous camps in that neighbourhood surrounding the headquarters of the Southern Command of the British Army.

Top right - Pre-grouping information about the facilities available at Southampton and post-grouping the GWR office in Oxford St, Southampton. [D J Hyde]

Right - GW vessel SS Sambur (a Channel Islands cargo boat) under repair at Thorneycroft's in April 1937 at the Inner dock at Southampton.

could achieve that was important and as soon as the railway was in place to take passengers and goods to London, Southampton developed quickly.

Unlike other ports it served, the GW had neither lines of its own nor a goods depot within the Southampton dock estate, and the GW's relationship with the dock owners (the LSWR after 1892) was different from elsewhere. Consequently, the history of Southampton docks is not given in any detail in this book; the reader is referred to the bibliography for titles. Nevertheless, those activities at Southampton that affected activities at Weymouth, Plymouth and Fishguard are described.

A great deal of coal was brought in by train from GWR territory. The broad gauge branch from Reading to the LSWR at Basingstoke opened in 1848, and was intended as a short cut for coal from the Midlands and the North to Southampton. One transfer from 'narrow' to broad gauge wagons at Wolverhampton might have been acceptable, but the need to re-transfer the same loads back from the broad to the 'narrow' at Basingstoke could not be seriously contemplated. Thus, mixed gauge was installed from Wolverhampton, via Didcot and Reading, to Basingstoke between 1852 and 1856; this necessity sounded the death-knell of the broad gauge on the GW. On 9th January 1886, an experimental coal train of 14 wagons ran from Aberdare through the newly-opened Severn Tunnel to Southampton, so that 'coal which had been raised at the colliery in the morning was delivered at the port in the evening of the same day'. This was the first commercial train through the tunnel (the running of regular goods and mineral traffic had to be delayed until September 1886, owing to the need to install a large 40ft diameter ventilator fan). All traffic from the GW via Reading was exchanged at Basingstoke from where trains were hauled by LSW (later SR) locos.

The Royal Mail service to the Channel Islands had been transferred in 1845 from Weymouth to Southampton when the South Western Steam Packet Company was formed to run steamers to the Channel Islands, and to Le Havre and St. Malo. While these steamers ran in connection with the LSW trains, the shipping company was independent of the LSWR. Later, after the GWR and LSWR both opened their railway routes to Weymouth in 1857, the South Western Steam Packet Co. detached one of its steamers from Southampton to Weymouth to start up a service to the Channel Islands. The Great Western responded by encouraging and helping businessmen from Weymouth and the Channel Islands to form the independent Weymouth & Channel Islands Steam Packet Company to carry passengers and goods between Weymouth, Guernsey and Jersey, the shipping timetable to connect with the Great Western's London &Weymouth trains. This turned out to be an unsatisfactory operation, not only because (a) the LSWR made vast improvements in its vessels on the Channel Islands run from Southampton, but also because (b) the Southampton route took goods traffic that might otherwise have gone to Weymouth, since Guernsey and Jersey traders were reluctant to send via the broad gauge because of delays in transhipment of goods to other parts of the country.

The GWR and LSWR competed strongly for Channel Islands traffic in the last quarter of the C19[th], the Great Western taking over the Weymouth & Channel Islands Steam Packet Co. in 1887 and building new ships for the service. The two companies began to realise, however, that competitive working was expensive, and an agreement was entered into during October 1899 whereby each company provided steamers on alternate days of the week during the winter. In the summer (June to September), the GWR ran an outward-bound daytime service, and the LSWR an outward-bound night run; both companies' vessels returned by day. Apart from the suspension of the service during the Second World War, similar arrangements lasted right up to nationalisation. However, the two companies continued to operate their own cargo boats separately to Weymouth and to Southampton.

In addition to passenger traffic, general cargo was landed at Southampton, including Jamaican bananas and frozen goods. The LSWR carried imported frozen meat to London in an imaginative way: instead of employing railway meat vans, the meat was loaded into horse-drawn road vans, which were then loaded two at a time onto flat wagons for the comparatively short journey to its Nine Elms depot in London, from where they were quickly driven directly to market by road.

Two lines established at the end of the C19[th] that the GW later took over ran into Southampton, (a) the Didcot, Newbury and Southampton Rly (DNS); and the Midland and South Western Jct Rly (MSWJ).

The promoters of the Swindon, Marlborough & Andover Railway (later MSWJ) had envisaged a line from Cheltenham down to a new harbour at Stone Point on the western side of the Solent. Traffic from the midlands and the north to the new port would travel via Cheltenham, and lucrative coal traffic from South Wales by a junction at Fairford/Cirencester with the East Gloucester Rly. Lack of funds stopped the port being built and while a number of through rates were established, that for the hoped-for Aberdare-Southampton through coal traffic was not. Nevertheless, after the opening throughout of the MSWJ line in 1891, a fast goods ran each weekday between the Midland Rly goods depot in Cheltenham and Andover, from which through traffic for Southampton Docks (such as Burton beer) was taken on by the LSW. The MSWJ obtained running powers from Andover (Red Post Jct) to Southampton late in 1892 for passenger trains to the Terminus station and goods trains to the adjacent sidings (from where dock shunting engines took over). A south-bound overnight/early morning fast goods train featured in MSWJ timetables from that time. The running powers were inherited by the GWR at the Grouping. There was one regular goods train between Cheltenham and Southampton Docks in each direction, with perishable and other special services as and when necessary, an arrangement that continued largely up to nationalisation and beyond.

While DNS passenger trains ran to the Terminus station, there was little through goods traffic and it would usually be exchanged at Winchester. However, during WW

Landing stages at Weymouth. The tramway runs alongside the River Wey, with the sharp bend at Ferry Corner indicated.

II, these patterns of traffic were altered by the sending of 'block goods trains' of military materiel direct from ordnance factory to quayside without change of loco.

At the turn of the C19th/20th, the biggest liners in the world were owned by North German Lloyd (viz: *Kaiser Wilhelm der Grosse*, *Kronprinz Wilhelm* and *Kaiser Wilhelm II*); they variously held the Blue Riband record for Atlantic crossings, and all called at Southampton. The White Star Line responded with bigger ships, and by 1914 three liners bigger than 40,000 tons deadweight were using the port, viz: the *Olympic* of 1911 and Hamburg-Amerika's *Imperator* and *Vaterland*; *Olympic's* sister ship, the *Titanic*, had sunk on her maiden voyage in 1912 (*Britannic*, the third sister ship, completed in 1916, was sunk in the Aegean serving as a troopship). In 1907, White Star had transferred its express services to Southampton from Liverpool, and the new, large Ocean dock (named the White Star dock up until the Grouping) was opened in 1911 for its large ships.

During the First World War, Southampton was designated 'No. 1 Military Port'. Except for a reduced Channel Islands service from the Outer Dock, all commercial traffic ceased. By the end of WW I, 7½ million men had passed through Southampton docks, as well as 850,000 horses and mules, 175,000 vehicles, 7¼ million mailbags and parcels, 14,500 artillery pieces, and 3¼ million tons of stores, all involving over 16,000 ship movements.

In 1919, Cunard moved its express services from Liverpool (its biggest liner at the time being the *Aquitania*), whilst the Canadian Pacific Steamship Co likewise based itself at Southampton in 1920. The large German liners were given over as reparations (the *Imperator* became Cunard's *Berengaria*, for example). The ascendancy of Southampton,

and the withdrawal of sailings to and from Liverpool, meant that there were no liners passing Fishguard, and the GWR's hopes of developing the port for ocean-going liners were dashed. However, the number of ocean liners calling at Plymouth increased, bringing business to the GW.

After the Grouping, the Great Western bought the property at 20 Oxford St in Southampton to house its recently-appointed District Agent. The new Southern Railway was keen to develop the port of Southampton, and an entirely new set of docks was begun in 1927 on 400 acres of mud upstream of the Town Quay. One-and-a-half miles of deep-water berths were eventually constructed by 1934, together with all the associated sheds, cranes, railway lines and so on.

In the inter-war period, Southampton possessed the largest floating and dry docks in the world, and handled 50% of the world's ocean passenger traffic, with sometimes as many as 17 boats per day arriving or leaving. Ever-bigger liners such as the *Normandie* used these facilities; the *Normandie* called at Southampton outward bound from Cherbourg, but at Plymouth inbound (to allow a speedy transit of passengers and mails to London via the GWR), as did many other liners outward and/or inward bound. In 1935, the French Line substituted Southampton for Plymouth on its North American and West Indies routes.

The economic depression of the '30s caused the Cunard and White Star companies to combine, and the *Queen Mary* was eventually finished with government assistance. Some ships calling at Southampton did not bother to berth, and were serviced by tenders in Cowes Roads. Unlike the tenders at Plymouth (and at Fishguard before the First World War), Southampton tenders were operated by private tug companies such as the Alexandra

The collier SS Calchfaen discharging Cwmgorse anthracite at St Peter Port, Guernsey on 11th Sept1901. Cwmgorse colliery was near Gwaun Cae Gurwen, Swansea, and was owned by Amalgamated Anthracite Collieries Ltd. The coal had been loaded in South Wales on 8th Sept, and was to heat Guernsey's greenhouses. The coal is being unloaded by quayside crane using a bucket (above and to the right of the 'Williams Esplanade' sentry box). Notice the size of the lumps of coal and how high they are stacked. [Amgueddfa Cymru National Museum of Wales]

Towage Co. and Red Funnel Tugs, rather than by the railway.

Passengers and general cargo through the port up the Second World War were as follows:

	1892	1913	1923	1933	1938
Passengers (1000's)	122	379	414	481	560
Cargo (1000's tons)	422	1,320	1,010	882	1,085

At the beginning of the Second World War, Southampton again became a military port, serving the British Army and the Royal Air Force in France and the Low Countries. Big ships went off to safer ports - after the fall of France in 1940, Southampton became vulnerable to bombing and would have been a target for invasion; apart from some coastal traders, the docks were closed to shipping for fear of submarines and air attack. Indeed, aerial bombardment in 1940/1 caused extensive damage to the Southampton dock area. In 1942, the docks reopened to receive food and war equipment from North America, and then, from 1943, Southampton played a significant role in the preparations for the Normandy landings, including the construction of the Mulberry Harbours within the dock area. Following D-Day, a train ferry terminal was established near the King George V dry dock to take railway vehicles to France. By the war's end, over 4 million troops had passed through the port and nearly 4 million tons of stores and military equipment.

WEYMOUTH & THE CHANNEL ISLANDS (Served)

Construction of the independent broad gauge Wilts, Somerset & Weymouth Railway started in 1845; it commenced on the Paddington to Bristol main line at Thingley Junction, about 2 miles south-west of Chippenham, and went south via Trowbridge, Westbury, Frome, Yeovil and Dorchester to Weymouth. In the early days of railways, facing junctions were avoided when possible so, at first, down trains from the GWR main line were backed into a siding at Thingley before proceeding forwards onto the Wilts & Somerset line.

The L & SWR had running powers over the final seven miles of the line from Dorchester to Weymouth, and this part of the line was mixed gauge (until 1874). The running powers had come about in a curious way: the GWR had given strong support in 1844 to the promoters of the Southampton & Dorchester Railway, which was to be built partly on the bed of the old Southampton & Salisbury Canal, abandoned in 1805 owing to lack of funds. However, when the BoT ruled that the line should be to the 'standard' gauge and not the broad, the GWR dropped it like a hot potato. The Great Western agreed that their interest should pass to the LSWR on condition that the latter maintain a strictly neutral position in regard to the broad gauge line from Thingley to Weymouth. Following the collapse of the money markets after the 'railway mania', the GWR had given £750,000 to the financially-strapped Wilts & Somerset so that it could complete the railway from Frome

Top - *Ford & Jackson's PS Great Western(I) of 1867, taken over by the GW in 1872. Normally on New Milford Irish services, she is photographed at Weymouth some time between 1878 and 1885 when operating a service from there to Cherbourg. [STEAM Swindon]*

Centre *- The South of Ireland and the Aquila at Weymouth in 1883. [STEAM Swindon]*

Bottom - *Weymouth harbour about 1909. Single track at passenger station where boat train is standing. Pavilion to the left. SS Roebuck(I) or Reindeer at quay.*

to Weymouth (and also the line from Westbury to Salisbury), and wanted no encroachment of this territory by the LSW. The GWR and LSWR opened their railway routes to Weymouth on the same day in 1857.

In 1845, the port of Weymouth had lost the Royal Mail service to the Channel Islands (see Southampton). As soon as railways arrived in Weymouth, the South Western Steam Packet Co. detached the *PS Express* from Southampton to start up a service to the Channel Islands from Weymouth. In response, businessmen from Weymouth and the Channel Islands (with help and encouragement of the GWR) formed the independent Weymouth & Channel Islands Steam Packet Company to carry passengers and goods between Weymouth, Guernsey and Jersey, the shipping timetable to connect with the Great Western's London &Weymouth trains, and through parcel rates were instituted.

The service started with two 120-ton paddle steamers called *Cygnus* and *Aquila*, chartered from May to November

Left - GW town offices in Bond St Jersey, June 1925. [D J Hyde]

Bottom - The GWR quayside offices at Jersey in June 1925. Travelling dockside crane to the left; GW station trolleys to the right. Man with white shirtsleeves transferring goods from motor lorry backed up to loading bay. Horse and cart (driver with white hat) is waiting to unload baskets of fruit. [GWR]

The 1,150 ton Ibex as delivered from Laird's in 1891 arriving at Jersey. [STEAM Swindon]

1857, and subsequently purchased. In 1858, they were augmented by the 180-ton *PS Brighton* (ex-LBSCR, sold off because the Brighton company had been fined for deviously owning ships and operating them to Dieppe through a disguised, but wholly-owned, subsidiary company which contravened the LBSC's Act of Incorporation). Boats left Weymouth at 8.0 a.m. on Tuesdays and Saturdays, and at 3.0 a.m. on Wednesdays and Fridays every week for the approximate 10-hour journey to Jersey. The service provided by the Packet company was just about adequate and was maintained for many years, but the private firm lost money and had to be bailed out financially by the GWR a number of times, even though the LSW's *Express* had been wrecked in 1859 so that there was no competition at Weymouth. Nevertheless, in 1865 the company claimed that its summertime 6.0 a.m. service by the 'well-known, fast, iron paddle steam ships' gave 'day passages and the shortest sea route by several hours' without 'the unpleasantness and dangers of Night Travelling.'

In the meanwhile, the LSW had made vast improvements in its vessels on the Channel Islands run from Southampton, and had taken goods traffic that might otherwise have gone to Weymouth. The bother and delay of trans-shipment from the broad gauge made Guernsey and Jersey traders reluctant to send, via Weymouth, goods to those parts of the country served by standard gauge lines. The GWR was losing business despite having the shorter sea route: Weymouth to Jersey 98 nautical miles;

Southampton to Jersey 125 miles; the trip between Guernsey and Jersey was 31 miles.

Parliament repealed, in 1862, that part of the Railways Act prohibiting railway companies from owning ships, and the GWR obtained permission in 1871 to operate ships on services to Ireland, the Channel Islands, St Malo and Cherbourg. Although the Great Western put its own steamers on the Irish services from Milford Haven straight away, it left the Channel Islands service in private hands since business had picked up after the Weymouth/ Dorchester/Chippenham/Bath/Salisbury lines were converted to standard gauge (in 3 days) during June 1874. Jersey potatoes for the Midlands and the North could now go directly from Weymouth.

In 1875, the Midland Railway and LSWR took on a 999-year lease of the Somerset & Dorset Railway, which gave access to the Midlands and the North via Bath. Initially, the GWR lost some of its Weymouth traffic to the S & D, but this setback was short-lived, and disappeared after the opening of the Severn Tunnel in 1886.

Nevertheless, the finances of the shipping company based at Weymouth continued to be precarious, and matters came to a head in 1887 after the *Brighton* sank in fog en route to Guernsey. It became clear that the packet company could not bear the expense of replacing the *Brighton*, leave alone provide up-to-date new vessels to compete with the LSW. The GWR therefore took over the sea run (the packet company was wound up in 1891) and ordered three new

Lengthening and widening of Weymouth quay in January 1932. Contractor's steam travelling crane on right; bucket of spoil in right foreground. [GWR]

twin-screw steamers. The new ships were the *Lynx*, *Antelope* and *Gazelle*, which were delivered from Laird Bros at Birkenhead in 1889 at a cost of £25,000 each. The three ships were identical 672-tonners, capable of 17 knots, and could each carry over 400 passengers. The new ships took 6¼ hours to Jersey (10 hours by the old vessels), 2½ hours faster than any other sea route to the Channel Islands at that time. The faster ships attracted so much new traffic that another, bigger vessel was soon ordered: the 1,150-ton *Ibex* was delivered from Laird's in 1891, and could carry 600 passengers at a speed of 19 knots. Within two months of the introduction of the new ships in 1889, the Weymouth route carried more passengers than the LSWR from Southampton.

The *Ibex* (or its crew) was prone to accidents: in April 1897, she struck a rock off La Corbière lighthouse, Jersey, and had to be beached, the passengers being taken off in boats. She was returned to the builders, repaired, and was back in service three months later. Then, in January 1900, she struck rocks in the treacherous Little Russell Channel near St. Peter Port and sank; she was raised the following

summer, overhauled at Laird's and returned to service as an essentially new vessel.

There was continuing keen competition between the GW and LSW for Channel Islands traffic, not only for passengers but also fruit and vegetables. Frost was rarely experienced on the islands, so that out-of-season and even 'exotic' produce could be grown and supplied to the rapidly-increasing population of Victorian Britain. *Guernsey* grew its produce under glass: as early as 1830, it had more greenhouses than anywhere on the Continent. They were originally cold, and produced immense quantities of potatoes and broccoli which were exported in 1 cwt returnable barrels. After the 1880s, furnaces and small boilers were introduced and the greenhouses were in use all the year round. In the middle of February, the narcissi season began and at the same time early potatoes, peas and beans were dispatched to the mainland to be sold at a premium. Tomatoes followed in the middle of May and continued to be a significant traffic up until the beginning of November. Nearly three million baskets were in constant use, and tomatoes represented about three quarters of the produce exported from Guernsey. Tomatoes were picked at different stages of ripeness depending on their destination, so that produce for Scotland was despatched much less ripe than that for Covent Garden. Hothouse produce began to mature in June, and thence to the end of September grapes were sent off packed in boxes or baskets, with up to a thousand bunches in every consignment; similarly for melons, peaches, nectarines and figs. At the end of October, the chrysanthemum season opened. Flowers and early produce was sent in those Victorian days at passenger rates in order to ensure the quickest delivery to far-away markets. In 1890, it was reported that Guernsey 'feeds its own population and sends 400,000 packets of garden produce to Covent Garden annually'. Some 150,000 tons of South Wales anthracite was purchased annually in the interwar period by the island's 2,000-odd growers to heat Guernsey's greenhouses.

In contrast, *Jersey's* produce was grown out of doors and came into season as the Guernsey glass crop ended, thus prolonging the supply of Channel Islands fruit and vegetables from April until November. Two special trains a week of Jersey potatoes were being run from Weymouth in the 1860s. Jersey market gardeners realised that a second crop could be planted in the fields after the early potatoes had been lifted, so tomatoes also began to be grown.

The first GWR ventilated fruit vans built specially for the purpose (later 'Y2' in the *Wagon Diagram Index*) were outshopped in 1889. They were fitted to run in passenger trains (long buffers, Mansell wheels etc) and were employed at Weymouth to help move the gigantic amounts of fruit and vegetables. Some were fitted with the Westinghouse brake as well as vacuum so as to be able to work through to the NE and GE Railways, and to railways in Scotland. Early produce commanded premium prices, so that it was economic to consign such goods at passenger train rates up to the First World War. After the introduction of the partially-fitted C-headcode fast goods trains in the early 1900's, more and more perishable traffic began to be carried at goods rates.

A 'heavy' industry in Guernsey was quarrying, with the granite quarries of St. Sampson producing as much as 1,000 tons per day in Victorian times. Known as 'blue granite', it is harder than Aberdeen granite, and was used both architecturally (the Victoria Embankment in London, and the Royal Exchange Building) and for road chippings. A third significant business in the Channel Islands was cattle breeding and exporting, which had been the principal farming activity before market-gardening. For many years before the WWI, between 700 and 800 head of finest cattle were exported annually all over the globe, particularly to the USA. There is on record at least one transfer of cattle direct from the *Waterford* (a boat normally running on the Fishguard services) to the liner *Missouri* (outward bound for New York) in Plymouth Sound. To protect against infection of the indigenous herds, every live animal landed at St. Peter Port Guernsey and St. Helier Jersey for domestic consumption was immediately slaughtered in the public abattoirs. A further export from the Channel Islands before the First World War was wrack seaweed manure.

The GW and LSW had their own Agents in both Guernsey and Jersey each with a full complement of clerks, waterside staff, goods and parcels checkers and porters, ticket collectors, boatmen, quayside and harbour staff. Originally all the GW staff came under the auspices of the Marine Department, but the goods staff were moved on to the mainland establishment staff in January 1907.

In order to improve the boat service still further, the GWR introduced yet bigger and faster new steamers on additional daytime services. In 1897, the Naval Construction and Armaments Co (forerunners of Vickers Armstrong) of Barrow-in-Furness delivered the twin screw *Roebuck (I)* and *Reindeer*, each of 1,280 gross tons, carrying 842 passengers and capable of 21 knots. At that time, both the Great Western and LSW operated one boat in each direction daily (except Sundays).

During 1900, the GWR opened up a new, shortened railway route to Westbury, which not only improved the existing Berks & Hants Extension line from Savernake to Holt and Bradford-on-Avon (and on to Bath), but also built a new line from Stert Junction (Patney & Chirton), passing through the new stations of Lavington and Edington, to join the old Weymouth route from Thingley Junction at Westbury. The new section of line was 13¼ miles long, and shortened the old route via Chippenham by 14¼ miles; Weymouth thus became 154¼ miles from Paddington.

As time passed, both the GW and LSW began to realise that competitive working was expensive, and an agreement was entered into during October 1899, whereby each company provided steamers on alternate days of the week during the winter months (October to May). The LSW ran boat and mail trains to Southampton on Mondays, Wednesdays and Fridays, and the GWR on Tuesdays, Thursdays and Saturdays at 9.15 p.m. from Paddington; there were no Sunday services. GWR boats left Weymouth at 2.15 a.m. in the early 1900s to reach Guernsey at 7.0 a.m. and Jersey (St Helier) about 9.30 a.m.; boats left on the return journey from Jersey at 8.0 a.m., Guernsey at 10.0 a.m. and were due at Weymouth at 3.0 p.m. In the summer timetable (June to September) in the early 1900s, the service from Weymouth was by day, and that from Southampton by night. The outward-bound daytime service left Paddington at 9.30 a.m., boats left Weymouth at 1.45 p.m. and arrived at Guernsey at about 6.0 p.m. and Jersey about 8.30 p.m. Both companies' vessels returned to Weymouth and Southampton by day (GWR boats from Jersey at 8.30 a.m., Guernsey at 10.15 a.m., and were due at Weymouth at 3.0 p.m). For both, passenger fares were the same, and return halves of tickets were usable by either route on steamer and train. Similar joint arrangements carried on with the SR after the Grouping, and joint publicity material was issued (booklets such as *The Channel Islands where the Sunshine Comes and Stays*).

With the new *Roebuck (I)* and *Reindeer* on station, and with the altered services mentioned above, *Lynx* and *Antelope* were transferred to Plymouth to act as tenders for the ocean-going ships calling there. *Gazelle* remained at

Brand new Y8 goods fruit vans (telegraph code Fruit A) at Weymouth in June 1938. Hidden behind the left-hand open doors was, in GW italic writing, 'Return to Weymouth'. [GWR]

Weymouth as spare vessel. *Roebuck (I)* seems to have been employed in the summers only, for she was laid up for the winter at New Milford; while there in January 1905, she caught fire and sank at her mooring, caused by the weight of water used to put out the fire being retained aboard. She was repaired, however, in time for that year's summer services from Weymouth.

Other ports of departure for the Channel Islands in Edwardian times were London (East Dock, operated by the London & Channel Islands Steamship Company every Tuesday and Saturday) and Plymouth, Millbay Docks (operated by the Anglo-French Steamship Company, departing every Monday). Furthermore, every Friday a vessel belonging to the St. Malo & Binic Steamship Co. left Guernsey for Poole, via Alderney.

The harbour at Weymouth was a mile or so from the station and, at first, passengers and goods had to find their own way by whatever means they could. Shortly after the opening of the Weymouth line in 1857, Brunel met the town authorities to discuss building a tram line to connect to the harbour; the line eventually opened in 1865. In that same year the joint GWR and LSWR Weymouth & Portland Railway opened, and for both lines the track layout in Weymouth station yard had to be rearranged. The reconstruction has historical importance since one of the

first signal locking frames ever used on the GWR was installed at 'Portland Junction'. Adoption of locking frames meant the general introduction of signal cabins from 1875, and the inauguration of semaphore signals. Initially, the tramway was goods-only, and passengers still had to make their own way to and from the quay until 1889, at which time the line was upgraded for passenger traffic. The tramway (like the Weymouth & Portland Railway) was constructed as mixed gauge single line, and terminated in a pair of sidings at the harbour. It carried both GW and LSW goods traffic, but motive power was always provided by the Great Western.

The tramway left the main line at the north end of Weymouth goods yard, bypassing the terminal station, and extended for one mile 4 chains along the Commercial Road beside the 'Backwater', went under the town bridge which divided old Weymouth and Rodwell from Melcombe Regis, to terminate at Weymouth Quay station near Pulteney Buildings, where the passenger steamboats berthed. On the approach to the town bridge was located the ship coaling stage, served by sidings off the tramway, and used by the barges that replenished the bunkers of the GW steamers. Various businesses along the route of the tramway were also served by sidings.

The tramway followed an 'L'-shaped route, with a

severe 223 ft radius bend at the corner of the 'L' (Ferry's Corner). This restricted the length of stock that could run on the tramway; in the 1930s

carriages permitted to pass over the tramway were marked on their ends with 'W´Q' plates or by painting. Until 1938 when the sharp radius was relieved by reclaiming land 70ft out into the harbour,

special long loose couplings had to be attached to bogie vehicles. Horse traction was used on the tramway long after the conversion of the gauge in 1874, but the increase in traffic -- particularly after the introduction of the Great Western's faster rail and sea services to the Channel Islands --led to small GWR tank engines being employed from 1880 onwards. These were permitted to haul up to 40 goods wagons, or the boat train, typically consisting of 4 bogie carriages after 1889. A succession of light locos started with GWR No 2 (ex-Torbay & Brixham) dating from 1871, and rebuilt at Swindon in 1878 specially for Weymouth duties. Ex-B & E Culm Valley 0-6-0T locos Nos.1376 and 1377, dating from 1874/5, were also both rebuilt at Swindon in 1881 for the Weymouth tramway, and stayed there until scrapped in 1927. They were succeeded by ex-BP & GV 0-6-0ST Nos.2194 *Kidwelly* and 2195 *Cwm Mawr*, which in turn were replaced in 1939/40 by 0-6-0PT No.1371 (No.1367 of the same class had arrived in 1934), and No.1370 came in 1946 to assist in re-opening the Channel Islands route after the Second World War (No.2195 – by then nameless - also returned briefly in 1946). Other locos that served the quay at various times were ex-West Cornwall Railway 0-4-0T No.1391 *Fox* in the first decade of the 20th century; ex-Hook Norton Ironstone Partnership 0-6-0ST No 1337 *Hook Norton* at the same time; and ex-Whitland & Cardigan Bay Railway 0-6-0ST No.1386. Although horses were replaced as prime movers on the tramway in 1880, they were retained for shunting for many years; shunting was difficult in the restricted space of the tramway, and a special method of rope towing from the adjacent track was developed.

The harbour line, though maintained and operated by the GWR, was the property of Weymouth Corporation, to which a toll of 6d per passenger was paid in the early 1900s. The tramway had been offered to the GWR for £20 - the cost of the legal conveyancing - in the 1880s, but this was declined by the management.

Originally, the tramway did not extend on to the pier, but the tramway was lengthened at various times over the next half-century as quay and landing stage facilities were improved to cope with growing traffic. For example, a 200ft wooden landing stage with extra sidings was constructed in 1877. When the GWR began to run its own steamships, Weymouth Corporation built a new passenger landing stage, the harbour being dredged to accommodate the *Lynx*, *Antelope* and *Gazelle*. The tramway was then extended on to the pier to the new landing stage, permitting four bogie carriages to be placed alongside the vessels; access to the rest of the train had to be by steps from ground level. Inwards goods traffic from the Channel Islands continued to be dealt with near the original end of the tramway, but from

Spring 1892 the passenger landing stage was used for perishables unloading when required. By 1908, some 600 goods wagons were sometimes being dealt with daily over the line.

The siding accommodation on the branch was quite limited. On Commercial Road, the running line divided into an extended loop (with two outlets at one end) which held 11 and 6 wagons respectively, and a dead-end siding opposite, against the waterside, that held ten. Further on, the short siding just to the east of Weymouth Bridge accommodated two vehicles. At Customs House Quay, another extended loop held a run-around and nine wagons respectively, with a short spur beyond served by a 3-ton crane. Next to this, the cargo stage loop at the mouth of the jetty served a 470ft platform, whilst the single line beyond ran alongside the 200ft passenger platform, which had the baggage room behind, at the quayside. The greater portion of the jetty lay beyond, and formed Pile Pier, with a pavilion at the tip.

Passenger and goods traffic increased tremendously in the 1920s, and this led to the quay being completely rebuilt in 1931-33. It was lengthened and widened to allow two tracks in place of the former single line. Full-length boat trains could now be accommodated on the tracks behind the terminal building. When used for goods traffic, the new platform enabled far more wagons to be berthed for direct loading. New buildings were provided for customs, passengers and staff, and modern goods handling facilities provided on the quay - in particular six 5-ton capacity electric cranes by Stothert & Pitt running on tracks alongside the quay which could swing over the buildings onto the lengthened platforms. Previously, rail-mounted steam cranes had had to be brought in and lifted onto the quay in the high season to assist with loading and unloading: three 2-ton steam cranes were still listed as being available in 1936. The new passenger stage was 344ft long, and the new cargo stage 1,217ft , both having at least 14ft depth of water at the berths. Even after this rebuilding, the 'Achilles Heel' of the tramway – the severe bend at Ferry's Corner– still remained, not being eased until 1938.

In addition to Channel Islands traffic, the port of Weymouth had a considerable coasting trade in oilcake, coal etc. as well as foreign trade with America and the Mediterranean, added to which was fishing and the export of Portland stone. The timber trade was strong, too, with sailing ships from Scandinavia often being seen. There was a small shipbuilding yard, and a space was excavated in the late C19th for the GWR Marine Workshop and Stores, in which the Channel Island steamers were laid up for repairs and repainting. The GW Marine Dept Charge Code for the Weymouth workshops was 23B.

The GWR had other steamer services operating from Weymouth at various times. Indeed, the reason the Weymouth & Channel Islands Steam Packet Co. bought the *PS Brighton* in 1858 was to inaugurate a Weymouth & Cherbourg route; however, the service made a loss and was short-lived, ending in 1859. Then, in conjunction with the Western Railway of France, the Cherbourg service reopened in 1878, for which the *South of Ireland* and *Great Western (I)* were transferred from New Milford. In the event, that service, too, ceased at the end of June 1885, and *Great Western (I)* returned to the Irish routes; the *South of Ireland* had been wrecked in fog off Lulworth in 1883 and was replaced in 1884 by the 403-ton second-hand *Gael* dating from 1867 (an ex-Campbelltown & Glasgow day excursion paddle steamer). She was really too small for the job, and was soon transferred to summer excursion work between Portishead and Ilfracombe (the Portishead Railway had just been taken over by the GWR). These ceased in 1886, and *Gael* (still owned by the GWR) worked for the West Cornwall SS Co. between Penzance and the Scillies. Then she became the summer relief steamer at Weymouth (1889) and at New Milford (1890), though returning to Weymouth for the month of June. In 1891, she was sold to David MacBrayne to operate out of Oban. One reason for the discontinuation of the Cherbourg service was insufficient accommodation and customs facilities at Weymouth. Lack of facilities at Weymouth Quay led to various proposals at the end of the C19th for entirely new docks at Bincleaves (near Portland Dockyard), but none came to fruition.

Goods traffic between Guernsey and Jersey was some 500 tons annually in Victorian times, and was normally dealt with by the passenger boats, but they could not cope with the large and increasing volume of the perishable traffic dispatched to the mainland, so that by the beginning of the C20th additional ships had to be chartered. Eventually the railway itself had to provide dedicated cargo boats, the 412-ton screw cargo steamer *Melmore* being acquired second-hand in 1905 for this purpose. In 1909 she was employed to start a new weekly goods service from Weymouth to Nantes, but with provision for a limited number of passengers (the service featured in the GW's *Holiday Haunts* books). The *Melmore* departed Weymouth at 2.30 p.m. on Saturdays, and returned from Nantes on Tuesday afternoons; the 360 nautical mile passage took about 35 hours. Owing to the need for customs and the

provision of bonded stores, the Great Western opened a new building on the quayside at Weymouth. Even so, when the much larger *Bretonne* (an ex-GER boat that had run on the Harwich & Hook of Holland route) was bought for the Nantes service in 1910, the port of embarkation was moved to Plymouth. The *Lynx* also was employed on the Nantes service in 1910, the *Melmore* reverting to Channel Islands duties for a short time before being sold in 1912. The Nantes run was not profitable and was taken off after 1911, at which time the section on Brittany was removed from *Holiday Haunts*, and the *Bretonne* sold off.

Another way of obtaining cargo ships for the increasingly-busy Channel Islands service was to convert old passenger vessels into cargo carriers, and in 1908 the *Gazelle* (the spare vessel at Weymouth) and in 1912 the *Lynx* (by then a tender at Plymouth) were stripped of their passenger fittings, and the whole of their deck space and holds devoted to cargo carrying. These converted 1889-built boats, capable of a speed of 16 knots, were the fastest cargo ships afloat. *Antelope* remained at Plymouth as a tender until sold in 1913 – see Plymouth Docks.

To help speed up distribution of Channel Islands produce, a distinctive, yet simple, system of labelling was adopted; this had been recommended by Mr W. H. Smith, GW District Agent in Guernsey before the First World War. Every one of the 3 million packages exported bore a label with the station of destination printed in large black type. To the chief centres and markets, a system of colours was employed: the labels for all traffic for South Wales were blue; Scottish traffic was yellow; Birmingham traffic was green; Manchester traffic was red; London (Covent Garden) traffic was white, typeface black; London (Spitalfields) traffic was white, type red. Labels for other destinations were white, with print in bold black type. How the goods traffic grew in the first decade of the C20th is shown by the data below. Similar quantities were conveyed by the LSWR from Southampton, and the NER took some Channel Islands produce by boats to Hull. After the Grouping, there was a

Fast Train Traffic (passenger rated)					
Year	Sundries	Grapes, Fruit etc	Hot-house tomatoes and forced vegetables	Flowers	Total
1904	2,596	3,900	26,467.112,612	145,635	
1910	3,143	5,985	53,077	170,806	233,011

Goods Train Traffic						
Year	*Cases	Sundries	Grapes, Fruit etc	Outdoor tomatoes	Vegetables	Total
1904	3,300	4,011	42,931,506,563	84,381	641,186	
1910	7,001	4,405	16,298	984,637	111,461	1,123,802

* Average pf 20 baskets in one case

joint LNER/LMS service to Hull, which took as much as 20% of the Jersey potato crop each year.

The siding accommodation at Dorchester was very limited, so a large amount of marshalling took place at the Portland Branch Junction at Weymouth. The LSW provided a shunting engine, but most work was done by GW locos. At Dorchester, interchange of goods traffic was effected by a daily transfer train, provided alternately by the two companies. These arrangements changed in 1912: until then, while the GWR had controlled all traffic operations on the line to Weymouth, the LSWR maintained its own stationmaster and staff at Weymouth and other stations. Then, an agreement was reached whereby the entire staff south of Dorchester, including clerical departments, both goods and passenger, became GWR, and Weymouth no longer possessed two stationmasters. The quid pro quo was that that the Salisbury GWR terminus (opened in 1856) became an LSWR goods depot, and GWR traffic used the LSWR station and facilities at Salisbury.

Soon after the outbreak of war in 1914, *Roebuck (I)*, *Reindeer*, *Lynx* and *Gazelle* - including their captains and crews - were requisitioned by the Government, leaving the *Ibex* to perform all the passenger, mails and cargo duties from Weymouth. This naturally caused great disruption to the Channel Islands perishable traffic. It was the responsibility of the wartime Railway Executive Committee to find replacement ships, and *SS Vera* was loaned by the LSWR (but only for a month) as a stand-by boat, and to take the place of *Ibex* when she was out of service for boiler cleaning or repairs. It was intended thereafter that the LSWR *SS Normandy* and *SS Brittany* should replace *Lynx* and *Gazelle*, but as these LSWR boats were conveying military traffic at the time, the 1905-built cargo boat *SS Bertha* of 487 tons was used instead for Guernsey cargo; Jersey cargo was taken by the *Ibex* passenger boat. In addition, there were chartered boats including L & Y's *River Crake*. A year-round winter timetable was put in place, *Ibex* making three trips weekly alternating between Weymouth and Plymouth. The *Great Southern* from Fishguard also appeared briefly in 1916.

The 1880-built *Pembroke* (by then a GWR Fishguard tender) was roped in to help at Weymouth in 1916, although she was attacked by a U-boat soon after commencing duties. As a precaution, the daylight service was stopped and ships were fitted with a twelve-pounder gun at the stern. The *Ibex* was used as a troop transport to France at end of March 1918, and she distinguished herself by sinking a German submarine in the English Channel in April 1918 by a single shot fired from the gun. Proud of the achievement, the GW Directors placed a brass tablet at the top of the *Ibex*'s saloon staircase, bearing the record: *"During the Great War, 1914-1919, this vessel maintained the Great Western Company's Passenger and Mail Services between Weymouth and the Channel Islands, and on three occasions was attacked by enemy submarines, one of which she sank by gunfire. The Government requisitioned the steamer at various times for the conveyance of troops to France".*

The other GW Channel Island boats also had an eventful time in the First World War. The *Roebuck(I)* was armed and renamed *Roedean* by the Admiralty. At first she moved across to Portland, but then was sent to Scapa Flow with the Grand Fleet; unfortunately in 1915 she collided in bad weather with the French battleship *Imperieuse* and sank. The other three, *Reindeer*, *Lynx* and *Gazelle* took part in the attack on the Dardanelles in May 1915. The *Reindeer*, serving as a minesweeper there, saved most of the crew of the torpedoed battleship *Majestic*, and in June 1915 when acting as transport for the 4th Bt. Royal Scots, and steaming at 17 knots, she collided with and sank the ex-Great Central Railway steamer *Immingham*. The *Reindeer* saved the crew of the *Immingham* but with a 30 foot rent just above the waterline, had to return to the Island of Mudros (headquarters of operations against Turkey). A very curious event took place during the war in the Dardanelles in that the *Gazelle* recaptured the ex-GW *Antelope* (sold in 1913 to the Ionian Steamship Company and by then renamed *Anathometus* and sailing for the enemy) which was trying to run a blockade in the Greek islands. Immediately after the end of the war, the requisitioned *Reindeer* was used to bring home returning troops from Cherbourg to Weymouth. Eventually the *Lynx*, *Gazelle* and *Reindeer* returned to the GW. Considerable expenditure was incurred by the GW in reconditioning and modernising them as returned by the Admiralty.

Channel Islands traffic (both freight and passenger) increased even further after WWI; for example, about 8,000 tons of tomatoes and fruit were carried from Guernsey in 1900, but this had risen to 18,000 tons by 1920 representing over 2½ million baskets of tomatoes. At peak times, the roads on the Islands could be clogged with traffic transporting the perishable goods to the ports, and the harbour facilities at St. Peter Port, Guernsey, proved to be inadequate, even though 20-30,000 baskets of tomatoes could be loaded in a few hours. Improvements were made in the early 1920s by the Port Authority by the addition of extra berths and shore accommodation, and in 1922 electric platform trucks were introduced at St. Helier, Jersey, where the quays totalled nearly six miles in length.

Nevertheless, by the 1920s, the GWR fleet at Weymouth was antiquated, with 30-year old vessels still running on mail services. Furthermore, it had been found necessary to transfer steamers temporarily from Fishguard to the Channel Islands services to help out with cargo in the summer months. For example, the Jersey tomato crop for 1921 was a record, and the GWR's *Pembroke* took off 46,000 packages - the largest cargo of fruit ever exported up to that time. Of the 76,476 tons of exports in 1920, valued at just over £2 million, potatoes were the major contributor (61,296 tons with value just over £1 million). Again, in 1923 the *Waterford(II)* and *Great Western (II)* were brought in to help move the potato crop. New, larger ships could not be introduced until the berths in the Channel Islands were deepened by dredging. In fact, the design of the *Ibex*, *Reindeer* and sister ships at the tail-end of the C19th had been constricted by these draught limitations.

After dredging, in 1925 of two new mail and passenger

Above - St Julien as built with two funnels off Guernsey in June 1925.

Left - St Julien rebuilt with a single funnel in 1927.

boats, and two new cargo boats, were introduced. The 18-knot, oil-fired, geared turbine vessels *St. Julien* and *St. Helier* were built by John Brown of Clydebank; they were 1,885 tonners and, as built, had two funnels (the after one being a dummy), but in 1927 they become single-funnelled, and in 1937 the single funnels were shortened. They could carry about 1,000 passengers, including 120 berths. The *Ibex* was scrapped in 1925 upon the arrival of the *St Julien*, whilst the *Reindeer* subsequently became the spare vessel until 1928, when she was also scrapped. The new ships then maintained, in the summer, daily daylight services (Sundays excepted) with the assistance from the Irish route of the 1930-built *St Patrick(II)*, a 1,911-tonner that could carry some 900 passengers including 330 berths; in winter, the service was three times a week, at night from Weymouth, and three times a week by day from the Islands.

The two new cargo boats introduced in 1925 were built by Swan Hunter & Wigham Richardson at Newcastle, and were named *Roebuck (II)* (reusing the old name of the GWR boat sunk at Scapa Flow) and the *Sambur*. A feature of their construction was that three decks were available for storage of cargo, thus ensuring that baskets were not crushed by the weight of cargo placed on top. They were oil burners of 776 gross tonnage, carrying about 600 tons deadweight. The average speed of these 201ft-long vessels was about 12¼ knots. Their arrival made the 34-year-olds *Gazelle* and *Lynx* redundant, and they, too, were scrapped in 1925.

In the 1920s, there were also non-GWR boats to Cherbourg from Weymouth were running: traffic to and from Western France was shipped from Weymouth Quay on the regular service to Nantes, Brest and La Pallice in the Bay of Biscay. Seasonal traffic from Brittany - such as broccoli - was catered for by a cargo line running from Roscoff. All this traffic contributed to the growth in perishable goods handled by the GW at Weymouth between the wars.

After the Grouping, the vast majority of Docks Department staff were to be found at the South Wales ports, but a number from the Marine Section were stationed at Weymouth. In 1929, the Marine Office was staffed by a Traffic & Marine Agent with three clerks, with a shore staff of Berthing Master and Tubesweeper. A Foreman Carpenter, Clerk, and five various tradesmen were the establishment at the small marine factory. A steam launch *Armine* was stationed at the port, with a coxwain and 'driver' forming the crew.

There were sufficient establishment crew for *St. Helier* and *St. Julien* so that one would be a 'Running Vessel' and one a 'Standby Vessel'. The Running ship had a Master, Chief and Second Officers, Chief, Second and Third Engineers, Wireless Operator, two Quartermasters, nine Seamen, a Deck Boy, four Greasers and four Firemen. 'Below decks' were Chief, Second and After Cabin Stewards, two Assistant After Cabin and seven Assistant Stewards, a Mess Room Boy, Cook, Assistant Cook, two Stewardesses, a Superintendent of Cargo and two Night Watchmen, a total crew of 47 under normal circumstances. The 'Standby' crew was headed by another Master, with a basic crew of 15, comprising an example of most of the trades listed above. These were strengthened when circumstances dictated.

Cargo steamers *Roebuck (II)* and *Sambur* had a similar arrangement, but with far smaller crews. The 'Running Vessel' had a Master, with Chief and Second Officers, Chief and Second Engineers, a Quartermaster, four Seamen, a Deck Boy, three Greasers, a Fireman and a Cook/Steward, 16 crew members in total. The 'Standby Vessel' had a Second Officer, Chief and Second Engineers with five others.

Apart from Second World War service, *St. Julien*, *St. Helier*, *Roebuck (II)* and the *Sambur* remained on the GWR Channel Islands runs up to and beyond nationalisation. *Roebuck (II)* and *Sambur* were altered slightly in 1928 to allow twelve passengers to be carried on each. Although loading became easier with the new ships in service, some help was still required in the between-wars period. The 30-year old *Great Western (II)* assisted at Weymouth in the summer periods until 1932 when she was temporarily renamed *GWR 20*, before being broken up in 1933. She was the last coal-fired GWR ship to sail from Weymouth, so the now-redundant marine coal siding off the tramway could be used to store a few vans for the increased perishable traffic. (In 1899, the 7-ton *Amine*, an 1886 Cowes launch, had been brought to Weymouth by the GW to haul coal barges). The

St. Julien and *St. Helier* were reconditioned for the summer service of 1937, and more covered passenger accommodation was provided, together with more room for meals; the number of berths was likewise increased from 353 to 375.

By 1938 traffic had grown to over 4½ million baskets of tomatoes. Combined with the traffic carried by the SR, over 7 million packages of all types of market produce were shipped in that record year. The Guernsey cut-flower trade had developed to such an extent that a record 308,000 packages (21,500 tons) were sent in 1938 to the mainland (daffodils, tulips and irises from January to June, gladioli from July to October and chrysanthemums during the remainder of the year). In 1937 overall goods traffic from the Channel Islands had totalled some 50,000 tons, with 27,000 tons in the other direction to the Islands from Weymouth – including bananas (ex-Avonmouth) specially repacked in containers. Since much of the traffic was perishable, 200 specially-built ventilated covered vans (*Wagon Diagram Index* 'Y8') for express goods train working were introduced in 1937-8 to ensure the produce reached the markets in the best condition possible. By the later 1930s, as many as four cargo boats a day would leave Guernsey. In 1938, cargo boats made 212 special voyages, and 415 special fitted trains conveyed 15,024 vans to London and other parts of the system. At such peak periods, five 'C'-headcode vacuum-fitted goods trains daily left Weymouth during the afternoon and evening; all went initially to Westbury, then variously to Bordesley, Cardiff, Oxley, Paddington and Southall. Over 600 additional vanloads were dispatched by ordinary train services.

Loading and unloading the ships, and loading the railway vehicles, was very labour-intensive, and large numbers of men worked through the afternoon and into the night loading up the special trains. Many unmarried railway clerks were posted to Weymouth for three months to cope with the seasonal traffic, with large numbers of casual labour also being taken on. The increase in inter-war traffic is reflected in the harbour dues paid by the GWR: £4,000 in 1922, £8,500 in 1928 and over £10,000 thereafter. From 1932, the GWR and SR collaborated over the Channel Islands traffic in that the separate staffs on the Islands were amalgamated, Guernsey being run by the GWR and Jersey by the SR.

The Great Western's passenger service to the Channel Islands was stopped on 9th September 1939, after the outbreak of the Second World War, but goods traffic continued. At Fishguard, the *St. Andrew (II)*) (H C Bond, captain) on the Rosslare run had been requisitioned to become a hospital ship and the *St. Helier* (R R Pitman captain) went from Weymouth as a replacement, but she, her captain and crew were then also taken over by the government and conveyed troops and stores between Southampton and Cherbourg (later in the war, she served on the Gurock-Isle of Man service; at Dartmouth supporting Motor Torpedo boats; and was an assault ship at the D-day landings). *St. Julien* (L T Richardson captain) was requisitioned as soon as the Channel Islands service

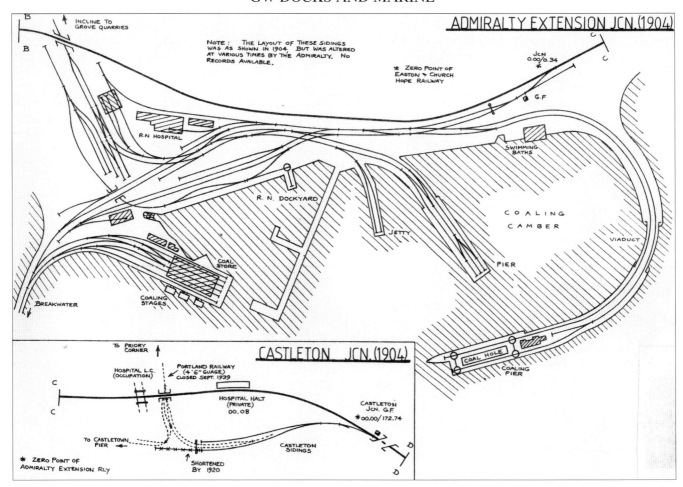

Map of tracks at Portland Dockyard [R A Cooke]

stopped, and took troops from Avonmouth to St. Nazaire before being converted to a hospital ship (No.29) at Southampton in which capacity she made trips between Newhaven and Dieppe. All of this took place before the evacuation from Dunkirk in late May 1940. *Roebuck (II)* (W Y Larbestier captain) was requisitioned in May 1940 and was rushed from Weymouth to La Panne near Dunkirk (with no charts!) for the evacuation. *St. Helier* was damaged at Dunkirk but, patched up, she, together with *Roebuck (II)* and *Sambur* (C W Sanderson captain), soon went to St Valery-en-Caux near Dieppe to try and rescue the Highland Division. Owing to German guns on the cliffs, not a soldier could be embarked. *St Helier* did bring 2,500 troops from St Malo to Southampton, before starting on a last and fruitless rescue mission to La Pallice.

The subsequent fall of Cherbourg and St Malo made it impossible to defend the Channel Islands from invasion and they were demilitarised. The Government hoped for a mass evacuation, and between the 20th and 28th June 1940 some 25,000 refugees were brought to Weymouth. The aeroplanes of Jersey Airways (joint property of the GWR and SR) did their bit, but when on the 28th June the Germans began to bombard Jersey and Guernsey, the last ships had to leave in haste. Following the end of hostilities in Europe, *Roebuck (II)* took supplies to the Channel Islands after the German surrender of the Islands in May 1945, and later joined *Sambur*, which had restored the GWR commercial cargo service between Weymouth and the Channel Islands in September 1945. The night passenger service was restored by the *St. Helier* in June 1946, and *St. Julien* returned in November. By 1947, things were back in full swing with passenger numbers and cargo tonnage at pre-war levels. A full complement of 60 GWR staff (the 1939 level) was employed at Weymouth Quay in that last year of the independent company; it had grown from 40 in 1929. New vessels - *St. David (III)* and *St. Patrick (III)* - had been ordered to replace the sunken ships of the same names. While the *St. David (III)* was delivered for the Irish services in 1947, the *St. Patrick (III)* - which, despite its name, was intended for daytime Channel Islands journeys - was not handed over until early 1948.

PORTLAND DOCKYARD, Royal Navy (Served)

In its heyday, Portland was an important naval base, being primarily a coaling station, although it also victualled vessels. Unlike Devonport, the dockyard had no graving docks, and did not construct or repair ships. Its origins lay in the construction of breakwaters in the mid-C19[th] to make Weymouth Bay a harbour of refuge for sailing vessels. The waters off Chesil bank are dangerous, and there was no place between Plymouth and the Solent for large ships to shelter in bad weather. At the time there were also fears of a French invasion, so massive defensive forts feature in the construction. One of the reasons for choosing Portland was that building materials were available on the spot: stone had been quarried on the island since ancient times and brought to a pier at Castletown for export. Long before the arrival of the GWR at Weymouth, blocks of Portland stone were being brought down on 4ft 6½in gauge railway inclines to a quay at Portland.

The Admiralty opened its own quarries in 1848 (using convict labour) with a 7ft-gauge incline that ran on to wooden staging out over the sea from which stones were deposited to pile up as the breakwater. Horses were employed at first, locomotives appearing in 1851. A line was put in between the foot of the old commercial incline and the Admiralty tracks, any stone used from the private quarries at Portland being transferred by crane from the wagons of one gauge to the other. All these lines were isolated until 1865 when the 5-mile-long, mixed-gauge GW and LSW joint Weymouth & Portland Railway opened. It left Weymouth over the northern section of the Quay line for a short distance through the goods yard. A branch was built from Portland terminus station to the foot of the incline belonging to the so-called Portland Railway (also called the Merchants' Railway) at Castletown. This enabled Portland stone to be conveyed overland by rail to new markets.

By the time of the breakwater's completion in 1872, steam was taking over from sail, and a need arose for bunkers coal for both navy and merchant navy ships within the harbour of refuge. In 1874, the line from Portland station to Castletown (by now standard gauge) was extended to the lines of the Admiralty workshops and small harbour, the broad gauge lines belonging to the navy (including those on the breakwater) being re-laid as standard gauge. The connecting line was built to passenger standards in case troops had to be conveyed, and was eventually opened to traffic in 1878. Even so, horse-drawn goods trains with coal, naval stores and equipment were the norm. Coaling facilities at Portland grew from that time with an Admiralty coal jetty, a second being built in 1893. Merchant ships were coaled from hulks out in the bay - these also had to be supplied with coal brought in along the branch line from Weymouth. The many steam cranes on site performed shunting on dockyard lines.

The intention of providing a harbour of refuge had been accomplished by the original design for the breakwater that swung round from Portland towards Weymouth, but left a two-mile gap at the Weymouth end. The gap became a weakness in defence after the invention of the torpedo in the late C19th, and in 1894 work began on extending the breakwater round to Bincleaves where the GWR had carried out reclamation work before abandoning a proposed new dock for Channel Islands services. The Admiralty quarry and incline was put to work again, and construction of the new breakwater system involved loading stone by crane into barges at the naval dockyard to be taken out to sea and offloaded. The breakwater was completed in 1908, but

before then the 5-mile-long Weymouth & Portland Railway (by now standard gauge) to Castletown and the dockyard was extended some 3½ miles to Easton and Church Hope. The line, reached by running a distance of 34 chains over the Admiralty railway, was opened to goods traffic in 1900. At the end of the Easton & Church Hope Railway, a gantry spanned a cutting to enable stone from adjacent quarries to be transferred to railway wagons. There was a 20 ton wagon weighbridge at Portland.

Early in the C20th, the establishment of a torpedo factory on the Portland branch south of Rodwell increased the traffic. While the LSWR and GWR ran passenger trains alternately on a five-year cycle on the extended branch, they operated independent goods trains. Signalling on the Portland line was the responsibility of the GWR.

In anticipation of Portland receiving hospital ships in 1915, requiring three ambulance trains per week, the dock lines were strengthened by the GWR, paid for by the Admiralty.

The *Helper* (ex-GWR *Sir Francis Drake (I)*, a tender from Plymouth sold by the company in 1910) was requisitioned by the Admiralty in WWI, and performed duties as a 'liberty' tender to the RN Fleet based at Portland Harbour. This same boat, later owned by the Alderney Steam Packet Co, was the last paddle steamer on inter-Channel Islands runs.

EXETER CITY (CANAL) BASIN
(Served)

The prospectus for the Bristol & Exeter Railway issued in 1835 was for '...a double line from the GWR in a certain field called Temple Mead at Bristol to Exeter's canal basin, with branches to Bridgwater Docks and Tiverton...' The Exeter canal basin had been built in 1827 at the time of an extension and widening of a canal - whose origins went back to 1567 - that had been built to by-pass the difficult-to-navigate top end of the River Exe; the canal enabled 200-ton vessels to be towed up to Exeter, horses replacing men hobblers. With operating costs coming down, trade at the basin increased rapidly, coastal craft no longer having to unload into lighters off Topsham. The price of coal at the quay, for example, was reduced by half. Up to the arrival of the railways, coal formed over half of the imports, with timber, slates, groceries from London and Bristol, and goods from the Continent making up the rest. Serge cloth was the principal export, sent all over the Continent (and to India during the Napoleonic Wars, when there was no access to Continental markets). But the Devon cottage industry in wool went into rapid decline when manufacture became concentrated in the more efficient mills of industrial Northern England.

The trade of the canal was immediately affected by the arrival of the B&E in 1844. According to the city council, '.....The whole of the trade from Bristol and Wales has totally ceased and that from Liverpool and Gloucester generally lessened and we must naturally look forward to further loss in the Plymouth and Cornwall trade when the South Devon line is in operation'. The Topsham coal dealer

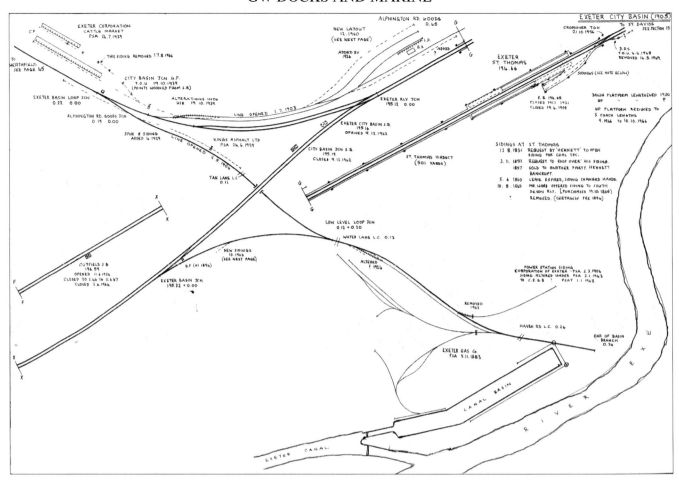

Map of Exeter Quay. [R A Cooke]

Richard Bussell told the Tidal Harbours Commission in 1845 that, before the Bristol & Exeter Railway arrived in 1844, his sale of coal alone amounted to nearly 6,000 tons per annum, for which his firm used 20 sailing ships. Afterwards it fell to 1,000 tons, for which only five ships were required. Furthermore, sidings were laid at Teignmouth Quay in 1851, and that port began to compete with the Exeter canal coal trade.

By the 1860s, the principal imports by canal were wines, hides and timber, with coal well down the list. By then it was realised - too late - that the locks should have been bigger and wider, a story repeated around the country at canals and docks. The canal surveyor had suggested on at least two occasions that the canal should have a link with the B&E, but his advice was ignored. In fact, Topsham quay received a rail link in 1857 via the LSWR, but it was not until 1867 that a broad gauge branch was opened to link the City Basin with the SDR at St David's station. Mixed gauge, though laid on the dock branch in 1870, was not sanctioned for use by the SDR until 1876. Timber was the principal traffic by rail.

After the loss of trade upon the arrival of the railways, Exeter Corporation could not pay the interest on the mortgage by which the improvements had been paid for, so the courts appointed a receiver. Over the years, the canal creditors were to exercise a stranglehold over canal expenditure. Eventually, a settlement was reached with the creditors in 1883 and Exeter City Council regained control. Trade had declined under the period of administration, and strong efforts were made to regain traffic for the canal. The tonnage carried on the canal did increase from just over 30,000 tons in 1888 to just over 50,000-tons in 1898, but no new patterns of traffic were generated, and less than 10% went for export. Trade declined in the early years of the C20[th] as ships were getting bigger and could not use the canal. After various enquiries, it was decided in 1910 that '…in view of the great expenditure required and the absence of any reasonable prospect of increase in trade……[the Navigation Committee]……is unable to recommend improvements……' Canal traffic fell rapidly during the First World War and the maintenance, particularly dredging, was neglected. Silting up had become so severe that the Council was advised that it might as well close the basin at Exeter if it did not tackle the problem so, in 1924/5, a new tug (*Venture III*) , dredger and hopper barges were purchased.

There were two rail connexions to the basin. The original was by a trailing connexion with the down mainline at Exeter Basin Jct, south of Exeter St Thomas station. This 34-chain-long branch ran to a corner of the basin where there was a wagon turntable that gave access to a short siding along the north side of the basin (4 or 5 wagons long) and also to another along the top end of the basin, off which another wagon turntable led to a long siding (24 wagons) on the south side. In 1904 a spur off the Heathfield branch was built to the basin. It passed back under the main line to join with the original branch.

As at Gloucester docks - whose story is in many ways similar to Exeter's - the need for petrol in the late 1920s presented hope for canal trade. Storage depots were established near the Exeter canal basin, and imports increased from some 40,000-tons in 1935 to over 50,000-tons in 1938; exports, on the other hand, were at about the 2,000-ton level. The need for petrol was a two-edged sword, of course: increased traffic by roads took away potential traffic from both canal and railway.

The Second World War saw a big drop in trade, petrol deliveries being virtually the only traffic. The basin was damaged during the blitz of 1942. After the war, trade was slow to pick up; only 46 ships entered the canal in 1945, but by 1948 there were 145 ships using the canal, with 30,000-odd tons of cargo plus nearly 1,000 stands of timber handled.

In 1948, the Exeter canal was already special in having been under single ownership for nearly 400 years. It escaped being nationalised, and remained under the control of local government.

TEIGNMOUTH
(Served)

The staple export of Teignmouth Quay was potters' clay (similar to china clay), which had been extracted since 1743 from the Bovey basin area around Teigngrace. All clay mined in the Teign Valley was known as 'ball clay' because it used to be dug in open pits and cut into rectangular blocks each weighing about 300 lbs, which were known to the miners as 'balls'. A major user of Devon clay was the Wedgwood firm in Staffordshire, to where it was shipped by coaster to Runcorn on the Mersey, and thence by canal. Clay was brought down by barge along the Stover Canal into the Teign estuary, where it was laboriously transferred by hand into sea-going vessels. Heytor granite was also exported along the Stover Canal. Demand for stone exceeded supply, particularly when London Bridge was under construction, so in 1821 the Teignmouth Harbour Commission was established to improve navigation on the Teign and build a quay to speed up the loading of granite blocks. The original facilities at Teignmouth dated from the days of the South Devon Newfoundland fishing fleets, and the connection

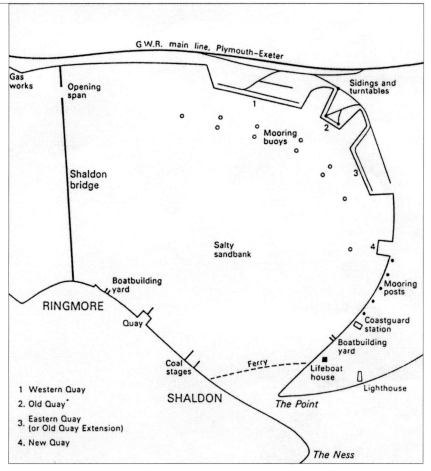

Map of Teignmouth Harbour [in Teignmouth: A Martime History].

with Canada continued with ships sailing outwards to Quebec with clay, and returning with timber.

In the early C19[th], the ports of South and North Devon were the biggest importers of culm (inferior coal) from South Wales, and that brought in by coastal vessels to Teignmouth was to raise steam for machinery at the ball clay mines around Bovey, Kingsteignton and Chudleigh; for the kilns of local potteries; and for lime-burning. There was sporadic traffic in different types of ore down the river and canal (depending on price booms and slumps), which was taken away by the returning culm and coal ships; this traffic had dwindled away by 1908.

Soon after the railway arrived in 1846, the Teignmouth Harbour Commissioners agreed to sidings being constructed on the Old Quay, which was strengthened for the purpose. The work was completed in 1851, whereafter coal imports doubled to 20,000 tons in 1852. Coal was now distributed locally by rail to places as far east as Cullompton and as far west as Brent. A feature of the restricted layout on the quay was the use (typical of the time) of wagon turntables to link tracks that ran at sharp angles to one another. Rail access to the new Western Quay dated from the turn of the C20[th]. During the period 1870-1920, coal imports through Teignmouth were consistently at about the level of 65,000 tons per annum. Imports of culm diminished in the late Victorian period when the estuary limekilns closed, it being easy by then to take dry lime around the country by rail from large 'factory' kilns. New sidings were provided particularly for coal traffic when different quays were developed before WWI. In the 1920s, Old Quay was accessed by trailing connections from each Main line to form a parallel siding, which held 33 wagons clear of pointwork. From this siding, a further seven were linked to serve the three sections of quay with their two small, intermediate basins. In the 1930s the number of sidings was increased to supply coal for the power station at Newton Abbot, grab cranes being employed for unloading. By this time the turn-tabled tracks on the Old Quay had been removed. There was a privately-owned 20 ton wagon weighbridge available to weigh GW traffic.

One of the most striking effects of the rail connection at Teignmouth quay was the establishment of a steamer service from London in 1853, which offered through transit to rail-connected towns in South Devon. There was even a sniff of ocean-going ships calling in 1851 when the *Comet* landed mails and passengers from Madeira for onwards transport by rail to London, as did the *Hannah* from South Africa a few months later. This was about the same time as ocean-going vessels began to call at Plymouth. Most ships using the port of Teignmouth were still sailing vessels at this time, and the steam paddle tug *PT Industry* was provided for their assistance; it was the only steam tug based between Plymouth and Portsmouth in those days. A number of different tugs were engaged over the years at Teignmouth: after the First World War, tugs were less and less required as by then most sailing ships had auxiliary engines and could enter, berth and leave port without help, but the steam tug *Kestrel* (and later the motor launch *Heron*) was employed to tow clay barges downriver to the harbour right up to Second World War.

While Teignmouth grew significantly in Victorian times, and shipbuilding and fishing became important, the arrival of the railway and the new works in the harbour did little to increase ball clay exports. This was in contrast to what happened at Fowey, for example, where trainloads of china clay were brought to jetties equipped with bulk tipping devices. Moving ball clay to Teignmouth ought not to have been difficult (the Moretonhampstead branch was opened in 1866 and the Heathfield & Christow line through Chudleigh in 1882), but one problem seems to have been the constricted area between the GW main line and the dockside into which sidings had to be fitted. Shunting in and out of the sidings blocked the main line, and there was little or no room for continuous belt conveyors of the sort found at Fowey. On top of that, ship owners seemed reluctant to pay wharfage, so that the clay continued to be loaded overside by hand with simple crane. Nevertheless, the importance of the export of ball clay to Teignmouth's harbour traffic is revealed by the fact that clay of value £21,000 was exported annually during 1911-13, when the value of 'all other articles' exported was a mere £71! By this time, additional uses had been found for ball clay, including in electrical porcelain, as a filler for rubber and as an extender for paint. The clay went to Belgium, Holland and Germany as well as

home ports such as Glasgow, the tonnage being some 80,000 annually. In 1904, foreign imports stood at 15,000 tons, which was double the tonnage of 1894; at the depth of the nation-wide depression in the mid-1880s it had been only about 1,000 tons.

Paper making was traditional in Devon, and wood pulp began to replace rags in the industry during the 1880s, which required ever-increasing imports of pulp from Scandinavia into Teignmouth. Ten thousand tons were brought in during 1904, in lots of 600 tons, for Reed & Smith's mill at Cullompton, and for the Hele Paper Co. of Silverton near Exeter, and taken forward by goods train. Occasionally there was traffic in cider apples from France when the home harvest was bad; in 1924, for example, about 5,000 tons arrived for Henley's of Newton Abbot, The Taunton Cider Co. and smaller local firms. Immediately after the First World War, and before competition from road lorries became severe, trade through Teignmouth increased because it proved to be a favourable distribution centre for the growing population of South Devon. Coal merchants as far away as Yeovil brought in coal via Teignmouth quay, but paradoxically the South Hams trade was lost to Brixham.

Trade picked up after the depression of the 1920s, the more so after a change of management of the Teignmouth Quay Co. in 1932. Within 20 years, the annual amount of water-borne traffic was quadrupled: 23,000 tons in 1931; 87,000 tons in 1939 and over 110,000 tons after the Second World War. In 1931, the total imports were 11,000 tons (coal, cement, oil-cake, flints, potatoes, sand, slates and timber); after WWII imports were 30,000 tons, mainly of coal, French apple juice, and timber, but also potatoes, bog ore and cement. Transport of ball clay by river came to an end during WWII, and since it was difficult to utilise the railway, conveyance by road was employed. Even before the end of the river traffic, lorries had begun to bring clay cheaply to Teignmouth for tipping directly into ships from the quayside (from ramps into bigger ships after 1937).

KINGSWEAR/DARTMOUTH
(Served)

The South Devon Railway branch line to Torquay from Newton Abbot (the 'Dartmouth & Torbay Railway') reached Torre in 1849, and was extended through Paignton to Churston (with its branch to Brixham) in 1860. The line's terminus was at Kingswear, reached in 1864. All these places lie to the east of the River Dart, whilst Dartmouth itself lies on the western bank, opposite Kingswear. The SDR wanted ultimately to serve Dartmouth, but wished to avoid either a monster swing bridge across the river (wide at that point, and busy with shipping) or the construction of a separate, additional railway line for nine or ten miles down the west bank from Totnes to serve only Dartmouth. The answer took the form of a ferry service timed to meet the arrival and departure of trains. It is well known that all the facilities of a normal railway station were built at Dartmouth, even though there was no railway line. The Dartmouth ferry pontoon on the

Sidings at coal tip (left centre) with wagon turntable access around the turn of the C19th/20th. Kingswear signal box at bottom centre (station buildings and tracks behind photographer). In front of the signal box is a small ferry beached on a hard-standing. At bottom right is the loco turntable with three roads running off, reached from the station. Between signal box and viaduct over creek was the location of a 'ticket platform' while in the far distance is the location of Britannia Halt/Steam ferry Crossing.

New cranes installed at Kingswear in June 1932. O29 GW Open C wagon No 121736 on extreme right was a brand-new wagon that year. Elsewhere some trucks are still lettered LNWR. The T & C Wilson ship berthed at the quay in the foreground is the Haytor of 1925. The vessel in the background is one of two troopships operated by the Bibby Line. They were the Dorsetshire of 1920, and the Somersetshire of 1921, both of which were laid up at the time at Dartmouth. According to the Maritime Information Centre at Greenwich, it is probably the Somersetshire. [GWR]

Kingswear side was at the southern end of the terminal station.

The ferry was first leased by the SDR to the Dartmouth Steam Packet Co., who employed various ships on the 300-yard crossing. They were the 101-ton wooden paddle steamer *PS Pilot,* followed by the 47-ton iron-hulled *PS Newcomin* that was specially built for the job. Also used at various times were the tug *Guide* and the river packet steamers *Dartmouth* and *Hauley* (the Dart was navigable to just above Totnes, and pleasure boats ran several times a day). In Victorian times, those rail passengers from Dartmouth wanting to travel in the Plymouth direction often took the pleasure boats up to Totnes rather than the ferry to Kingswear as that meant going back to Newton Abbot. The other boat specially ordered for the Dartmouth ferry by the lessees in 1869 was the 61-ton iron-hulled *PS Dolphin,* capable of carrying 300 passengers, which operated the run with the *Newcomin* until the latter was sold to a French Company in 1884. The *Dolphin,* re-engined in 1876 by her makers Harveys of Hayle, had two direct-acting oscillating cylinders. She did not run on Sundays, and any railway passengers had to engage a boat to cross the river.

There were other ferries across the Dart at that time, including a 'floating bridge' (pontoon) driven by steam at Sand Quay for vehicles and cartage traffic. For people travelling by Admiralty boat to or from the naval training ship *Britannia,* moored a mile up river from Dartmouth, a railway platform called 'Steam Ferry Crossing' had been erected at the level crossing between Kingswear and Churston. The replacement Royal Naval College dates from 1905.

The GWR itself took over the running of the railway ferry in 1901, inheriting the 32-year old *PS Dolphin.* The *Dolphin's* replacement was 117-ton *TSS Mew*; this came into service in 1908, when the *Dolphin* was broken up. The *Mew* (named after a local rock in the Dart) carried 543 passengers.

With motor cars increasing in numbers, the *Mew* was altered in 1921 to carry vehicles on the aft deck. In 1929, her GW Marine Section crew establishment comprised a Master, First and Second Engineers, Mate, four Deckhands, two Firemen and a Watchman.

In late May 1940, she set off at her maximum speed of 10 knots up channel, heading for Dunkirk, but arrived after it was all over. During 1946, she was given a new and shorter funnel, plus a foremast. She eventually came out of service in 1955, having steamed half a million miles and carried an estimated 23 million passengers, without having missed a sailing. She was replaced by the 35 tonners *Humphrey Gilbert* and *Adrian Gilbert,* the last vessels laid down for the Western Region.

As the number and size of steamers increased in the second half of the C19th, bunkers coal facilities were established at deepwater sites around the coast, and Dartmouth/Kingswear emerged as the principal South Devon coaling port for merchant shipping. In 1868, three coal hulks were moored in the Dart, and from then until 1914 the sale of bunkers coal from these vessels was the port's principal trade. Coal was loaded manually by gangs of 'lumpers' who received 2d per ton in those days. In the peak year of 1890, 750 ships called to be coaled. Ships for coaling were recorded as 'arriving' at the port; those actually berthing and loading/unloading cargo 'entered' the port.

In 1872, the Castle Line was set up and began a service to South Africa from Dartmouth. It was in direct competition with the Union Line sailing out of Plymouth, and it ran on alternate weeks, so that a weekly mail service was provided. Eventually, the two companies shared the government contract and, in 1900, merged as the Union Castle line. Before then, however, in 1891 Castle ships had abandoned Dartmouth for Southampton as home port, but still landed homeward-bound mails at Plymouth.

The north-west side of Kingswear Station was originally provided with two small jetties off the 360ft-long quay. In late Victorian days, the jetty very near to the ferry pontoon had two short sidings (two-wagon capacity each) accessed by wagon turntables from the main tracks parallel to the wharf; the tracks on the jetties were removed in the new station yard layout of 1929. The water along the quay was 24ft/10ft deep at spring/neap tides. Two 3-ton electric cranes equipped with grabs enabled coal to be emptied out of coasting vessels direct into railway wagons for distribution to other towns in the area. Forty-ton bogie coal wagons were marshalled in the weekly train (Saturdays Only) from Blaenavon to Kingswear (1908 Service Time Table) carrying bunkers coal. It is noteworthy that according to a 1911 GW pamphlet Kingswear had a 100 ton wagon weighbridge, comprising two 16ft long plates, spaced 8ft apart (which would accommodate bogie loco coal wagons), each plate capable of weighing 50 tons, or 100 combined. Timber was the other principal traffic unloaded at Kingswear Wharf.

TOTNES QUAY
(Served)

An old quay at Totnes dated from the Newfoundland trading days of the C18th. An extension of the Buckfastleigh, Totnes & South Devon Railway was authorised in 1865 and this included a railway or tramway to Totnes Quay '...on which no locomotive, stationary engine and ropes, or atmospheric agency was to be used...'. The single line, horse-drawn goods branch, just over half-a-mile long, was opened to the quay through the town in 1873. Despite the conditions of authorisation, locomotives were in use the following year from the main line station as far as the Tram Gate, where the line entered the streets of the town at The Plains, near Totnes Bridge. From there to the quayside, shunting horses handled all wagons, right up to and after nationalisation. The wharf (Marsh Quay) was situated on a narrow 'mill tail' off the River Dart, and despite its narrowness, small coasters could berth head-to-tail. There was a fixed goods yard crane at the quay (3-ton), located at the pointwork leading to the one trailing siding that ran along the quayside. Baltic timber and coal were important imports. There was a privately-

*Timber discharged at Totnes quay loaded on J14 Macaw B built on lot 797 in 1914 (wagon called Bogie Bolster after 1943 all
-railway telegraph code unification) passing through streets just after nationalisation. Load chained to wagon. Two shunting
horses with chains from harness collars attached to rings on wagon solebar. Leading driver carries a shunting pole. The
second view shows local traffic on the branch from the town to the quay.*

owned 20 ton wagon weighbridge available to weigh GW
traffic.

In addition to serving the quay, the branch dealt with
various businesses en route. Totnes was home to Symonds
Cider, and Harris's had a bacon factory alongside the
branch, whilst cattle feed was distributed from warehouses
along the line. There were no private sidings along the
branch (apart from a short siding for the Town Mill, north of
Tram Gate) and vehicles were simply left along the track for
loading and unloading. Some 18,000 tons of goods passed
over the line in the early 1920s, though this had fallen to
about 8,000 tons by the end of the 1930s.

A long, 1,100ft loop was added just before the First
World War on the stretch of the branch near Totnes
Racecourse, between the station and Tram Gate. A 1920s
diagram also shows a wagon weighbridge near the timber
yard on the southern part of branch, with a 2-ton crane
nearby.

Until 1915, the connection to the quay line was a
trailing junction from a headshunt at the mainline station,
after which a direct link was made. Much later, during the
Second World War, sidings were added at the racecourse in
the build-up for D-Day; at the same time, the far end of the
line was also extended to a small shipyard. The racecourse
sidings were later to serve Totnes cattle market, South
Devon Farmers Cooperative, and Staverton Contractors.

PLYMOUTH MILLBAY DOCK (Owned); SUTTON HARBOUR (served)

What is now called Plymouth was a merger, in 1914, of the
three towns of Plymouth, Stonehouse and Devonport; the
'Plymouth' of Elizabethan sailors was Sutton Pool and the
adjacent Cattewater Harbour on the River Plym. The first
railway in the district was the 4ft 6in-gauge Plymouth &
Dartmoor Tramway of 1819, the purpose of which was to

supply materials for Dartmoor Prison. The line ran from
Sutton Pool (later a proper harbour) alongside Cattewater
and past Laira. The line fell into disuse in the 1840s, but
later the track of the northern part became part of the GW
Princetown branch of 1883. The southern section was
connected in 1856 to the Lee Moor Tramway, built to
convey china clay from Dartmoor to Laira Wharf.

The SDR reached Plymouth in 1848, the 7ft broad
gauge line crossing the 4ft 6in tramway diagonally on the
level at Laira. The SDR bought up the part of the P&DT
near Sutton Pool, and gained broad gauge access to the Pool
by laying an additional rail alongside the P&DT tracks from
Laira in 1851 (mixed gauge, but not the usual sort!). Like
the rest of the P&DT, it was horse-worked, but in 1869, two
separate broad gauge tracks were installed and steam
traction was introduced. The broad gauge track was made
into mixed gauge in 1876, when the LSWR first entered
Plymouth over the Cornwall Railway's Launceston branch
that had been converted to mixed gauge south of Lydford
for that purpose; the CR had arrived at Plymouth in 1859
after the Royal Albert Bridge over the Tamar was opened,
and it amalgamated with the GWR in 1889.

In 1890, the LSWR opened its own line from Lydford
to enter Plymouth from the west, and used other sections of
the moribund P&DT to expand into the Plymouth area. This
gave rise to the LSWR branch to Turnchapel via Plymstock
(Act of 1883, line fully opened in 1897), and also
permission to build a line from Plymstock to Yealmpton
(Act of 1888). However, another Act of 1892 transferred
the powers for this line to the GWR, the line opening in
1898.

After the arrival of the railway, the ancient small
harbours and riverside wharves continued to deal with
coastal and Continental shipping, and local shipping on the
Tamar. In early days, the quays at Morwhellam and
Calstock used to land cargoes for Tavistock, and ship out

An aerial view of the GWR Millbay docks in 1926. Millbay Pier is at the bottom right, with the pontoon above (tenders berthed alongside) and Trinity Pier above that. The inner dock is at the top (north). Glasgow Wharf is to the right of the lock in the centre, and South Quay at the left. Graving dock off inner basin at top left. West Wharf is in the outer dock at centre left. [GWR]

copper ores to places like Swansea, but that traffic had gone by 1890.

The GW had operations in Sutton Harbour, but the significant commercial harbour at Plymouth was the extensive Millbay Docks, which was the largest of the Great Western's own dock properties before the Grouping. It consisted of an outer 31- acre basin and a 1,200ft by 500ft (13 acre) inner dock, with a dry dock off that. Owing to its location, the depth of water was little affected by tides (26/21 ft spring/neap tides), so that there were lock gates (80 ft wide) only into the inner dock at Millbay and into the railway-owned graving dock. Originally the entrance lock to the inner basin was to one side, but in 1902 it was made central. Plymouth docks had over two miles of quays with 10 acres of quay space and 40 additional acres of storage in the form of a timber float. There were 10 acres of sheds and 5 miles of dock tracks. In the outer basin there were three piers jutting out from the eastern (Millbay railway station) side, viz: the large Trinity Pier, the small Princess Royal

Pier and Pontoon, and the Millbay Pier that formed a sea wall. It was at the Millbay Pier and Pontoon that tenders berthed for ocean liner traffic.

Originally, the Brunel-designed docks belonged to the Plymouth Great Western Docks Company, an independent company in which the SDR, B & E and GWR each subscribed £17,600 in 1846. The outer dock was completed by 1848, and was soon served by a short branch line (1850) from alongside the SDR terminus at Millbay (opened 1849). The inner dock and graving dock were opened for commercial traffic in 1857. The three railway companies took over the Docks company into joint ownership in 1874 (dock tracks were made mixed gauge in the same year) and shortly after, in 1878, the Millbay Docks came wholly into GWR hands on its amalgamation with the SDR and B&E. At that time, the Great Western bought out all the warehouse owners around the docks, and soon dredged the West Wharf to take ships up to 21ft draught.

The SDR carried 940 tons of fish in 1854, yet 3,000

Plymouth Millbay station in broad gauge days. Goods depot on the right with line through to Millbay docks.

Until quick-acting hydraulic cranes were delivered, two travelling steam cranes were specially adapted in 1911 for coal traffic at the South Wharf, Plymouth docks. The special jibs, enabling the cranes to handle two tons at 40 ft radius, were designed and built at Swindon. The height of the jibs from rail level to centre of jib-head was 50 ft. These cranes remained at Plymouth performing general craneage duties. [A G Atkins collection]

tons in 1864; this included not only fish from the large fleets but also sprats, mackerel, herrings and shell fish landed by smaller vessels. By the end of the C19th, some 12,000 tons of trawled fish was being landed annually at Brixham and Plymouth.

Freight through Millbay Docks was both from overseas and coastwise. Up until the 1870s, Plymouth was the sixth busiest provincial port in England with regular sailings to ports in the UK. Coal was a significant import from early days: even before Millbay opened, some 80,000 tons of coal were brought into Plymouth annually, mainly from South Wales; in later years, the figure hovered around 50,000 tons coal per year. Total imports stood at more than 280,000 tons in 1870 and had risen to 653,000 tons in 1913. Vessels from the Black Sea, other Continental wheat-growing countries, Argentina and North America brought grain in large quantities, and lots of timber arrived from Scandinavia. Grain, flour and timber each contributed about 35,000 tons annually to import cargoes. In addition were iron and steel imports, while refined sugar from Holland and Belgium figured in the statistics for 1900, as did petrol from Romania. At the turn of the C20th, Plymouth was also a centre for the distribution of strawberries arriving by ship from Brittany. The traffic, arriving before home-grown strawberries were on the market and therefore realising high prices, was distributed by the GWR to all parts of the UK. As well as strawberries from Brest, fruit (including pineapples) came from the Azores.

In 1905, Mr J Rooney was the superintendent of the GW docks at Plymouth. He was in charge of all shipping arrangements, including the landing and embarkation of mails and passengers, clearance of baggage, loading/ unloading/warehousing of traffic and the management and control of the company's steamers at the port.

Machinery for handling the great quantities of grain passing through the port was introduced in 1919. It dealt with grain in bulk some of which needed to be bagged. Existing hydraulic cranes were equipped with 1-ton grabs that fed the grain into a hopper for weighing out portions for sacking. Four sacks/minute could be bagged after which a conveyor took sacks either to the warehouse or to sheeted wagons to be dispatched by rail. During the WWII, a 25,000 -ton grain silo was built at the dock.

The accommodation at Millbay was improved and extended as the years went by. For example, in the early years of the C20th, the 95ft-wide graving dock operated by Willoughby Bros was lengthened from 360ft to 454ft and new hydraulic double lock gates (80ft wide by 22ft deep) were installed in place of the former hand-worked gates. New steam-driven centrifugal pumps were installed in the graving dock in 1909 to replace the original 1856 beam engines. Their design was such that the dock without a vessel in it (containing some five million gallons of water) could be emptied in about 3½ hours using only one pump. When emptying the dock containing a ship to be worked on, the water level in the dock would drop as the tide fell by letting the water exit through sluices. When these were closed, pumping could start. If the job was urgent, the sluices would be closed and two pumps could rapidly empty the dock, enabling work to commence. After the First World War, the keel blocks in the dry dock were raised so that vessels of 55ft beam could be accommodated. The Royal Marine barracks were behind the dry dock.

Portal electric quayside cranes had been installed when the West Wharf at Plymouth was rebuilt in 1912. Even so, one of the special travelling steam cranes from 1911 with a kinked jib is seen working on the wharf in September 1924. Wagon in right foreground is from the Furness Rly, and the one behind that from the L&Y. [GWR]

The depth of water around the quays was increased by dredging, particularly around the Trinity Pier, which itself was widened and given additional warehouse accommodation for fruit and general traffic. West Wharf was re built in concrete and new hydraulic cranes installed on that side of the dock in 1912. The lifeboat station was at the end of West Wharf known as 'the Camber'. By the Grouping, the GWR had about £500,000 invested in the docks, and throughout the 1920s appliances to speed up the handling of cargo continued to be installed, including an electric belt conveyor for mailbags from ocean liners (see later) and up-to-date craneage. In the 1930s there were 9 hydraulic cranes (3 tons maximum capacity), 5 electric cranes (up to 3 tons) and 3 rail-mounted steam cranes of 5 tons capacity. At the Glasgow Wharf on the south side of the inner basin, the railway lines were altered and new crane tracks provided in order to create an additional timber discharging berth. The wharf's general cargo shed was remodelled with a new 3-ton electric crane and an additional siding. There was over 200,000 sq ft of floor space in the six transit sheds (42,000 sq ft) and four grain sheds (also 42,000 sq ft) at the inner basin; and 10 transit sheds (56,000 sq ft) and 12 grain sheds (74,000 sq ft) at the outer harbour.

The railway network inside the docks was quite complex, with sidings on all sides of the Inner and Outer basins. In all, the total capacity was around 600 wagons. Shunting work around the sharp curves of the docks lines employed a variety of small locos over the years. The ex-Torbay & Brixham Railway 0-4-0ST *Raven* (broad gauge No.2175; standard gauge No.1329) was stationed at Plymouth for this purpose at the end of the C19[th], and between the wars nearly all of the Nos.136x group of tank engines were shedded at Laira. There was a small engine shed (coded PLY) at Harwell Street, in the dock area, where a couple of small dock tanks were stabled over weekends.

Although later closed, the shed continued to be employed for servicing locos.

Although the 75-acre Millbay docks could take bigger ships than the other two harbours at Plymouth, its trade was mainly coastal. The other harbours tended to specialise in certain activities: sailing vessels most often berthed in Sutton Harbour, which was also the home of the fishing fleet, the fish market being at the adjacent Barbican. The Great Western had a share in the shipping business at Sutton Harbour where it maintained a depot, the tracks on the quays and wharfs being connected to the huge GWR marshalling yard at Laira that was also used by the LSWR; there were also traffic sidings at North Road station. Before and after Second World War, some 200,000 tons of coal from the North of England was the principal import at Sutton Harbour; the major export was coke destined for the Channel Islands. Cattewater (LSWR), where most trade was done, connected with the Lee Moor Tramroad, and continued to deal with china clay, and also fertiliser and bulk petrol in later years. At nationalisation, there were over 450,000 tons of imports there, of which coal and petrol were each 175,000 tons (the coal was for a new power station at the northern end of the Laira wharf). Exports were some 90,000 tons, mostly china clay and stone.

For over a century, Plymouth was a port of call for British and foreign ocean liners travelling to and from North America, Australia, India and South Africa, and ships continued to call at Plymouth long after nationalisation. The origins of the Plymouth ocean liner traffic lay in government mail contracts (see Falmouth). Using the railway, late mails for overseas could be sent from London by train to Plymouth and put on board ships that had already sailed from London or Southampton, and homeward-bound mails taken off at Plymouth could be in London long before the ship had even reached Southampton. The first mail contracts at Plymouth were to South Africa in 1850, and to Australia in 1852. The Royal Mail Line serving the West Indies and South America began to call homeward-bound in 1860, and the Hamburg-Amerika Line outward bound in 1869 (both ways in 1899). The Compagnie Générale Transatlantique (the 'French Line') started to call both inwards and outwards bound in 1875 from Le Havre and Cherbourg. Other shipping lines calling included Norddeutscher Lloyd, the Peninsular Line and the Union Line. The Duke of Cornwall hotel was built in Plymouth especially to cater for the ocean liner traffic, and others followed soon after. It was a special broad gauge express from Plymouth, with passengers that had arrived from South Africa, which was involved in the collision with a 'narrow' gauge goods train at Norton Fitzwarren in 1890.

At first, the mail ships berthed in Millbay, for which the Great Western had dredged a deep channel, but later ships became too big and had to stop within the Sound, requiring private tenders to be hired to transport mail and passengers between ship and shore. The process was, in fact, quicker than docking. When the docks came under the joint control of the GWR, B & E and SDR in 1874, they provided a tender: the 170-ton *PS Sir Francis Drake (I)* was built by Allsupp & Sons in Preston in 1873, and taken over by the GWR in 1878. It had compound diagonal 350 HP steam engines, was 131 ft long by 20ft beam by 10 ft deep, and could carry 292 passengers. A second tender was introduced at Plymouth in 1876, the 174-ton *PS Sir Walter Raleigh (I)*. When taken over by the Great Western two years later, this tender was given an upper landing deck to work with high-sided French Line vessels. Passengers and mail were picked up or dropped off, some outward-bound passengers having come over specially by ship from ports in Northern France, to which there were train connections from Switzerland and other parts of the Continent. A third tender was the 700 HP 369-ton *Smeaton* of 1883, which was an enlarged *Sir Walter Raleigh (I)*, also built by Allsupp's, except that she was not a paddle steamer but had twin screws. The *Sir Richard Grenville (I)* of 1891 from Laird Bros was also twin screw, and the biggest tender yet, at 420 tons; in design, the ship was a small version of a contemporary Mersey ferry boat. Behind its funnel was a platform to receive gangways from taller liners (height seems to have been a problem with the early tenders).

The traffic grew tremendously: two dozen outward-bound ships, and the same number again inward-bound, called in 1880, with some 4,000 passengers. There were 10,000 passengers in 1890; 20,000 in 1906; and 30,000 in 1913. Numbers declined during WWI, but picked up again to reach 25,000 in 1924 and just over 40,000 in 1930, during which year about 800 ocean vessels called at Plymouth. The number of mailbags hovered at the 200-300,000 level from 1900 until 1948. It was claimed that one passenger in nine reaching the UK by sea entered through Plymouth.

Turnaround time of the ships calling at Plymouth was remarkably fast. The arrival time of the ship was telegraphed ahead, thus alerting the tenders, and when the ship arrived in Cawsand Bay and had dropped anchor, the

waiting tenders came alongside, one on each beam, that to port for passengers and mails, that to starboard for baggage, parcels, bullion, specie (coinage) and more bulky stuff. The liner would be underway again within half an hour! A typical 'transaction' might involve 100 passengers and associated baggage, 400-500 mailbags, plus bullion.

The boat train would have been made up on the dock lines (shunting would start when, for example, an incoming transatlantic ship was signalled off the Scillies). The train was in two halves on parallel tracks, with the passenger vehicles on the inside track, and the mail, baggage and bullion vehicles on the outside (bullion vans were odd in having doors on one side only). The two sets of vehicles were coupled up when all loading was completed, and the train sent off - it took about half-an-hour after the tenders landed to get the train away. The practice of boat trains departing from the dock began in 1882; before that, passengers had to take cabs to Millbay station. In the early C20th the typical make-up of an ocean special was six eight-wheel coaches.

A new landing pier for the increased ocean traffic was built in 1907. The reason for gold shipments featuring from the beginning of the Ocean Mails traffic was that gold was being brought continually to London from the Australian

The corner of the inner basin at Plymouth where the East Quay (straight ahead) joins Glasgow Wharf (on left) in September 1924. The single track across the picture proceeds on right to Millbay and the mainline. Warehouses Nos 48/49/50 on the right set back from tracks. Trestle up against first floor of warehouse to assist loading/unloading of goods by travelling steam crane. Warehouses 1-4 in distance closer to sidings. [GWR]

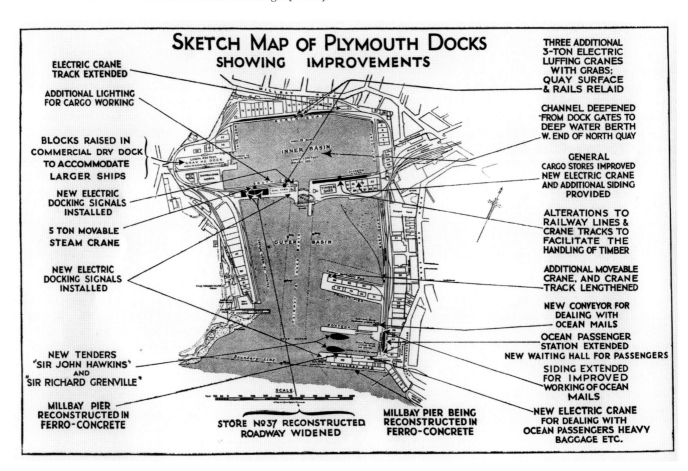

SKETCH MAP OF PLYMOUTH DOCKS
SHOWING IMPROVEMENTS

ELECTRIC CRANE
TRACK EXTENDED

ADDITIONAL LIGHTING
FOR CARGO WORKING

BLOCKS RAISED IN
COMMERCIAL DRY DOCK
TO ACCOMMODATE
LARGER SHIPS

NEW ELECTRIC
DOCKING SIGNALS
INSTALLED

5 TON MOVABLE
STEAM CRANE

NEW ELECTRIC
DOCKING SIGNALS
INSTALLED

NEW TENDERS
"SIR JOHN HAWKINS"
AND
"SIR RICHARD GRENVILLE"

MILLBAY PIER
RECONSTRUCTED IN
FERRO-CONCRETE

STORE No37 RECONSTRUCTED
ROADWAY WIDENED

MILLBAY PIER BEING
RECONSTRUCTED IN
FERRO-CONCRETE

THREE ADDITIONAL
3-TON ELECTRIC
LUFFING CRANES
WITH GRABS;
QUAY SURFACE
& RAILS RELAID

CHANNEL DEEPENED
FROM DOCK GATES TO
DEEP WATER BERTH
W. END OF NORTH QUAY

GENERAL
CARGO STORES IMPROVED
NEW ELECTRIC CRANE
AND ADDITIONAL SIDING
PROVIDED

ALTERATIONS TO
RAILWAY LINES &
CRANE TRACKS TO
FACILITATE THE
HANDLING OF TIMBER

ADDITIONAL MOVEABLE
CRANE, AND CRANE
TRACK LENGTHENED

NEW CONVEYOR FOR
DEALING WITH
OCEAN MAILS

OCEAN PASSENGER
STATION EXTENDED
NEW WAITING HALL FOR PASSENGERS

SIDING EXTENDED
FOR IMPROVED
WORKING OF OCEAN
MAILS

NEW ELECTRIC CRANE
FOR DEALING WITH
OCEAN PASSENGERS HEAVY
BAGGAGE ETC.

Mailbags being transferred by hand to the boat train at Trinity Pier from the tender Cheshire. This ex-Mersey ferry boat dating from 1889, and still registered at Liverpool, was purchased by the GW in 1905; she was broken up in 1913. [GWR]

gold rush, from the Cape in South Africa, and from West Africa. In the 1870s, coinage (over $300,000 at a time) was brought from the USA. In 1904, as the US payment to France for purchase of the Panama Canal, *Kronprinz Wilhelm* of the Norddeutscher Lloyd line landed bullion at Plymouth, which then travelled on the *City of Truro*'s 100 mph record-breaking run.

Sir *Walter Raleigh (I)* was sold in 1896, and when the *Gazelle* became the reserve boat for the GWR Irish services from Milford in 1900, she was used as a tender at Plymouth. A second-hand ex-Mersey ferry boat of 1889 was acquired in 1905 as a tender: she was the 387-ton *Cheshire*. Two new twin-screw tenders were introduced in 1908 to replace the aged paddlers *Sir Francis Drake (I)* and *Sir Walter Raleigh (I)* reusing their names. The *Sir Francis Drake (II)* of 608 tons was built with an extremely tall funnel, and could take 1,200 passengers, together with mails and baggage. The *Sir Walter Raleigh (II)* of 478 tons was similar; this vessel went to Fishguard for the first call of the *Mauretania* in 1909. The original *Sir Francis Drake (I)* was renamed *Helper* in 1908, and remained in the GW fleet until sold in 1910.

The LSWR was always trying to increase its trade through the docks at Sutton Harbour and Cattewater in Plymouth, and had ambitions at the end of the C19th to create an ocean liner port by developing the Cattewater right up to Laira Bridge but the scheme, and others similar, was vetoed by the Admiralty. But, in 1904, the LSWR obtained a contract to handle American Line passengers at Plymouth, and set up an 'Ocean Quay' station on its Stonehouse Pool goods branch from Devonport, running its own tender (a 1907-built 577-ton Southampton & Channel Islands vessel named *Victoria*). The GPO insisted that the GWR still handle all the mails, so tenders from both companies served the American Line ships, and competing trains raced to London by their different routes. GW tenders proclaimed 'Royal Mail Route to London'. However, after the LSWR Salisbury boat train crash in 1906, in which 24 passengers were killed, things quietened down, and in 1910 the two companies agreed on a pooling agreement, including that tender services should be run solely by the GWR. The *Victoria* was thus removed by the LSWR to Southampton, but it was soon acquired by the Great Western, renamed *Atalanta* and employed on tender services principally at Fishguard, but also on relief tender work at Plymouth.

Opposite bottom - *GW Sketch map of Plymouth docks showing improvements of the 1930's. The 'new tender' referred to in the bottom left corner is Sir Richard Grenville(II) introduced in 1931.*

PLYMOUTH, DEVONPORT, STONEHOUSE.

In addition to the central Station at Millbay, which has been recently reconstructed at great expense, and equipped with modern appliances for the quick despatch of business, the Company's Stations at Devonport, Keyham and Sutton Harbour afford all necessary accommodation for the trade of the District.

The Company's carts collect and deliver goods and parcels, and Receiving Offices are established in prominent positions in the three towns. There are fast trains to and from all parts of the Great Western Railway System, and, by arrangements with other Companies, through services convey goods and parcels at through rates to and from all parts of the Kingdom.

THE GREAT WESTERN DOCKS AT MILLBAY cover an area of nearly 60 acres, and comprise extensive transit shed and warehouse accommodation, steam and hydraulic appliances for the landing and shipment of goods of every description, including hydraulic cranes up to 25 tons lifting capacity, deep water berths for vessels of large size, a graving dock 454 feet long, and 80 feet wide, and ample uncovered space for the storage of Coal, Timber, Ores, etc. The Docks are in direct connection with all parts of the English Railway System.

A share of the Shipping business is dealt with at Sutton Pool, and the Company's Station at SUTTON HARBOUR is fully equipped for the prompt handling of goods of all descriptions, their trucks running alongside the vessels.

The Company's Stations at DEVONPORT and KEYHAM are situated near to, and in direct rail communication with His Majesty's Dock Yards which, by the completion of the immense extension works undertaken by Sir John Jackson Limited, and opened on February 21st, 1907, by their Royal Highnesses the Prince and Princess of Wales, has now become the largest Naval Station in the world.

The Royal Naval Barracks are immediately opposite the Company's Keyham Station.

Above - Conveyor belt for handling mailbags installed at the head of the pontoon situated between Millbay Pier and Trinity Pier. Castle class 4-6-0 at head of boat train. The deck of Sir Walter Rayleigh(II) is packed with mailbags. This tender (new in 1908) was sent to Fishguard in 1909 for the arrival of the RMS Mauretania. [GWR].

Opposite - South Quay in September 1924. Ship's derrick dealing with sacked grain. Hand crane on quay behind lamppost with steam crane beyond. [STEAM Swindon]

There were, at different times, GWR cross-channel services operating out of Plymouth. In 1907, the fruit growers of Brittany chartered a GWR vessel for the season to bring their produce to Plymouth; the Channel Islands boat *Antelope* was employed between Millbay and Plougastel/Brest in Brittany. The Great Western Publicity Department at Paddington issued its *Beautiful Brittany* descriptive pamphlet at that time to encourage business, and Brittany was included in *Holiday Haunts*. It became a regular service for a few years. Another route involved the 412-ton *Melmore*, which had been acquired by the GWR in 1905 to avoid having to charter cargo ships for the heavy seasonal Channel Islands perishables traffic to Weymouth. She was an 1892-built boat formerly employed on a Glasgow-Northern Ireland service, and carried out a variety of jobs for the Great Western including, in 1909, a Weymouth & Nantes service. The 1653-ton *Bretonne* (ex-GER Harwich & Hook boat, formerly named *Chelmsford*, dating from 1893) was purchased in 1910 to replace the much smaller *Melmore*, at which time the Nantes service was transferred to Plymouth from Weymouth. The 18-knot *Bretonne* could carry up to 500

tons of cargo, 800 passengers and was fitted with 200 berths. However, the service lost money and was taken off in 1911. The *Bretonne* was then sold, and although *Melmore* had carried on working from Weymouth, she too was sold in 1912. The Great Western's service to Brest from Plymouth was also taken off in 1911 as a result of the 'peace' between the LSWR and the GWR; the hostility between the two companies in Edwardian days is illustrated by the LSWR's introduction of a Southampton & Cork service to irritate the GWR, just because the latter had introduced the services to Brittany.

PS Cheshire was sold to the breakers in 1913. At the outbreak of war in August 1914, the Plymouth tenders Sir *Francis Drake (II)*, *Sir Walter Rayleigh (II)*, *Sir Richard Grenville(I)* and *Smeaton* were requisitioned by the Admiralty at Plymouth, but were available to meet the ocean liners by arrangement. Requisition was not just of the vessel, but the captain and crew as well. In the case of the Plymouth tenders, for example, the GWR was paid £100 per week by the Government, from which it paid the wages of the crews (including special allowances/increased wages owing to additional work thrown on the men). The Admiralty had to find coal, oil, water, stores etc. for all the boats requisitioned from the company, which itself had to

take out special war insurance on all its ships. The *Atalanta* was fitted up for salvage duty, and the *Smeaton* was lent to the US Army when its troops arrived to cross to France in 1917.

After the First World War, the transfer of Cunard and White Star operations to Southampton brought increased traffic with boat trains and Ocean Mails specials, and the setting up of new record journey times to London. The tenders at Millbay remained the 39-year-old *Smeaton*, the 31 -year-old *Sir Richard Grenville (I)*, along with the *Sir Francis Drake (II)* and *Sir Walter Raleigh (II)*, both 14 years old. *Sir Richard Grenville (I)* was offered for sale in 1921 but, with no takers, was taken back into service. The *Smeaton* was sold in 1929 to be replaced by the coal-fired 930-ton twin-screw *Sir John Hawkins*, which could carry 800 passengers and had a cargo hold. Soon after, in 1931, the 896-ton *Sir Richard Grenville (II)* was commissioned to replace its 39-year-old namesake (it was similar to the *Sir John Hawkins* but was oil-fired and had a smaller funnel). The old boat was renamed *Penlee* in 1931 just before being sold to the Dover Harbour Board (Penlee Point is a headland in Plymouth Sound). Earle's Shipbuilders of Hull constructed both new tenders.

GW Marine Section staff were stationed at Plymouth to

The twin-screw tender Smeaton of 1883 photographed at Millbay Pier. "GWR" on funnel. 'Great Western Railway' and 'Royal Mail Route to London' emblazoned on deck rails. Smeaton was lent to the US Army when its troops arrived to cross to France in 1917; she was scrapped in 1929. A GW bullion van (no doors this side) is seen on the quay at the left of the picture. [GWR]

Lock entrance to inner basin (on right) at Plymouth. South Quay runs in-and-out of the picture at the far side of the lock. The photographer stands this side on Glasgow Wharf. One of three electric luffing cranes with grabs on the South Quay is discharging the steamer. West Quay is in the distance on the right, with gates to the GW graving dock to the left of the white pitched-roof building. Electric ship docking signals are on the pole to the left of the crane. [GWR]

run the tenders. In 1929, the four vessels were each provided with a Master, First and Second Engineers and a Mate, with eleven Deckhands, six Firemen and three Watchmen between them.

Right up to 1939, the four tenders were hard at work dealing with some 40,000 passengers per annum to and from the 800 or so liners that called at Plymouth. Many dignitaries coming to Britain disembarked at Plymouth; in the case of Royalty, senior GWR officers greeted them and accompanied them to London (e.g. when Edward, Prince of Wales, returned from India in 1925 he was met by the Chairman, Lord Churchill, and the General Manager, Sir Felix Pole).

All the Plymouth tenders were requisitioned as RN boarding party examination vessels in the Second World War, still based at Plymouth. The port received its share of soldiers evacuated by sea from France in 1940, some 80,000 troops being rescued from Brest. *Sir John Hawkins* was damaged by bombing in August 1940. When repaired she was taken over by the Government and manned by the navy. *Sir Walter Raleigh (II)* was damaged in December 1940 in an air raid, and was afterwards altered into a torpedo and midget submarine trials vessel; later, the vessel served as a fleet tender at Scapa Flow. During the 1941-45 period of WWII, the town and its docks suffered continual bombing. Damage from heavy raids in 1941 led to Millbay station being closed, buildings and refreshment rooms being badly damaged, and the goods shed, goods offices, and stables were destroyed by fire, with 32 horses being killed. The loco shed was also destroyed by fire with a number of passenger coaches and goods wagons destroyed or damaged. North Rd station was similarly affected, two people being killed. At the docks, many sheds, warehouses, stores and offices were destroyed. The quay wall of the inner basin was damaged; two tug boats were burnt out and sunk at the West Wharf and two trawlers were sunk. It was in the 1941 raids that 'Hall' No. 4911 *Bowden Hall* was destroyed at Keyham; amazingly, while the bomb blew the loco and tender off the line, no carriages were touched. The raid ruptured all communications with the Plymouth Control room.

All the requisitioned boats were returned to the GWR in 1945/6. However, before any of the tenders had been released, *SS Empire Chieftain* and *SS John Ericson* disembarked passengers at Plymouth who were brought ashore by the Admiralty paddle tug *PS Camel*. The altered *Sir Walter Raleigh (II)* was immediately sold off, leaving the *Sir Francis Drake (II)*, the *Sir John Hawkins* and the *Sir Richard Grenville (II)* to serve into nationalisation. *Sir Richard Grenville (II)* was the last tender to work at Millbay: she was withdrawn in 1963 when the French Line stopped calling at Plymouth.

DEVONPORT DOCKYARD, Royal Navy (Served)

Northwards up the eastern shore of the Hamoaze (the estuary of the Tamar and the Tavy), Devonport Dockyard stretched for two miles, almost to the Royal Albert Bridge. Plymouth was not an operational naval port, but was used for refitting, reconstruction and new construction (the last ship built at Plymouth was the aircraft carrier *HMS Terrible*, completed in 1942).

The royal dockyard started life in 1690 with the construction of a dry and a wet dock for ships of the line. The activities and size of the site expanded throughout the C18th and expanded again when the Royal Navy accepted the idea of steam propulsion, with the opening of the Keyham Steam Dockyard in 1853. A tunnel (with a bend in it) linked Keyham to the rest of the old dockyard; the dimensions of this tunnel anticipated a possible tramway running through. At the end of the C19th, some 2,000 people were employed at Keyham alone, which had boiler shops, platers'shops, pattern shops, foundries, millwrights and so on. There were proposals as early as 1817 to install a tramway within the dockyard to move around stores and equipment, but it was not until 1860 that a broad gauge tramway was laid at Keyham. The rails were brought from Ebbw Vale, and extensive use was made of wagon turntables in the layout. The first line laid in the yard was for moving boilers from the boiler shop to the dockside for installation by crane. As well as moving equipment within the yard, the tramway was used to move stores and coal unloaded by crane from ships at the dockyard's river wharf. In addition to the broad gauge lines, an 18in-gauge tramway was installed in part of the yard, and trans-shipment facilities had to be provided.

The Cornwall Railway made an agreement with the Admiralty to connect its line with the dockyard system by a single line branch from Weston Mill viaduct, between Plymouth's North Road station and Brunel's Saltash bridge. Just short of a mile long, the private line was opened in 1867. Part of the agreement was for the CR to maintain the Keyham Steam Yard railway, and to provide shunting locos if requested for the dockyard, which it did until the Admiralty purchased its own Aveling & Porter steam loco in 1869. Subsequently, traffic in and out was dealt with through exchange sidings.

Plans were already in hand to extend the broad gauge railway throughout the whole dockyard by means of a line through the tunnel, but the tunnel would have had to be enlarged and the curvature eased, and discussions about costs went on for many years. The Admiralty was not only conscious of the impending arrival of the standard gauge LSWR at Plymouth, but was also affected by trans-shipment delays from broad to narrow, and it took the decision in 1872 that the extension of the dock railways would be to the standard gauge. Construction of the new lines around the whole dockyard was nevertheless carried out by the CR, as per the agreement. An internal dockyard passenger train service was later set up between the different parts of the complex.

When the LSWR arrived at Plymouth in 1876, a third rail was laid on the CR main line from Devonport Jct. out over Weston Mill viaduct, enabling narrow gauge trains to reach the dockyard, the old lines in which (including turntables) were also converted to mixed gauge. In 1889, the Royal Naval Barracks was opened at Keyham, and a platform was provided on the west side of the branch, off which a coal siding for the barracks also led. The problem of the gauges ceased in May 1892 with the removal of the broad from Great Western metals.

The barracks and housing developments in the area led to the opening, in 1900, of a new station at Keyham, at the time when the line westwards from Plymouth was doubled. Considerable enlargement of the whole dockyard took place about this time - completed in 1907 - and with it the extent of the dockyard railway grew, as well as the number of Admiralty shunting locos. It grew further during WWI, when there was a large increase in the number of goods wagons passing in and out of the yard, as well as the need to run troop trains into the dockyard. Bunkers coal required by the navy had traditionally been brought by sea to the dockyard from South Wales but, owing to the submarine threat, an increased tonnage (some 2,500,000 tons) was conveyed by rail.

For most of the C20th, both the Great Western and LSW railways operated a couple of goods trains each day to the dockyard exchange sidings. GWR trains were made up at Laira or Tavistock Jct and, for the LSWR, at Kings Rd. Typical goods passing into the yard would have been timber, steel plate and sections, wire rope, stores, foodstuffs, explosives, torpedoes, ships' propellers, guns and so on; passing out (and far less in quantity) would be stores cleared out from ships docked for refit to be taken to inland depots, stores for other naval depots and scrap metal. Goods trains bringing armour plate for the dockyard were instructed in the GW *Service Timetables* at the end of the C19th to minimise work at local Plymouth stations, so as to not to delay delivery.

The dockyard railway had its own internal wagons, but main line railway wagons were exchanged continually. The bend in the tunnel between the yards meant that a special loading gauge had to be employed for vehicles taken through. Some wagons with sloping loads had to be reversed before passage through the troublesome tunnel, and in many cases goods had to be trans-shipped as the wagons that they were on could not go through. Conveyance of large naval gun barrels from manufacturers to dockyard often formed special or 'out-of-gauge' loads for the railways.

LOOE
(Served)

The port of Looe experienced a renaissance in the C19th, becoming the main outlet for the rich mining area to the north of Liskeard. A six-mile-long canal (the Liskeard & Looe Union Canal) had been opened in 1828 to extend navigation on the East Looe river from Terras to Moorswater (near Liskeard) to load copper ore and blocks of granite. The material had been brought down from the Cheesewring and other quarries by strings of pack animals, and road wagons drawn by oxen and horses. Increasing traffic led to the opening, in 1846, of the Liskeard & Caradon Railway to replace the animals. The railway descended from 800ft to 150ft above sea level in its six-mile length and, at first, the daily output of the mines and quarries was sent down each evening in separate loaded wagons, each under the control of a brakeman. At Moorswater there was a stone-dressing yard belonging to the quarry owners and a nearby china clay works served by a short siding. It was found that the canal could not cope with all the traffic presented by the railway, so the canal company built its own Liskeard & Looe Railway alongside the canal in 1860, with an end-on junction to tracks on Looe Quay. The quay sidings were owned by the Harbour Commissioners and by the China Clay Co, but were maintained by the railway.

The increase in traffic is shown by the fact that while the canal carried some 45,000 tons in 1858, the railway carried over 62,000 tons of ore, coal and granite in 1863. Unfortunately, Looe did not have enough wharfage to deal with the increase: in 1861, it was reported that £4,000-worth of copper ore was lying unshipped on the quays and, at times, there were as many as 30 ships waiting to load or

The Liskeard & Looe Rly at Looe in the 1880's. The bridge across the picture connects East Looe (on left) with West Looe. The masts of ships in the left centre distance show that the main quay is beyond the bridge. Loco water tower at centre left.

discharge. Congestion was relieved somewhat by seawards extensions of the quays in the 1860s.

Granite from the moorland quarries was supplied for forts or docks at Plymouth, Spithead, Portsmouth and in the Medway; for Westminster Bridge and the Thames Embankment; for breakwaters at Alderney, Dover and Portland; and for the base of the Albert Memorial in Kensington Gardens. Imports at Looe were sand, limestone and coal.

In 1895, a branch from Coombe Jct to Liskeard provided a connexion with the GWR. 1909, the Great Western acquired the L & C, and worked both the Liskeard & Looe and Liskeard & Caradon Railways from the same time. The L & L was not absorbed until the Grouping of 1923. In later years, the output of the remaining Caradon mines fell off and traffic declined, which affected the port. Lines to the north of Moorswater were abandoned in 1916, the last traffic on the line being two or three trips per week to the Phoenix mine (then being dismantled) and the Cheesewring quarry. Typically the trains consisted of a GW 0-6-0ST, a few wagons and a Toad.

The railway layout was very confined, with the town of East Looe on one side, and the river/harbour on the other. The quay was located to the south of the passenger station and goods yard, beyond the town bridge to West Looe, and ran for little over a quarter-of-a-mile alongside the water. The main quayside was served by a long loop from the quay line for about half of that length. A 30-ton wagon weighbridge was available.

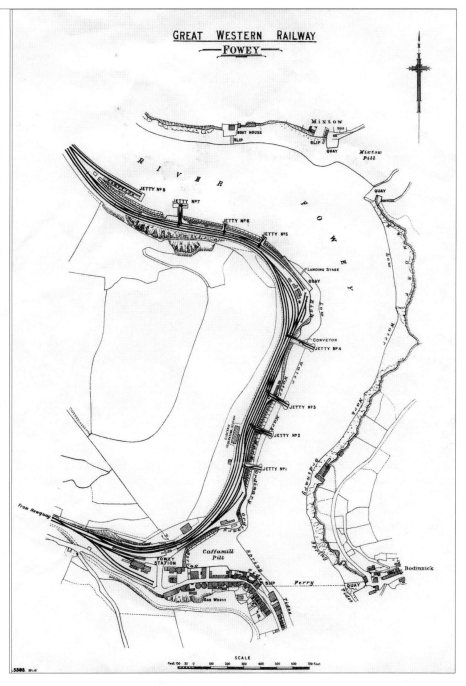

The commercial fishery at Looe sent wagons to the main line at Liskeard for collection by long-distance express freight trains. Pilchards in barrels were sent away in great quantities in Victorian times, before the shoals failed to return to home waters. In the 1930's ray, skate and haddock were being landed, the harbourmaster acting as auctioneer at the fish market, but the quantities were much reduced from former times.

FOWEY
(Owned)

Commercial working of china clay (kaolin) in Cornwall and North Devon began in the middle of the C18th, with the Stannon Moor deposit in Cornwall ranked the largest in the world. Some of that clay was shipped out of north Cornish ports, the LSWR employing special, long wheelbase flat wagons that each took four containers of clay between Wenford Bridge and Padstow, but traffic from the northern deposits also came to the south coast for shipment, running over the Great Western's Bodmin branch. Clay from the Lee Moor district of Dartmoor was shipped out of Plymouth. By the middle of Victoria's reign, the principal port for china clay shipments was Fowey, close to the St Austell area where there were large deposits. The china clay industry was rapidly expanding, and the older harbours at Charlestown, Lostwithiel and Pentewan were no longer capable of handling all the traffic, and also suffered the recurrent problem of silting up by sediment precipitated

34020 Fowey Loading Jetties. C.N.

Opposite top - *Jetty No 2 (near) and jetty No 1 (in distance) at Fowey in 1905. Short-wheelbase GW wagon numbered 34438 (To carry 8 tons Tare 4-7-2) loaded with casks of china clay on wagon turntable. Grey shunting horse in attendance. Masts of ship at Bodinnick quay around bend at left centre.*

Opposite bottom - Fowey passenger station and goods yard in 1911. Open wagons loaded with casks of china clay waiting to be shipped at the jetties on the river, reached along the tracks passing under the station footbridge. Different types of wagon, including end-tippers and short-wheelbase iron-bodied GW wagons on extreme right. The South Wales 'Federated' private-owner shipment coal wagon is being employed far away from its home. [GWR]

This page, top - *GW dumb-buffered china clay wagon being tipped at Fowey's No 2 jetty in 1911. Plate 399 in GWR Goods Wagons is a close-up of this wagon that pre-dates the GW O12/13 china clay wagons. The contents of wagons were tipped on to an endless belt that elevated the material before tipping down a shoot into the hold of a ship (in this case, a barque). The track to the left on which shunting horses are standing is for wagons containing barrels of clay that are loaded by the steam crane at the end of the jetty. That track was accessed by means of a wagon turntable. [GWR]*

Right - Tippler in action at Fowey. Wagon is a single-ended private-owner tipping vehicle. This is a posed photograph since the tip end should be down below rail level feeding the conveyor belt, not up in the air. Note that the lever brake is held by a toothed ratchet that is under the tipping end this side. [GWR

Above - 0-6-0PT No 1746, with K headlamps, leaving Fowey for St Austell with china clay empties in July 1921. *Photographed from station footbridge. Note the check rails. [H L Hopwood]*

Opposite top - Number 7 jetty at Fowey in April 1919, showing foundations of No 8 jetty, begun before WWI, in the left *distance with rake of loaded china clay wagons in nearby siding. Steam cranes at head of No 7 jetty unloading coal by bucket from a barque into GW open wagons (diagram O4, with 5 equal planks). Note the positioning of the two wagon turntables and the cross-over roads on the jetty. Grounded body near hut at right, behind loaded wagon. [GWR]*

Opposite bottom - Jetty No 1 in December 1936. This jetty had no conveyor belt. Shows wagon turntables, and capstans and *reels (which had replaced shunting horses) for moving wagons to tipplers. Wagon No 92641 on right is a GW O13 china clay tipping wagon dating from 1914. It is fitted with an either-side Dean-Churchward type II single-ended lever brake with both levers just out of the picture to the right away from the tipping end, thus avoiding gumming up from spilled china clay upon tipping. [GWR]*

from the clay 'streaming' workings.

In the first stage of production, clay was washed out of the ground by hoses or cascades of water, and was fed into boxes or 'drags' that filtered out the sand that was mixed with the raw clay; this waste sand formed the high surface tips characteristic of the landscape. The milky-looking clay-water mixture, which held the china clay in suspension, passed on to further filters, after which the wet clay was then dried ready for shipping. By the beginning of the C20th, most clay was handled in bulk; the GWR built special zinc-lined open tipping wagons before the First World War (wagon diagrams O12/13) to avoid contact with ironwork that would stain the china clay, but former methods of packing in casks or bags were still employed.

The perceived uses for china clay in the manufacture of china and porcelain took, in fact, only 30% of the output; the paper, paint and textile industries were also significant users. Next to coal, china clay was the most important mineral export of the UK, and well over 750,000 tons were

produced annually in the 1930s, of which 300-400,000 tons was exported to India, USA, Germany, Belgium, France, Italy and Spain. Later, some 2 million tons was being produced, of which 600-700,000 tons on average was annually shipped from Fowey; most of this was for export, but some was for the home market, being carried in small coastal vessels.

Fowey was reached by rail either from the east (Lostwithiel) or from the west (St. Blazey) the two lines together forming the 'Fowey Loop'. The broad gauge Lostwithiel & Fowey Railway opened a line for clay as far as Carne Point (just short of Fowey) in 1869, the year in which the Fowey Harbour Board was constituted. The line was worked by the Cornwall Railway, but it closed in 1880 as, trying to compete with the Cornwall Minerals Railway (see below), the CR had not charged enough to pay its way. Five years later it was re-opened as a standard gauge line extending to Fowey. It was transferred to the CMR in 1892, and absorbed into the GWR in 1896. The CMR had been

formed in 1873 by a speculator (W. R. Roebuck) to take over Treffry's tramroads in the area (see Par) and to build new locomotive-hauled lines such as that from Newquay to Fowey via St Blazey (1874). The GWR worked the 47-odd miles of the CMR from 1877.

The railway yard above Fowey station was constructed alongside the River Fowey, partly by hewing out rock and partly by filling in the Caffer Mill Pill, a creek where Treffry had built a small dock. In 1874, three timber jetties (Nos.1 to 3) were built out into the river from this yard; all had a water depth at the berths of some 19ft at spring tides. A fourth (with 25ft-deep berth) was added in 1890. The jetties were T-shaped, vessels lying alongside the short head. The first three jetties were used originally for exporting iron ore, but a china clay boom occurred soon afterwards, which coincided with a decline in the ore business and altered the use of the jetties completely.

Above the fourth jetty, the river bends in a westerly direction creating a very sheltered harbour; in the deep water made by the bend, three more jetties (Nos. 5, 6 and 7) were built in 1896 for unloading coal, loading clay in casks, and for general cargo. The depth of water at No.7 jetty was 21ft, but much later the dredging was such that at Nos.5 and 6 jetties the depths were only 5 ft. Most clay at that time was shipped from jetties Nos.1-4 that could berth vessels up to 300 tons; clay in casks and bags was loaded by a steam crane at each jetty head, and clay in bulk was tipped down a telescopic shoot beside each crane directly into ships at all states of the tide.

By the 1890s, more steamers than sailing vessels were transporting china clay. As the size of steamers increased, the Fowey Harbour Commissioners dredged shipping channels in 1897, thus permitting 3,000 ton ships to berth, capable of carrying up to 7,000 tons of clay. These bigger steamers could now sail directly to the USA rather than having to carry clay to Liverpool and elsewhere in small coasters for transhipment to ocean-going ships. However, the heights of the Fowey jetties limited the size of boats that could be dealt with: 1,000-ton ships could be tipped into at low water only, and 3,000 ton ships never. In consequence, all clay and stone, whether in cask, bag or in bulk had, most of the time, to be loaded into the bigger ships by buckets on the cranes, and this was a slow and uneconomic process. Direct tipping into small 300-ton vessels proceeded at a rate of about 500 tons per 10 hour shift ; this included time taken to marshal wagons, shifting the vessel to trim it, filling through different hatches and separating, if requested, different parcels of clay from each other by walls of casks or other means. The rate dropped to 15 tons per10 hour shift for larger steamers. Loading of casks of china clay proceeded at 200 tons per10 hours, and the loading of bags of clay at 130 tons per 10 hour shift.

To allow for continuous loading of larger vessels at all states of the tide, the GWR in 1908-11 equipped jetty No.4 with an electrical elevating conveyor to supply a high-level shoot. It consisted of a tipping frame for discharging wagons into a hopper below the level of the sidings (wagons being secured by chains during tipping), from which a regulated flow of clay fell on to a covered 350ft-long endless belt moving at up to 150 ft/min,. The angle of elevation of the framework containing the belt could be adjusted to suit different size ships, the greatest height attainable being 35ft above the jetty. An adjustable steel shoot with trimming nose was hung from the head of the conveyor to direct the flow of clay into the holds of the ships, and the labour and time of hand trimming was almost entirely saved. The tipping frame and conveyor were made by Spencer and Co. of Melksham. The conveyor usually worked at 110 tons/hour, but was capable of 200 tons/hour and more. An electric crane, with luffing jib capable of lifting four half-ton casks at one go from a railway wagon, was installed at the end of jetty No.4 at the same time as the conveyor, to load casks when required to create bulkheads between different types of clay.

The Great Western built a coal-fired steam turbine generating station to power all the new electrically-driven equipment. Only small anthracite coal brought from the Swansea area was burned, in order to keep smoke to minimum levels; smoke from bituminous coals was likely to damage the clay lying in the wagons awaiting shipment. Even so, the steamers berthing at Fowey burnt bituminous coal, and they were bunkered there.

Since the greater part of the ground for sidings had been blasted out of solid rock in the original construction, there was little room for extra capacity at Fowey. Even so, to the original 11,800 yards of siding an extra 1,200 yards was added in 1909. In all, the accommodation provided for over 400 wagons. Before the electrical installations at No.4 jetty, horses had always been employed to draw loaded wagons, one by one, to the jetty heads for tipping from the trains brought into the sidings by steam locos. The last of the 1909 improvements was the installation of 16 electric capstans and 63 reels at Fowey for wagon shunting to and from the jetties, and this displaced all horse haulage. According to a 1911 pamphlet there was a 20 ton wagon weighbridge at Carne Point.

The improved rate of loading at jetty No.4, along with reduction in delays and time spent in harbour (demurrage payments), induced freighters to employ still larger vessels for overseas shipments of china clay. The entrance channel was dredged to 20 ft, and vessels of 8,000 or 9,000 tons began to be employed. A conveyor belt system was soon installed at No.3 jetty, too, but the other old jetties were not suitable for alteration. Demand was such that new china clay workings were opened up. Construction of an eighth jetty was begun before the First World War, but had to be postponed. This partially-built jetty was commandeered by the Admiralty in 1917. It is remarkable to note that, owing to the shortage of coastal shipping immediately after the First World War, more china clay was carried away by rail per month in 1919 in a single month than in a whole year before the war.

At this time, the harbour was served by rail initially from a 'Goods Road', which ran alongside the Lostwithiel branch (itself positioned against the wooded hillside) from the station to Carne Point signal box, a distance of about a mile. Outside this was a series of storage loops and sidings, from some of which wagon turntables gave access to the jetties.

The early 1920s saw jetty No 8 completed, fully equipped with a conveyor as on the improved jetty No.4, but with even more modern equipment. The site for No 8 jetty gave a 30ft deepwater berth. The 500ft-long structure was built at a sharp angle to the shore in the bend and, not having a T-head, vessels berthed alongside. The new jetty was 50ft wide and of steel, concrete and brick construction. Total quayage by this time was about 2,400 ft. The 1909 electric generating station was enlarged to cope with the increased loading. Owing to the ships berthing completely alongside the new jetty, the elevator did not transfer its load directly into the ship, but instead onto a second endless belt running parallel to the side of the ship, from which a moveable tower traversing along the side of the structure took bulk clay to feed various hatchways in succession. At the other jetties, ships had to be moved to bring different holds into position for loading. Two sidings ran the length of the new jetty, from which clay in casks and bags could be loaded by crane if required.

In order to maintain a continuous flow of wagons to be tipped into the hopper that supplied the elevator, storage sidings for an additional 200 wagons were laid down on land purchased for the purpose. By the time No.8 jetty was finished, there were in all 6 electric cranes of three-ton capacity at Fowey, along with 3 rail steam cranes of two-ton capacity. A new office on the jetty frontage was built in 1925 for the controller and dock superintendent.

In addition to improving the harbour at Fowey, the GWR assisted the china clay trade by the construction of new railway lines. Near St. Austell, the Trenance Valley Railway, the construction of which commenced in June 1914 but was not completed until after WWI, was about 1¾ miles long and served 16 china clay 'dries' at Bojea, Lower Ruddle and Lansalson. Previously, clay from that area had been sent to St Austell by road, the vehicles returning loaded with coal. The single- track line ascended almost continuously alongside the St. Austell to Bodmin road to the terminus at Lansalson, and included sections of 1 in 40, the total rise being some 163ft. A feature of the line, remarked on in a 1922 *Railway Magazine* article shortly after its opening, was that the telegraph poles along the line were smaller than the usual height; this was because locally-grown larch poles were employed, owing to the much higher cost of timber following the First World War - some sizes of Baltic telegraph poles had increased in price as much as nine times over pre-war figures.

Fowey had been a port since the 14th century, so it is not surprising that it had other business as well as china clay. Indeed, even before its own connections by rail, it experienced a boom in the 1850s during the construction of the Cornwall Railway. For example, in 1858, more than 16,000 loads of timber had been discharged between June and September for railway construction, which was more than five times the normal quantity for the period. Trade fluctuated over the years: ships' (bunkers) coal was listed at 90,000 tons/year before the First World War, falling to 24,000 tons/year in 1937; and 1,000 tons annually of 'other traffics'.

After the Second World War, Fowey lost some of its china clay trade because berthing facilities were improved at Par, where vessels having a shallow draught preferred to load.

PAR
(Served)

The silting of rivers and estuaries, and the flushing of waste products from the mines, caused many ancient seaports in Cornwall (such as Pentewan) to be left high and dry, or fall into decay. Par is an example of the *reverse* process.

At the beginning of the C19[th], the area covered by Par docks, the town of Par and parts of St. Blazey, was all under the sea. A local entrepreneur, J. T. Austen (who later assumed the surname Treffry, and who became chairman of the Cornwall Railway), owned rich copper mines at nearby Lanescot, and he wanted a port nearer and easier to get to than Fowey where, prior to developments at Par, he had made a small harbour at Caffa Mill Pill. In 1828, he decided to build an artificial tidal harbour at the far end of a sandbank (that later became Par beach) which was building up across the mouth of St Austell Bay. In addition to the formation of the sandbank, river-borne silt and mining waste was beginning to fill up the broad estuary itself. A long breakwater formed the harbour, and Treffry established many industries on the site, among which were a lead smelters, a brickworks, granite cutting and dressing yards, a pilchard fishery, a shipbuilding yard, sail lofts, a candle factory (for the Cornish mines), a ships' chandlery, limekilns and a flour mill. The harbour as built could accommodate 50 vessels of up to 200 tons. The reclamation was extensive, and very ambitious.

In 1847, Treffry had opened a two-mile long canal alongside the Luxulyan river from Par to Ponts Mill, and from there he built a standard gauge horse-drawn railway to Wheal Virgin mine by way of a 1 in 10 incline at Carmears, and a magnificent 98ft-high, 650ft-long viaduct over the Luxulyan valley, thus connecting the china clay district inland with the port of Par. In 1855, the tramway was extended alongside the canal to Par harbour. Treffry had built a similar standard gauge horse-drawn tramway in the late 1840s between Newquay harbour and East Wheal Rose mine; later, these were taken over by the Cornwall Minerals Railway, and were converted into a new line for locomotive haulage right across the county, connecting Fowey and Newquay. The canal functioned until 1873.

As at many South Cornish harbours around St. Austell (Charlestown, Devoran etc.), export of china clay and import of coal soon surpassed the export trade in copper ore. At Par itself, although served by rail, much of the china clay was brought in by horse and cart, later superseded by motor lorry in the 1920s.

The harbour was served by trailing connections off the adjacent main lines, forming a loop alongside, to which the extensive private sidings of the dock were connected. In

Newham Quay in the early years of the C20th. 'Great Western Goods Depot' behind loco on left. Wooden-jibbed hand crane at centre. Loco appears to be a '3251' outside-framed 4-4-0.

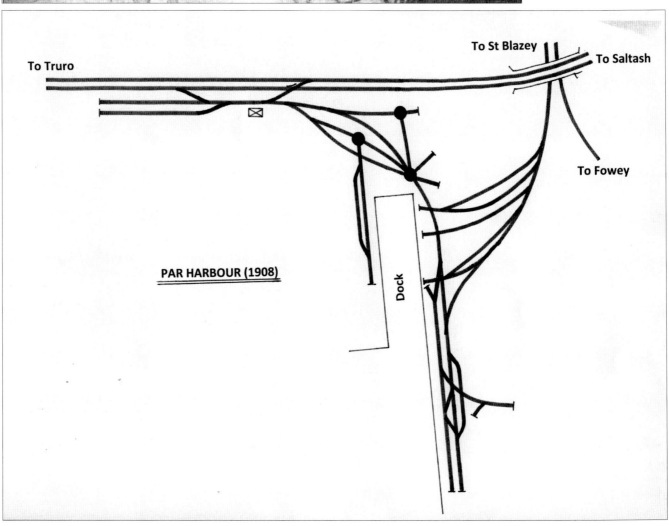

Map of Par Harbour in 1908. Not to scale. [based on R A Cooke]

addition, the harbour estate was served by a line off the nearby Fowey branch from St. Blazey.

After the Second World War, there were two large china clay drying plants on the dock estate; large storage tanks for liquid china clay fed by pipeline; storage space for several thousand tons of dried clay; a mineral grinding plant; dumping grounds for imported felspar; a railway wagon repair shop; coal yard; gas works; an extensive railway network; and the only dry dock between Falmouth and Plymouth. Treffry granite was shipped from Par for many structures and erections in Victorian London, and for the monument on the battlefield at Waterloo in Belgium. In addition to market goods, hardware and groceries, imports at Par in those days were mainly confined to mining. Thus timber, iron, coal, machinery, tallow, sail cloth etc. figure prominently.

The Treffry Estate sold Par Harbour in the late 1940s; a report by the UK Chamber of Shipping in 1930 on the financial problems of small West Country harbours had said of Par:

'...Reconstruction of two berths is urgently needed. The owner of the harbour although anxious to   proceed   with the work...is unable to do so owing to financial difficulties in connection with recently incurred death duties...'

Even so, after WWII, 1,300 ships a year typically called at Par, travelling from and to ports all over the Continent and further afield. For its limited number of berths, Par was one of the busiest ports in the country at that time.

TRURO NEWHAM QUAY
(Owned)

In 1852, the standard gauge West Cornwall Railway was extended as a single line eastwards from Redruth to Higher Town (Truro Road), and in 1855 a further 2½-miles to Garras Wharf (Newham) on the west bank of the Truro River. Newham's wooden passenger station, with a two-track all-over Brunel-style roof, was the terminus of the WCR for Truro.

Near the Newham station, the WCR built a quay wall (4ft above spring tides) on the mud lands down-river from the existing Garras wharf to give about 930ft of quayage, with an extensive flat area for buildings and storage. A 15ft-wide public landing place was incorporated between Garras Wharf and the railway quay proper.

IN 1859, the WCR and the CR were joined by a line from what became Penwithers Jct. on the WCR to the new CR station for Truro; this gave a through route from Plymouth to Penzance, but with a break of gauge. The part of the line from Penwithers Jct. to Newham Quay became a branch, and the old WCR station was closed to passengers in 1863, the passenger station becoming a goods depot. A single-line through goods shed had been, in fact, the first structure erected at Newham, and was used originally by passenger trains, so that when the line became a goods branch, there were two other buildings on the site available for goods traffic and warehousing. Facilities provided for

Private.—For Company's Servants only.

GREAT WESTERN RAILWAY.

CHIEF GOODS MANAGER'S OFFICE,

Circular No. R.1014
R.F. 9/759.

Paddington Station,

London, W.

April 23rd, 1894.

NEWHAM GOODS DÉPÔT (TRURO).

On and after this date, the Rates to and from the above-named Station for all traffic—**excepting Coal and Coke**—in Classes A, B and C, and any other Merchandise in full truck loads, charged at Station to Station rates, will be the same as are in operation with Truro.

Traffic for Newham must be labelled and invoiced direct to that place; consignments in quantities of less than truck loads must be invoiced and sent to Truro in the same manner as hitherto.

Please acknowledge receipt of this Circular to your District Goods Manager.

J. L. WILKINSON.

rail and quay work included a 5-ton crane in 1864, reduced to a 1½ ton unit by the 1920s.

Although a third rail was added to the standard gauge WCR main line tracks westwards from 1866 (see Hayle), so that broad gauge trains could reach Penzance, the Newham Quay branch never was converted.

There was a 16 ton wagon weighbridge, and the goods line and quay remained in use right through into nationalisation. In 1913 when the Bath & West and Southern Counties Agricultural Show was held at Truro, Newham Quay became the railhead into which all show traffic arrived and departed.

FALMOUTH
(Served)

Falmouth, like Milford Haven, is a magnificent natural harbour and, before the railway came, was a busy port with imports of coal, timber, salt, limestone and general goods, and exports of minerals, agricultural produce and fish. It was strategically placed as a safe anchorage at the entrance to the English Channel and, before the days of ship-to-shore wireless, was a calling point for orders for merchant ships in

Falmouth docks under construction. [D Barnicoat collection]

the channel. For similar reasons, it had been an important packet station for mail ships, since the prevailing winds made progress very slow when sailing westwards along the English Channel, and road journeys from London were quicker than by sea. In 1688, Falmouth became a packet station to Corunna, and a hundred years later over 40 small, speedy brigantines were sailing to the Mediterranean, North and South America, and the East and West Indies.

Inwards cargo by sea from London consisted of market goods and groceries; charcoal for tin smelting came from Southampton; and salt, earthenware, coal and general hardware from Liverpool. From France came wine, brandy, salt, grain, flour and fruit; from Russia and Baltic ports hemp, pitch, tar, tallow, iron, sail-cloth, linen, grain and timber; from the Netherlands cheese, gin, grain and butter; from Spain and Portugal salt, wool, fruit, brandy and wine; from North America tobacco, barrel staves and timber, wheat, rice, and flour; and from South America wool, cotton, sugar and hides. Exports included tin, pilchards, pilchard oil, and copper ore. To go with all this trade were all the ancillary activities found in a busy seaport such as ship-chandling and victualling.

The coming of steamships and railways meant that there was no longer a need for packet ports to be situated in the far west. Southampton became the new packet station, the last Post Office packet sailing from Falmouth in 1852; this change had a long-term effect on the port, but general shipping continued as before and the Falmouth Harbour Commission began to build proper docks in 1860.

In 1872, some 4,000 vessels entered the port from overseas, and about the same number of ships in the British coastwise trade called. In fact, the Trinity House pilotage receipts at Falmouth at that time were greater than those for Liverpool, Glasgow and Hull, and were exceeded only by the Port of London.

The Cornwall Railway's single broad gauge line to Falmouth from Truro was opened finally in 1863; it had been partly completed in 1852, but was then left in order to concentrate on finishing the Plymouth & Truro section (1859) that joined up with the West Cornwall Railway line that had reached Truro in 1855. In 1864, the railway was connected to the new docks, which lay immediately to the north of the passenger station. The extension of the CR to Falmouth was inspired by a belief in the future importance of the docks but, as a general cargo port, Falmouth never

Flowers from the Scilly isles being unloaded from the 2.00pm ferry boat SS Lyonesse on to a GW one-horse lorry to be taken to Penzance station in the spring of 1899. [F E Gibson]

developed, probably owing to its remoteness from centres of industry and population. The number of ships using the port had dropped to some 2,500 in 1912 and, while many were larger than in earlier years, general trade was in decline. However, fishing was flourishing, with about 200 vessels in the fleet just before WWI.

To combat the decline in general trade, the Falmouth Harbour Commission saw an opportunity in ship repairing and overhauling. It was the first port of call for returning ships that had suffered storm, or other, damage en route. From 1860, facilities were built up to handle the largest ships afloat and this enterprise became the major activity of the port. Thus, while Falmouth continued to deal with some import and export cargoes, its principal function became that of a ship-servicing station, and ship repairing gave rise to goods traffic to the docks for which there was a 20½ ton wagon weighbridge. By 1878, the Falmouth Dock Co. had an extensive private broad gauge rail network, with lines to the East and West Piers, and serving works on the dock estate; two dry docks had already been built. In 1889, the CR system was absorbed by the GWR, and in 1892 it

followed that the gauge of the private dock lines had to be converted. It is amusing to note that this work was contracted to the LSWR by the dock company!

Two more dry docks were brought into use after WWI, together with a North Pier (off the end of the West Pier); and the Empire Jetty, also off the West pier, but built in the opposite direction. All piers, jetties and basins had rail connections, and the dock facilities and tracks elsewhere were considerably extended; the Great Western had a few sidings adjacent to the passenger station that were connected to the dock system, holding around 60 wagons.

The repair of oil tankers became a speciality of the port from the 1930's. Having unloaded at ports around the UK coast, tankers would proceed empty to Falmouth with screens opened up on deck to let air fully ventilate the tanks so that welding could safely take place.

PENZANCE and NEWLYN
(Served)

Penzance, at the western end of the GWR main line, had been the principal port of Mount's Bay from mediaeval

PENZANCE (G.W.R.) STATION AND HARBOUR.

Opposite top - *Penzance station with ships berthed at the Albert Quay along which runs a railway track that is an extension of a line through the goods shed situated right on the sea wall.*

Opposite bottom - *lower boxes, all for dealers at Covent Garden Market and marked 'charged 6d', have arrived at the loading dock at Penzance station goods yard (passenger station to the left) to be put aboard the special train of six oil-lit passenger ventilated fruit vans (Wagon Diagram Index Y2) hauled by Dean goods No 2428. Four-wheel ducketted brake van (Carriage Diagram Index V2) carrying red-bodied side lamps showing white to the front and red to the rear.Dealers at Covent Garden include G H Craze, W S Everson, J D Pankhurst and J D Thomas. The one-horse lorry is a private carter's vehicle with advertisements for Lifebuoy Soap and Sunlight Soap on the tilt. It is different from the GW lorry in the adjoining picture in that its rear wheels come above its floor [F E Gibson]*

times. Before the decline in tin exports in the 1870s, nearly half of Cornwall's tin was shipped through Penzance, the principal markets for which were Turkey, Italy, France, Holland, Russia and Denmark. Incoming vessels brought a wide variety of goods ranging from coopers' hoops and wine to timber and salt. Fishing for pilchard was also strong, and that figured prominently in exports from Penzance until the fishing fleet moved just along the coast to Newlyn (see later). The Albert Pier, one end of which was located where the railway station would later be built, formed a breakwater for the new harbour, opened in 1845 and completed in 1853. Construction of a new (northern) pier was commenced in 1847 and improvements continued throughout the C19th, culminating in extensive works in the 1880s, including the Ross swing bridge of 1881 that improved road access and a wet dock (1884) constructed by Penzance Corporation for grain ships. An old graving dock dating from 1810 was destroyed in the new works, but was replaced by Holman's Foundry's much bigger private dry dock.

The standard gauge West Cornwall Railway arrived in Penzance in 1852, and after the opening of the Royal Albert Bridge at Saltash in 1859, Penzance was connected to London, albeit with a break of gauge at Truro. Thereafter London time (which was 22½ minutes earlier than Penzance time) was kept at all WCR stations. Broad gauge arrived in 1866 (see Hayle). The railway brought great benefits to the local farmers and fishermen by getting their produce to faraway markets much faster than before.

Although there was a great deal of activity and traffic in the harbour and dock, there was only one railway line that ran along the Albert Quay at Penzance: it was a private siding, reached by an extension of the line through the original goods shed alongside the passenger station (the back wall of the goods shed was right on the edge of the sea wall). Penzance Town Council took out a private siding agreement with the railway in 1869, and it was renewed in 1925 when the track was realigned. Sandwiched between the main road and the sea, the Great Western site at Penzance was quite cramped, and it was difficult to get lines to the other parts of the harbour except by passing along public roads. It was not until the late 1930s that the railway layout was considerably improved between Penzance, Ponsadane and Marazion, (including a new goods depot at Ponsandane) but that did nothing to improve access to the quaysides. Indeed, by the end of the 1930's, the Albert quay line had been removed. Hence, a great deal of heavy goods such as coal and cement was carted to and from the quays in

Penzance, and all the fish from Newlyn. Even some traffic that was conveyed into Penzance by rail was transhipped to road vehicles between the station and the Albert Quay, such as wooden boxes being returned to the Scillies for flowers (and vice-versa for the flowers, carried by express train from Penzance). Sometimes up to three 'flower specials' were sent off from Penzance at the turn of the C19th/20th, with special instructions for the line to be kept clear. The trains were normally only stopped at Bristol and Didcot detach vans for markets in Manchester and Birmingham.

From just before WWI until the 1930s, china clay from new pits at Leswidden (near St. Just) was shipped from Penzance, brought to the quays in sacks by Foden steam wagons and horse-drawn carts.

The port was the mainland terminal of the Scilly Isles packet service. The first iron-hulled ship on the route was *SS Little Western* of 1858, followed by *SS Lady of the Isles (I)* of 1875 and *Lyonesse* of 1889, both built by Harvey's of Hayle. Between 1886 and 1889, the *PS Gael*, bought second hand by the GWR in 1884 to replace the wrecked *South of Ireland*, was chartered for the Penzance & Scillies route. In 1926, a new boat - the *SS Scillonian* - came on to the run. A full history of these services may be found in Duckworth & Langmuir, and in *The Port of Penzance*. While the packet boats were not the concern of the railway, the GWR nevertheless put on special express goods trains to enable flowers brought over from the Scillies to speed to the principal markets.

Newlyn, served by Penzance station, eventually became the principal fishing port in Cornwall after the railway connected Penzance with the rest of the country. Mackerel and pilchard fisheries were the most important, but as early as 1826, Newlyn had gone into the herring fishery off Ireland and sold their catches to merchants in the Irish Sea, who marketed them in Northern England. Newlyn fisherman worked the year round: they fished for mackerel off South Devon at the beginning of the year, and then followed the shoals westward to Mounts Bay; then to Irish waters for herring, returning in July to catch pilchards until the end of the year. A great deal of fish was sent to London: before the arrival of the railway, catches were sent by sea to Portsmouth for onwards conveyance by land to London, and when the original GWR main line was opened between Bristol and London, fish was sent across Cornwall by cart and wagon to Hayle to catch the steamer packets to Bristol to connect with the GW at Bristol.

Newlyn's successful growth was aided by extensive harbour works between 1866-88, giving an all-weather port with water area of 40 acres protected from the south-easterly gales found on this part of the coast. One claim to fame for Newlyn is that the harbour was chosen to be the reference 'mean sea level' for the Ordnance Survey of the UK, when mapping commenced towards the end of the C19th. In addition to fishing, there was a busy coastwise trade in road chippings quarried at the nearby Penlee Point and Castle-an-Dinas. Vessels were loaded via a narrow-gauge railway running along the south pier.

Just over 1,000 tons of fish were sent off from Penzance in August 1861 and thereafter fish traffic grew rapidly. Steamers belonging to the West Cornwall Steamship Co. picked up fish from sailing boats still at sea some 60 miles offshore, and brought the stock to harbour. Speed to market was essential and to meet the demand for rolling stock, fish wagons were converted from the underframes of old six-wheeled carriages which could be attached to the mail train or enabled fish specials to be run at passenger speeds (see *A History of GWR Goods Wagons*). Special fish trains could be organised at 3 hours notice provided the minimum load was 20 tons. In 1891, the total catch at St Ives (some 5700 tons) exceeded that at Penzance/Newlyn (about 4100 tons) but by 1895 St Ives had dropped to just under 4000 tons while Penzance/Newlyn had risen to nearly 7000 tons. That trend continued as St Ives and some other fishing ports became destinations for tourists and holiday makers. By 1938, for example, St Ives accounted for only 3% of the total catch among Brixham (15%), Plymouth (11%) and Newlyn (57%).

Despite the heavy fish traffic, Newlyn itself was never connected by rail to Penzance. In 1898 two different applications for light railways to the west of Penzance were made that would have put Newlyn on the railway, but neither was built. Consequently all fish had to be brought by a 'baggage train' of carts to Penzance station.

In 1937, when rebuilding of the main line terminus at Penzance began, considerable additional sidings were provided between Penzance and Marazion, not only to cope with the storage of passenger vehicles and to handle the extensive local agricultural produce, but also to handle the fish traffic from Newlyn. In 1947, twelve fish wagons per week were required at Penzance to take forward fish from Newlyn which was, by then, the most important commercial fishery in the South West, catches being landed from Belgian, French and East Coast vessels as well as by the local fleet.

LELANT QUAY (ST IVES branch)
(Served)

Long before the coming of railways, fish landed at St. Ives was taken by pack animal to the markets at Marazion, Penzance and Mousehole. In those early days, however, it was not only fishing that bolstered the trade of the port: the growth of tin and copper mining in the region meant that, by the middle of the C18th, the harbour at St. Ives could no longer accommodate all the shipping wanting to use it. Smeaton built a pier in 1770 and Trevithick a rubble breakwater early in the C19th, whilst the pier was lengthened in 1890. In 1894, the west pier was erected for shipping roadstone from a local quarry at Man's Head.

Trade peaked at St. Ives in the 1830s and 1840s, the size of the harbour limiting subsequent development. Even so, in 1871 there were 286 pilchard fishing seines at the port, and in that year more than 106,000 hogsheads of fish a year were exported, selling at over £3 10s per hogshead. Pilchards were cured in salt and pressed to extract the oil,

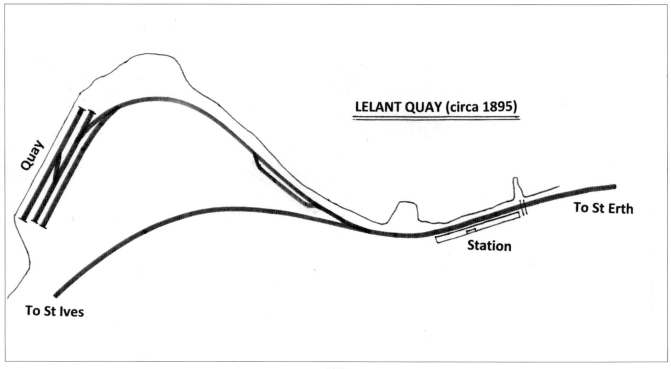

LELANT QUAY (circa 1895)

Quay

To St Ives

Station

To St Erth

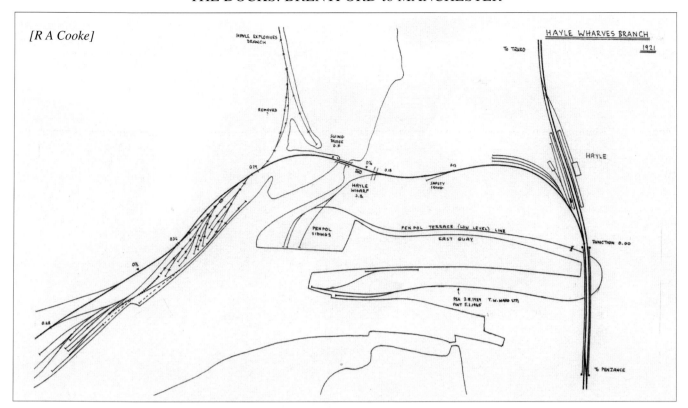

[R A Cooke]

most of which was shipped to Italy. Mackerel and herring were sent by steamer for the Bristol, Bath and London markets, and tin was also being exported. Pilchard shoals moved away from Cornish waters at the beginning of the C20th: the last catch of pilchards by seine net was made in 1908.

Imports during the C19th at St. Ives included fruit from Spain and Greece; hides from South America; barrel staves from the Baltic; brandy, sailcloth, grain, flour, hemp, wool and groceries from other countries, including France. The greater part of the port's trade was with foreign countries.

The 4½-mile-long branch from St. Erth to St. Ives opened in 1877, and was the last-ever length of new broad gauge construction. The branch was on the western side of the River Hayle estuary and there was a quay at Lelant, served by a short line from Lelant station and dating from the opening of the St Ives branch. The granite quay was about 600 ft long and possessed a warehouse, steam crane and weighbridge. In 1888, an agreement was made between the Trustees and Guardians of Roger W.G. Tyringham -- who operated the quay -- and the GWR for a third rail (mixed gauge) to be installed between St. Erth and Lelant Quay to permit standard gauge goods trains to reach the wharf. The line remained broad gauge beyond to St. Ives until the final gauge conversion in 1892. The business of the quay followed the fortunes of the Cornish mining industry, and the track to the wharf was closed about the time of WWI.

Unlike Lelant Quay, St Ives harbour was not rail-connected. Even so, like Brixham, a great deal of fish was taken away by rail, meeting the main line at St Erth for onwards delivery to market.

HAYLE
(Owned)

The town of Hayle, on the eastern side of the River Hayle estuary, was typical of the ports established to export copper and tin, originally obtained from 'streaming'; mining came later. At first, local timber provided fuel for smelting, but later coal had to be imported from South Wales, not only for smelting but also to supply the mine pumping engines. The engineering firm of Harvey's, which supplied mining equipment, and on which the prosperity of Hayle in the C19th was founded, was established in 1779. A rival firm (the Cornish Copper Co) had been established earlier in the Copperhouse district half a mile from the Hayle river estuary, but was eventually taken over by Harvey's in 1875. The CCC foundry made the chains for Brunel's Clifton suspension bridge and the Royal Albert bridge. After the harbour and quays had been improved, Harvey's established a packet steamer service to Bristol in 1831. When the GWR was opened to Bristol in 1841, exports from Penzance (broccoli, early potatoes, fruit and fish) were carried the few miles overland by road to Hayle for shipment by steamer to Bristol and thence to London.

An Act was obtained in 1834 to build the Hayle Railway, to serve mines near Redruth, Tresevean and Gwennap. A branch, opened in 1838, went from Redruth to the harbour at Portreath and brought coal and mining timber into Hayle's hinterland as well as bringing down ore; beforehand, over 1,000 pack horses and mules had been required for this work.

The new Hayle Railway was standard gauge and locomotive-hauled, but had four inclines worked by ropes driven by stationary steam engines. Horses were used from

Opposite top - *Looking towards the sea from Hayle passenger station (behind photographer). Line to harbour drops down behind the white-roofed GW Toad goods brake van (marked 'Hayle') to Hayle Wharf signal box where a branch to the left went to the Penpol sidings and the East Quay at centre of picture. The original line passed over a swing bridge and proceeded to quayside sidings and a sand pit on the other side of the river at the far right centre. The WWI Hayle explosives branch (old Hayle Rly route to Redruth with incline at Angarrack) formed a trailing junction with this line. At one time there were sidings on the spit of land to the left of the ship used by the Hayle company and Thos W Ward. Notice the way the GW buffer stops are painted. Great Central Rly wagon at right on end of rake of vehicles. GW 4-planker 44397 built in 1890. The GW 5-plankers are to diag O3 or O9 and date from 1904-6*

Opposite bottom - *Horse shunting at Hayle during BR days. [Mark Warburton courtesy Mrs M Warburton]*

Hayle through Phillack to one of the inclines at Angarrack to be taken onwards by locomotive to Redruth. The other inclines were on the branch to Tresavean mine, at Penponds, and down to the harbour at Portreath. The Hayle Rly crossed the 9-mile long, 4ft-gauge Redruth & Chasewater Railway (later 'Chacewater'), one of the other local lines dating from 1828 that led to the harbour at Point Quay (Devoran), sited on the east bank of Restronguet Creek, off the River Fal in the south, but there were no interchange facilities. Devoran had been the major mining port in the area, more important than Hayle or Portreath, but after the opening of the Hayle Rly it began to decline. The Redruth & Chasewater was horse-drawn until 1854, when locomotives were introduced. It closed in 1915.

The West Cornwall Railway was authorised to take over the Hayle Railway by an Act of 1846 with a view to extending it westwards to Penzance and eastwards to Truro. The new company originally intended its track to be broad gauge, as was the Cornwall Railway that would connect Truro with Plymouth, but later it obtained permission to retain the standard gauge of the Hayle Rly on the understanding that the broad may have to be accommodated later. In 1852, the old Hayle Railway was closed for reconstruction, including some re-routing of tracks and replacement of the inclines at Hayle, Penponds and Angarrack. Removal of the 1 in 10 Angarrack incline at Hayle meant that the new line was carried high above the old lines situated down on the wharves. It was originally intended to transfer rail vehicles from the new viaduct down to the old station sidings and harbour lines by means of a wagon lift, but the Hayle Wharves branch was built instead from a trailing junction at the station. One of the first-ever sand-drags in the UK was installed on the line owing to its steepness of up to 1 in 30 over a section near the main line.

In 1855, the West Cornwall Railway reached Truro (Newham), whilst the Cornwall Railway arrived at Truro from Plymouth in 1859. The break of gauge at Truro caused the usual delays, and in 1864, the Cornwall Railway insisted - as it had a legal right to do - that a third (BG) rail be laid to Penzance. Since the West Cornwall Railway was not in a financial position to comply, in 1865 it was leased jointly to the GWR, B & E, and SDR companies, who took over joint ownership completely the following year; the line and harbour connections came to the GWR proper in 1878. Local goods traffic continued on the 'narrow' gauge, and through goods traffic used the broad. From 1871, freight trains having wagons of both gauges *in the same train* were

run. The last WCR loco in service was 0-4-0T (GWR No.1391, *Fox*) which stayed in Cornwall until 1897 when it was rebuilt at Swindon and afterwards worked the harbour line at Weymouth. It lasted until 1948.

The extensive rail network around Hayle Wharves remained in place, substantially unaltered, until nationalisation. Because of the Angarrack incline, horses were originally used for wagon movement at Hayle, but even before rebuilding by the West Cornwall Railway, locomotives were permitted down the incline attached to the ropes. After the opening of the steep branch down from the new main line in 1852, locomotives went directly to the wharves.

The layout involved sidings at Penpol Terrace not far down the branch, which had a lengthy private siding that looped under the main line and back again to terminate on the opposite side of East Quay. At one time, fish was landed at Hayle: in 1868 for example 20 tons of fish were sent to Billingsgate, but that traffic died out with the growth of Newlyn.

Many of the 20 sidings in the main (north-western) section of the harbour were used by Harvey's, and ultimately gave accommodation for around 200 wagons. The fortunes of this firm ebbed and flowed with those of the Cornish mining industry, and in the 1860s, at the time of the mining slump in Cornwall, Harvey's turned to the building of iron ships, including two used on the Scillies route (see Penzance). Their foundry, over which the Hayle viaduct was built, was closed in 1904, as was their shipyard. Coal and, much later, oil and petrol became the major traffic through the port. In addition, Thos. W. Ward had private siding agreements with the Great Western on the dock estate; among other things, they were shipbreakers, and dealt in scrap. There was also a gasworks at the northern end of the harbour nearest the sea.

During WWI, an explosives factory was established alongside the abandoned route of the old Hayle Railway: the National Explosives Co.'s railway left the GWR Hayle Wharves branch about halfway along its length, running north-eastwards to the works; it was linked by exchange sidings at dock level, and this brought traffic to the line both from inland and by sea.

In 1917, the Great Western transferred movement of some of its loco coal to sea from land, and 400 tons per week were shipped to Hayle which, with the 800 tons/week sent to Fremington (see Barnstaple), provided all the loco

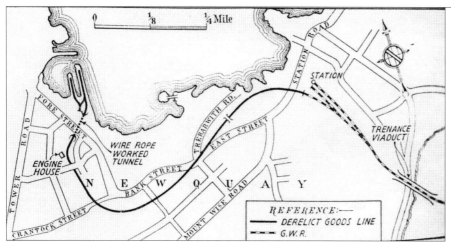

Left - Map of the Newquay harbour branch.

Bottom - View of Newquay harbour showing track emerging on the left down the incline (in tunnel) to the harbour wall and on to the bridge that connected with the stone quay.

coal needs between Bodmin and Penzance, and a third of loco coal consumed east of Bodmin to Exeter.

ICI (Alkali) Ltd. were provided with a siding in 1939, and in the Second World War a dynamite factory was established and sidings were put in for the Ministry of War Transport to deal with special barge traffic (removed 1948).The British Ethyl Corporation also had a private siding arrangement with the GWR at the harbour.

PORTREATH
(Served)

The horse-drawn Portreath and Poldice 4ft gauge tramroad linked the harbour at Portreath with copper mines up the valley around Scorrier and St. Day, with a branch to

Treskerby mine. Begun in 1809 and finished in 1818, it was the first railway in Cornwall. A pier at Portreath dated from 1760, and a basin from 1800, both of which were improved in 1824. When the mines at Poldice became exhausted in about 1860, the tramway ceased to operate, although the tracks remained in place for many years afterwards.

In 1838, the standard gauge Hayle Railway opened to traffic. Although the new railway was locomotive-hauled, it did have a number of rope inclines, including the final 1 in 10 length of track down the branch from the cliffs to Portreath harbour, where wagon movements were performed by horse power.

The Hayle Railway was taken over by the West Cornwall Railway in 1846 and reconstructed in 1852, when

a number of the inclines were eliminated, but not that at Portreath. The branch from the main line at Carn Brea to Portreath generated much new goods traffic, and carried to the harbour large quantities of copper and tin ore to be shipped for smelting in the Llanelly and Swansea districts. On return trips, coal was brought in by the boats from South Wales for the steam-driven mining equipment. For example, during March 1840, the St. Ives schooner *Bristol* sailed from Portreath to Swansea with 140 tons of ore and returned with 147 tons of coal, which were sold at Portreath harbour for 13s 9d per ton. A profit of £30 was made on the round voyage, which took 23 days. So much ore and coal was brought through to Portreath harbour that an inner basin was added in 1846.

Right up to the beginning of the C20th, over 200 boats a year were still calling at Portreath, and the railway branch to the port (marked 'goods only' on GWR maps and documents) was kept busy with goods traffic. The layout below the incline included ten or so short sidings, mostly to the west of the two docks, worked by shunting horses. There was a privately-owned 11 ton wagon weighbridge that was available to weigh GW traffic when required.

The entrance to the harbour was long and narrow, however, limiting the size of ships, and the harbour could only be used in good weather, so that traffic dwindled and regular railway freight ceased about 1930; as late as 1929, a new agreement for the use of a private siding alongside the inner harbour was entered into. The incline down to the harbour closed in 1936, and the rest of the branch from the main line to North Pool siding closed in 1938.

NEWQUAY (Cornwall)
(Owned)

Newquay possessed a breakwater in the C15th that was rebuilt to provide a 'new quay' in 1586, but it was really a 'harbour of refuge' to escape storms.

Pilchard fishing became established later, and in 1833 Richard Lomax completed a proper 4-acre harbour that was developed for minerals, china clay and general goods by J.T. Austen (he later took the name 'Treffry'), who purchased the port in 1838. Trade built up, and Newquay began to export ores of copper, iron, and lead, as well as china clay, in fairly substantial quantities; shipbuilding had also developed. Coal was imported particularly to drive the machinery at the East Wheal Rose lead mine. Treffry's horse-drawn tramroads provided the inland transport, the Newquay Railway (a tramroad) from the harbour to St. Dennis having a branch to the lead mine. Clay workings were situated at Pontsmill, and china clay mines at Luxulyan and Roche, all connected by tramroad in 1849.

Later, the Cornwall Minerals Railway took over Treffry's tramroads, converted them to locomotive haulage and linked them through new lines, so that in 1874 a single line was opened across Cornwall from Newquay to Fowey. The harbour branch at Newquay was a continuation of one of the goods yard tracks at the station, running through the greater part of the town to reach the harbour through an 80 yds-long tunnel under Fore St down a wire-rope-worked

incline of 1 in 4½. It branched out on to the harbour quays and on to a 100yds-long wooden bridge that connected with an isolated stone jetty built about 1870 to increase capacity for loading and unloading. The harbour had 880ft of quays in all.

The opening of the main line railway through Cornwall in 1859 started the decline of small seaports. Newquay's sea-borne trade, already dwindling by the 1870s, lingered on until just after WWI, the demise accelerated by the exhaustion of the East Wheal Rose lead mine at the end of the C19th. In 1905, Newquay was joined to Perranporth and Chacewater by a new railway; it connected with the mineral line from Tolcarn Jct. to Treamble and Gravel Hill, enabling through trains to be run, but this did not produce a revival in the fortunes of the harbour.

GWR publicity in the 1920s maintained that coal was still being imported at the tidal harbour, with china stone and china clay being exported. In fact, the last outward cargo left the port in 1921, and a year later, the schooner *Hobah* brought in a load of fertiliser that was the last cargo to be discharged at Newquay. The branch closed in 1926. In 1931 the town Council bought that part of the branch from the station to Crantock St, and at the same time the GWR presented the incline and harbour itself to the town as a free gift.

WATCHET
(Served)

Watchet had a tidal harbour from ancient times, and landed the usual 'necessities' for living, and also wool from Milford in Wales for local weaving communities. Another local trade was the burning of seaweed to produce kelp that was used in the manufacture of coarse bottle glass.

Trade at the port received a boost when iron ore began to be exported to South Wales. The ore was mined in the Brendon Hills, and traffic increased a great deal when the standard gauge West Somerset Mineral Railway opened fully in 1859 to link mines at Gupworthy (some eight miles to the south-west) to a pier on the north-western side of the harbour, where there was a hoist to tip wagons into the holds of vessels below. The harbour was improved at the same time so as to accommodate 500-ton vessels, and soon after, the Ebbw Vale Steel, Iron & Coal Co leased the railway for a 55-year period. The West Somerset Mineral Railway was an isolated line, not connected to the rest of the railway system.

In 1862, the West Somerset Railway reached Watchet from Norton Fitzwarren, and built lines on the south-eastern side of the harbour, where formerly there had been limekilns and a shipbuilding yard. The harbour lines were at a lower level than the station, and were reached by reversing down to them. The line was broad gauge and was extended to Minehead in 1874. It was worked by the B&E (by the GWR after 1876). The West Somerset line was converted to narrow gauge in 1882. By 1911 a 20 ton wagon weighbridge had been installed.

Bringing in goods by rail was detrimental to the coastal harbour trade that also received a blow when, after 1882, it

Broad gauge B&E Rly 4-4-0ST No 74 on loco turntable at Watchet Harbour. Western Pier (used by the isolated West Somerset Mineral Rly) across the water with breakwater extending across the picture. Wagon turntable at right centre to access line along sea wall. [The Stephenson Locomotive Society]

became cheaper for Welsh iron and steel works to import Spanish ore. Until then, the mineral railway had regularly brought down about 3,000 tons of ore every month to the harbour. The Brendon Hills mines closed down, and the WSMR itself closed in 1898.

Problems for Watchet continued when severe gales in 1900 and 1903 damaged the harbour, washed away the pier and wrecked the first reconstruction. There was a short-lived mining boom in 1907-10, during which the SMR to the Brendon Hills was reopened (but not the furthest Gupworthy section) and a new jetty was built in the harbour. But it was again abandoned. The rails were lifted in 1917 for military lines in France, and in 1919 the Ebbw Vale Company's lease finally ran out.

In 1911, A.R. Angus demonstrated his system of automatic train control on the lines of the WSMR, employing two ex-West Midland Railway 2-4-0s (Nos. 212/3), bought from the GWR.

By the early 1920s, the GW dockside layout saw half-a-dozen sidings on the south and east sides of the harbour, a couple of which were formed off three wagon turntables. The West Somerset Railway had been promoted as a means of distributing coal and goods imported by sea through Watchet harbour. 'Sea-coal' from across the Bristol Channel had been imported since the 1840s at the private wharf at Dunball, near Bridgwater, and was already being distributed around the West Country by the B&E, so that very little coal came into Watchet by sea at first. Some began to appear in the 1880s, and imports grew sporadically to a peak of 17,000 tons in the early 1930s, but thereafter declined rapidly.

On the other hand, general freight through the harbour built up and was steady. Between the two world wars, a major import at Watchet was wood pulp and esparto grass for paper making. A private siding was installed to the premises of the Wansborough (Reed & Smith) Paper Mill in 1929. Esparto is a tough grass grown in Spain and North Africa, and was taken by rail to paper mills in Somerset and Devon. One consignment of 1,450 tons from the Panamanian *SS Flamenco* needed 351 railway wagons to clear the traffic from Watchet harbour. Imports of esparto featured at many other Great Western locations, including Penarth Dock for the Ely Paper Mills in Cardiff. Some of the coal arriving at Watchet by sea was for the boilers of the paper mills, which was taken forward by rail. This traffic in esparto and coal continued into nationalisation.

BRIDGWATER and DUNBALL WHARF
(Canal and Privately-Owned; then B&E/GWR Owned)

The River Parrett and its tributaries, running through the heart of Somerset and passing through Bridgwater and Dunball to its outlet on the Bristol Channel near Burnham-on-Sea, had been a trade route long before the coming of the railway. Bridgwater was the lowest crossing point over the Parrett, and housed a number of important merchant families owning ships. The established patterns of pre-railway shipping trade in and out of Bridgwater included coal imported from Cardiff, Lydney and Newport; culm from Swansea for calcining limestone; salt from Droitwich, shipped from Worcester; roofing slates from North Wales; oats from Carmarthen and Cardigan; oak bark for tanning from Minehead; and gin from Bristol. Some of these goods would be transhipped to small boats that could pass under the town bridge and get to places up river. Outwards, tiles and building bricks as well as agricultural produce were sent to Ireland, Cornwall, South Wales and London. Scouring bricks made from the black, sticky mud found along the banks of the Parrett (often called 'Bath Bricks' after their inventor, whose family name was Bath) were a peculiar

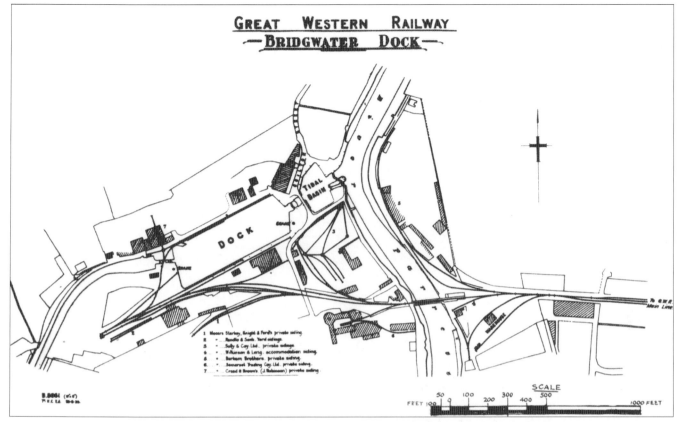

export from Bridgwater; among other things, they were used to clean rust from cutlery before the days of stainless steel implements.

While that type of mud may have had its uses, most of the mud in the winding river, together with the Bristol Channel extremes of tidal levels, was a nuisance to shipping. The town berths in Bridgwater had to be periodically scoured and flushed free of slime and, at times of low tides, ships over 100 tons were unloaded down river. Various ambitious schemes were proposed in the early C19[th] to straighten the river with ship canals, and to provide a floating harbour as had recently been built at Bristol, but the economics weren't right and the Bridgwater Corporation would not go ahead.

However, a little later the Bridgwater & Taunton Canal Company was building its part of the grand waterway planned to connect Exeter to Bristol and London, and the end of the canal included a dock at Bridgwater. Measuring 625ft by 215ft, the 3-acre dock opened in 1841 and was connected to the Parrett by a 150ft by 195ft, ¾-acre tidal basin; total quayage was 2,855 ft. The depth of water in the dock was 16ft at spring tides but only 6ft at neap tides. To conserve water, there were two locks into the Parrett from the basin: a small one for barges, and a 180ft long by 31ft wide entrance lock for ships. The ship entrance was not, in fact, a proper lock, only a pair of gates from the canal into the basin, and this caused tremendous problems soon after opening when it was found that mud was accumulating in the dock at the rate of one foot a month! A scraper had to be purchased, similar to the one designed by Brunel for Bristol's floating harbour; it hauled itself back and forth across Bridgwater dock on chains attached to the quays with a blade below, which guided the mud out of the dock into the tidal basin from where it was sluiced out with dock water into the river. The problem was a continual nuisance to owners of the dock, and the scraper (preserved at the Falmouth Maritime Museum) did valiant work for over 100 years.

The canal company built a large, three-storey brick warehouse alongside one of the quays, together with other facilities around the dock. Ships' chandlers, block and rope makers etc. were established on the site. After the opening of the dock, shipping on the Parrett picked up considerably. The coming of wooden steam paddle tugs - the Bridgwater Steam Towing Co.'s *PT Endeavour* of 1837 and *PT Perseverance* of 1840 - had already reduced some of the tidal problems that delayed ships by being able to tow one or more sailing vessels all the way up to Bridgwater on one tide (formerly, under sail, or being towed by men 'hobblers', it had sometimes taken three tides to get up river from the mouth of the Parrett at Burnham). Even so, being canal-related, the Bridgwater dock was not on the railway and this was to its disadvantage, as illustrated by what was happening three miles downriver at Dunball.

The B&E arrived at Bridgwater in 1841, the same year that Bridgwater dock was opened. The line passed first through Dunball, on the eastern bank of the Parrett, on its way south from Bristol. Civil engineering works in the making of the B&E route had revealed clay and limestone deposits, which could be utilised in brick, tile, pottery and cement manufacture; as a result, new industries were founded in the Dunball area. These factories required

113

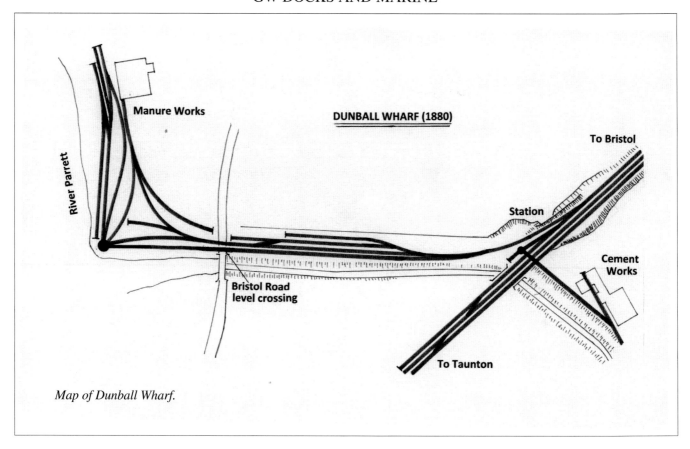

Map of Dunball Wharf.

inwards coal for their machinery, and their products became outwards goods. Given that Dunball was downriver of the twisting stretch nearer Bridgwater, a local industrialist and director of the B&E (John Browne) realised that a wharf at Dunball, with a connection to the railway, could avoid the traditional movement of goods to Bridgwater and transfer to the canals and navigations. So, about 1844 he built a river wharf and broad gauge horse tramway at Dunball to link with the new railway. The tramway tracks ran across the main Bristol road and round to a goods loop on the Up side at the Dunball passenger station (that had the unusual feature of having staggered platforms, divided by the railway bridge across the waterway from Sedgemoor). Later a level crossing was installed where the railway crossed the Bristol road (subsequently the A38). Keys for the crossing had to be fetched from the Dunball signal box, and road traffic was halted by showing a red flag. Movements were permitted only in daylight and the length of later loco-hauled trains was limited to 25 wagons.

The wharf eventually had over 1,000 ft of quay, and had tidal water depths of 17ft/7ft spring /neap tides. While, as expected by Browne, the existence of the wharf benefited the pottery, cement and manure factories in the area (many of which came to have their own private sidings), it was the landing of sea-coal and its onwards distribution by rail that was really significant. By 1849, the B&E 'Old Dunball Coal Train' was taking coal on weekdays to Taunton, Wellington, Tiverton etc. on its way to Exeter, and from there it was conveyed further westwards by the SDR. This broad gauge rail traffic was the death-knell of the Bridgwater & Taunton,

and of the Grand Western Canals, which (with the dock at Bridgwater) were later taken over by the railway. In fact, the opening of the extended Bridgwater & Taunton canal link preceded the arrival of the B & E at Taunton by only 16 months, so the canal was going to be in commercial trouble even before it opened. The rail traffic became such that after mixed gauge was installed in 1867 three Up and three Down narrow gauge goods trains called at Dunball, and depending on whether the midday Exeter & Manchester train could (or could not) clear all the waiting wagons, the late evening Taunton to Bristol goods train 'called if required' ('CR' in the timetables). In addition, there were two down broad gauge goods trains: the Bristol to Penzance fast goods, which stopped between 2.20 and 2.35 a.m., and the 1.0 p.m. goods train (the Dunball-Exeter coal train) which started at Dunball.

Despite the activities at Dunball, shipping at Bridgwater nevertheless thrived in the 1840s, both at the Corporation-owned town wharves and the canal-owned dock. Seeing the success of Dunball's rail connection, the Corporation in 1845 built a half-mile-long horse tramway (its so-called 'Communication Works') from the East Quay wharf on the Parrett to the B&E station at Eastover. Thereafter, all shipping traffic at Bridgwater intended for the railway used the corporation wharves since the canal dock was on the other (west) side of the river, and was not yet rail-connected.

The increased shipping activity in the Parrett at this time is shown by one day's arrivals in 1851, comprising 22 colliers from Cardiff, 19 from Newport, seven from Lydney

Clearing mud from the dock at Bridgwater [GWR].

and one from Swansea; four vessels from Gloucester (salt and flour); and one from Bristol with general cargo transhipped from ocean-going ships. The B&E wanted to play an even bigger part in all this trade, and in 1859 leased the tramway from Bridgwater Corporation (buying it outright in 1863), and in 1865 extended the town landing stage and sidings, and provided a steam crane for loading and unloading: but it was still a horse-drawn tramway, and did not at that time connect with the canal dock.

Meanwhile, although trade at Bridgwater dock was good, the parent canal company had been sinking further and further into financial difficulties because it was unable to pay interest on the loans it had taken out for extending the canal and building the dock. The Corporation had been keen for some time that the railway should build a bridge across the Parrett, and take a line into the dock; given the canal company's deteriorating situation, the canal proprietors eventually agreed to sell out to the B&E for £64,000 in 1866. The B&E immediately started on the task of repairing the dock gates, and converting the horse-drawn tramway into a mixed gauge railway, on which steam locos could operate. A 'rolling telescopic bridge' to carry the new railway across the river was installed in 1871. It was opened at high tides for shipping, originally by hand winch and later

by steam power. Some 200 tons of freight was taken over the bridge in the first month of operation, and the dock branch itself went on to spawn sidings to a coal yard, brewery, timber yard and saw mills. As the dock itself was not designed with railways in mind, space was limited, and wagon turntables were employed in the earliest track layout to give lines to the quays.

In 1890, the Somerset & Dorset Joint Railway arrived in Bridgwater, and put in a connection to the GWR dock line; it also built a separate wharf of its own further down the river.

Trade at Dunball Wharf had also become so active that the B&E sought to buy it as well, and did so in 1867 (a year after taking over at Bridgwater), while in 1869 the by-now mixed gauge track serving the wharf was converted to take steam locos. An extension to the wharf was opened in 1874. When the GWR took over the B&E two years later, Dunball Wharf was landing about 100,000 tons of coal and timber each year, and also salt and lime. As well as the coal forwarded to the West Country by rail, a great deal was imported to feed the clay-firing furnaces. Indeed, in 1873, the port of Bridgwater/Dunball was fifth among English ports for the importation of coal and culm. In comparison, the outwards tonnage of cement, bricks and tiles was

Junction of branch to Dunball Wharf from the GW mainline running across the bottom of the picture. The signal box was moved to the up side (as shown) in June 1905. Dunball station had separated platforms: the down platform is at the bottom centre of the picture; the up platform is out of the picture to the left. Note the flat crossing from the bottom left of the picture to a wagon turntable on the siding to the right of the signal box. The line (from a cement works behind the photographer) was later replaced by a direct connexion from the line on the branch nearer the Sedgemoor Drain that passed back under the mainline to the left of the signal box.

The tidal basin for Bridgwater dock. Four-masted ship in dock at rear. [STEAM Swindon]

relatively small, even though the production of clay goods that were exported to all parts of the world was the staple industry of the area in the late C19th.

Dunball rarely dealt with general cargoes, and these tended to be taken upriver to Bridgwater for unloading. At both places, after coming into railway ownership, vessels were berthed by railway employees who then controlled the unloading operations on the wharf, as well as associated wagon shunting. The loading and unloading of goods, as at other places at this time, was labour intensive: coal, for

many years, was shovelled into baskets or tubs by the ships' crews (perhaps just a master, mate and boy) to be lifted by hand-crane out of the trows or other vessels into wagons on the wharf and quayside. Use of grabs and cranes did not come until the 1920s. With no dock at Dunball, ships grounded on the mud at low tide, and the B&E/GWR had a team of 'mud-rakers' to remove silt and level the berths. That was a very arduous and unpleasant job.

The railway arrangement at Dunball was quite modest, with six sidings on the approach to hold about 90 wagons, and another six on the wharf to hold around 60 more. There was a wagon weighbridge of 20 ton capacity on the wharf line.

While it is too simplistic to say that the opening of the Severn Tunnel in 1886 signalled the demise of Bridgwater dock, the number of vessels entering the Parrett and the tonnage of cargo handled did, nevertheless, begin to decrease thereafter: in 1878, just over 4,000 vessels with nearly a quarter of a million tons of goods arrived, whilst in 1900 this had declined to just over 2,000 vessels conveying 130,000-odd tons. Local ship owning had peaked even earlier - 160 vessels had been registered at Bridgwater in 1876.

The Bridgwater & Taunton Canal also began to cease operations at that time, not only because of lack of traffic, but also because of lack of water. The River Tone Conservators continually complained about the low levels in the river caused by the B&E/GWR's taking water periodically from the river into the canal in order to flush out the mud accumulated in the dock and tidal basin into the Parrett. The railway was statutorily entitled to extract water from the Tone, and one reply from the B&E to the Conservators said that '.........when a longer time is consumed [by barges] it is generally caused by boatmen wasting time by the way in drinking, etc........' -- not because of low water! Nevertheless, some 600 men in 1886 extracted an estimated 130,000 tons of mud from the 14½-mile- long canal, and the GWR had to attend to the Bridgwater dock gates. The water rights issue came to a head in 1905 in the House of Lords, where judgement was given against the GWR in favour of millers who had complained about extraction of water from the Tone above their water mills; this made the railway rethink the system of scouring the dock of mud, and soon afterwards there was a complete reconstruction of the culvert system and an overhaul of the dock equipment including realignment of tracks on the quays. Traffic on the canal during the rebuilding was limited to restricted trips: in fact, between 1905 and 1912, there were only 23 canal journeys of loaded barges carrying coal, sand and bricks.

At Dunball, a search for coal in 1909 found salt instead, and brine pans were established; but it proved to be a short-lived industry, and was abandoned in 1922. Through Bridgwater dock itself, traffic continued to decline during the first half of the C20th. The S&D ran a steamer service to Cardiff from Bridgwater. After the Grouping, an additional vessel (*Radstock*) was launched in 1925 for the Joint Committee, and the service continued until 1934. Thereafter, its wharf fell into disuse, although the tracks continued in use for wagon storage until 1942, when they were lifted. The GWR kept the canal facilities in repair, despite the fall in trade, and reconstruction of the dock gates was again necessary in 1936.

The railway layout at Bridgwater in the 1920s was rather more complex than Dunball. A series of loops alongside the Docks Running Line accommodated around 140 wagons before the east bank of the Parrett was reached, at which point sidings diverged to both sides, holding 100 more, to serve the bank. Beyond the bridge, a complex of sidings and wagon turntables served the dock and Sully's yards.

In 1933, Bridgwater took over its own running from the Port of Bristol as far as shipping matters were concerned. To offset losses, wharfage charges were increased by the GW in 1937 to 1d per ton for general goods and ½d per ton for coal. A fillip to coal imports at Dunball came when a Royal Ordnance Factory was built at Puriton in 1939, but for the railway it was only short-haul traffic. About this time there were 20 men employed on the wharf, with a gang of six being required to moor vessels. There were no quayside dock cranes as such at either location and, although there was a 10-ton hand crane at Bridgwater, lifting was mostly performed by three 2-ton capacity rail steam cranes at each place.

Locomotives for shunting at Bridgwater and Dunball were sent up from Taunton on a daily basis in broad gauge days, but in 1893 part of the old B&E carriage workshops at Bridgwater was turned over to become a small sub-shed, where locos remained during the week. A variety of 'uncoloured', short-wheelbase saddle and pannier tanks were employed on the dock branches and for shunting (and also '517' class 0-4-2T No. 834 in 1920), but allocations to the shed included Dean tender goods engines in the 1920s. The ex-BP&GV 0-6-0ST *Kidwelly* was also to be found between the wars and, from 1945 into nationalisation, the ex-Cardiff Railway Kitson 0-4-0ST No. 1338, dating from 1898. GWR Simplex petrol shunter No. 23 also resided at Bridgwater for many years.

In the inter-war period, Bridgwater suffered financially like many other small West Country ports. A UK Chamber of Shipping report in 1930 wrote:

'...Of recent years the tonnage handled has much diminished due, it is stated, to the severe competition from road and rail transport, which has resulted in a considerable loss of revenue and consequent lack of funds to prevent silting up of the channel and approaches, and to maintain or improve facilities at the port...'

Between the wars at Dunball, petrol imports displaced coal; as early as 1871, strict regulations about mooring ships carrying petrol and other inflammable liquids had prevented such a product being handled in the town at Bridgwater. With the upgrading of the national road system, roadstone began to be imported to Dunball, and was distributed to local council dumps by a Great Western Sentinel steam wagon. A change also took place throughout the country in the feeding of cattle: hay was displaced by 'cattle feed', made as a by-product of sugar processing. The British Oil Cake Mills (BOCM) and other firms built factories at various locations, such as Liverpool and Bristol, and a small plant was constructed at Bridgwater from which oil cake was taken by train to warehouses built at country stations such as South Molton and Wiveliscombe; this provided much-needed goods business for branch lines.

The dry dock on the East Quay at Bridgwater, owned

by the GWR, was rented out in the 1930s to Carver & Son. It was last used in 1940, since during WWII the rolling telescopic bridge was fixed in position which prevented ships getting up to the graving dock. There were proposals to make the bridge capable of opening again after the war, but these came to nought.

Just before nationalisation, in 1947, Plaster Products built a new wharf at Dunball for the import of gypsum from Rouen, but the enterprise did not last. At nationalisation, the tonnage of imports at Bridgwater was roughly as follows:

Coastal Traffic: sand 45,000 tons; coal 35,000 tons; flour 2,000 tons; general cargo 2,000 tons. F o r e i g n Traffic : timber 4,000 tons.

Dried milk came in from Ireland for the chocolate factory at Wiveliscombe, and there was also traffic in fertiliser and wood pulp. After WWII, some traditional traffic, such as hides for tanneries and seeds for cattle cake, died out.

BRISTOL CITY DOCKS
(Served)

Bristol had been a port from Anglo-Saxon times, and was important in the growth of transatlantic traffic to and from the 'New World': John and Sebastian Cabot had discovered Newfoundland in 1497, sailing from Bristol. Under various monopolies, Bristol's overseas trade originally specialised in West India sugars and rum, and Virginia tobaccos. But, as at the port of London, these monopolies eventually lapsed, and Bristol had to diversify into other commodities during the C19th. Bristol was the major port in the channel, and was the place where much of the iron, copper and tinplate from Wales, destined for overseas markets, was trans-shipped from coasters into ocean-going vessels before the growth of the big coal docks in South Wales made that unnecessary.

Owing to the winding nature of the Avon up to Bristol, and the large rise and fall of the tides, it was difficult for ships to get up to the city under their own sail. They were usually towed up by horses, by rowing boats, or by men ('hobblers') walking along the banks. The first steam tug at Bristol was the *Fury*, of 1836 and its appearance caused riots at Pill where the towing men lived.

Bristol's earliest wharves were in the city alongside the tidal Avon and its tributary the Frome, the latter providing soft mud berths as opposed to the stony bottoms of the original Avon berths. In 1804-09, this part of the Avon and the Frome flowing through the centre of Bristol was converted into a 'floating harbour', the tidal river being channelled along a navigable bypass called the 'New Cut', designed to take away the flood waters of the Avon. There were three locks into the floating harbour: one at each end of the New Cut (Cumberland Basin (Hotwells) on the west - the principal entrance - and near the Cattle Market at Temple Meads on the east, together with a central entrance via Bathurst Basin (with a feeder canal with entrance lock from the Avon above the Netham weir further east again). The design and construction of the floating harbour and new cut were performed by William and Josias Jessop for the

Bristol Dock Company established under an 1803 Act of Parliament.

While it was the wealth of its merchants and their forward-looking attitudes that prompted the proposal for a railway to connect Bristol to London (the GWR), it is surprising to find that although the railway was opened throughout in 1841 the Bristol City Docks were not connected by rail to the system until some 30 years later. The site of Temple Meads station was adjacent to the original course of the Avon and the new Cut, but the only convenient access to the Floating harbour was above Bristol Bridge, thus preventing direct transfer from ship to rail. The first railway in Bristol was the Bristol and Gloucestershire Railway of 1838 having a tramway to the River Avon at what became known as Avonside Wharf. There was a complication that the Kennet and Avon Canal Company owned the navigation rights on the River Avon from Netham to Bath and so the preferred route for coal from the mines north of Bristol was via the eastern branch of the Avon and Gloucestershire tramway. In later years, the Midland Railway (that had arrived in Bristol from Gloucester in 1845 and as standard gauge in 1854) continued to use this Avonside Wharf as the principal point of transfer to rail from barges.

Apart from a small wharf adjoining Temple Meads Goods Depot which could only deal with small vessels, all goods passing by rail from the GWR and B&E to and from the docks had to be carted through the city to and from Temple Meads. Railways ought to have been vital to a major port within 120 miles of London, and even closer to the Midlands. In 1872, however, and probably prompted by the perceived competition for traffic from Avonmouth and Portishead Docks (see later), the ¾ mile, broad gauge Bristol Harbour Railway from Temple Meads via Redcliff to Wapping Wharf was opened. It was a joint venture between the B&E/GWR, who built the railway, and Bristol Corporation, who built and extended the wharf and the depot there. One of the two lines was mixed gauge when first opened, although by that time the GWR had decided to pursue standard gauge for its lines in Bristol. The connexion was so successful that three additional wharves, including Prince's Wharf, were opened soon after in 1876, by which time the B&E had been absorbed into the Great Western.

This first rail-connected development in the Bristol City Docks was on the south side of the river. Few, if any, facilities existed on the northern side, in particular in the Canon's Marsh area opposite Wapping Wharf. The Midland Railway had first proposed to use the area in 1891 but the cost of tunnelling through Hotwells from the Port and Pier station (see later) made it uneconomic. By the Bristol Harbour Lines Act of 1897, the GWR obtained powers to connect the Bristol Harbour Railway with its Portishead branch (see later) at Ashton Gate. This involved a new double-decker hydraulic swing bridge over the New Cut near Ashton. The line over the bridge from the Portishead branch direction curved back sharply eastwards along the side of the New Cut to make an end-on junction with the GWR Bristol Harbour Railway sidings at Wapping

GREAT WESTERN RAILWAY.

LIST OF

TOWNS & PLACES

TO AND FROM WHICH THE

GREAT WESTERN RAILWAY COMPANY

CARRY GOODS

FROM AND TO

BRISTOL,

AVONMOUTH DOCK & PORTISHEAD DOCK.

JAMES C. INGLIS,

General Manager,

Paddington Station.

February, 1910.

BRISTOL, AVONMOUTH DOCK, AND PORTISHEAD DOCK.

The G.W.R. Company's arrangements are of the most complete character. No fewer than 32 Stations and Receiving Offices are provided for the accommodation of the town and dock traffic.

The Company have their own extensive wharves with Rail and Crane accommodation adjoining the Floating Harbour, and have access by their railways to all parts of the Docks in Bristol. Their own teams collect and deliver in all parts of Bristol, and they also have access, over the Corporation lines, to the Avonmouth and Portishead Docks.

The Goods Stations and Depôts are :—

TEMPLE MEADS ...	... For General Goods (except for and from the West of England).
PYLLE HILL ...	... For truck loads of General Goods, Coal, and other Minerals. Also for Live Stock for and from the West of England.
CANONS' MARSH ...	... For General Goods in any quantity for and from the West of England, and in truck loads for and from all other parts. For Shipping traffic, Coal and other Minerals.
WAPPING WHARF ...	.. For Shipping and General traffic in truck-loads, and for Coal and other Minerals.
REDCLIFFE WHARF ST. PHILIP'S MARSH ...	} For Truck loads of General traffic, Coal and other Minerals.
KINGSLAND ROAD ...	... For Truck loads of General traffic, Coal, and other Minerals. Also for Live Stock except for and from the West of England.
LAWRENCE HILL ...	... For General Goods, Coal and other Minerals.
STAPLETON ROAD ...	... For Station to Station traffic, Coal and other Minerals.
MONTPELIER CLIFTON DOWN ...	} For Station to Station traffic, Coal and other Minerals.
CLIFTON BRIDGE ...	.. For Station to Station traffic.
AVONMOUTH TOWN ...	.. For General Goods, Coal and other Minerals.
AVONMOUTH DOCK ...	.. For Shipping traffic.
PORTISHEAD DOCK ...	... For Shipping traffic.

Wharf, thus making a full circle back to Temple Meads from the Portishead branch junction near Bedminster, on the main line to the West Country. Perhaps more importantly, a second line ran on northwards from Ashton Gate Swing Bridge to cross the floating harbour at the Cumberland Basin locks, and so reach Mardyke Wharf, the Gas Works and the Canon's Marsh area. Rail-connected quays were then established by Bristol Corporation on the northern side of the Floating Harbour, and a large new GWR goods depot was also built on the site, which relieved Temple Meads and Pylle Hill depots of West of England goods traffic.

There were 83 acres of deep water in the City Docks, with an average depth of 23 ft, the largest lock into the floating harbour being 350ft x 62ft (the Horseshoe bend between Shirehampton and Sea Mills limited the length of vessels to 333 ft between perpendiculars). Nearly three miles of quays fronted the docks, with some 40 acres of quay space on which there were some 14 acres of sheds, with another 14 acres of tobacco warehouses. By 1908, the GWR had berthing rights for 1,600 ft of quay served by the depot at Wapping, and an extensive grain traffic from ship

to rail was dealt with there. By this time, the Bristol Corporation had also erected a large granary adjoining the depot, at which Black Sea steamers discharged grain. In addition, there were two spacious transit sheds and more warehouses built in 1929, all of which were rail-connected with the depot.

Redcliff Wharf sidings, on the route from Temple Meads to Wapping Wharf, was also a mileage depot which daily handled a large number of wagons, as many as 350 wagons a day being loaded sometimes. There was a large amount of timber, flour and feed cake traffic loaded at Redcliff from mills in the vicinity, and inwards there was a regular heavy coal traffic. Before WWII, the Redcliff side of Redcliff Wharf was used as a sand-and-ballast wharf, delivered by Bideford ketches up till the 1930s. Barges belonging to the Midland Railway also waited at this wharf for traffic, since only the GWR had access to the quays below Bristol Bridge. To get any rail traffic at all, the MR had to maintain a fleet of barges and two tugs which transhipped cargo to its Avon Street Wharf at St. Phillips.

There was varied activity at the large open wharf

Canon's Marsh in about 1912. The large goods shed, parallel to the sidings in the foreground, is out of the picture to the left. Transit sheds go across picture and behind them are seen masts and funnels of steamers in the floating harbour and buildings on its far side. The two lines curving in front of the transit sheds pass through gates to cross over Butts Rd and eventually turn through a semi-circle to serve quays and transit sheds on the floating harbour. There is a large yard crane at centre left and a variety of wagons including an LBSC van, a PO Coal wagon, a Fry's cocoa container on a flat wagon (under loading gauge) with a GW Serpent flat wagon (holes along solebar) at bottom right. [Railway & Travel Monthly]

known as the Railway Wharf. From North Africa came esparto grass for paper making (for the banknote paper mills at Cheddar, among other places), and schooners brought in valonia (acorn cups used for tanning). There were three or four mobile steam cranes on the railway track which could be used anywhere on the sidings, not necessarily on the quayside, and all manner of cargoes were handled there, either being put into railway wagons or taken from them to load vessels. The railway sidings on this quay were not level with the surface, so cargo could not be dumped on the quay as it could be at Narrow Quay on the north side of the dock where, early on, iron ore from Bilboa and French cider

A view from Prince's Wharf looking down the floating harbour to Cumberland Basin. Wapping Wharf and sidings on the left and Canon's Marsh on the right. The rear of the Fairburn steam crane, built in 1876 by Stothert & Pitt of Bath for the City docks, is behind the nearest ship moored at Wapping Wharf on its special jutting-out piece of quay. Ship berthed at Canon's Marsh is using its derricks to load into barges. Date is uncertain, but GW 4-planker at extreme right has pre-1936 painting style. [Port of Bristol Authority]

A goods train working from Wapping Wharf sidings towards the tunnel under Redcliffe. The train has just crossed over the Prince Street level crossing and is approaching the bascule bridge at Guinea Street. The building in the background is a bonded warehouse. The dock in the foreground is Bathurst Basin which opened in 1809 as part of the floating harbour. The loco may be a Wolverhampton 850-class 0-6-0ST. [G Nichols]

apples were discharged. At Wapping Wharf, china clay was loaded into Hill's City Line steamers from rail wagons that had come from Fowey as an alternative to sending the ships in ballast to Fowey to load china clay directly.

Details of the cargoes at particular wharves (not all of them were rail-connected) are reported in *Bristol City Docks Remembered 1900–1993*. For example, immediately below Bristol Bridge, on the Welsh Back side, the Irish sailing boats used to unload. Alongside was the berth of Norwegian steamers that brought block ice cut from frozen lakes; this traffic disappeared when a factory for artificial ice was established in Cumberland Road in Bristol.

Graces' flour mill was situated on the Welsh Back. In those days, it seems that it was a common sight to see horses in difficulties, having slipped down either in being backed, or in drawing a heavy load up the incline from Baldwin Street, or on to Bristol Bridge. To help this problem, the Great Western and Midland Railways had a shed just off Bristol Bridge which contained two or three trace horses and men for the purpose of dealing with heavy loads.

At the south side of Cumberland Basin was berthed the twice-weekly service from Cork in Ireland (the Cork Steam Packet Company and the Bristol Steam Navigation Company). Behind were the Corporation cattle lairs, to which animals from the Irish steamers were driven on the hoof. There had been - and continued to be - a considerable traffic in Irish cattle at Bristol. Upon a 1912 outbreak of foot-and-mouth disease in Ireland, Bristol (along with Birkenhead and Glasgow) was designated a quarantine and slaughter centre for Irish cattle. The Corporation pens were served by a backwards extension of the railway line along the New Cut, which crossed the Canons Marsh line on the level at Ashton Swing Bridge North signal box. There was a slaughterhouse just to the north of the junction lock at the east end of Cumberland Basin. In early days, some Irish cattle used to be discharged at Broad Quay, and were taken on the road by drovers to the cattle market at the back of Temple Meads, near Totterdown Lock. Cattle from Belfast were also brought into Bristol on boats from Glasgow. Some

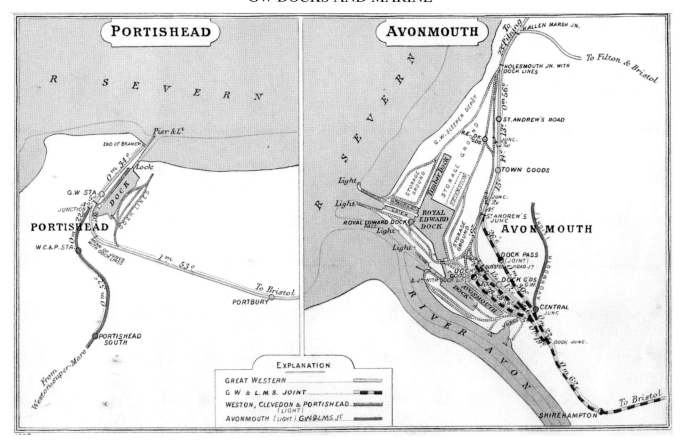

RCH map of Portishead and Avonmouth docks.

of Bristol's imported meat was sent to Smithfield, particularly after the Second World War.

On the north side of Bristol City Docks was Merchant's Dock (that pre-dated the building of the floating harbour), the dry dock and building yard of Stothert & Co., then some coal wharves and the open quay at Mardyke. The gasworks on this Canons Marsh side had a wooden pier on which a steam crane loaded coke into vessels. On the Broad Quay was the Dublin ('Guinness') shed, usually occupied by ships from Wexford, or Welsh ships from Tenby. The Narrow Quay was used by a number of regular traders from Bideford and Hayle.

All the open quays around the dock accommodated those vessels whose cargo did not require cover, such as timber ships from the Baltic countries. In 1913, a paperboard mill was opened at St. Anne's in Brislington: it was supplied with wood pulp imported from Sweden on Bratt Line ships, which was transferred overside into lighters and taken to the mill along a feeder canal.

After connecting Wapping Wharf with the railway from Temple Meads in the 1870s, further developments at the City Docks took time to resolve because ocean-going ships were getting bigger, and the biggest steamships of the day found it difficult to navigate the Avon. The seven winding miles of the river increasingly became a stranglehold in Bristol's efforts to remain a thriving and prosperous port. The Avon also had steeply sloping mud banks so that if a ship became stranded, there was a danger

of her settling awkwardly and breaking her back, particularly when fully loaded. The *SS Gypsy*, en route to Waterford in 1878, broke in two from this cause - the fracture of the hull, it was said, sounded across the city like an explosion.

The long tradition of Bristol's shipbuilders was also under threat as ships became bigger. Some of the world's biggest ships such as the 236ft-long, wooden-hulled, 1,340-ton *PS Great Western* of 1837 and the 322ft-long, iron-hulled, 3,400-ton *SS Great Britain* of 1843, had been built in Bristol in the Wapping group of yards, and successfully got down river, but when the 3,000-ton *Demerara* for the West India Mail Steamship Company was launched in 1851 from the same yard, she stuck in the Avon mud only 2 minutes out from the Cumberland Basin, and swung across the river. Despite being refloated, she again became stranded across the river and was abandoned by the underwriters. While, in fact, she survived to be repaired and converted into a sailing ship under the name *British Empire*, it was a serious blow to the reputation of Bristol.

In the years following, the Corporation and its merchants were faced with options of either developing the City Docks, or investing in new docks at the river mouth on the Channel. But the choice was not that simple, since the private docks at Portishead (on the Somerset side) and Avonmouth (on the northern, Gloucestershire bank) were both contenders.

Eventually, the Bristol City Docks became home only

A 1947 aerial view of Portishead dock showing the extensive timber grounds on the Portbury (left) side and, on the right, the granary (with four roof-top pipes connecting to the quayside. The old Pier station is at the bottom centre and the GWR station at the top. The chimneys of the 'A' power station are clear to see. [CEGB]

to those small vessels of coastal and near-Continental trading which could pass through the locks into the floating harbour.

PORTISHEAD AND AVONMOUTH
(Served)

In 1863, the Bristol & Portishead Pier & Railway Co. opened a 9-mile, broad gauge, single line branch along the west bank of the Avon to Portishead, diverging off the B&E main line a mile to the west of Bedminster. The line was operated by the B&E. Portishead Pill was a landing place for Bristol Channel pilots, and had been a 'harbour of refuge' for centuries. Just off Portishead was the ancient anchorage of Kingroad, where sailing vessels out of Bristol let go the hobbling ropes, shook out their sails and waited for a favourable wind; inward-bound ships waited there for tides to get them up the Avon. Some local trade at the Portishead parish wharf had to be relocated since the new railway embankment cut off the top of the creek. Portishead was already a favourite destination for river excursions, the Royal Hotel (of 1830) being a watering place of Bristol merchants.

The Avonmouth line was opened in 1865 by the Bristol Port Railway & Pier Co ('The Port & Pier'), and ran along the east bank of the Avon. This 6-mile long line was originally not connected to any other railway, and did not purport to serve any dock, as the intention of its promoters was to establish a holiday resort like those at Weston and Clevedon. The Bristol terminus of the Port & Pier was directly below Brunel's suspension bridge at a station called Clifton (later called Hotwells), and it was hoped that fashionable visitors to the hot wells would take excursions to the resort, where not only a pier, but a also a hotel, was built on the foreshore. The name 'Avonmouth' for the place was first employed after the opening of this hotel in 1865.

Various schemes were put forward to join the Port & Pier with the main railway lines, one of which would have included a station in the centre of Bristol (in the event, Temple Meads was rebuilt during 1871-8 jointly for the Great Western, B&E and Midland Railways). Since none of its schemes received outside backing, the BPR&P pressed on itself, and in 1868 began the 3-mile Clifton Extension Railway; this climbed from the Port & Pier line at Sneyd Park Jct., up through tunnels, passing through stations at Clifton Down and Montpelier, to Narroways Hill Jct., just to

Bailey's flour mill on the Portishead dock estate. Tarpaulined open wagons and vans, nearest of which is a GW Mink C.

the north of Stapleton Road on the GWR Bristol & South Wales Union line to New Passage Ferry. A spur crossed this line to connect the CER with the MR at Kingswood. Redland station, between Clifton Down and Montpelier, was opened 30 years later.

At the same time as the building of the Extension Railway in 1868, the promoters of the Port & Pier Railway formed a separate concern (the Bristol Port Channel Dock Co) to construct a dock at Avonmouth, in response to the growing difficulties of bigger ships reaching Bristol City Docks. The Portishead company also decided to build a dock on their branch, and there were great divisions - fisticuffs even! - within the Bristol community as to which scheme to support. Eventually, the Corporation subscribed to the Portishead dock (where it owned land), and gave no support to the Avonmouth scheme.

Avonmouth Dock was opened in 1877, and had 16 acres of water originally, with average water depth of 28ft, the lock being 450ft x 70ft. A couple of miles to the south-west, the dock at Portishead opened in 1879, and was 1,800ft long by 360ft wide with just over a half-mile of quays, 12 acres of water of average depth 30ft, connected by a 445ft x 66ft lock. The heavy cost of completing both docks was borne by the two independent railway companies, and placed them into increasing debt; in fact, the Port & Pier's effort to build the Clifton Extension Railway had already made it bankrupt in 1869, and in 1871 the CER had been taken over jointly by the Great Western & Midland Railways who finished the line in 1874. The line had been planned as broad gauge but was built to the narrow as the 'host' B&SWU line was converted in 1873. Although the CER became joint GW and MR, the Port & Pier railway line

from Clifton/Hotwells to Avonmouth remained a separate concern under an Official Receiver, its troubles continuing as the years went by.

When both docks opened for traffic, trade was in a depressed state and the three docks now serving Bristol found themselves in cut-throat competition for what available trade there was. Avonmouth in particular took a lot of grain traffic from Bristol City Docks; the first trading vessel to berth at Avonmouth was the *SS Evelyn*, with barley from the Danube. Bristol Corporation could not permit this to continue, and since both docks were in debt, and not profitable, the Port of Bristol Authority (PBA) decided to offer to buy up both concerns in 1884. Avonmouth was bought for £550,000 and Portishead for £250,000, both less than their costs of construction.

As this took place, the Portishead railway was vested in the Great Western (it had been converted to narrow gauge in 1880), together with the pier at Portishead. The long-standing summer pleasure services to Ilfracombe were continued, the Portishead Railway's *PS Lyn* being replaced by the GWR's *PS Gael* in 1884, the latter having proved inadequate on the then Weymouth & Cherbourg route (see Weymouth). The Great Western's Portishead excursion steamers ceased in 1886, but the traffic was taken over by P. & A. Campbell's White Funnel Fleet. Local excursion boats from Bristol to Portishead had ceased when the railway arrived, since passengers much preferred a timetable independent of the tides.

The financially-troubled Avonmouth & Hotwells line was eventually taken over jointly by the Great Western and Midland Railways in 1890. The part from Hotwells to Sneyd Park Jct. was closed in the early 1920s to enable a new, level road --the 'Portway'-- to be built linking Bristol with Avonmouth (opened in 1926).

Trade picked up at the end of the C19th, so much so that in 1894 an extra four acres of water was added at Avonmouth to bring the total area to 20 acres, with nearly a mile of quays. Owning all three docks, Bristol Corporation had to decide which to develop - or even to do something different again, which was to make the whole of the Avon into a floating harbour with lock gates at the river mouth, and wharves and subsidiary docks all the way up the Avon - an idea going back to the 1850s. Finally, in 1900, it was decided to build a second dock at Avonmouth to the north of the existing one; this became the Royal Edward Dock, opened in 1908, with 25½ acres extended to 44 acres, a 33ft average depth of water, and a new 875ft x 100ft lock. The original dock at Avonmouth was thereafter called the 'Old Dock'. The new scheme involved a graving dock 850ft long, and over a mile of quays, along with 23 acres of shed area (about the same again as the covered accommodation in the old dock) and additionally silos for 150,000 quarters of grain; the open quay space in both the Old and Royal Edward Docks was similar, at some 13 acres. There were about 34 miles of dock railway after the Royal Edward opened, compared with 13 miles before. At the Old dock there was a 20-ton truck weighbridge: at the Royal Edward dock a 25-ton wagon weighbridge. Since the new dock was parallel to the River Severn, but the old dock parallel to the Avon, they were at right angles, and some realignment of railway tracks was necessary where they joined.

Also in 1900, the 7-mile long Avonmouth & Severn Tunnel Railway was built to bring bunkers coal from South Wales to Avonmouth docks via the Severn Tunnel. It is surprising that, when the old dock was opened, no coal bunkering facilities were provided and steamers had to call at the South Wales docks across the channel as required. The new line ran up the shoreline of the Severn Estuary to Pilning to join the South Wales & Bristol Direct line. Passengers were not carried on this line until 1922, when Severn Beach station opened for excursion seaside traffic. The GW established a sleeper depot near where the Royal Edward Dock lines joined the line to Pilning.

The reason why Bristol Corporation altered its initial support for Portishead to Avonmouth, and had authorised the 1894 small extension, and later the new dock at Avonmouth, may have had something to do with Avonmouth being served by two rival railways (the Midland and the Great Western), rather than by only the GWR. There had been some criticism of the Great Western 'not trying hard enough' with traffic on the Portishead branch, over which it had complete control. While the building of the Royal Edward Dock ensured that Portishead Docks would never be enlarged, developments did take place there: an extensive timber wharf was built on the under-used Portbury side of the dock, with stacking grounds for some 80,000 tons of timber, and in 1908, BP built petrol storage tanks. Both ventures brought lots of freight traffic to the line. Eventually, there were 6 acres of quay space and 11 acres of sheds at Portishead.

A rail connection at Portishead Dock between the Great Western and The Weston, Clevedon & Portishead Railway was made in 1907/8. There were exchange sidings, but it seems that WC & PR locos did not work on to the dock tracks as such. A power station was built at Portishead in 1929 as part of the government's national electricity plan; this led to a fleet of steam and motor colliers being regular visitors to the port from South Wales to supply the station with the 2,000 tons of coal required per day. At nearby Avonmouth, the Royal Edward Dock was enlarged twice: (i) the so-called Eastern Arm in 1928 with cranage on both sides; and (ii) the Oil basin in 1939 on what had been the timber dock. The Avonmouth dock passenger station (joint GW/Midland) that dated from 1877 was rebuilt in 1926.

One commodity that Avonmouth was famous for was bananas. At the turn of the C20th, the banana was still a comparative rarity in Britain, but the Colonial Office wanted to develop Jamaica, and offered a £40,000 annual subsidy for a mail/passenger steamship line to run a boat service between Britain and Jamaica, part of the arrangement being that 20,000 bunches of bananas would be brought back each trip. The Elder-Dempster Line won the contract, and the SS Port Morant refrigerator ship (the first of a purpose-built fleet) sailed from Avonmouth in February 1901 on the inaugural voyage. She returned a month later with 14,000 boxes of oranges as well as the bananas. Never before had such perishable fruit been carried such a long way. A weekly service in summer (fortnightly in winter) was begun in 1904 between Port Limon (Jamaica) and Bristol, and the association between Bristol, Elders & Fyffes and the railway lasted beyond nationalisation in 1948.

The Railway Magazine of 1906 showed a picture of a clerestory corridor convertible coach that had been attached to the 4.30 ex-Paddington express and ran to Avonmouth. The accompanying note said that the 'Jamaica boat train' earned great kudos for the GWR but, in the event, the service was not well patronised and was discontinued in 1914. For the royal visit to name the new dock, a passenger station for boat trains was opened in 1908 on the South Pier near the entrance locks of the Royal Edward Dock. It began to be used by ordinary passengers in 1910 for a new service to Canada inaugurated by the Royal Shipping Line. With the growth in the number of special trains for the West Indies boats and other services sailing to and from Avonmouth, a direct connection to the cut-off route through Badminton for London traffic was desirable, since the use of the CER required reversing, at Narroways Jct. as the connection faced Temple Meads. Hence, the Avonmouth & Filton Railway was opened in 1910; running west-east, it bisected the area between the CER, Patchway and Pilning, passing through Hallen and Henbury to Stoke Gifford. Passengers and mails landed from the RMS Port Kingston from Jamaica reached Paddington in 2 hr 8 min after leaving the docks station on the first train over the new route; by the old route it had been just over 3 hrs. A Bristol Port Authority loco brought trains from the dockside to Avonmouth exchange sidings at which point the GW engine took over.

By 1910, over 200,000 bunches of bananas were being

'Avonmouth from the docks' postcard, showing a variety of pre-grouping wagons on the sidings. Gerry Nichols dates it to 1905. At the right centre is Avonmouth Dock signal box that was later incorporated in the extended platform at Avonmouth Dock passenger station. The church on the right is Avonmouth Congregational Church that was opened in 1902. The engineers department wagons in front of the houses at left centre are standing on additional sidings put in during 1904-05 when a bay line was added to Avonmouth Dock station.

Avonmouth from the Docks.   Harvey Barton's Series.

imported per week at Avonmouth, whereas in 1884 only 10,000 bunches had been imported in a whole year: a bunch is the long stalk containing from six to nine 'hands', each of which has about 15 'fingers', i.e. individual bananas. Avonmouth Docks became the principal centre for the European banana trade, and by 1939 was handling over six million bunches a year.

The GWR pioneered the railway conveyance of bananas as the following extract from the November 1905 *Railway Gazette* shows:

'... The great initiative ability of the officers of the Great Western Railway is shown by the arrangements made in anticipation of the arrival at Avonmouth of the *SS Chickahominy*. Two special express banana trains, with 14,000 bunches, were despatched as soon as possible after the arrival of the steamer, and reached Paddington Station a little before 6 am on Tuesday morning, October 3rd. The two arrival platforms flanking the 850ft covered carriage-way were reserved for these trains and some 300 men ... loaded ... 100 cartage vans ... covering the bananas with straw and blankets. The road vans, bearing labels 'Jamaica bananas' in huge letters ... started at 8.15 am to cross London, in a procession extending some half a mile, for Stratford, Spitalfields, the Borough and Covent Garden markets. Fifty smaller one-horse vans left subsequently to supply the various lesser distributing centres, as far out as Finchley, Croydon, East Ham and Teddington ... The Great Western Railway is now having built a banana train, embodying all the improvement which the working of the traffic has suggested ...'

The two special trains were made up of Dia.Y1/2 fruit vans; the special banana vans mentioned at the end of that extract (Dia.V8 in the *Wagon Diagram* book, later Y6) were the first vehicles to have adjustable shuttered louvres. Further details may be found in *GWR Goods Wagons*. All

banana traffic (with the exception of that for the Channel Islands, which went in containers) was carried in these specially-designed vans, and by the 1920s, six hundred were allocated to Avonmouth. In later years, an interchange arrangement existed with the LMS, under which vans were lent by one company to the other should the traffic on any particular occasion have been unbalanced. Also, LMS banana trains to St. Pancras commenced their journey over Great Western lines from Avonmouth Docks to Yate, via Holesmouth Jct., Henbury, Stoke Gifford and Westerleigh West Jct., joining the LMS West of England main line at Yate. This route relieved the Clifton Down line, which was not only crowded with suburban passenger traffic, but moreover had a 1 in 75 rising gradient through Clifton Down tunnel, which was challenging for heavy freight trains. The LMS had no running powers over the GWR lines taken by the banana trains: it was merely a mutually-convenient arrangement.

Importers aimed to get the temperamental banana to the consumer in perfect eating condition at the time of purchase, and careful control of ripening was necessary from the time of cutting in the West Indies. Bunches would be green when cut (on the morning when a boat would be arriving), and it would be three weeks before they were on sale in the UK. Temperatures in the tropics for the first part of a ship's journey would have rapidly ripened the fruit, so the refrigeration plant on the ship cooled the holds and kept the temperature at about 52-56°F. As the ship travelled into the cooler air closer to Europe, refrigeration gave way to gentle heating to maintain the temperature of about 50°F, for controlled ripening. While the ship was still at sea, the captain radioed his owners at Avonmouth advising them of the condition of the fruit. On this report, and on the orders received from the trade, Elders and Fyffes worked out their programme.

On the day before the boat was due, they telephoned the GWR Avonmouth yardmaster giving provisional details for the numbers of vans required, and the stations for which they were to be consigned. Banana vans were both insulated, and could be steam heated. Depending on the precise stage of ripeness of the bananas, on the length of the journey to the wholesalers, and on the likely weather during the rail journey, experts from Elders & Fyffes decided what temperature on the train would be required for each consignment. The times at which the vans were collected into the railway yard allowed a sufficient margin of pre-heating to be carried out before setting off, but if the weather were cold, the vans would be steam heated en route as well. The normal steam-heating capacity of the train engines employed at Avonmouth was seventeen vans from cold, but as a rule the dock pilot, or an engine sent down specially for the work, lent a hand. With an engine on each end, thirty-four vans could be dealt with at a time. On the rail journey, sixty vans was the maximum capacity of the train, but this number was reduced to a limit of 34 vans if steam heating was necessary.

The fruit was handled in single bunches, and carefully stowed in the vans on beds of straw. Before the First World War, the unloading was done manually, some 500 men being employed at Avonmouth in carrying the stems from the ship to the waiting wagons; casual labour was brought in from all over the area. Bunches were raised from the holds by steam (later electric) elevators working on endless chains. Three lines of vans would be loaded simultaneously, gangways being left between wagons on the first and second lines to give access to the third. Even in later times, when conveyor belts were employed to move the bananas right to the railway vans, some 300 men were still required. As many as 400 or 500 vans might be loaded from a single cargo: typical Elders and Fyffes banana boats in Edwardian days were able to accommodate 60,000 bunches. The record unloading at Avonmouth (with later, bigger ships) was 77,679 bunches in an eight-hour day; and, on the average, a railway banana van left the shed, fully loaded, every minute.

The work of loading and dispatch was simplified by the fact that all banana trains were 'specials', and shown with scheduled paths in the service timetable. The aim of the importers was to make delivery of the bananas to the wholesalers on the morning after unloading, and in several cases the GWR exceeded even that requirement, with Paddington and Birmingham consignments, for instance, being delivered in the early afternoon of the same day. There were two unusual regular banana consignments from Avonmouth: the first was for the Channel Islands, and travelled in containers packed with wood fibre; arrangements for passing this traffic forward were made direct with Weymouth Quay. The other unusual consignment was despatched in the first place to Hull or Newcastle, there to be re-shipped for Scandinavia.

Being on the western side of the country, both Avonmouth and Portishead were used to overcapacity in both world wars. During WWI, Portishead became the principal depot for the supply of canned petrol to France and Belgium: 116 million gallons of petrol were imported and 72 million gallons exported, most of which was distributed by rail. Also during the First World War, Shell built a toluol distillery at Portishead from which it was taken by rail to various factories to make TNT. After the USA entered the war, the government abandoned the large munitions factory being constructed at Henbury, even though much building work had been done, including additional sidings at Stoke Gifford, doubling of the Henbury line, and work on the GWR & MR Jt. Clifton Extension Lines (maintained by the MR). The government did, however, proceed with a picric acid factory and zinc works at Avonmouth, and the sidings prepared for the Henbury munitions factory were retained for these new factories. After the war, railways could buy such new sidings at a knock-down value, or they were removed by the government if of no use to the railway.

In 1917, the Government approved the setting up of a National Shipyard Company, to speed up replacement of cargo ships lost by enemy action (see Chepstow). Three yards were to be built, viz: at Chepstow, Beachley and Portbury, but all ships were to be fitted out at Avonmouth. The scheme was overtaken by the end of hostilities, by which time some considerable construction and installation of a rail connection and extra sidings had taken place on the Portishead branch; these sidings proved to be extremely valuable in WWII for storing stock. During WWI, Portishead took overflow traffic from Avonmouth so that, for example, even some banana traffic was handled.

Various GWR steamers took troops to France from Avonmouth early in Second World War, before the evacuation from Dunkirk. *St. Patrick (II)* was requisitioned for a troop transport in September 1939, and sailed between Avonmouth and France until the October, when she returned to the Rosslare route (see Fishguard). *St. Julien* was requisitioned as soon as the Channel Islands passenger service was suspended on 9th September 1940, and took troops from Avonmouth to St. Nazaire before being converted to a hospital ship (No.29) at Southampton.

The increase in traffic at Portishead during World War II is illustrated by the fact that, in 1939, imports were 294,000 tons and exports 6,140 tons, while in 1945 the figures were 455,000 tons imports and 95,000 tons exports. The increase was not only related to the armed forces, but also occurred because coastal shipping was used in the Second World War to relieve traffic on the railways. Besides coal, foodstuffs (cattle feed and human) were stored and distributed from Portishead. During the conflict, trains of china clay in sheeted open wagons came to Portishead from Cornwall. After WWII, grain landed at Avonmouth was sometimes brought by train to Portishead for storage in the granary there, owing to lack of accommodation at Avonmouth.

The Royal Edward Dock passenger station was destroyed in an air raid in 1941 and its job was thereafter conducted in the S-transit shed at Avonmouth. Rubble from bomb damage in Bristol was taken to Avonmouth for tipping, to reclaim land for development at the docks. A great deal of imported petrol was taken from Avonmouth to Norwich by through train during World War II to supply the many aerodromes of East Anglia.

This page, top - *The first Avonmouth Dock of 1877 looking eastward from the original entrance lock. The photograph was taken about 1900 and shows from left to right, Royal Mail steamers Arawa (5,060 tons), Ikbel (5,434 tons), Monterey (5,455 tons), Potomac (3,868 tons), and Tergest (2,000 tons).*

This page, bottom - *An aerial view of Sharpness dock in 1933 showing the tidal basin and entrance lock at the bottom, with the dock proper beyond, and the canal passing to the top of the picture. The old entrance is at the top left, just below the Severn railway bridge. There are jetties out into the dock over the sloping banks in many places. Sidings on the left serve both coal tips, the original tip being at the old entrance at the top left, the later one in the middle right of the picture.*

Opposite - *The later coal tip at the Sharpness dock in 1901. Coke (wagons have coke rails) being loaded into the Wolfe, a barque bound for Havanah. The timber viaduct was reconstructed with reinforced concrete in 1908. To the left, the quay where the 30-ton steam cranes travelled. To the right, lines to the timber stacking grounds.*

SHARPNESS and GLOUCESTER
(Served)

At the turn of the C18th/19th, the River Severn was an important artery for the conveyance of goods to the growing industrial midlands, and there were regular market boats operating between Bristol, Tewkesbury, Worcester, Stourport and other locations. Wheat, oats and barley imported from Ireland, the Continent and Black Sea ports, was taken on canal boats from Gloucester into the Midlands for milling, mainly for the burgeoning towns of Birmingham, Wolverhampton and Walsall, using the extensive canal system around those towns. This traffic, particularly from overseas, increased significantly after the passing of the Corn Laws. There was also significant trade in timber from North America and from Baltic ports. Salt from Droitwich and Stoke Prior brought by barge from up-river was about the only export cargo from Gloucester, often for Ireland and sometimes for the Continent.

The problem for Gloucester as a port was that the Severn was very narrow and winding between Gloucester and around Sharpness where the river widened out into the Bristol Channel. This stretch of river was navigable only by small vessels, and then only for a few days around spring tides. To bypass this bottleneck, the 16-mile Gloucester & Sharpness Canal was built, and this later gave rise to a dock at Sharpness. The original intention was for the entrance to and from the Severn to be at Berkeley, not Sharpness, which is why the canal was known as the 'Gloucester & Berkeley' Canal until 1935, when its name was officially changed. Construction started during the height of the canal mania in 1794, but owing to shortage of funds, the Napoleonic Wars,

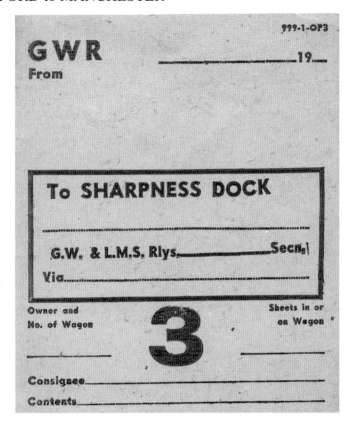

and failure of one of the contractors, the canal did not open until 1827. The canal was different from most at the time in that it was wide and deep enough to take sea-going vessels, up to perhaps 400 tons, and it was envisaged that this would

Cranes running along the quay near the graving dock at Sharpness.

enable Gloucester to rival Bristol.

Ships were towed along the canal by horses, one horse being capable of towing a single barge as on ordinary canals, but up to a dozen being required to tow a sea-going vessel. The River Severn was entered at Sharpness via a tidal basin having two locks to limit the loss of water: a small one for barges, the other for large vessels. The market boats between Bristol and towns in the Severn Valley passed along the canal after it opened, and wharfs built along the canal served local communities. Regular passenger steamers ran on the canal from the 1850s.

As constructed, there was no dock at Sharpness, as boats were expected to proceed directly by canal to Gloucester, where warehouses and other facilities for merchants were provided around its one large basin, off which there was also a small dry dock. As trade grew, with large quantities of iron, copper and tin coming in from South Wales, as well as more and more timber, encouraged by the government's Free Trade policy, a second basin (Victoria dock) was opened at Gloucester in 1849 along with additional warehouses and timber stacking yards. In turn, this led to flour mills, sawmills and other industries, including shipbuilding, being set up round the dock estate in the middle of the C19th. Samuel Moreland, one of the Gloucester timber merchants, later specialised in *England's Glory* match manufacture.

Railways came to the dock area during this period, the Midland Railway first arriving on the east at High Orchard, followed soon by the Forest of Dean Railway (later South Wales Railway, then GWR) on the west side of the dock at Llanthony Yard. The dock owners were keen to get the connection from the west, as it would provide Forest of Dean coal for export. When the line along Llanthony Quay was opened in 1854, the SWR erected one of the earliest hydraulic wagon hoists for the shipment of coal; its capacity was 36 tons, and it was first used to load 120 tons of coal from Nicholson's colliery at Parkend into an Irish schooner bound for Wexford. The MR also began to bring salt to

Gloucester by rail, and to carry road stone traffic formerly taken by the Gloucester & Cheltenham tramroad. The Gloucester Carriage & Wagon Works, which in later years was the largest employer in Gloucester, were established along the canal on the MR side. There were some hand-operated cranes on the quayside, but mobile rail steam cranes were in general use.

In the 1860s, further land was developed within the dock estate, and the multi-storey Great Western warehouse was built on the Llanthony site. The building was privately owned, and the name was adopted long before the GWR began to use the building from the 1890s as a store for sugar brought in from the Low Countries and Hamburg. The Great Western opened a sheet (tarpaulin) factory at the Llanthony yard in the 1880s.

Tugboats took over from horses on the Gloucester & Sharpness Canal in the 1860s, and hence its throughput was increased. However, in the years following, more and more sailing vessels and steamers were arriving at Sharpness that were too big to pass through the lock into the canal. Their cargo had to be transhipped into lighters in the Sharpness basin for onwards delivery to Gloucester. Not only was this inconvenient but it also congested the basin, so that smaller ships that could have locked into the canal could not get through, and had to queue up in the estuary. Vessels began to go elsewhere.

In consequence, the canal company built an extensive 'New Dock' at Sharpness with a new lock entrance, which opened in 1874. The new tidal basin had a 60ft-wide entrance, the length of entrance lock and tidal basin being 900ft, with water area of 20 acres. The depth of water in the lock was 29/24ft spring/neap tides. A new dry dock was also provided as part of the developments. The smaller locks at the old entrance to the canal remained in use until 1910, after which they were blocked off. When the new dock opened, the company changed its name to The Sharpness New Docks & Gloucester & Birmingham Navigation Co. (in the previous year, it had bought the Worcester &

Top - *The Sharpness gas works on the far bank of the canal with coal wagons, two tar tank wagons and a travelling steam crane. The 'Gloster Steam Packet Wharf' is on the right. On this side long planks have been placed across the nearer barge to reach the one moored alongside.*

Centre - *Flour mills adjacent to the quay at Sharpness dock just before WWII.*

Bottom - *The swing section of the Severn & Wye Joint Rly bridge over the canal opened to allow passage of a tug pulling a ketch and other vessels from Gloucester.*

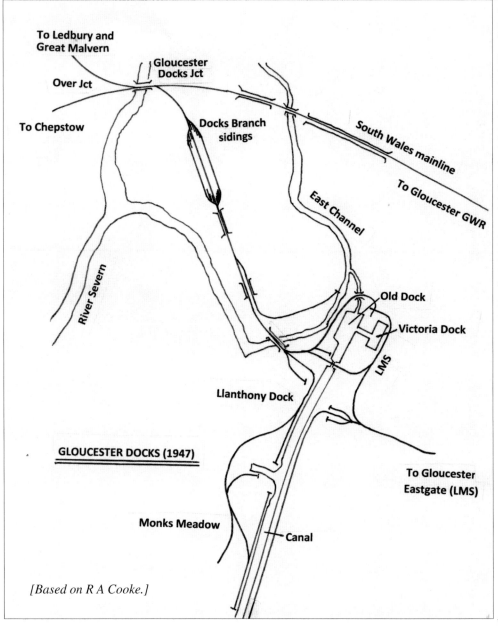

To Ledbury and
Great Malvern

Over Jct

Gloucester
Docks Jct

To Chepstow

Docks Branch
sidings

South Wales mainline

To Gloucester GWR

East Channel

River Severn

Old Dock

Victoria Dock

LMS

Llanthony Dock

GLOUCESTER DOCKS (1947)

To Gloucester
Eastgate (LMS)

Monks Meadow

Canal

[Based on R A Cooke.]

the railways. Part of the problem was that the Great Western and Midland would not cooperate in extending their lines, although things got better when, in 1876, the Dock Co. took responsibility for the tracks on its own land, and later built a new bridge over the lock so that the lines of the two companies could be joined. Much later still, the MR built a swing bridge over the canal in order to gain access to the new Monk Meadow Dock of 1892, below Llanthony Quay, that at first was served only by the GWR. This dock was originally rented by Birmingham timber merchants.

Unfortunately, the new-found prosperity at Gloucester was short-lived. In 1877 and 1879 respectively, Avonmouth and Portishead docks were opened. Both had good rail connections and could compete for midlands traffic. Gloucester suffered more than Sharpness, so it is not surprising that the Gloucester Dock Co. welcomed an entirely new type of cargo in the 1880s, viz: petroleum products such as benzoline and naptha in barrels from North America, which were stored and distributed from licensed warehouses at Hempstead nearby. Much of the oil was used for lamps for domestic lighting.

Birmingham Canal). Extensive facilities were then provided at Sharpness in terms of warehouses, timber yards and a railway network, connecting with the MR at Berkeley Road station on the Gloucester & Birmingham main line. A coal tip was erected alongside the old dock for ships' bunkers and export coal. Tugs were bunkered off a siding near the junction of the canal and the new dock. Housing for dockworkers was created nearby: considerable labour was required at that time for handling foreign corn imported in bulk, which had to be transferred into sacks by hand using wooden shovels before transfer to lighter or warehouse.

While freight continued to be taken up the canal to Gloucester, some goods bypassed the town altogether, being taken directly by rail from Sharpness Dock. Nevertheless, there was increased traffic through Gloucester Docks after the new dock at Sharpness opened, so much so that Gloucester merchants complained about the performance of

Most Forest of Dean coal was shipped at Lydney, and some at Gloucester, but it became possible to ship such coal at Sharpness after the opening of the railway bridge over the Severn in 1879 (see Lydney). The bridge also passed over the canal, and had to have an opening section for tall vessels. The Severn & Wye Railway & Canal Co. and the Severn Bridge Railway were two concerns who amalgamated in 1879 as the S&W&SBR, and connected Lydney to the Sharpness dock lines. The dock at Sharpness was deeper than the dock at Lydney, and to take advantage of the larger vessels that could berth at Sharpness, the S&W&SBR immediately rented quay area and built its own 'high level' coal tip at the new dock; it extended into the dock on a wooden (much later, concrete) jetty, and could tip 150 tons of coal per hour. Eventually, there were two 150-tons/hour tips at Sharpness, together with a coal tipping cradle worked by a 30-ton crane. Instead of bringing coal across the rail bridge just to Sharpness, coal could also be taken all the way by rail to Bristol and further afield via the Midland Rly branch. Nevertheless Sully's, the big firm of coal factors based in Bridgwater, continued to employ their own private-owner rail wagons to bring coal from the collieries in the Forest to Lydney, to be tipped into their own coasters that sailed to Bridgwater, long after railways provided a faster route. Given that at least some onward distribution of the coal from Bridgwater would have been by rail, it is presumed that all the double-handling made economic sense at the time, and was part of the delicate balance between freight rates for coastal shipping and for rail.

As is explained in the Lydney Docks section, the S&W&SBR Co. was not a financial success, and became bankrupt in 1893. In 1894 the whole undertaking, including the docks at Lydney, was vested jointly in the Great Western & Midland Railways to form the Severn & Wye Joint Railway Co. The volume of trade at Sharpness Docks was rather less than at Lydney Docks, but whereas Lydney was mostly a coal exporting dock with few imports, Sharpness and Gloucester were importing docks with few exports; there was little return loading for vessels returning from Gloucester and towns along the Severn, apart from Droitwich salt handled at the Victoria dock (the 'salt quay'). For return loads, ships would have gone down to the South Wales coal ports, or to the docks around Bristol. Some cargoes arose at locations along the canal: for example, gravel used in the building of the Royal Edward Dock at Avonmouth in the early 1900s came from Frampton-on-Severn. Later, Cadbury's had a factory in this village, from which 'chocolate crumb' (a mixture of ground cocoa, sugar and milk from local farms) was taken by boat up the Severn to their Bournville factory in Birmingham.

Although not, of course, part of the S&WJR, information was given on the privately-owned Sharpness dock in GWR literature, where it was advised that information on rates, shipment of coal, and other information could be obtained not only from the dock company itself, but also from the Great Western's District Goods Manager at Gloucester.

In the years before WWI, steamers continued to increase in size, and some could only enter the Sharpness dock after having part unloaded their cargo outside. Larger ships just did not bother to come up Channel, and stopped at Avonmouth. In consequence, the Canal company set up a regular towing service between Avonmouth and Gloucester for lighters bringing transhipped goods for places further up the Severn.

Trade through Gloucester and the canal declined markedly during WWI (the Black Sea was closed to trade, and many Baltic ports were enemy-held): combined imports had been nearly 700,000 tons in 1913, but fell to about 200,000 tons in 1918, whilst exports that had been 268,000 tons in 1913 were only 112,000 tons in 1918. Traffic picked up again in the 1920s, with timber traffic returning to pre-war levels; most was taken up the Severn for use in the

The Gopsill, Brown sack warehouse at Gloucester. This firm was the GWR's supplier of grain sacks (see GWR Goods Services). After closure of the docks this building saw service as an antiques warehouse for several years before being converted into apartments. [A G Atkins collection]

midlands. At that time, small tankers and tanker barges used the canal as a conduit for petrol to the midlands (it was two tanker barges that, in dense fog, struck and demolished one of the Severn railway bridge piers much later in 1960). The Monk's Meadow dock on the west side of the canal below Llanthony Quay became the home of a number of petrol importing and distributing companies, many of which picked up supplies at Avonmouth and delivered them to depots in Worcester, Stourport etc.

The layout of the GW Docks branch at Gloucester involved a set of marshalling sidings on both sides of the running lines at the Over Jct. end, comprising seven loop and five dead-end lines accommodating around 480 wagons, and another set of 17 (Llanthony Yard) on the approach to the docks, holding another 370. There were three parallel sidings along the quay itself, with others serving the sugar shed etc. A 23-ton wagon weighbridge was available.

Facilities were improved in the inter-war years at Gloucester and Sharpness, including the introduction of pneumatic elevators for bulk grain, but the amount of grain going further inland by boat fell off completely as a result of competition from the railways. In consequence, the extensive grain warehouses were under-used. In fact, since

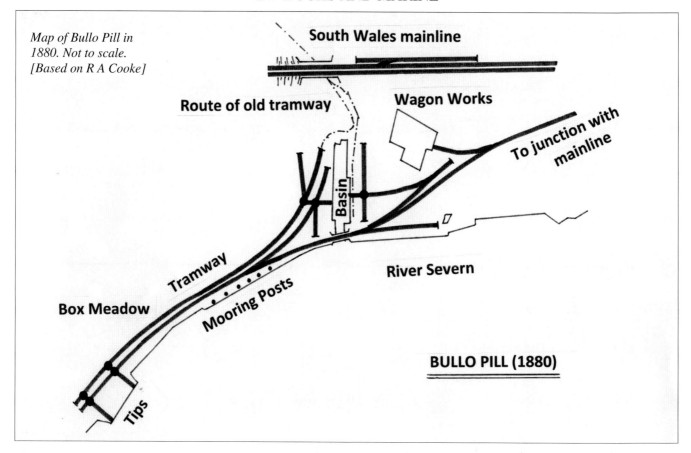

Map of Bullo Pill in 1880. Not to scale. [Based on R A Cooke]

South Wales mainline

Route of old tramway

Wagon Works

To junction with mainline

Basin

River Severn

Tramway

Mooring Posts

Box Meadow

Tips

BULLO PILL (1880)

the 1880s, the GWR freight rate for grain to Birmingham from Avonmouth had been much lower than its corresponding rate to Birmingham from Birkenhead. This was because the river and canal route to Gloucester was much more efficient than any canal route to and from the Mersey, and railway rates were made lower when there was effective competition on a route. Mersey traders therefore complained that Avonmouth could take trade away for reasons that had nothing to do with the respective merits of the two ports. It was higher tolls on northern canals that made it economic for many years to take Welsh slates to the midlands via the Bristol Channel and Gloucester, rather than directly from the Mersey.

There was an increase of 'other traffic' during WWII, where the canal took goods inland from ships diverted to the Bristol Channel from London and other ports. To speed up the traffic, a quay wall was built on the west side of Sharpness new dock, and electric cranes were installed; a large grain silo was built at Gloucester in 1944 for home-grown grain. The Castle Meads power station on the River Severn, opened at that time, had regular supplies of coal from Barry. In preparation for the D-Day landings in Normandy during June 1944, Sharpness was one of a number of 'oil ports' from where the liberating armies were supplied.

In 1945, the Great Western warehouse at Gloucester was being used to prepare breakfast oatmeal, and a dust explosion caused a fire which destroyed all but the ground floor. Traffic, except for timber, fell off again after the war.

THE FOREST OF DEAN: BULLO PILL and LYDNEY

The Forest of Dean had been an industrial area since Roman times; iron ore had been mined, and timber was felled for charcoal burning used in smelting the ores. In mediæval times, wood was felled for local shipbuilding, and coal was mined from the middle of the C18th. Tinplate mills were later set up. Packhorses with panniers would bring iron, tinplate and coal out of the forest, as the roads were not good enough for carts or wagons. Transport of these products to the outside world used the creeks ('pills') leading into the Wye, and into the Severn. Because the Wye was shallow, and difficult to navigate towards its junction with the Severn at Chepstow, some traffic (coal from Lydbrook, for example) was sent upriver to Ross, Monmouth and Hereford: southbound traffic from the Forest came down to Lydney which gave access to the Severn and places further away. The type of boat almost invariably used to forward the products was the Severn trow which was flat-bottomed and open-holded, which sat easily on the mud up the various pills at low tide for loading and unloading, and floated off at high tide. Trows were often ketch rigged as it did not require too many crew (a ketch is a two-masted, fore-and-aft rigged sailing ship in which the mizzen mast is stepped forward of the rudder post). Trows were a long-lived design, lasting well into the C20th, and could be found at all the ports on both sides of the Severn estuary and Bristol Channel. Many were later derigged, and an engine installed to serve out many more years in coastal, and even Continental, working.

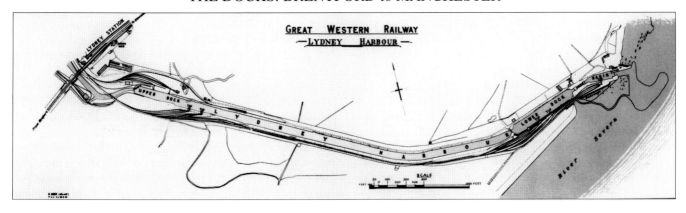

BULLO PILL
(Owned)

Colliery tramroads had been constructed in the early 1800s on the eastern side of the Forest of Dean, the natural outlet for which was southward along the Cinderford valley to Bullo Pill, some seven miles upstream of Lydney (the later Severn railway bridge crossed the river between the two). There was a modest (and originally incomplete) single, stone-lined basin, 90yds long by 20 yds wide, with lock gates into the Severn, and wharves and tips fronting the river to either side of the basin. The Bullo Pill Railway (a tramway) dated from 1807, but was on hard times in the recession after the Napoleonic Wars, and was bought up in 1827 when the name was changed to the Forest of Dean Railway. A new, deeper-water wharf with tips was built downstream at Box Meadow in the 1830s.

The South Wales Railway bought up the FoDR in 1847, and when the SWR main line was opened in 1851, interchange sidings with the tramroad were constructed. A broad gauge SWR branch left the main line at Bullo Pill Jct., descended to cross the mouth of the basin over a drawbridge to the Box Meadow wharf, where there were two tips served by turntables and a crane. Sidings also connected with the basin, other wharves and, in 1873, to Boucher's wagon works (the wagon works operated under various owners until it closed in 1916). Despite the siphoning-off of minerals to the railway, coastal vessel traffic through Bullo Pill remained strong, with typically 1,000 tons of coal being sent out on spring tides to Bridgwater and Dunball, and considerable quantities of pig-iron to Stourport by barge.

In the 1850s, coal traffic on the FoDR might average 40 wagons daily, generally taken down to Bullo Yard for onwards delivery to Swindon. As new collieries were opened, the daily haul of coal trucks went up to about one hundred. Owing to the steep gradients near the collieries, train lengths were limited, depending on location, to 15 or 25 wagons. Four locos were shedded at Bullo Yard, the single-road shed being on the Up side, next to the branch.

In the last quarter of the C19[th], Bullo Pill took trade from Lydney and the Severn & Wye Rly by offering preferential rates. However, it did not last. Whereas there were 35 sailings in an 18-day period in 1892, there were only 25 during three months in 1902. The tips at Box Meadow were removed in 1904 and the bridge over the dock entrance was removed in 1907, thus limiting access to only the east side of the basin.

Nevertheless, as late as 1922 an occasional trow took coal from Bullo to Framilode lock on the Gloucester & Berkeley Canal for mills in the Stroud valley. At this time, the dock had a loop line to each side of the running line, accommodating a total of 45 wagons, and a dead-end siding with a capacity for 15 more. A single wagon turntable served the three primary lines at the dock, with single spur passing beyond to a jetty, and a short siding for 4 wagons running alongside the dock.

The last vessel passed through the lock in 1926, and thereafter the dock was available only as a tidal basin. The remaining sidings were much simplified in the 1930s. Remarkably, parts of the tramroad survived into the C20[th].

Sidings alongside the mainline at Bullo Pill were regularly employed well beyond nationalisation by all sorts of goods trains for examination purposes and stops for water.

LYDNEY DOCKS
(Jointly Owned)

Water-driven iron forges were established in the early C18[th] down the Cannop Brook towards Lydney, some of the products of which (including tinplate) were shipped down Lydney Pill and over to Bristol. In 1790, Pidcock's canal was built to join the tinplate works to the top end of Lydney Pill in order to gain access to the Severn, and the canal carried iron and coal for over a century. But it was the building of tramroads that made a massive difference to transporting goods to the river for onwards shipment, and the establishment of proper docks at Lydney came about because of the tramroad.

In 1809, the Lydney & Lydbrook Railway Company was formed to link the rivers Severn and Wye, with branches to collieries in the Forest of Dean, using a 4ft gauge tramway. It was soon realised that facilities at the town dock in Lydney were inadequate for the increasing amounts of coal and other goods being exported, so a new dock and basin were constructed out in the Severn with a canal connecting the old and new docks. The dock and outer harbour were finally completed in 1821, with associated wharves and cranes. The enabling Act of 1810 also changed the name of the company to the Severn & Wye Railway & Canal Co. The original Town (Upper) Dock was 908ft long by 88ft wide with 383ft of quayage, and the new Lower

Dock was 780ft long by 105ft wide, having some 4 acres of water area; the canal joining the two was nearly two miles long. The Lower Dock was entered from the Severn by a 270ft by 75ft tidal basin through a lock 100ft long by 24ft wide, the entrance gates between the river and basin being 33ft wide. Water depth in the tidal basin was 24/12ft at spring/neap tides; in the Lower Dock it was 13½ft and was 12ft in the Upper. Three-hundred-ton boats could enter the canal, and 400-tonners just the outer dock.

The tramway was worked by horse until 1865, after which locomotives were employed. Being lower than the height of the wharf, coal could be placed into trows by up-ending wagons at coal tips. The line was a success, and paid good dividends. By 1867, despite the continuing limitations on the size of vessel that could enter the docks at Lydney (and the tidal problems of entering the harbour, which like many harbours on the Bristol Channel, was also prone to silting-up), some 200,000 tons of coal, pig iron, bark and timber, and quarried stone were being sent out annually.

Meanwhile, the South Wales Railway had been incorporated in 1845. There was a number of proposals to connect the GWR with South Wales, but the river crossings mostly ran into objections from the Admiralty or from Parliament. Consequently, the SWR, thwarted in its attempts to cross the Severn, used the powers it did have to buy the Forest of Dean Railway (see Bullo Pill) and constructed a railway from Chepstow up to the southern extremities of the FoD Rly and from thence to Gloucester. It had been arranged at the outset that this railway (and other 'feeder' lines to the SWR, including the proposed Ely Valley Railway, the Llynvi Valley Railway, and the South Wales Mineral Railway) should be broad gauge. On its arrival in 1851, the 7ft SWR thus crossed the 4ft tramway on the level at Lydney Junction.

At the SWR shareholders' meeting in 1853, approval was given to constructing new lines in the Forest of Dean, including a branch to Monmouth. At Lydney Junction station, there was a railway interchange wharf at which coal brought down on the tramway was tipped into broad gauge wagons. The SWR thus provided an outlet by rail for Forest of Dean coal, at first to Gloucester, and later to South Wales, after Brunel's Chepstow rail bridge had been completed.

The presence of all the broad gauge lines surrounding the tramroad eventually made it necessary for the S&WR&C in 1868 to lay down a broad gauge railway (all its lines had been hitherto laid with tram plates) between Lydney and Wimberry Slade. Further broad gauge construction extended the line to Cinderford, and also put in an important loop line to Drybrook Road with connexions to many collieries round the eastern side of the Forest. Some of the gradients on the branches were quite steep. At the Lydney docks, nine new mechanical tips for the bigger and heavier railway wagons replaced the old tramroad tips. Eventually, all the remaining tramway was converted to a railway, and in 1872 an Act of Parliament permitted the railway to carry passengers, the same year that the old tramroad, and the BG SWR, were both converted to

standard ('narrow') gauge. By the end of the C19th, Lydney was shipping out 300,000 tons of coal per year. Given the restricted size of vessels that could enter the docks, this meant over 40 vessels per week.

An important clause in the 1872 Act was the incorporation of the Severn Bridge Railway Co. with the purpose of making a railway from Lydney across the River Severn to the (privately-owned) Sharpness Docks on the MR. The bridge (the bowstring spans of which were constructed in Liverpool) opened in 1879, and the S&WR&C built a coal tip at Sharpness to enable Forest of Dean coal to be shipped from the larger vessels that could enter the deeper dock at Sharpness. The coal could also be taken directly by rail from Sharpness to Bristol. Even with all the alternative competition for this traffic, the tonnage of coal shipped from Lydney Docks continued to increase.

The renamed Severn & Wye Bridge Railway Co. was not a financial success, however, and became bankrupt in 1893. In 1894, the whole undertaking, including the docks at Lydney, was vested jointly in the Great Western & Midland Railways to form the Severn & Wye Joint Railway Co. - neither company by itself wanted to take over the debt-ridden and run-down S&W. By the same Act, the MR transferred to the Joint Committee their Gloucester & Berkeley New Docks branch from Sharpness to Berkeley Road on the MR Gloucester-Bristol line. The total length of the S&WJ was just over 38 miles, of which 11 miles were mineral traffic only. Management alternated between the two owners, while the Great Western supplied the locos and managed the running department, and carriages were supplied equally by both companies.

At the turn of the C19th/20th, there were within the Forest of Dean over 40 collieries, two tin-plate works, several iron ore mines and numerous quarries. By 1890, the S&W company was transporting nearly 700,000 tons of traffic annually, whilst in 1898, after the formation of the joint company, over 1 million tons per annum was recorded (including then, of course, traffic from the Berkeley branch, and all that exchanged with the independent Sharpness Dock Co. as well). In 1897, over 2,000 sail and steam vessels were loaded with a tonnage of over 250,000 tons; a few years later it was nearly 3,000 vessels and 337,000 tons. The coal went to many destinations: for example, coal was taken to Hayle in Cornwall, where it was mixed with Welsh steam coal for the boilers of the tin mines. There were nine coal tips and three cranes at Lydney Docks in 1900.

Traffic began to decrease after WWI, and some Forest of Dean collieries closed in the 1920s. At this time, the Upper dock at Lydney comprised two main banks of sidings, one on each side of the waterway. The northern sector comprised seven loops serving two wagon turntables, with two connections thence towards the basin, and a single siding. Outside these, another siding ran on to serve the quayside, with its crane. The southern part, alongside the line to the Lower dock, had eight short loops serving two wagon turntables near the quayside, with three loops and a dead-end siding giving storage capacity off the branch. The Lower dock itself had three wagon turntables supplied by ten loop lines, with quay spurs off two of them, and a dead-end storage siding.

In 1927 two very old small coal tips used by small boats at the town end of the Lydney canal were dismantled, leaving the port with seven tips, and gradually only the tips at the bottom of the canal and the one in the outer basin were employed, simply because boats did not then have to pass up the canal. In 1932, there were five 12-ton coal tips still in use and a 2-ton capacity hand crane. The tinplate traffic from Richard Thomas & Co's Lydney works, which for years had been taken from the Upper dock to Avonmouth for shipment all over the world, had dwindled away by the Second World War. The works were requisitioned by the Admiralty from 1941-46. The opening of Pine End plywood factory in WWII (to fabricate the plywood from which the de Havilland Mosquito was made) brought some new life to the docks, logs being tugged over in dumb barges from Avonmouth, and that business continued beyond nationalisation, but the docks were in continual decline.

CHEPSTOW
(Served)

The timber trade in all its aspects (supply of shipbuilding timber to the naval dockyards at Plymouth, Deptford and Woolwich, sale of bark for tanning, manufacture of tree-nails for ship building, import of Baltic deals and masts and North American woods) was important at Chepstow in the C18th/19th. Iron ore brought from Cumberland for the furnaces at Tintern was another significant import, the ships returning north with timber. Dried fish ('stockfish') from Iceland, and wines from France and Portugal were also imported.

The Wye used to be navigable for many miles inland,, and local trading up and down the tributaries, and along the Bristol Channel, was performed by a fleet of Severn trows. There was a weekly market boat for passengers, perishables and parcels between Chepstow and Bristol. Steam packet boats started to ply between these same ports from the 1820s, one of which, the *Wye(I)* of 1827, was the first steam vessel built, engined and completely fitted out at Bristol.

A feature of the port of Chepstow was its connection from ancient times with ferry crossings over the River Severn. There were two, one called the Old Passage between Beachley (on the spit of land between the Wye and the Severn) and Aust on the Bristol side, and the other from St. Pierre (on the Welsh side, near the later Severn Tunnel's Sudbrook pumping station) to the place called 'New Passage' on the English side. Rival ferries operated on both routes; both operators had Welsh mail contracts, which formed a major part of their incomes. But after the opening of Brunel's rail bridge over the Wye at Chepstow in 1852 which completed the SWR/GWR route from London to Carmarthen, the Post Office moved the mail contracts to the railway. The arrival of the railway was propitious for the Wye salmon fishery, however, which began regular deliveries to London.

Even with the opening of the SWR/GWR line, the journey from South Wales to the South-West of England by rail via Gloucester was still tedious, and various schemes to shorten journey times were put forward and ultimately the Severn Tunnel would be opened. One idea was to run a line from Bristol to the south side of the Severn, and connect to Chepstow by ferry. The short-lived Bristol & South Wales Jct. Railway took an option in 1846 on both ferries, but it went into liquidation in 1853, not having got further than the survey stage. Six years later, however, a different company (the Bristol & South Wales Union Railway) was formed to build a single track railway line from Bristol (11½ miles long through Lawrence Hill, Filton and Pilning) to the end of a new pier built at New Passage, with a steam ferry to cross the 2 miles of the Severn to another new pier at Black Rock, on the Chepstow side, with a one mile branch to connect with the SWR main line at Portskewett station. The broad gauge B&SWUR opened in 1863 and the New Passage route gained a new lease of life, the Old Passage ferry company selling up in 1864.

A contractor, John Bland, operated the ferry boats provided by the B&SWUR: the wooden-hulled *PS Gem* (of 1853), the iron-hulled *PS Relief* (of 1862), the wooden-hulled *PS President* and iron-hulled *PS Christopher Thomas* (of 1864, the latter name being that of the chairman of the company). All were registered in Bristol. Before absorption by the GWR in 1868, the B&SWUR had disposed of the old wooden vessels, so the Great Western took over the *Relief* and the *Christopher Thomas*. They ordered a new vessel (the iron-hulled *PS Chepstow*) in 1874 to replace the *Relief*, which was sold on to become a Mersey excursion boat. The gauge of the B&SWUR was narrowed in 1872/3, and the line doubled for the opening of the Severn Tunnel in 1886; Temple Meads to Ashley Hill had already been doubled for the Clifton Extension Railway in 1874 (see Bristol).

Early in 1881, the pier at Black Rock was damaged by fire, and the ferry for rail passengers moved to a quay at Chepstow itself. During this period, at least one Bristol-Cardiff train was routed from Temple Meads up the MR to Berkeley Road station, to reverse and cross the Severn & Wye rail bridge to join the SWR at Lydney. Repairs were complete by the summer of 1881, and the ferry service continued to operate until the opening of the Severn Tunnel in 1886, after which it ceased and both the *Christopher Thomas* and *Chepstow* paddle steamers were sold in 1890. Even after the Severn Tunnel opened, boats that had run between Cardiff and the S&DJR pier at Burnham, to shorten the distance between South Wales and the West Country, continued to operate into the early C20th.

The builder of Brunel's bridge over the Wye was Edward Finch, who remained in business at Chepstow, his Bridge Works afterwards constructing various iron boilers, cassions etc., and eventually iron ships: Daniel and William Gooch both had part ownership of the 132-ton *Alma* screw steamer built by Finch in 1855. At its peak in the 1880s, Finch's had a workforce of nearly 500. Another railway contractor, Robert Sharp, built a large, steam-driven flour mill in the town in the early 1850s; this later became a malthouse, and was in operation until the 1920s. The

Admiralty buoys built by Fairfield Engineering loaded on Crocodile F wagons ready for shipment (probably to Newport docks) in the 1920's. Works tracks, including the National Shipyard No 1, were on the south side of the South Wales main line (on embankment) to which there was a connection west of Chepstow passenger station.

Brunel's bridge over the Wye which opened in 1852 was a precursor for the Royal Albert Bridge at Saltash. The tubular portion was on the English side and the iron viaduct on the Welsh. The contractor for the bridge was Edward Finch who subsequently remained in business as shipbuilders until WWI.

contractor of the Severn Tunnel, Thomas Walker, also remained in business at Sudbrook, near Chepstow. His riverside yard was rail-connected (originally from Portskewett, and after 1878 by a new branch from Caldicot Crossing). Many small ships were built there until 1922, when it closed owing to the post-WWI depression. Walkers had been the contractors for the Prince of Wales dock at Swansea in the late 1870's.

In 1876, the Wye Valley Railway opened from Monmouth to Chepstow. Always operated by the GWR, it was eventually taken over by the company in 1905. It joined the South Wales main line at Wye Valley Jct to reach Chepstow's GWR station ¾-mile distant over the bridge.. Convinced that a revival of trade was just around the corner, in 1878 the company began to build a rail-connected 800ft-long wharf on the river; the first import was a cargo of corn that was unloaded into railway trucks and taken up the line to the flourmill at Redbrook. But trade at Chepstow did not

revive, and the foreign and coastal trade continued to fall dramatically.

Neighbouring ports grew at the expense of Chepstow. For example, the Monmouthshire Canal to Newport deprived Chepstow of some of its hinterland, and Newport had coal that Chepstow did not. However, as ships became larger, it became more economical to send ocean-going vessels to Bristol rather than Chepstow. By 1881, designation of Chepstow as a separate customs port was no longer justified, and its Customs House was closed. Nevertheless some shipping continued, and vast quantities of limestone from the quarries at Lancaut were taken by trow at various times for building the docks at Bristol, Avonmouth, Newport, Sharpness and Gloucester, and sloops carrying coal to Chepstow sailed up to the beginning of the C20th. In WWI, the Ministry of Food had a large storage warehouse in the 'Buffer Wharf' area of Chepstow Dock, which continued in use long afterwards.

The tradition of shipbuilding continued at Chepstow, even if it was running down as a commercial port. In 1917, alarmed at the loss of ocean-going cargo steamers (the allies had lost 500,000 tons of shipping by early 1917, of which 250,000 was British), the government began the National Shipyard scheme in several parts of the country. In the Bristol Channel, extensive yards with over 30 slipways in total were laid down at Chepstow, Beachley and Portbury (Portishead), and ship workers were brought down from established yards in the north to get things going. National Shipyard No.1 was built on land immediately to the south-east of Chepstow station, where sidings forty private sidings were installed in an area measuring about half-a-mile in length to serve the slipways and workshops. National Shipyard No.2 was built at Beachley, on the spit of land between the Wye and Severn, again with a very extensive private rail system stretching over some 2½ miles, connected to the GWR about half-a-mile above Wye Valley Jct. A crossover on the mainline was installed between Chepstow and Portskewett for the Admiralty.

Construction of some 2,500-ton and 6,500-ton ships to standard, part-prefabricated, designs began, but the Armistice was signed before any were launched. At the end of WWI, Finch's and the Chepstow National Yard amalgamated to complete those vessels still on the slipways, and to seek further work. Owing to the post-war slump, business was bad, and the yard closed in 1925. Rail connection to the Beachley Yard was removed in 1928, as were the sidings at Finch's yard at Chepstow. However, the site of National Shipyard No.1 was taken over by the Fairfield Engineering Co. of Glasgow, who carried on crane building and general engineering. Indeed, Fairfield's constructed wagons for the GWR (e.g. 250 of the 5,000 Dia. N32 'Pole' steel mineral wagons, built in 1933-36 by outside contractors for colliery hire purchase). The yard also provided the Great Western with many 'exceptional loads' such as long, built-up girders and train-loads of Admiralty buoys. During WWII, Fairfield's were building three tank landing craft a month in the run up to 'D'-Day; these were the last vessels launched at Chepstow.

There was a demand to transport cars through the Severn Tunnel, to shorten the road journey between Wales and the West, even in Edwardian days, and in 1912 the GWR advertised *Road Motor Cars - Conveyance through the Severn Tunnel*, cars being carried on 'Scorpion' and 'Serpent' carriage trucks and similar vehicles on timetabled trains. Indeed, the June 1909 *GWR Magazine* highlighted a '1,000 mile motor car drive through England, Wales and Ireland' with established petrol sheds on either side at Pilning and Severn Tunnel Jct. Old Ferry Passage was revived commercially in 1926 with a motor boat, and became the Beachley & Aust vehicle ferry from 1931. Schedules depended on the tides but, even so, the ferry survived until the first Severn Road bridged opened in 1966.

NEWPORT (owned; formerly ADR)

Newport's history as a port goes back to Roman times when vessels sailed up the River Usk to Caerleon, but it was the South Wales iron and coal trade that made the town an important commercial centre. After the completion of the Monmouthshire Canal in 1796, pressure from iron masters such as Samuel Homfray culminated in the construction of the first wet dock at Newport (later known as the Town Dock). It opened in 1842, two miles below the castle and road bridge over the River Ebbw where the SWR would later cross the river. It had a water area of 5 acres, an inner basin extension of 1858 increasing the area of the dock to 12 acres with a corresponding increase in the number of wharves. The lock was 220ft long x 60 ft wide. There was a 26 ft average depth in this dock which had a mile of quays, five acres of quay area and in later years about one-third of an acre in shed area. (An indication of how dock and lock capacity grew over the years at Newport is that the giant New Lock entrance to the final dock opened in 1914 was 11 times larger than the 1842 lock for the Town dock).

Trade grew tremendously between 1855 (when 562 vessels docked and 154,000 tons of coal and 53,000 tons of iron were shipped, and 13,000 loads of timber imported) and 1865 (when 1011 vessels docked and 336,000 tons of coal and 75,000 tons of iron shipped and 33,000 loads of timber imported). There was great congestion in the port and a need for more dock accommodation. Old wooden wharves along the river used by the ironmasters of the C18[th] and C19[th] were improved to help increase capacity but, as at London Docks, the Commissioners of Customs permitted only a limited number of 'legal quays' and 'suffrance wharves' for imports and exports so that increased capacity was limited.

Iron ore from Lancashire and Cumberland had been imported at Newport for many years by coastal vessels for ironworks in Monmouthshire, such as those at Cwbran, Nantyglo, Tredegar, Rhymney and Ebbw Vale. Soon after the West Somerset Mineral Railway opened in 1859 to bring iron ore from the Brendon Hills to Watchet harbour, the Ebbw Vale Steel, Iron & Coal Co leased the line for a 55-year period. When extra furnaces in the north of England took the dwindling supply of Lancashire and Cumberland ore, ore had to be imported from Spain, more cheaply in fact than Somerset ore. Nevertheless, British ore continued to be brought by iron ore trains to South Wales up to and after WWII (from round about Hook Norton and Bloxham, Oxfordshire, on the Banbury & Cheltenham Rly opened in 1887; from Barton Dassett on the Edge Hill Light Rly off the Stratford-upon-Avon & Midland Jct Rly; and from Northamptonshire) but more and more ore had to be imported. At Newport, the so-called Great Western wharf, on the east bank of the Usk, in 1875 began to import 30,000 tons of Spanish ore per annum for transit to Staffordshire. The Great Western Wharf & Railway was a private concern, with its own railway connecting to the GWR. There were four large steam cranes capable of discharging 1000 tons of ore per day, appliances for shipping 800-1000 tons of coal per day, and a 'keel berth' (grid iron) 500 ft long. The company had two locos and 500 mineral wagons carrying goods for those collieries and iron works located mainly in the Eastern and Western valleys. In addition to iron ore, iron pyrites, pig iron and pitwood were imported, with steam

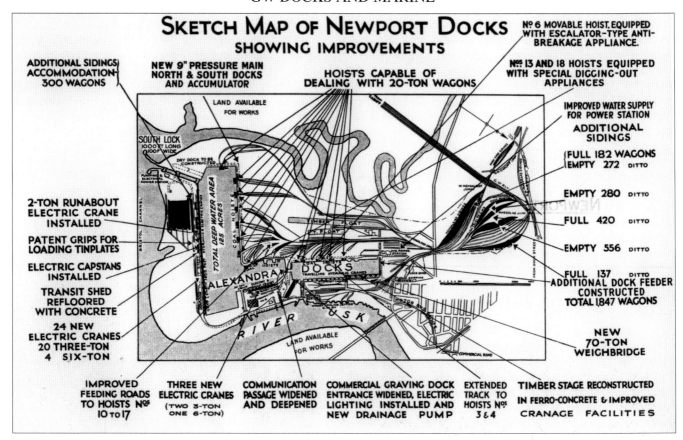

coal, artificial manure and heavy engineering plant being exported.

Before all this, however, it was clear that something new had to be done about dock accommodation and the new Alexandra (Newport) Dock Co was formed in 1865 to build a large new dock (the first Alexandra dock, later known as the North Dock) some 3½ miles downstream from the Town Dock. Hampered by financial difficulties, it did not open until 1875. It was a great leap forward, having 29 acres of 30 ft-deep water, with 1½ miles of quays and ¼ acre of sheds. The dock company built railways from the dock to join up with the GW, the (then separate) Monmouthshire Rly, the B&M and the LNWR, all of whom were granted running powers. Once the new dock opened, each succeeding week saw shipping records broken. In 1877, 4189 ships carrying 698,233 tons of goods arrived at the port and 9133 ships sailed with 1,110,046 tons of export cargo. Imports were some 343,000 tons of iron ore; 82,000 loads of timber; 49,000 loads of pitwood; 15,200 tons of flour and grain; and 9000 tons of potatoes. Exports were 611,000 tons of coal to foreign ports and 823,000 tons coastwise; and 99,000 tons of iron. In 1880, pressure of business made the Alexandra Dock Co erect coal tips on the river bank and to construct the Alexandra Wharf. The transition from sail to steam was proceeding rapidly and iron ore was arriving in steamers of the largest tonnage. The day of the up-river port, such as the Newport Town Dock, was already declining and future docks had to adjoin deep water channels.

Before the Grouping in 1922, the GW's only presence at Newport was Gloucester Wharf at which there was a 20 ton wagon weighbridge listed in a GW pamphlet 1911 (the same document said that there were two at Pill Bank, each of 60 tons capacity). The GW installed new capstans and reels at the wharf in 1914.

The Alexandra Dock company changed its name to 'The Alexandra (Newport and South Wales) Docks and Railway Company' (known as the ADR) in 1882 and immediately after, in 1883, it bought the Town Dock. The immediate cause of the sale was that the Town dock company's fortunes had taken a knock in 1882 after a bizarre accident in its lock: two ships were being passed through but managed to get jammed in the lock entrance. They could not be separated, and since the lock gates could not be closed, the water ran out of the dock with the tide, leaving the ships stuck in the air preventing other vessels from entering and leaving.

Between 1884 and 1890 the trade through Newport increased by a third, and various firms established themselves on the dock estate manufacturing anchors, chains and other ironfounding, and even building ships (eg by the Orb steelworks in 1888). Construction of the first part of another new dock (the Alexandra South Dock) had started in 1882 and opened in 1892. It was a 20 acre extension of the Alexandra North Dock with a 57 ft junction channel between, with a new and larger lock entrance from the river. The entrance, later called the East lock, was 503 ft long by 72 ft wide, and had a hydraulic roller bridge over which ran a roadway and two lines of railway. The East lock had a 35/25 ft depth of water at spring/neap tides.

Armstrong Whitworth coal hoists of 20 ton capacity were installed in 1895 having a height of lift of 40 ft. In 1907 the South Dock was further enlarged, and enlarged yet again in 1914, the two additions giving a total water acreage of 95 acres. Three weeks before the outbreak of war in 1914, a new sea lock entrance was opened which, at 1,000 ft long by 100 ft wide, was the largest lock entrance in the world. It had 45/35 ft of water at spring/neap tides and was divided into two compartments, the one closer to the sea being 400 ft long and the other 600 ft. Of course the whole 1000 ft length could be employed when required, but less water was lost on locking when it was possible to use the smaller part only. A disaster occurred during its construction in 1909, when a trench collapsed killing 38 men. After the opening of the big South Lock, the lock of the original Alexandra North dock was converted into a dry dock by installing a concrete dam at its river end; the East and South locks remained. Later, in 1937, the East lock of the South Dock was closed permanently as trade had fallen so much and fewer ships were passing in and out.

The continuous total water area of the North and South Alexandra Docks became about 125 acres, with water depth some 33 ft. The up-river 12 acre Town Dock was additional but as the years went by it was used only by small vessels engaged in coastal shipping, and by steam trawlers (a fish market was opened at Town dock after WWI). The Town Dock was closed by the GWR in 1929, at which time the two remaining coal hoists were removed and taken by floating crane to be erected in the South Dock. The Town dock was later filled in. There were five dry docks in total at Newport of which one (the Commercial Graving Dock Co) was railway-owned. Overall there were some five miles of quays in the dock estate, with 36 acres of quay space and 5 acres of sheds; there was a 14-acre timber float. The equipment of the docks in the shape of coal tipping appliances, and facilities for loading and discharging general cargoes, kept pace with the extensions of the deep-water area. General import and export cargo was discharged and loaded by hydraulic cranes before WWI, of which there was a range from 3 to 30 tons capacity. There were about 100 miles of railway sidings provided at the docks for storage of coal and other traffic awaiting shipment. Passenger landing stages were also provided for pleasure steamers.

The Monmouthshire section of the South Wales coalfield was Newport's hinterland, and before the Grouping coal from the Eastern and Western valleys was brought to Newport by the GWR, B&M, and LNWR. The Eastern Valley ran to Pontypool and Blaenavon; the Western to Risca and Ebbw Vale. With the increasing inability of Cardiff Docks to cope with all the export coal traffic in the mid-late C19th, a route for Glamorgan coal to Newport was effected by the opening of the Pontypridd, Caerphilly and Newport Railway in 1884 (which involved running powers over the lines of five other companies, see the Introductory Volume of *GW Goods Services*). The ADR purchased the line in 1897. The direct service from all sections of the South Wales coalfield allowed mixing of different coals at Newport on shipment.

NEWPORT.

The facilities afforded to Newport by the various lines of the G.W.R. which converge there have led to a remarkable development of its natural advantages as a port for the Midlands and the Coalfields, and Ironfields of Monmouthshire and North Glamorganshire.

The River Usk is lined with extensive Wharves and Docks which, by means of the Great Western Railway, are connected by rail with all the leading railways of Great Britain.

The Company's Stations and Depôts are :—

HIGH STREET ... For General Goods, Furniture Vans, and Live Stock.

DOCK STREET ... For all descriptions of traffic (except Coal).

MILL STREET ... For Coal, Minerals, and other Station to Station traffic.

LLISWERRY ... For Coal, Minerals, and other heavy traffic for the Districts of Cross Hands and Lliswerry.

The Company's teams collect and deliver merchandise in all parts of the town and Docks, and traffic charged at the ordinary C. & D. rates is collected and delivered from or to ships in the Docks free of charge.

Ocean Liners for India, China, South Africa, and South America call regularly at the **ALEXANDRA DOCKS**, and the largest vessel can enter and leave the Docks in safety in all weathers.

The facilities for weighing and shipping Coal, etc., are of the most up-to-date character.

The construction by the Great Western Railway Company of a branch railway on the East side of the Usk to the mouth of the river has been the means of opening up a District hitherto practically undeveloped, and rendering it eminently suitable for industrial purposes, accessible by rail and water, near to Coalfields, and having a good supply of water. **Manufacturers in search of eligible sites for building new works will find the conditions here very suitable.** Some very large concerns have already taken advantage of the facilities afforded.

In 1875, when the first portion of the Alexandra Dock was opened, the coal shipments amounted to 394,000 tons, while the total imports and exports amounted to 565,000 tons. By 1894, when the first extension of the Alexandra Docks was opened, the coal shipments had increased to 3,620,000 tons annually, and the total imports and exports to 4,120,000 tons. Between 1901 and 1906 a levy of 1/- per ton was charged by the government on export coal to pay for the Boer War. This affected business at all coal exporting ports. Small coal was, however, duty free and Newport exported a great tonnage to France and Italy where briquettes were manufactured for railway use.

By 1913, exports amounted to 4,600,000 tons of coal to foreign parts with 725,000 tons coastwise; 200,000 tons of iron; 14,000 tons of coke; and 147,000 tons of coal briquettes. Coal imports and exports were 7,130,000 tons. There was in addition 2 million tons of general cargo in 1914. The registered tonnage of the vessels using the docks in 1913 amounted to 3,130,000 tons, as against 1,875,679 in 1894, and 296,927 in 1875. These figures were surpassed only in the short-lived boom period following WWI, the highest being in 1923, viz: imports: 875,000 tons; exports:

Wagon weighbridge at Gloucester Wharf, Newport, in 1919. Gloucester Wharf was the only GW riverside presence in Newport until the Grouping. First 2-plank wagon is Furness Rly; next is a 4-planker labelled 'CR'; third is a L&Y 2-planker. Wagons are being moved up to the weighbridge (out of the page) by a rope attached to the axleguard the L&Y wagon, taken round the capstan in the foreground (being used as a reel) and back to the operated capstan in the middle distance. Wagon turntables and rail steam crane in distance. [GWR]

6,800,000 tons of coal and coke, and 314,000 tons of 'other'.

Throughout WWI export coal traffic was maintained both for the Admiralty and for the French government. General cargo traffic decreased however (as at many other ports) but its place was taken by the import and export of hundreds of thousands of tons of war materials and tens of thousands of tons of foodstuffs, including one or two exceptionally large consignments (eg over 43,000 barrels of grapes). Before WWI little or no foodstuffs had been handled at Newport. The government built at Cardiff, Swansea and Barry, as well as at Newport, large new sheds to deal with this sort of traffic and later these were taken over by the GW for use as transit sheds for general merchandise. Another government enterprise at Newport in WWI was the so-called Salvage Box Factory erected near the South Lock entrance for the reconditioning of brass shell cases brought back from the Western Front after firing. It occupied 13 acres and there was a regular line of ships bringing back used 4.5 inch howitzer and 18-pounder shells. Millions of reconditioned shells were sent off to filling

factories. At one time 5,000 women were employed at the factory. After the war, it was converted into a refrigerated cold store and ice-making factory.

During WWI Newport docks took on extra tasks. The *Belgia* of the German Hamburg-Amerika Line had left the USA in a hurry but had not managed to reach her home port before the outbreak of war on 4 August 1914, so she came up the Bristol Channel and virtually offered herself as a prize. She was the first German ship to be captured in WWI and was taken into Newport Docks through the new lock entrance and her valuable cargo moved into government warehouses. Other captured cargoes were taken to Newport, one comprising complete trains of Turkish locos and passenger carriages, and large quantities of medical stores and officers kits (relics from the Turkish retreat from Serbia). Belgian steamers unable to return home after Antwerp fell into German hands were laid up in the North Dock. Some passenger and mail traffic came to Newport when ships' home ports were congested. In 1915 the Cunard *Ascania* docked at Newport as her home port was being employed for troop movements. Special trains from

North dock Newport in 1927, with ex-ADR 0-6-0ST loco No 3 (Robert Stephenson, 1900) now GW No 676, alongside small fixed-jib hydraulic crane. Wagons belong to the Tredegar Company. [GWR]

Paddington ran alongside the vessel to take the 600 passengers. The large new entrance lock enabled big liners of the Cunard, Union Castle, Royal Mail, Leyland, P & O and Pacific Steam companies to use Newport (some had been converted to auxiliary cruisers or hospital ships).

Three tugs (*Horace* and *Wolfhound* both dating from 1904 and *Lady Tredegar* from 1913) were inherited from the ADR by the GW at the Grouping, along with *Bruce*, a 141-ton bucket hopper dredger of 1905 and three old hopper barges. After the GWR took over, it added to the accommodation and machinery at Newport docks, and brought old equipment up to date. A dumb bucket dredger *Foremost IV* with two hoppers was built in 1928 for use at Newport. One of the hoppers, *Foremost 45*, struck a mine in 1941 and sank off Newport. She was replaced by the *Francis Gilbertson* a 275-ton grab dredger which had been built in 1928 and which had served where required in the Bristol Channel. *Foremost 27* of 1925 was 512-ton self-propelled hopper barge.

By the 1930's Newport was listed as having seven transit sheds round the South dock, having a total floor area of 709,000 sq ft. In addition to the usual sort of general cargo at Newport between the wars, specialist goods comprised iron ore, timber and steel bars (imports) and steel rails, steel sleepers, carriage and wagon work, galvanised iron and tinplate. A great number of out-of-gauge loads for export were shipped through Newport, such as from the Birmingham Carriage & Wagon Co. The general cargo quays might handle up to 40,000 tons of cargo per week, shipped and discharged. The record for a day's working was over 9,000 tons. The Arrow Fuel Works manufactured patent fuel briquettes on the dock estate between the wars. In 1931 a belt coal conveyor, similar to those at Port Talbot, was installed at Newport. In 1932, the South Dock had 11 coal hoists with lifts up to 75 ft, eight of which could deal with Pole 20-ton mineral wagons (two of the older hoists had been removed by 1936 to leave 9 in total); cranes had lifting capacity from 3 to 10 tons, of which 11 were hydraulic and 27 electric (up to 6 tons); and one 30 ton hydraulic crane. The North Dock had nine coal hoists in 1932 lifting to 60 ft, five of which could deal with 20-ton

wagons (three older hoists had been removed by 1936 to leave 6 in total). Eighteen cranes (all hydraulic, none electric) were situated on the general cargo quays of the North dock and in addition 9 steam cranes (up to 10 tons capacity) were available over the whole dock estate. At the 300ft long Riverside Jetty, where the water depth was 25/15 ft (spring/neap tides), there were two coal hoists (lifting to 25 ft); on the 403 ft long Riverside Wharf (30/20 ft depth of water) there were 4 hydraulic cranes (2 tons capacity).

CARDIFF (owned; formerly Bute Trustees; then Cardiff Rly)

Cardiff between 1870 and 1914 was a boom town: the village of less than 2000 inhabitants in 1801 had a population of 10,000 in 1841; had burgeoned into a city of 130,000 in 1893; and 200,000 just before WWI. It had become the biggest town in Wales in 1881, outpopulating Merthyr, Newport and Swansea. Right through to WWI, the Bristol Channel teemed with ships bound for the customs port of Cardiff (which included Penarth and Barry after they opened). Cardiff increased its trade through the docks 20-fold in less than 50 years. Although the UK's third largest port in terms of water area, Cardiff came top of the league of all UK ports in terms of volume and tonnage of export trade. The coal exported exceeded the total of all the Tynside ports, so 'carrying coals to Newcastle' is nonsense. In its first complete year of operation (1840), the coal and coke traffic from the first Bute (West) Dock amounted to 43,651 tons; iron and steel to 1,916 tons; and general merchandise to 24 tons. By 1880, the annual import trade of the docks had reached about 1 million tons, and in 1907 had more than doubled to 2,161,818 tons. Including exports as well, Cardiff docks in 1905 handled a total of 10,189,831 tons.

There were fortunes to be made by operating steam colliers. From about 1860 there was a great increase in shipowning: iron vessels and steamers were purchased in great numbers by ambitious businessmen. Only a few of the old Cardiff shipowners made the change from sail to steam and from wooden to iron vessels. Shipowning in the port was soon in the hands of immigrant capitalists: the Gueret

Cargo of old locos from the Gold Coast Rly being unloaded for scrap from SS Beldis at Newport in May 1934. C22 Crocodile G wagon no 41953 of 1921 was later sold to the Admiralty in 1940 as gun carriage, but was returned to the GWR in 1943. [STEAM Swindon]

70-ton weighbridge at Newport in 1927. J21 Macaw B no 107027 built in 1924 has a load of I-beams. At the extreme right is GW ventilated vac-fitted Mink A van No 85487 built about 1910 The wagon in front of the crane in the right background between the shed and the Mink van is still labelled 'Alexandra Docks & Railway Newport'. [GWR]

Non-luffing 30-ton hydraulic crane located at the end of the East Wharf, South Alexandra dock Newport, near the inner gates of the East lock. Picture taken in June 1927 showing a large flywheel in course of being loaded on to timber packing already in place a GW Crocodile H trolley wagon [GWR].

family from France; the Cory, Gibbs, Tatem, and Reardon-Smith families from the West of England; and the Morel and Hacquoil brothers from Jersey. One of the largest and most prosperous ship owners was Evan Thomas of Aberporth who went into partnership with Henry Radcliffe of Merthyr. The Evan Thomas Radcliffe ships were all tramp steamers, not plying fixed routes, but sailing wherever charterers wanted. Cardiff tramp steamers took coal to coaling stations all over world for naval and merchant shipping, and returned with general cargo.

But it was the growth of the *iron* (not coal) industry in Cardiff's hinterland that had been the main stimulus to the development of the port, ironmasters building the 25-mile long Glamorganshire Canal down from Merthyr in 1794. The canal was connected by horse-drawn tramroads to the Penydarren, Dowlais, Cyfarthfa and Plymouth (Duffryn) ironworks: in 1804 it was on such a tramroad between Merthyr and Abercynon that Richard Trevithick's steam loco was the first ever to haul a load on rails. In 1798 the canal was extended at the Cardiff end to a basin equipped with a sea lock that was the first, rudimentary, wet dock in Wales. A great deal of iron was sent to Bristol or Liverpool for transhipment to the USA and other remote places. However, the channel to the open sea was shallow and the dock narrow, so only small vessels could be dealt with, larger vessels having to be loaded in the roadstead from 20-ton canal barges. Even so, trade flourished and by 1830 some 200,000 tons were being conveyed, despite the canal lock and basin being too far from deep water. Improvements to the canal lock and basin could only be made by purchasing adjacent land from the

2nd Marquess of Bute. Since he had his own plans to create a dock at Cardiff to get a slice of the action, he would not sell.

The second Lord Bute was the fourth-richest man in Britain at the time and owned much of the land at Cardiff through marriage. He personally financed the first dock (what was later called the Bute West Dock) that opened in 1839. It was designed by Robert Stephenson and had an area of nearly 20 acres, was between 13-19ft deep with a 152ft long x 36ft wide lock connected to a 1½ acre tidal basin having a 45 ft wide entrance. To enable traffic brought down by canal to be shipped from the dock (and vice versa), a junction canal was dug from the canal basin to join the new dock at its northern (town) end.

Meanwhile in 1836, since the Glamorganshire Canal was inadequate and could not be improved, the

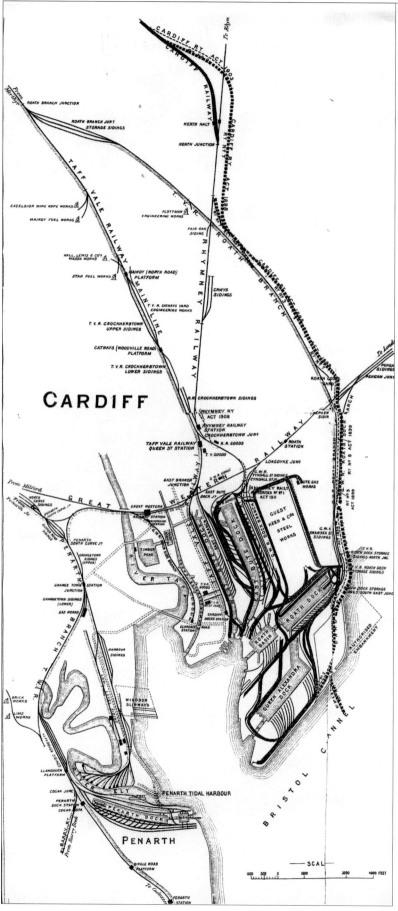

Merthyr ironmasters had promoted the Taff Vale Rly. Brunel, in his 1835 survey, indicated that the foremost object of the proposed TVR was the conveyance of iron. Coal, used for smelting, was ancillary to the iron industry and apart from collieries owned by ironfounders near their works, there were at that time very few other mines from which coal was extracted for general sale. (Indeed many parts of South Wales, including most of the Aberdare and Rhondda valleys, had yet to be prospected for coal). To transport 'sale-coal', a few tramways were built to connect isolated pits with the Glamorganshire Canal.

Authority was obtained to construct the railway from Merthyr Tydfil to Cardiff, with a branch to Cogan Pill, on the river Ely, the site of the later Penarth Tidal Basin and Dock. After the opening of the TVR, the tramways connecting the few mines to the canal made easy connexions with the railway. The coal industry eventually surpassed the iron trade after about 1850, and TVR branches were extended further up the Aberdare and Rhondda valleys to enable new collieries to be opened, after which the tramways became redundant.

The construction of the Bute dock and of the TVR mainline to Cardiff proceeded simultaneously, and the railway line between Cardiff and Merthyr was opened in 1841. Materials for the construction of both the Bute dock and the TVR were landed at the 'Little Dock' which led off the Glamorganshire Canal basin in Cardiff and was on Bute land. Opened in 1836, and operated by the TVR, this half-acre dock connected to the TVR terminus by wagon turntables with horse haulage across Bute St. The TVR built its West Yard workshops alongside the Little Dock. In addition to construction materials, iron ore from Cornwall, tin for the Melingriffith works, and ordinary market goods began to be landed as well. The TVR began to ship coal from its Little Dock (originally loaded by hand, later with appliances) and also from the west side of the first Bute dock where in 1842 it installed a hydraulic wagon hoist designed by Robert Stephenson; two more were built the following year, by Bute himself and by Thomas Powell a coal owner. Despite these activities, it was not intended that the Bute dock in Cardiff should be the principal port for shipping iron and coal brought down the valley from Merthyr. The intention of the TVR was still to extend its line to a new dock of its own at Cogan Pill.

That branch was not constructed, however, because in 1846 an arrangement was made with Lord Bute, whereby the TVR agreed

Arrival of one of the special passenger trains at the Queen Alexandra dock in connexion a sailing in June 1929. Bogie Siphon used for baggage. [GWR]

to abandon the branch altogether in exchange for access to the Bute dock at Cardiff. To 'obtain access', the TVR undertook (i) to construct a branch line to the new dock from just south of its Queen St station from the line down to its dock terminus (later called Bute Street) near the Pier Head; (ii) to take a lease, at a heavy rental, of a large part of the east side of the dock; (iii) to construct and maintain coal shipping appliances there; (iv) to abandon their own powers to construct a line to Cogan Pill; and (v) to 'cause and procure' that all shipment traffic carried over their railway be 'shipped or unshipped' at Lord Bute's dock or, in default, to pay the dues as if such traffic had actually used the dock. This was a strange, one-sided, arrangement with all the benefits on the Bute side: probably the TVR thought it was securing the exclusive right to ship coal at Cardiff. Little did the TVR realise that the 1846 agreement would cause trouble when it began to ship coal from the new Penarth Dock (see Penarth).

The 2nd Marquess of Bute died in 1848 and since his heir was only one year old, his affairs had to be run by trustees. In 1859 they completed a second dock at Cardiff --- the Bute East dock ---which had a water area of about 46 acres, with a 25 ft deep, 200 ft by 36 ft (later 49 ft) lock leading to a 2½ acre tidal basin with a 220 ft long entrance (whose width later became 55 ft). The Bute East dock ran parallel to the West dock (and was joined to it by an

extension of the junction canal) and both were parallel to the TVR line to its dock terminus. The new dock was fully provided with railway lines and coal shipment appliances. Much to the TVR's surprise, the Bute trustees gave unrestricted access to the Rhymney Rly but *not* to the Taff. (The RR had been promoted indirectly by Lord Bute to exploit pits on his lands to the northeast of Cardiff. The TVR had opposed the RR's first attempt to get its own direct line to Cardiff from Caerphilly, so the Bute/RR interests were perhaps getting their own back). The RR had four appliances on the east side of the East dock and the Taff had three on the west side. The Bute trustees obliged the TVR to pay a toll for every ton of coal it conveyed to its three appliances. After arbitration, the TVR got independent access to the dock in 1866. Nevertheless, as explained under Penarth, the situation was unsatisfactory and made worse by the inability of the two Bute docks to cope with the massive increase in shipment coal traffic. This led to the construction of the Penarth Tidal Harbour and Dock (opened in 1859 and 1865 respectively), which was reached by a new railway coming in westwards from the TVR main line at Radyr.

The SWR built a branch from its mainline at Long Dyke Jct to the east side of the East dock in 1859, and rented two coal tips near the basin.

The TVR opened a branch from Abercynon to

Above - Shipment coal storage sidings at Tremorfa, reached from the GW mainline at Long Dyke Jct, serving the Bute Roath dock. Owing to the narrowness of the South Wales valleys, these sorts of sidings were sited near the entrances to the various dock lines Various private-owner single-end-tip wagons belonging to Nixon's Navigation, David Bevan & Co, D Davis &Sons Ltd, Bwllfa. Tip ends are facing to the left, so this 1927 photograph was taken looking away from the docks.

Right - Landing cattle from South Africa at the Bute Roath dock cattle lairs in 1920's.

Above - *Pitprops being unloaded by crane at the Queen Alexandra dock before WWI. Loaded wagon on railway line between tracks of portal crane. Dumb-buffered 'CB' Cory Bros end-tipping coal wagons on right. Funnel of vessel on left being painted by man up ladder. [A G Atkins collection]*

Opposite bottom *- Meat from GW Mica vans being put into a new cold stores at Cardiff in November 1941. [GWR]*

Aberdare in 1845 to open up new coalfields. In 1855 the first train of steam coal from the Rhonnda Valley ran down to Cardiff. The quality of steam coal from the Rhondda was superb and was in demand by navies all over the world. New collieries were continually opening, so that by the late C19[th] the TVR alone was connected to over 80 mines, and the 9 million tons of coal carried by the TVR in 1885 had grown to 19 million tons by 1914. Long before that, however, there were continual arguments between the coalowners, the railways and the Bute Trustees over dock accommodation and dock charges. The Trustees argued that dock revenue did not earn enough to pay off the cost of building the two original docks, which were already becoming obsolescent, so that there was no money to invest in the new docks that were clearly required. Various promises were made by the Trustees after 1866 to construct a new big dock (the later Roath dock) but little was done, apart from a reluctant building in 1874 of the 12 acre Roath basin (originally tidal) parallel to the foreshore and thus perpendicular to the Bute West and East docks, and the erection of some coal staiths on the east bank of the River Taff for colliers that could safely lie aground at low water. By then Penarth was working at full tilt and was enlarged a little in 1884, but the volume of shipment coal traffic coming down to Cardiff was growing so rapidly that all the existing docks were just incapable of dealing with it. Frustration with the Bute docks and its commercial outlook led to the promotion of both the Barry Dock and Railway and also the Rhondda & Swansea Bay Rly (this line would take coal westwards for shipping at Briton Ferry and Swansea, away from the Cardiff area altogether). The threat of new railways had been in the air for some years and eventually W.T.Lewis, the Bute dock manager, got on with the building of the long-promised Roath Dock that was eventually opened in 1887. That same year the Bute Docks Co was formed: the enterprise had become too big for the Bute Trustees to take sole responsibility. The new dock led off the Roath basin through a set of locks and had a water area of 33 acres. The entrance lock was 600 ft long by 80 ft wide, with a 36/26 ft spring/neap tides water depth at the outer cill; the lock to the Roath basin became 350 ft long by 80 ft wide. The Lewis-Hunter coaling crane, intended to reduce lump breakage, was devised for the new Roath Dock; Hunter was the dock engineer. The 1882 Parliamentary bill for the building of the Roath dock had said that shipping rates for coal at all the Cardiff docks would be increased by 1d/ton and this was "the straw that broke the camel's back" as far as David Davies of the Ocean Collieries was

concerned, and led to his promoting the Barry Dock & Rly in 1883.

The year 1882 saw the building by the GWR of the Riverside goods branch from near its main line passenger station to Clarence Road on the west of the commercial area of Cardiff docks. In 1894 the branch was upgraded to carry passengers as well, and both TVR and BR trains ran over it. The branch served wharves and industries on the west side of the Glamorganshire Canal. Previously the canal company had its own standard gauge tramroad serving the wharves and much of this remained in operation even though the new branch took in a part of the tramroad. The branch also served old coal staithes on the River Taff and timber ponds linked to both the river and the canal.

Numerous firms were rail-connected from the branch at various times, such as timber and builders merchants; an ice factory; wagon repairers, foundries and so on. Firms came and went, the firm of Edward Curran expanding into a giant complex of factories for hollow ware in the 1930's; in WWII munitions were manufactured on the site.

As the C19[th] closed, all traffic at Cardiff, and particularly coal, continued to increase and the need arose for yet more dock area. This led to the opening in 1907 of the South (Queen Alexandra) dock, parallel to the Roath dock, on reclaimed foreshore. Its water area was 52 acres, 37 ft deep, with an 850 ft long by 90 ft wide lock having a 40/30 ft spring/neap tides water depth at the outer cill. The water area of the QA dock formed nearly one-third of the whole of the Bute Docks. As at the Roath dock, there were coal appliances (including Lewis-Hunter coaling cranes) on the south side of the new dock and general cargo quays on the north. Lock sizes on the newer docks were progressively larger to cater for the ever-increasing size of steamships. There were intercommunication channels between the QA, Roath and Bute East docks by which ships could pass from one dock to the other without having to go out into the tideway.

There was a regular pattern of trade routes by the colliers: outward cargoes of coal destined for Mediterranean railways, or to bunkering ports in the region, would unload in Italy or Egypt, say, then proceed in ballast to load Black Sea grain as return cargo; alternatively typical return cargoes for ships having taken coal to Spain would be iron ore or pyrites, some from North Africa. Ships also sailed to South America with coal, and with rails from the South Wales ironfounders, to supply the expanding British-built railway systems, again returning with grain. Vessels after being unloaded at one side of a Cardiff dock would be

Opposite top - A heavy casting at the Bute docks in 1913, carried on the unique GWR Totem A roll wagon No 41910 (B2 in the diagram index and rated at 45 tons) dating from 1899. The depth of the I-beams forming the underframe is 1ft 4 ins as can be seen from the space above the coupling hook where '41910' is painted. Side stanchions have been removed as the casting forms an over-wide load. Capstan with foot pedal control in left foreground, reels behind. Stacked pitprops on quay at left. [D J Hyde]

Opposite bottom - Boxes of Canadian salmon being unloaded by crane into GW FX refrigerated containers. The method of lowering cargo first on to flat wagons then swinging across into vans was often used at docks across the system. Cardiff, October 1934. [GWR]

Canadian pine being craned ashore at the Queen Alexandra dock in October 1935. Shorter planks go into open wagons; longer on to bolster wagons. [GWR]

warped across to the other side and in a few hours loaded with coal. In this way, in addition to coal, there was considerable traffic in other goods at the Bute docks.

Warehousing had been provided from the early days, and on the north side of the Queen Alexandra dock and at the Roath dock, there were extensive transit sheds and cold stores. Imports of tea, fruit, dried fruit, groceries and so on, together with live cattle and frozen meat were not restricted to the needs of the immediate neighbourhood of Cardiff, much of it being forwarded by train to destinations such as Birmingham for distribution in the Midlands. (There were 8 million people living within 90 miles of Cardiff before WWI).

Spillers had established in 1854 a steam-driven flourmill (the Atlantic Building between the top ends of the West and East docks) where the grain trade came to be centred for many years. The flourmill was extended but, as ships became yet larger, a new mill with tall concrete silos (served by suction elevators to the ships) was erected in 1936 at the east end of the Roath Dock. It had the capacity to produce 13,000 sacks flour/week as well as manufacture ships biscuits and animal feed. The grain suction elevator bought by the GW after the grouping helped reduce the amount of grain barged from quay to mill. Still on the food side, Messrs Neale & West had established in the 1880's a commercial fishing fleet in the Bute West dock with an ice factory alongside. In the 1930's, about 6,000 tons of fish were being landed annually, much of which was taken off by GW train.

The enormous coalfields of Glamorganshire and Monmouthshire required vast quantities of mining timber (pitwood), pit-props, and sleepers. Sometimes, pitwood was loaded direct into railway wagons for its journey to the collieries but fluctuating trade conditions made stacking of pitwood a necessity, and there was extensive storage ground for both pitprops and pitwood at the docks and nearby. Import of French pitwood was very big business at the Bute docks (500,000 tons per annum in the years leading up to WWI). During 1922, over a million tons of pitwood and

mining timber were imported, a figure which nearly matched the pre-WWI tonnage. One of the largest single cargoes of mining timber brought to Cardiff was 8,500 tons in 1937 from Newfoundland. An extensive trade was also carried on by general timber merchants who had sawmills on the dock premises (Cardiff was the second most important timber-importing docks in the UK).

Cardiff was the only Welsh port licensed to import cattle from overseas (see Birkenhead for the background to licensing). In 1891, 1,600 head of cattle were imported from Chicago. Live and slaughtered cattle were distributed to Wales, the Midlands, London and other parts of the country. Lairage was situated on the north side of the Inner Lock between the Roath basin and Roath dock proper. There was accommodation for 500 fat cattle (ie those ready for slaughter directly on being landed) and nearly 1,000 head of store cattle (ie those to be put out to graze around Britain to fatten up before slaughtering). Facilities were available for weighing live cattle on the hoof, along with an auction ring. After selling, store cattle were loaded directly into Mex cattle trucks and sent off. Adjoining the lairs were abattoirs for fat cattle. Chill rooms (capable of storing 10,000 tons of meat) formed part of the accommodation, and carcases could be transported by overhead rail conveyors to the chill rooms or to railway refrigerated wagons (Mica vans). Cold storage was also provided later at the Roath dock jetty warehouse where there were three large floors for the storage of frozen mutton.

After the Grouping, the GWR made special efforts to encourage cattle breeders in Canada, and buyers in Britain, to use Cardiff docks. The first shipment arrived in July 1922 and in the following 12 months 1,530 head of cattle were dealt with. Farmers and dealers from all over the country purchased the beasts upon arrival at Cardiff, and special trains were run direct to all parts. For example, in October 1923, 150 head of cattle were loaded for delivery to farms in Norfolk, and left Cardiff by special overnight through train. Rhodesian cattle began to be imported through Cardiff in 1931. The 3.50 pm Cardiff-Hanwell

Bridge Sidings 'C' headcode goods was nicknamed 'The Stock'. Cattle were exported also for breeding purposes.

Near the docks at the end of Bute St in Cardiff were the Coal Exchange, Shipping Offices and all the rest of the commercial resource necessary to keep trade going. Nearly all the coal mined in S Wales was sold on the Cardiff Coal Exchange, even when not exported through the Bute docks. The success of coal factors in winning orders was reported in the press, e.g. the *Railway Magazine* of 1905 stated that a Cardiff firm had secured, for the third year running, the locomotive coal contract from the GSWR of Ireland, which involved the supply of 120,000 tons of large Monmouthshire coals at a price of 11s per ton 'free on board', delivery to extend over 12 months. The Italian State railways had an office in Cardiff whose job it was to purchase locomotive coal, and colliers belonging to the French Paris, Lyon & Mediterranée Rly (PLM) were regularly to be seen loading in the docks.

On the dock estate, in addition to the large flour mills, there were many industries and factories including copper works, wagon-building and repairing shops, foundries, paint works, biscuit factories, and various workshops. A wire rope factory began manufacture on the dock estate as early as 1857, followed by two more at the end of the C19th. Demand came from the mines as well as ships. In addition to the usual 'patent fuel' briquette factories (such as the Crown Preserved Fuel Works at the entrance to the Roath dock), one of the most important industries was the integrated iron and steel works established in 1891 on a 100-acre site within the docks at East Moors. The demand for steel in tonnage quantities could be satisfied after Bessemer and Siemens-Martens introduced their processes in the 1850's after which the demand for iron fell off. The Cardiff steelworks was built to replace the inland iron works around Merthyr which were suffering the handicap of having to transport imported ore the 30 miles up to Merthyr and a similar journey in reverse for finished products. (Merthyr, with the greatest concentration of ironworks in the world at the turn of the C18th/19th, once had a population greater than Cardiff, Newport and Swansea combined). When iron companies found that they could not compete with the new steel companies, they turned to exploiting coal seams on their lands: hence the many PO coal wagons with iron companies' names. The East Moors works were known as 'the Dowlais' (named after the original Dowlais Works near Merthyr from where workmen travelled to Cardiff even up to WWII). Ore and other traffic for these works were dealt with through the Roath Dock, from where finished products such as steel rails and sleepers were exported. Also on the docks estate was the Bute Works Supply Co that dealt in second-hand railway equipment. It was from this company that the Cambrian Rlys purchased two ex-GW 2-4-0's (Nos 212 and 213) as stop-gap replacements for the locos destroyed in the Abermule single-line collision of 1921. The GW bought 140 12-ton wooden coal wagons in 1907 from the same firm; they were later used as loco coal wagons and indexed as N33 in the Wagon Diagram Book (see *GWR Goods Wagons*).

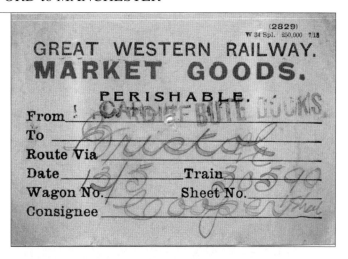

Pre-Grouping Railway lines into the Bute Docks

As explained in an article in the Railway Magazine, after the completion of the Queen Alexandra dock in 1907, there were some 120 miles of railway line within the one-mile square Bute docks estate, at which time the Cardiff Railway had 29 locos. The first engine shed dating from 1861 was at Bute Yard (Tyndall St) between the East and West docks; in 1881 a new loco depot was opened on the other side of the dock at East Moors (closed 1926). The Cardiff Railway's locomotives dealt with all general goods traffic handed to them at the various junctions for delivery alongside vessels, or distribution to the steel works and other industries located upon the dock premises.

Before the Grouping, the railways having direct rail access to the Cardiff docks were the GWR, TVR, and the Rhymney. In addition, the LNWR gained access via running powers over the RR; and the B&M, Midland, and ADR also gained access from Caerphilly, over other companies' lines. In addition to coal traffic, through goods rates were in operation to all parts of the country, and before 1922 there was rivalry between the different railways to take goods forward to the Midlands and the North of England by their own different routes.

The story of the connexions into the dock lines from the different companies, and the traffic exchanges between them before the Grouping, is fascinating.

TVR

The first railway to be connected was the TVR that approached Cardiff from the north west, the complete line to Merthyr being opened in 1841. Access to the west side of the first (Bute West) dock was obtained from the main TVR line running to its docks terminus. Near the passenger terminus was the TVR engine shed and works (until 1884 when Cathays shed was opened), and a goods yard and exchange sidings, from where most imported traffic was dispatched, not only around the Taff system but also elsewhere around the country. The 'East Branch', opened in 1848 from just south of Queen St station, accessed coal tips leased by the TVR on the east side of the first Bute dock. After the Bute East dock was opened in 1859, the East

Branch also connected with the west side of that new dock. At East Dock Junction, the TVR built extensive sidings that held some 800 wagons for the reception, sorting and dispatch of wagons returning after being tipped. At this point also most general goods for export from the TVR was delivered to the Cardiff Railway for conveyance to ships' sides.

For the opening of the Roath dock, the TVR constructed in 1888 a new line about 4½ miles long which left the TVR mainline at Roath Line Junction south of Llandaff station, and which skirted Cardiff on its east and south sides. The branch passed under the RR main line about a mile before the branch crossed over the GWR main line by a three-span bridge near the Taff's Roath goods depot, eventually to join the dock railway system by end-on connexions at the south and north ends of Splott Jct. At the Llandaff end of the branch there were sidings for some 2000 wagons; at Splott Jct the sidings could hold about 1300 wagons. The Roath branch was worked by the TVR on the time interval system. In the early years of the C20th, some 3 million tons of coal and goods annually found their way to the docks over this branch.

RR

The Rhymney Railway, as originally sanctioned in 1854, was a 9 mile line running south from the town of Rhymney (pronounced 'Rumney') to a junction with the Newport, Abergavenny and Hereford Rly. An extension through Caerphilly was authorised in 1855 to join the Taff Vale Railway at Walnut Tree Junction (Taffs Well) six miles north of Cardiff, beyond which the RR had running powers over the TVR as far as Crockherbtown Jct, just north of Queen St station in Cardiff, where the RR picked up its own line, 1¼ miles long, to the Bute East dock. (The TVR enjoyed reciprocal running powers to the East dock over this line). The original RR passenger and goods station in Cardiff was on this line at Adam St. The construction of the RR was strongly supported by the Bute Trustees as the RR could open up undeveloped coal fields to the north east of Cardiff and bring the coal to the new Bute East dock then being constructed. Furthermore, Pwllypant Quarry, owned by the Bute estate and about 10 miles north of Cardiff, was situated on the RR and many millions of tons of stone and ballast were carried over the line for reclaiming the foreshore and making the later Roath and Queen Alexandra docks. In 1871, the RR's own independent route into Cardiff from Caerphilly via Llanishen was opened. At this time it opened a new passenger station in Cardiff (Parade station), Adam St remaining as its goods depot. The RR also made a number of connexions with the GW that gave it running powers to Merthyr and Aberdare, all of which made the Rhymney a serious competitor with the Taff for bringing coal down to Cardiff for shipment.

South of Crockherbtown Junction and the Adam St goods depot, the RR passed over the GWR main line near the GW Newtown goods depot, by means of a viaduct of 11 spans, to reach Tyndall Street High Level Jct. Here the line divided to give RR traffic access to both sides of the Bute East Dock. On the east side, the main RR line descended at 1 in 147 down to the level of the East dock quays, where there were end-on junctions with the dock lines. On the west side the line continued at high level over the dock company's Bute Viaduct. On both sides of the railway, from the Adam St passenger station to the end of the line in the dock, there were sidings capable of accommodating over 500 wagons. At the dock terminus, the Rhymney's locomotive running sheds were situated (opened in 1857) with accommodation for 71 engines. The RR also had there a dock goods depot for the reception of general merchandise traffic, carted from business premises in the neighbourhood that were not directly connected by rail with the dock lines. Between 1868 and 1919, the RR also ran a line to a pier in the tideway near the entrance to the Roath Basin from which passenger steamers ran to Bristol.

LNWR

The LNWR reached Cardiff by running powers over the RR from Rhymney, granted in recognition of the financial help given by the LNWR for the construction of the Caerphilly Tunnel, opened in 1871, that gave the RR its direct route into Cardiff. In the same year, a single line joint connexion between Rhymney station and Nantybwch Junction on the Merthyr, Abergavenny and Tredegar section of the LNWR joined the two railways. Although the LNWR had to travel over 23½ miles of 'foreign' line to reach Cardiff, it recognised the importance of the place, by having its own three-storey goods depot (Tyndall St) within the dock area. It opened in 1875, and was situated at the head of the Bute East Dock, north of the feeders from the Glamorganshire canal. The 'isolated' half-mile long line to the depot ran from a trailing junction (for down trains) with the RR, a quarter of a mile north of the Rhymney's dock terminus. One LNW 0-6-2T engine was stationed at Cardiff for shunting at the depot. The LNWR acted as carting agent for the Rhymney Railway, for both goods and parcels traffic, at Cardiff, Caerphilly, and Rhymney. At the inaugural meeting of the Cardiff & District Railway Clerks Improvement Society in 1904, the LNWR goods agent, Mr C W Lodge, lectured on 'Canvassing'.

There were regular goods trains to and from Cardiff and the LNWR system (five down from Rhymney and six up), some calling at Energlyn Junction (for traffic to and from Barry Docks), and at Caerphilly (for Newport and the ADR reached by the B&M via Bassaleg). The destination of the up trains was Crewe, where the trains were re-marshalled and despatched to all parts of the northwest. Since the goods service was competitive with the GW, the LNW goods trains were classed 'express', carrying a white light at the foot of the chimney, and a green light on the left hand buffer. During the season there was a large import of new potatoes into Cardiff, and the LNWR obtained a good share of the traffic destined for Birmingham, the Midlands, Liverpool, Manchester, and other towns in the north. The LNWR had through passenger traffic from the Rhymney station in Cardiff, excursions being run as far as North Wales, Liverpool, Manchester and Blackpool. Since the

Rhymney Railway was a Westinghouse-braked system, special dual-fitted locos had to be provided.

GWR

The GWR, while having no docks in S E Wales before the Grouping, nevertheless carried an enormous amount of coal traffic for shipment at Cardiff, Penarth or Barry Docks as ordered by the coal factors. Whereas the TVR and RR carried coal from the valleys immediately to the north of Cardiff, the coal traffic over the GWR came from the collieries in the Eastern, Western and Sirhowy valleys centered on Newport, and the Llynvi, Ogmore and Garw valleys centred on Tondu. From 1858, the SWR leased two coal tips at the south end of the Bute East Dock that were reached by a 1¼-mile long branch to the West and East Bute docks from Long Dyke Junction on the main line on the east of Cardiff which joined the dock railway at Tyndall St Low Level Jct. Before the conversion of the gauge in 1872, coal from the Eastern and Western Valleys (on NG lines) had to be transhipped at Newport. In the early days, a great deal of coal was shipped from the GW tips at the East dock to the GW locomotive coking plant at Bristol; (the invention of the firebox brick arch in the 1860's made it possible to use coal instead of coke on locomotives thereafter). In 1874 the GW leased a third coal tip at the new Roath Basin reached by an extension of the line from Long Dyke. According to a 1911 GW circular on weighbridges across the system, there were two wagon weighbridges at No 1 coal tip; one at No 2; and two at No 3, all of 20 ton capacity. There was a very large tonnage of Newport coal brought to Cardiff, as it was much used for 'mixing' purposes, since Monmouthshire coal had a greater proportion of volatile matter that permits quick steam raising. After the conversion of the gauge, the GW tried to get as much traffic as possible for shipment at the three tips leased to it within the Bute docks, and a good deal of the coal shipped at them was brought down by the RR and TVR.

The GW had a second approach to the dock estate following the opening of its Roath Dock Branch in 1904. It left the main line further east at Pengam and was also 1¼-miles long, the middle ¼-mile being owned jointly with the dock railway. The new line was necessary as otherwise the GW had no direct access to the new Queen Alexandra dock.

GW traffic from the direction of Newport had a clear run over both GW branches into the Cardiff docks to the junctions with the Cardiff Rly, but coal from the west of Cardiff had to be run into the sidings at the junctions alongside the GW main line, and worked down by pilot engines attached at the other end of the trains. To marshal and shunt its immense traffic for the Bute docks, eight GW pilot engines were regularly employed round the clock before the Grouping, with another four engines during daytime, with yet more at busy periods.

Operations within dock lines

By means of statutory powers the Bute Trustees were able to compel all the railways bringing coal down for shipment to store the wagons of coal until required for shipping, to marshal them in the order required at the tips, and to shunt away the empty wagons after they were handed back by the dock railway engines. This accounts for the miles of different storage sidings provided by the pre-Grouping companies alongside their lines into Cardiff. Before the Grouping the GW alone had accommodation for some 6,000 wagons or about 13 miles of sidings. The Crockherbtown sidings of the TVR (between Cathays and Queen St station) could accommodate about 650 wagons, and the Cathays (Maindy Bridge) sidings even more. These sidings were used for the relief of the main lines should traffic be held up awaiting orders from ships in the docks, and for transferring the coal trains to the dock pilot engines.

Locomotives of the docks railway marshalled all traffic unloaded from vessels, and delivered it to the reception sidings of the 'foreign' railways for forwarding to destination. The dock railway owned 976 goods wagons; an inspection saloon was the only coach possessed originally by the Cardiff Railway. Imported goods consigned to places on other railways were loaded in the wagons of the 'foreign' railways, vehicles of the Cardiff Railway rarely leaving the dock estate. Reception sidings for imported traffic were as follows: traffic going on to the Taff Vale Railway (and Midland Railway via Taff Vale) was exchanged at East branch; and on to the Rhymney Railway at the Roath Basin interchange sidings. Great Western (and Midland Railway via GW) was exchanged at Tyndall Street Junction (Low Level); and traffic for the LNWR at its goods depot at Bute East dock.

For shipment coal traffic, incoming GW, TVR and RR locos took some of the trains right to the coal hoist reception sidings. At Tyndall Street (Low Level) and Roath Basin junctions, Cardiff Railway engines took charge of any traffic brought by the GW for both sides of the Bute East dock. The RR engines also hauled large quantities of iron ore (nearly 750,000 tons in 1907) for the original Dowlais Works near Merthyr some 25 miles north of Cardiff. The total tonnage of all descriptions of traffic carried over the Rhymney Railway in and out of Cardiff docks was about 3¼ millions per annum in the years before WWI.

The opening of the Barry Dock and Railway at the end of the C19[th] diverted a good deal of traffic from the Bute Docks, even though the BR did not really enter the coal field. The Bute company thought it could emulate the Barry undertaking, and construct its own railway to feed its docks. Indeed, the Glamorganshire canal had been bought by the Bute Trustees in 1885 with a view to converting it into a railway, but that never happened. Instead in 1896 a Parliamentary Bill was deposited seeking powers to construct five branch railways some 12 miles in extent, commencing with a junction with the RR at Llanishen, and terminating by a junction with the TVR near Pontypridd. The Bute docks railway became the Cardiff Railway Company in 1897, but the actual Bute docks port organisation (including ownership of tugs, dredgers etc) did not pass to the Cardiff Rly until 1919. Some of the new line was built and railmotors were run from Rhymney Parade station to Rhyd-y-felin (Treforest), but the connexion to the

TVR was prevented from opening by delays and blocking tactics by the TVR in 1916. The venture was a white elephant and after the Grouping was completely unnecessary as the lines no longer competed. Although the Cardiff Rly came into being in 1897, The Cardiff Rly was not as profitable as other South Wales coal railways. In 1921 when the Rhymney paid a dividend of 9% to ordinary shareholders, those of the Cardiff Rly received 1%. As a war measure, the overall management of the Cardiff Rly, the Rhymney and the Taff was combined under E.A.Prosser, the RR general manager from 1917.

After the Grouping

When the GWR took over Cardiff Docks, there was a total deep water area of 165 acres (including 17 acres of basins) and quayage of over 7 miles. Twenty-three acres of sheds were available for goods needing covered accommodation. There were 59 coal hoists and coaling cranes, comprising 28 fixed and 13 movable hoists (15 coal appliances in the Bute West dock and 19 in the East dock; and ten fixed and movable hoists in the Roath basin) and 19 Lewis-Hunter coaling cranes (11 at the Roath dock; 8 at the Queen Alexandra dock). The maximum gross capacity of each hoist was at that time 23 tons, meaning a wagon load of up to 15 tons of coal. The dock permanent way was in a bad state when the GW took possession, and the hydraulic power plant needed updating. There were 19 dry docks and slipways, but most were private, only two having been inherited from the Cardiff Rly. The original ship repairing yards were the privately-owned Mountstuart Dry Dock near the Pier Head, the Channel Dry Dock, a second Mountstuart Dry Dock and the Commercial Dry Dock (the latter railway owned) both at the Roath Basin, and Hills Dry Dock at the Bute East dock.

As dock shunting no longer proceeded independently, the separate locomotive sheds were initially concentrated at the former RR shed, and then a new shed nearby was opened in 1931 (Cardiff East Dock).

The GW inherited one tug at Cardiff (*The Earl(I)* of 1887), *Ferry No 2*, two dumb dredgers (*Marquess* and *Duchess* from 1903/4), and five hopper barges, one of which dated from 1877. *The Earl(I)* was renamed *GWR No 127* in 1931 to make way for its replacement *The Earl (II)*, the original tug being scrapped in 1932. A second tug was built for Cardiff docks by the GW in 1927 (*Lord Glanely*, renamed *Baron Glanely* in 1946, and named after W J Tatem, the Cardiff shipowner) and a third in 1940 (named *Cardiff*). The two ex-Cardiff Railway dredgers continued in operation until they were scrapped immediately prior to nationalisation, but had been assisted from 1924 by the *Mudeford*, a grab dredger ordered by the GW from Holland. Most of the hopper barges were scrapped or sold on by the GW (*Hopgarden* and *Hoptree* both 320-tonners of 1887 were disposed of in 1930/31) and replaced by new vessels some of which had the names of company directors, eg the 735-ton *Viscount Churchill* self-propelled hopper barge of 1924 was the first vessel built for the enlarged GWR and was named after its chairman. There were also the 753-ton

Sir Ernest Palmer and 735-ton *Sir Henry Mather Jackson* hopper barges. All three were scrapped in 1947. The GW inherited other vessels from the other South Wales docks and although they (or their replacements) tended to remain at their 'home dock', there was some interchange. The *Simson III*, a 125-ton (later 100-ton) floating crane purchased in 1925, was based at the Queen Alexandra dock but was employed all over the GW dock system as required. Soon after the Grouping, the GW ordered a grain elevator for use at Cardiff. *GWR Grain Elevator No 1* dated from 1924 and could suck up, weigh and discharge as much as 120 tons an hour. In 1925, over five and a half thousand ships entered Cardiff docks having a net registered tonnage of about 4 million tons.

To make coal shipment traffic more efficient in South Wales, the GW introduced the Pole 20-ton mineral wagons in the 1920s and 1930s, and invested considerable sums in modifying hoists and reception sidings to handle these higher capacity wagons. To encourage their use, rebates were offered off the rates charged on coal carried in these wagons. Opportunity was also taken at Cardiff under the GW's modernisation plan to replace the Lewis-Hunter coaling cranes with 20-ton wagon hoists (some with traversers at the Queen Alexandra dock). Some coaling cranes were still in place in 1932 but all were gone by 1936. Coal was in decline, however, and the weight shipped went down inexorably. Even so, in 1928, of 13.5 million tons of all types of cargo through Cardiff, over 7 million tons was still shipment coal. One factor in the reduced demand for Welsh coal after the First World War was the change to oil burning ships, the Admiralty reducing its coal purchases from about 2 million tons in 1913 to less than 300,000 tons in 1927. Another important factor was the Treaty of Versailles under which Germany made reparation payments in the form of coal to France, Belgium and Italy. In pre-war days those countries had been among the largest purchasers of Welsh steam coal for naval and railway purposes.

As part of efforts to diversify trade through the port, there was a short-lived attempt in the 1920's to get transatlantic liners to call at Cardiff, and one or two did. But these were often associated with special events such as bringing Americans of Welsh extraction over to Eisteddfodau. The lure of liners obtaining the best bunkers coal as cheaply as possible was not a sufficient incentive to bring liners to Cardiff, and was of no interest to the new oil-burning ships.

To broaden handling ability, as part of its modernisation programme new cranes were installed at the Bute docks by the GW and a new train traffic control system was introduced in the Cardiff area. By the 1930s, Cardiff docks were listed as having six transit sheds of total floor area 378,000 sq ft at the Queen Alexandra dock and also a 33,000sq ft cold store there; two sheds at the Roath dock (120,000sq ft); five at the Bute East dock (248,000 sq ft); four at the East dock basin (16,000 sq ft); four at the Bute West dock (37,000 sq ft); and one at the West dock basin (10,000 sq ft). Many shipowners developed new trading routes as their coal business declined. As an example, the

Passenger luggage being embarked at Cardiff in August 1946 on the RMS St Hilary bound for West Africa. The GW Thorneycroft van has delivered the luggage to the loading platform at A shed, Queen Alexandra dock. [GWR]

Cardiff shipowner Sir William Reardon Smith & Sons began to carry Californian grapefruit and canned fruit via the Panama Canal in 1934. Similarly, the import of Jaffa oranges grapefruit and lemons from Palestine grew after 1933 – some 207,000 cases (over 8,000 tons) being brought in during the winter of 1936. Cardiff's claims as a distributing centre also involved produce such as Canadian salmon: in 1934 a consignment of over 1,700 boxes of salmon and halibut was received, the GW providing 28 insulated 'FX' containers with 'Drikold' refrigerant which moved the goods by special train to London.

In 1931 a belt coal conveyor, similar to those at Port Talbot, was installed at Cardiff and a second in 1936. The facilities available in 1936 were: 4 hoists in the Bute West dock that rose 22 ft, none of which could deal with 20-ton capacity wagons; 8 in the Bute East dock lifting through 59 ft all of which could handle 20-ton wagons; 3 at the Roath Basin rising 60 ft above the coping of the quay (2 could lift 20-ton wagons); 7 in the Roath dock elevating to 37 ft (2 handling 20-ton wagons); and 9 in the Queen Alexandra dock all lifting to 70 ft and all handling 20-ton wagons. A

new timber quay was established on the eastern side of the Bute East dock in 1939 on land formerly occupied by coal hoists.

The 1936 audit of cranes stated that there was one hydraulic crane for general goods in the West dock (1¾ ton) and 21 in the East (up to 6 tons), all company-owned; in the Roath dock there were 22 hydraulic cranes (of which 16 were privately-owned, up to 7 tons capacity, the rest GW, up to 6 tons) and 4 electric cranes up to 3 ton; in the Queen Alexandra dock, 14 hydraulic cranes (4 private) all up to 2 tons and 21 electric up to 15 tons capacity. There were no cranes in the Roath Basin. All the dry docks remained in business and by this time crude oil was being imported at the Queen Alexandra dock. Guest, Keen & Baldwin's began to rebuild the East Moors Dowlais works on the dock estate and bring it up to date in 1934.

Cardiff was also the principal British port for importing potatoes (cf the 9.45pm Cardiff-Saltney 'C' headcode express goods train was nicknamed 'The Spud'). The Cardiff wholesale fruit and vegetable merchant Messrs J E England wrote to the GWR in appreciation of the speedy discharge of 4267 cwt of new French potatoes from ship to rail in less than 5½ hours, the potatoes reaching destinations 200 miles away in less than 12 hours after the steamer had tied up at the Queen Alexandra Dock. Their letter was published in the *From People We Have Pleased* feature carried by the GW Magazine in 1927. A famous 'export and re-import' in 1927 was the King George V loco sent in August from the Roath Dock across the Atlantic to Baltimore docks for the centenary celebrations of the B&O on the *SS Chicago City*. The loco returned in October that year.

While the LMS continued the LNWR presence in Cardiff docks after the Grouping and continued to operate its separate goods depot at Tyndall St, the GW eventually took over the operation under a traffic pooling operation in 1933. Joint cartage fleets were established during the interim period. In 1933 also, tanks capable of storing 4,000-tons of imported oil in bulk were built at the Queen Alexandra dock.

In 1943 the Ministry of War transport (MOWT) took delivery of five 40-ton crane barges, built at Fairfields (Chepstow), one of which (*MOWT No 5*) was managed by the GWR. Twin-screw crane steamer *MOWT No 10* was built by Fleming & Ferguson of Paisley in 1943 and this too was managed by the GWR in Cardiff. There was also crane steamer *MOWT No 28* (*GWR No 28*) used at Cardiff and Port Talbot, and derrick barges *MOWT Nos 30 and 31* (*GWR 30* and *31*), all built by the Barry Graving Dock Co in 1944, which were managed and, from 1946, owned by the GW. After the war, *MOWT No 5* was sold to Poland and *MOWT No 10* to the Clyde Navigation Trustees. In February 1942, the streamlined LMS 4-6-2 Princess Coronation loco returned through Cardiff docks from the USA where it had gone for the 1939 World Fair.

The collapse of the South Wales coal export trade after WWI, from 40 million tons in 1913 to 19 million tons in 1938, continued after WWII when it fell to minimal proportions, and this had a lasting effect on Cardiff Docks owing to the port's dependence on a fairly narrow basis of trade. In 1913 Cardiff shipped over 10½ million tons of coal (and another 11 million tons were shipped from nearby Barry in the same year). That was the zenith: in 1946 coal shipments were only slightly in excess of one million tons per annum, and such a comparatively low figure had not been recorded since 1854.

PENARTH (owned; formerly TVR)

Penarth Dock had interesting origins the history of which was repeated some years later when Barry Dock was built. In the original TVR Act of 1836, it was proposed to build a harbour at Penarth, but the idea was abandoned when the 2nd Marquess of Bute in 1846 persuaded the TVR to ship its coal from his first dock at Cardiff. By the 1850's, however, colliery owners had more coal to ship than the existing two docks at Cardiff could cope with. Led by John Nixon of Aberdare, they revived the original TVR scheme of a harbour at Penarth (see Cardiff). Despite strong opposition from the Bute Trustees, an Act was passed in 1855 allowing

a tidal harbour to be constructed at Cogan Pill on the eastern bank of the River Ely, together with a connecting mineral railway about 6 miles long from the TVR main line at Penarth Branch Jct (Radyr), north of Cardiff which swept south and then south east to reach Penarth. Coal began to be shipped from the tidal harbour in 1859. A second Act, in 1856, permitted a wet dock to be built on the western bank of the River Ely which opened in 1865. This dock was reached by a two mile branch from a junction at Grangetown on the railway to the tidal harbour. Twelve coal tips of 150 tons/hour capacity were installed at the tidal harbour, with 10 of 300 tons/hour capacity at the dock itself and two more in the dock basin (these had been transferred over from the tidal harbour) to give 22 tips in all of 15 tons gross capacity (ie about 8 ton wagon loads). The dock was 30 ft deep, 2100 ft long by 370 ft wide and the basin 400 ft by 330 ft. Ships up to 60 ft wide could pass through the 270 ft long lock. The water area of the dock was 17½ acres; including the tidal wharves it was 20½ acres.

An Act of 1863 had empowered the TVR to lease the tidal harbour, dock and the branch railways from the owners, the Penarth Dock & Harbour Rly. When the TVR took up the lease trouble began, because a clause in the 1863 Act preserved all the rights of the Marquess of Bute under the old agreement with the TVR relating to the West Dock at Cardiff (see Cardiff). The Bute Trustees claimed that the shipment of coal at Penarth by the TVR was an infringement of the agreement, and an action was commenced to recover from the Taff Vale the whole of the dues and charges received by them on the traffic shipped and unshipped at Penarth. Eventually the TVR won the case: a decision the other way would have set up a very peculiar situation------the TVR, while being obliged to work and maintain the Penarth Dock, and pay a heavy guaranteed rental to its proprietors, would have been expected to hand over the entire earnings to a third party (the Bute Trustees), for the reason that the traffic had not been shipped at a dock in Cardiff, which was wholly incapable of accommodating it! Nevertheless, the Taff won on the technicality that it did not actually own the harbour, dock and railways at Penarth, and to avoid further action from the Bute Trustees, this remained the state of affairs right up to the Grouping.

Coal exports out of Penarth built up gradually: over 100,000 tons were sent off from the tidal harbour in 1860. By 1870, over 900,000 tons were shipped from the dock and harbour together, the million tons per annum figure being attained in 1873 and over 2 million tons in 1881. The Rhymney Rly began to send trainloads of coal for shipment at Penarth after 1864 (15,000 tons in 1864, but 130,000 tons in 1869 and 230,000 tons in 1873). Up till then all the coal the RR carried had been shipped at the Bute Docks. The Rhymney transferred its coal trains destined for Penarth to the TVR at Radyr. These trains had to be hauled from Radyr by Taff locos as the RR had no running powers to Penarth. The tonnage built up so much that in 1866 an engine shed and storage sidings had to be put in by the Taff at Radyr to cope. The RR coal traffic fluctuated with dock availability at Cardiff, falling somewhat after the Roath dock was opened

Aerial view of Penarth dock in 1930 showing coal hoists on left and general cargo quay on right. Entrance basin with set of four moveable hoists at bottom right. River Ely at mid and upper right. One of the sites of the Penarth Pontoon, Slipway and Ship Repairing Co Ltd is situated on the 'bulge' of land, at the right centre of the picture, with their wharf and gridiron in the river. Their floating dry dock can be seen moored at the top right end of the dock proper. The chimneystack of the dock hydraulic power house is just to the right. The tidal wharves are across the river on the right, where coal hoists and some of the quayside moveable cranes may be seen. [Amgueddfa Cymru National Museum of Wales]

in 1887. Even so, by 1907 over three-quarters of a million tons of coal was being passed over to the TVR from the RR at Radyr. This involved 3000 loaded and empty wagons per day. At that time three and three quarter million tons of all the coal produced in the valleys above Cardiff passed down the branch from Radyr to Penarth. (In 1900, of some 28 million tons of coal raised in the Rhondda, Ferndale, Aberdare and Merthyr valleys, over 15 million tons was conveyed by the TVR; and in 1904, of the TVR's total revenue of £951,731, the contribution from goods, mineral and livestock traffic was £618,246, the goods mileage of 1,643,696 being double that of the Taff's passenger train miles).

The Penarth Branch of the TVR from Radyr crossed the GWR near the Ely Paper Mills (dating from 1865) on the western side of Cardiff. Both railways had connections to the private sidings at the Ely paper works. It was the largest paper mills in Great Britain, and at the turn of the C19th/20th the London dailies were largely supplied with paper manufactured there and brought to Paddington. The raw material was chiefly imported through Penarth Dock in bales or logs (as was esparto grass, also for paper making).

The GW too brought coal to Penarth from Monmouthshire, and from the Ely, Llynvi and Ogmore valleys after the narrowing of the gauge in South Wales in 1872. Two connexions and exchange sidings were completed in 1875 from the South Wales main line just to the west of Cardiff passenger station to the existing Radyr-Grangetown-Penarth Dock line which ran south of the GW main line. The TVR already had storage accommodation in this location for about 700 wagons of coal awaiting orders from ships at Penarth. The GW connexions left the South Wales main line as a single junction facing west and then split. One line swung around almost in a semicircle to join

159

Views of Penarth's coal hoists taken at different times from almost the same location.

Left - *The earliest picture from May 1883 shows the dock full of square-rigged sailing ships (one steamer at the lower left). Covered-in coal tips at the ends of jetties built out into the dock and fed with wagons from turntables. All tracks at the same level.*

For the other three pictures, the building with a clerestory roof along half its length (the dock hydraulic power house) is a useful reference.

the harbour line in the direction of Penarth just before Grangetown station; this was Penarth Curve East. The second line (Penarth Curve North) left the first line facing west, ran south of Canton loco sheds, and joined the harbour line in the Radyr direction near the later Ninian Park Halt. The base of the triangle (Penarth Curve South) was the original Taff line to Penarth dock.

Each leg of the triangle of lines so formed had adjacent sidings at which traffic was exchanged between the companies. Between Penarth North Curve and South Curve the Taff Vale Railway had a series of sidings on the eastern side for the reception of shipment coal, and a series of reception and sorting sidings for returned empty wagons and imports from the Penarth dock on the western side. These

were capable of dealing with many thousands of wagons daily. In 1907, 3½ million tons of coal passed over this portion of the Taff line (350,000 loaded 10-ton wagons). Traffic from the GW for Penarth Dock was conveyed to the GW's own Penarth North Curve sidings, from which GW locos placed the full wagons in the Taff Vale Railway's sidings on the west side of the triangle; vice versa for returning empty wagons. Traffic for the Barry Railway (after its opening in 1889) from the GW (and vice versa) was placed on the Penarth East curve sidings. (A more important exchange between the BR and GWR was at St Fagans). GW trains heading for the Penarth Curve sidings from the east had a clear run, but traffic from the west was more difficult to deal with, as the trains had to run almost

In this picture taken in 1912, two old covered-in hoists remain at the centre and right of the picture, with newer 'open steelwork' hoists at the left and on the extreme right.

In the next picture (above) taken from further to the right since the hoist with cranes on top is omitted, the covered-in hoists are being replaced by open-framework hoists.

The final picture (below), in which the hoist with cranes on top reappears, is taken after the Grouping (GW 'Cathays Yard' Toad goods brakevan at lower left); Pratts Spirit storage tanks may be seen at the tidal harbour across the River Ely.

Note in the last three pictures that empty wagons returned from hoists are at a lower level than the loaded wagons (the coping stones of the retaining walls of the lower level tracks appear white in the picture) [Amgueddfa Cymru National Museum of Wales and GWR]

Top - *Overhead tracks leading to wooden framework hoists at Penarth. Picture taken after 1904 (large 'G' and 'W' on engineers' Mink van on right, and on 4-planker open wagon on track below). Entrance and exit roads both at high level connected by the wagon turntable at the left centre of the picture. Capstans and reels for moving wagons. Great Central and LNWR wagons on lower tracks [GWR]*

Bottom - *Discharging woodpulp at Penarth dock for the Ely Papermills, Cardiff, in the 1920's [GWR].*

into the GWR passenger station, and then set back into the sidings. The GW coal traffic brought for the Taff or Barry Rlys represented an extra 2 million tons (over and above the 3½-million tons mentioned above).

Traffic destined for the Barry line from locations on the TVR above Treforest was exchanged at junctions further up the valleys and then travelled over the Barry main line, but traffic originating below Treforest was exchanged at the Penarth Curve. Taff and Barry passenger trains from the GW Clarence Rd and Cardiff stations passed along Penarth Curve East to join the TVR at Grangetown station; Barry trains then left the Taff lines at Cogan to head for Dinas Powis and Cadoxton. This was the route to Barry taken by coal trains exchanged at Penarth Curve (see Barry). An alternative route existed in principle through Penarth Town station whereby the TVR could have retained haulage all the way to Biglis Jct (near Cadoxton) before handing it over to the Barry, but that was prohibited by a restriction imposed on the TVR when its coastal line through Penarth Town, Lavernock, Swanbridge and Sully was opened in 1888, whereby it was to be used only for local traffic. In fact, working that line was difficult. It had severe gradients, rising from Penarth Dock at 1 in 40 for a distance of about 50 chains through Dingle Road. Eighty-two tons was the load for one engine up this bank in fine weather, whilst in greasy or frosty weather it was reduced to 33 tons. The maximum load for two engines was 20 loaded 10-ton wagons. Beyond Penarth Town station the line to Biglis Jct had some severe gradients falling in both directions before Lavernock, the steeper bits varying between 1 in 45 and 1 in 81: the speed of mineral and goods trains down these banks was limited to 8 mph.

The increasing export coal traffic in the last quarter of the C19[th] meant that Penarth Dock was under strain. In 1884 therefore it was lengthened by 270 yds to give a new length of 2900 ft having 26½ acres of water including the 3-acre outer basin. (Later a pontoon floating dry dock for ship repairing was berthed at the eastern side of this extension).

This page - *Bulk timber being discharged at Penarth in August 1945 from SS Madras City on to bogie bolster wagons. Modern cargo cranes have been installed for use in WWII [GWR]*

Aerial view of Barry docks. Number 1 dock is at the top right of the picture with oil storage tanks behind. Dock No 2 is along the middle showing coal hoists on the right quays and cranes for general cargo on the left. Railway tracks from both sides of the dock join in a semicircle at the bottom of the picture. The Cadoxton river runs out to sea at the far left. Docks Nos 1 and 2 are joined by the Junction Cut at the top centre, above which is the entrance basin (called no 3 dock) running horizontally across the picture, beyond and parallel to which is the Lady Windsor deep water lock and the Commercial Graving dock (the two other dry docks are off No 1 dock at the right of the Junction Cut. Barry Island resort (Whitmore Bay) is at the top centre left. [Amgueddfa Cymru National Museum of Wales]

There were 2 miles of quays and 26 acres of quay space. Since it was essentially a coal port, there was minimal shed area for general cargo (one transit shed of 2,000 sq ft, 9 hydraulic cranes of 3 ton capacity and three 3-ton hand cranes). Shipment coal from all sources grew by leaps and bounds and at Llandough (pronounced 'Landock'), just outside Penarth Dock, extensive new storage sidings for loaded wagons were laid down in 1885. Eventually the running lines between Grangetown and Cogan were quadrupled (up and down passenger and up and down mineral, with crossovers at both Llandough Upper and Lower Junctions).

After the opening of the line to Penarth town station and beyond, the original 1½-mile long Penarth Harbour line, commencing at Grangetown and leading to the tidal harbour, became a branch. In addition to shipping coal, an oil tank farm was opened at the Victoria wharf on this line

and in 1890 the *SS Lux* landed the first cargo of petrol from Philadelphia. Other works with rail connexions ran off this branch such as the Cardiff Gas Works; Cardiff Rope Works; the Windsor Ship Repairing Slipway, There were several petroleum distributing companies, including the Anglo-American Oil Co which had a 500 ft long wharf at which 600 ton vessels could berth; an iron ore and general cargo wharf. The South Wales Public Wharf and Storage Company had a locomotive, which worked over a portion of this branch under the supervision of Taff Vale officials. At Grangetown TVR station were sidings for storing about 400 loaded or empty coal wagons.

The capacity of the coal tips at Penarth altered over the years as they were rebuilt or modernised. After the dock enlargement, there were 16 tips and in 1905 there were 15 high-level hydraulic coal tips, some specially-designed for bunkering large empty (high out of the water) ships. Penarth

Steel tubes being loaded aboard SS Loch Lomond from bogie bolster wagons at Barry. [GWR]

frequently set records: several steam collier vessels were loaded at one tip with 1,500 tons or more of coal and sailed on the same tide. In 1904, four new moveable tips were erected on the east side of the dock basin which could be worked simultaneously into one steamer. Since vessels could enter and leave the basin with the inner dock gates remaining closed, this speeded up matters no end. Steamers of up to 2,500 tons capacity could be loaded at the new tips in less than 2½ hours. One ship loaded 2115 tons of coal plus its own bunkers in 1 hour 57 minutes; another loaded over 4000 tons of coal in 3 hours 40 minutes. The sidings feeding the quartet of rapid-loading tips were such that the whole cargo for a 2,500 ton collier could be held ready for immediate loading. The best year's record for the set of four tips was 900,000 tons. Despite the fierce competition from other South Wales docks and railways from the 1880's onwards, the coal trade expanded at such a rate that coal exports at Penarth reached a peak of over 4 ½ million tons in 1913.

Hydraulic power at the Penarth docks was supplied from the engine house where there was one accumulator with another at the eastern end of the tips. Water was pumped by three pairs of compound tandem steam engines, collectively capable of delivering 1440 gallons/minute. The Taff Vale Rly had one bucket dredger, the 317-ton *Robert Vassell* launched in 1912, which it passed over to the GWR at the Grouping.

After WWI there was a post-war boom which carried over into the first years of GW ownership after the Grouping. Coal exports at Penarth Dock were nearly at the 3 ½ million tons level in 1923, but soon a recession set in, and by 1927 coal shipments had fallen to 2 million tons (in the previous year of the miners' and General Strike, it had only just exceeded 1 million tons). In 1929 the ex-TVR engine shed at Penarth dock was closed, traffic having dropped so much. In 1932 there were 18 hoists still in operation (four of which could handle 20-ton wagons) but finally in 1936 the dock was closed to commercial shipping, except for ships laying-up or needing repairs at the dry dock/slipway. By that

time, there were only six coal hoists left in operation within the dock itself (all 50 ft elevation, four capable of dealing with Pole 20-tonners) and two of 45 ft elevation (not 20 ton wagons) in the basin. The tidal harbour remained open for coal exports (there were three hoists there in 1936) and oil/petrol imports (the National Benzole Co had established a depot). In the late 1930's, total trade was at the 400-500,000 tons level, of which over 90% were still coal exports.

The dock was reopened in 1940 during WWII for general war cargo, with coal and oil remaining at the tidal wharves. The peak year was 1943 when the total trade at both dock and harbour was about 550,000 tons, of which coal again contributed some 90%. The dock closed again for commercial shipping in 1947 but was used for laying up surplus ships.

BARRY (owned; formerly Barry Railway)

Export of superb quality steam coal grew so much by the 1880s that the Bute docks at Cardiff began to be overwhelmed. Although the Bute trustees enlarged Cardiff Docks somewhat, the facilities became altogether inadequate for the enormous traffic of the district. The tidal harbour (1859), and the dock (1865), at Penarth had relieved the situation, but ships still had to wait in the Bristol Channel roads for berths, and coal was held up in colliery wagons for days and even weeks. Not only were the losses to shipowners extremely high, but also shippers and coalowners alike regarded terminal charges at the Bute Docks as excessive. Like those who, in frustration, had got the tidal basin and dock built at Penarth, an Act was obtained as early as 1865 to construct a tidal harbour at Barry with a line northwards to join the SWR main line at Peterston, but it received little support. Nevertheless 18 years later, in 1883, a similar scheme was promoted by a group led by David Davies the former railway contractor (who had sunk extensive collieries in the Upper Rhondda and Aberdare) seeking powers to build a dock at Barry with a railway connexion to the valleys. There was strenuous, but

RMS Nagra loading bunkers coal at a 20-ton hoist on the south side of No 1 dock Barry, adjacent to a moveable hoist, both installed as part of the GW's improvement scheme for the South Wales docks. The shoot at the side of the hoist was for recycling screenings (spilled coal). Returned empty coal wagons are at a lower level than main tracks. [GWR]

ultimately unsuccessful, opposition from the TVR and RR and a scheme was authorised in 1884 for a dock between Barry Island and the mainland, and a 19-mile long main line running north from Barry to connect with the TVR Rhondda branch at Trehafod (between Pontypridd and Treherbert). On the way north, another connexion was made with the TVR at Tonteg Jct near Treforest (for coal coming from the Aberdare and Merthyr districts) and with the the GW at St Fagans.

Originally there was no line towards Cardiff from Barry, but this was rectified by the line to Cogan (next to Penarth Dock) that joined the TVR and which then also gave a route into Cardiff from Grangetown over the GWR. This was in fact the first part of the BR to be opened in 1888. In 1893 arrangements were made for Barry passenger trains to run through to the Cardiff Riverside station (even at that time really part of the main GW station at Cardiff) and on to Clarence Rd station in Cardiff's dockland. Previously the GW Clarence Rd branch had only been used for mineral and goods traffic connecting with firms alongside the Glamorganshire canal. The agreement with the GW enabling BR (and TVR) passenger trains to run to Clarence Rd also gave the BR a right to run goods trains over the

branch. It is not clear whether this was ever taken up.

The location of Barry for a dock was attractive because it had the great advantage of having its entrance not only close to deep water, but also situated under the high land of Barry Island and thus was sheltered from the prevailing westerly and south-westerly winds. The original dock was designed to be 40 acres in extent, but it was enlarged to 73 acres during construction, making it the largest enclosed dock in the country when opened. It was built within two breakwaters, so that vessels approaching the entrance could be admitted into a 7-acre tidal basin in still water, free from the influence of wind and tide; the depth of water in the lock at high water was 38 ft.

Modern for the time, electric light was installed by the contactors so that construction, started in 1884, could proceed round the clock. The dock and railway main line were both opened in 1889. There were 17 coal tips at first. It was immediately successful: in the first half-year 598 vessels, with aggregate nett registered tonnage of 567,958 tons, entered the dock and 1,106,402 tons of coal and goods were shipped or discharged. The traffic increased by leaps and bounds, as shown by the table below:

	Total Imports and Exports Tons	Total number of ships	Total registered ship tonnage
1890	3,265,296	1,753	1,692,223
1895	5,266,548	2,278	2,516,122
1900	7,486,996	3,115	3,776,828
1905	9,071,864	3,225	4,278,759
1914	11,572,373	3,456	5,061,869

Barry Dock was included in the customs port of Cardiff, and already in 1892, it was handling one-third of the coal tonnage dealt with at Cardiff. Over a period of ten years up to WWI, Barry exported more than 10 million tons annually on six occasions; and in 1913, Barry exported more coal than Cardiff and Penarth put together. Of the 11 million-odd tons of goods passing through the docks, coal formed by far the major part, 'other minerals' being only at the 100,000 tons level with general merchandise some 750,000 tons. (When making comparisons between docks in the heyday of Welsh coal exporting, care should be taken about whether the data relate to *coal only* or to *all cargo* passing through a port. Thus, taking all other traffic into account, in the best year (1913) for the Bute docks 13,700,000 tons were dealt with, against 11,750,000 tons at Barry and 7,500,000 tons at Newport).

The Barry Rly was extended by the construction of the Vale of Glamorgan Rly opened in 1897 from Barry to join the GW at Coity and at Bridgend. Over this railway, coal traffic from the Llynvi, Ogmore, and Garw Valleys, and from the anthracite districts in West Wales was brought for shipment at Barry. The line enabled the Aberthaw Lime Co to start up business again, making lime from beach pebbles. It also served the mid-C19[th] Aberthaw cement works: Smeaton had used cement made from Aberthaw limestone in the construction of the Eddystone lighthouse in 1759 as it had the special property of setting quickly. Although the Aberthaw works were abandoned in 1910, they were replaced by a new cement works at nearby Rhoose in 1912. Where the BR crossed the GWR mainline on a viaduct at St Fagans, a BR line (with a facing junction from the north) dropped down to a goods yard near the GW station. Connexions were made there with the GW, and in 1900 another was made between Peterston futher to the west on

the GW mainline and Drope Jct (facing from the south) on the BR. Also branches were made from Tynycae Jct to the Walnut Tree Viaduct spanning the valley of the Taff to the Rhymney Railway at Penrhos and Energlyn Junctions, near Caerphilly (1901); and with the Brecon & Merthyr's main line from Newport northwards, at Barry Junction north of Bedwas station (1905).

When two companies wanted voluntarily to exchange traffic, they would usually keep such railway traffic on their own lines as far as possible to an appropriate common junction, even though there may have been a shorter route which involved a third railway company. For example, the goods and mineral traffic exchanged between the Barry Rly and the GWR east of Cardiff did not follow the same route as that taken by the passenger trains between Cardiff and Barry (ie not via the TVR through Cogan) and took place at St Fagans where the north-south Barry mainline crossed the east-west GW mainline. This avoided the TVR taking a share in the receipts, and kept up the wagon mileage on the BR and GWR for which they would get extra money. The exchange siding accommodation at the Canton/Grangetown Penarth Curve proved too limited to use it as a regular exchange point between the BR and GWR (see Penarth).

A curious feature of the BR was that it hardly entered the coalfield itself, traffic consigned to Barry being brought to it by other railways. This prompted the Cardiff Rly (formerly the Bute dock railway) just before WWI to try and construct five small branch railways to get new coal traffic to Cardiff, but the scheme was a white elephant (see Cardiff).

New traffic was brought to Barry by its new lines and junctions but even beforehand it had been necessary to build an additional dock at Barry (the 34 acre Dock No 2), east of the original dock, opened in 1898. There were ten high-level

Soldiers boarding a troopship at Barry No 2 dock in WWI. GW Mica refrigerated meat van at right. [GWR]

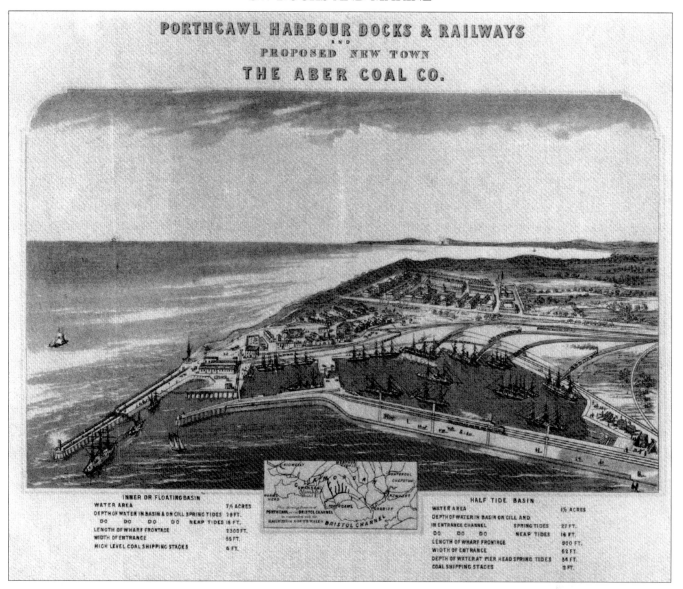

Above - An artist's impression of Porthcawl dock about 1890 taken from a brochure by the Aber Coal Co listing port charges. According to railway maps there were only three elevated coal hoists on the far side, instead of the four shown. The sketch gives a good general idea of the dock layout but points of detail do not match. Aber No 3 colliery at Ogmore Vale was also called Cwmfuwch colliery according to the 1932 List of Collieries on or connected to the GWR. [Amgueddfa Cymru National Museum of Wales]

coal hoists erected on the north side of the dock, and opportunity was taken to cater for general cargo on the south side (practically the whole of No 1 dock was lined with hoists). At that time a new deep-water lock (the Lady Windsor Lock) for the largest steamers then afloat was brought into use; it was 647 ft long by 65 ft wide and constructed parallel to the original tidal entrance basin. Fitted with three pairs of gates, it could be divided into two compartments, each sufficiently large to accommodate a more than average-sized steamer. The lock enabled large steamers to enter or leave the dock at very low water and was unique, so far as the Bristol Channel was concerned (even the later giant entrance lock built in 1914 at Newport's Alexandra South dock did not have such depth of water at low tide). The adjacent basin was 80 ft wide, and

was a tidal entrance. All of this gave a total water area at Barry of 114 acres. Subsequently a pontoon was constructed within the breakwaters, at which Bristol Channel passenger steamers berthed. The pontoon was served by an extension of the railway line to Barry Island opened in 1896. (The BR ran its own paddle pleasure steamers from 1905–11 for which it had built the paddle steamers *Gwalia*, *Devonia*, *Westonia* and *Barry*. It also subscribed to the Burnham Pier Co (S&DJR) to generate traffic but owing to a legal dispute about whether the BR was entitled to run such services, the operation was wound up; the pier continued however to be employed by P & A Campbell's paddle pleasure steamers).

Along the south side of dock No 2 there was a large transit shed (500 ft long by 156 ft wide) having cellarage,

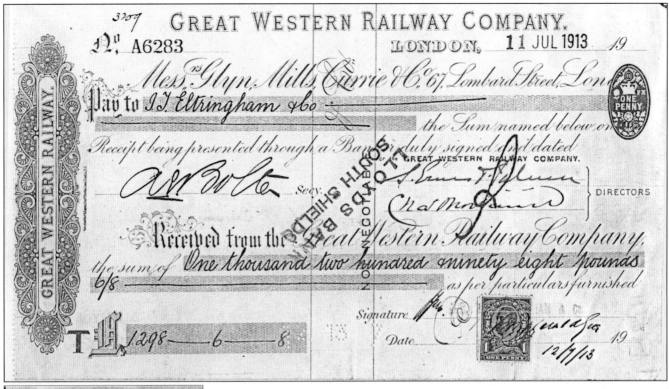

Above and left - Cheque and receipt for £1298 : 6 : 8d paid by the GWR in July 1913 to Messrs Eltringham of South Shields for the building of PT Pen Cw(I), launched in October 1912. The paddle tug was used as a tender at Fishguard until sold in June 1927. [D J Hyde]

Below - Map of Port Talbot dock. [GWR]

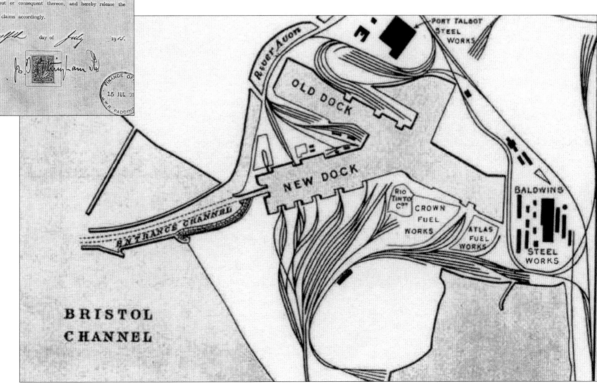

1920' s aerial view looking up the entrance channel from the River Avon towards lock for the New Dock. Old Dock on left, with the Port Talbot Steel Works behind. The Margam Steel Works are at the top right, beyond which the South Wales main line runs across the top of the picture. [GWR]

ground and upper floors, and bonded stores. At the basin there was a transit shed having 4,500 sq ft of floor area. There were, in total, nearly five miles of quays and over nine acres of sheds at Barry. Merchandise traffic was quickly received into the sheds, either from ships or rail wagons, or was loaded from the warehouse into wagons or vessels. A fixed 50-ton hydraulic crane, travelling cranes from 12 tons down to 30 cwts, and 47 movable hydraulic cranes were originally provided. The BR also had a steam floating crane. Close by, Joseph Rank Ltd erected the huge 7-storey Atlantic Flour Mill in 1906 which provided a large traffic for the BR; the flour mill was extended in 1934. Frozen foodstuffs could be discharged direct from a ship's hold into railway wagons and dispatched to the consuming centres, or quickly transferred into the cold store adjacent to No 2 dock. When first built, the store could accommodate 80,000 carcases of sheep and other goods. Around the dock estate, large areas of land were reserved for the storage of pitwood and timber. A considerable quantity of the heavier timber was water-stored, there being 41 acres of timber floats available. In 1914 a new briquette factory was constructed at nearby Sully.

Between Barry Island and the town, the railway described almost a half circle, within which were the docks, with many miles of running lines and about 100 miles of sidings: in fact the sidings extended north as far as Cadoxton from where there was a direct low level line into the docks, running down an incline and tunnel under the sidings. This line enabled coal trains to avoid passing through Barry passenger station. There was accommodation for approximately 6000 loaded and 3000 empty coal wagons.

By 1906 there were 37 hydraulic coal hoists at Barry, many of them being served by high level tracks, equipped with pairs of sloping lines for the laden and empty wagons. Capstans could be used to haul the wagons on to the hoists. A feature of coal shipment at Barry from the outset was that wagons were weighed both before and after tipping, thus not taking for granted the indicated tare of the wagon; not weighing before and after had caused disputes in other ports. This practice was later adopted at most other docks in South Wales. Hydraulic power worked the lock gates. Work at the docks was carried on by day and night, quays and wharves being electrically lighted, the power for which was generated by eight pairs of vertical compound engines, together giving 970 h.p. Improvements were continually put in place, eg in 1914, six new tips designed for 20 ton wagons enabling an extra 2 million tons of coal to be handled per year; and three fixed and two movable Armstrong-Whitworth coal tips were installed in 1918.

There were three graving docks, two private (run by The Barry Graving Dock and Engineering Company) and the other belonging to the railway. Within the docks there were 44 large buoys, to which vessels not requiring immediate quay berths could be moored. To move vessels in the docks, the Barry Railway had one screw tug (the *Clive*, built at Barry) when the dock was opened in 1892; the 164-

Small coal coming off the end of one of the conveyors at Port Talbot and falling into the hold of a collier. [GWR]

ton *Archibald Hood*, built at Falmouth, was added in 1898; and the 177-ton *St Baruch* in 1916, also built at Falmouth. All three came into GW ownership. Barry was essentially a railway-made town, a large population growing up around the docks. Where once there had been green fields and sandy wastes, with about 100 people living in the neighbourhood, there were some 5,000 people in 1891 and a thriving town of over 35,000 inhabitants at the end of WWI.

The building of the Barry Docks and Railway put the other independent South Wales docks and railways on their mettle. Rates for transporting coal came down and it was said that the traders in South Wales and other parts of the country had had their carriage rates reduced by some £500,000 per annum. By 1918, the Barry owned and/or worked some 68 miles of double-track railway, with about 143 miles of sidings. The BR 'stole' large quantities of traffic from Cardiff's Bute Docks. In 1907, for example, 2 million tons of coal was transferred at Barry Junction (Treforest) most of which was from the Aberdare and

Merthyr valleys, but some also came from the southern part of the Rhondda.

By 1924, after the Grouping, there were 41 hoists many with lifting capacity from 20 to 30 tons gross (ie loads of 12 to 20 tons of coal), all of which could elevate wagons 60 ft into the air. The GWR took over the BR Commercial graving dock, and the two private dry docks continued as before. An additional tug *Windsor(II)* was built for Barry in 1932 replacing an 85-ton tug of the same name dating from 1889; *Windsor(II)* was a sister ship to the tug *The Earl (II)* based at Cardiff. An up-to-date hopper dredger *David Davies* was delivered to Barry in 1925, named after the former chairman of the Barry Rly. By 1932 there were 40 hoists in operation, but only 34 left in 1936: 22 in No 1 dock (of which 13 could handle 20 ton loaded wagons) and 12 in No 2 dock (four 20-tonners). Even so, those remaining had increased capacity, as only nine in total could handle 20-ton wagons in 1932, so eight had been upgraded in the intervening years. The basin at Barry was called 'No 3

171

Dock' at this time: it had no coal hoists but did have hand cranes. Craneage provision had also changed, with the 50 ton hydraulic crane at No 1 dock being still in use, but with only 31 10-ton hydraulic cranes at No 2 dock. The basin No 3 dock did however have 7 hydraulic cranes of 2-ton capacity. There was a number of rail-mounted steam, and hand, cranes also available around the dock system. There were no electric cranes at Barry until after nationalisation.

PORTHCAWL (served)

The dock at Porthcawl, to which the SWR had a connexion, is an example of a harbour which rose briefly from obscurity owing to the efforts of a local entrepreneur, only to decline afterwards. A tidal basin, which admitted small vessels when weather and tides permitted, had been completed in 1828 to connect with the 1825 Duffryn, Llynvi & Porthcawl Railway (a tramroad). The DL&P was the first combined dock and railway venture in the world (not the Llanelly Railway & Dock Co of 1828 which is usually given that soubriquet).

Facilities at Porthcawl remained minimal until the 1860's when Alexander Brogden purchased the Tondu ironworks and some nearby collieries. The Llynvi Valley and Ogmore Valley Rly (as the tramroad had become named) obtained an Act in 1864 authorising the construction of a 1½-acre inner wet dock joining the existing tidal basin that was also improved to give 7½-acres in total. The wet dock opened in 1867, had depth of water of 26ft/16ft Spring/neap tides, and was equipped with coal tips etc and was able to berth vessels up to 2,000 tons. Exports were coal and iron (including rails and chairs); imports were pitwood and some general cargo. In 1864, only about 17,000 tons of coal were exported; in 1871, the new inner wet dock shipped over 165,000 tons.

As long as the ironworks prospered, so did the dock. Depression in the iron industry in the 1870's resulted in Brogden's bankruptcy and trade through the port waned. But later North's Navigation Collieries took over Brogden's interests and trade revived. As an example of the sort of craft calling at Porthcawl, the 37-ton smack *Elizabeth Ann* built at Cardigan in 1875 and owned by John Thomas & Co of Aberporth, took 46 tons of coal from Porthcawl to Cardigan in early October, 1884. The freightage was 5/11d per ton.

In 1873, the GW took over management of the Llynvi Valley and Ogmore Valley Rly and during 1884 the dock was vested in the GWR. Activity rose to a peak in 1892 but then trade collapsed because of the opening of the large new dock at Port Talbot along the coast which was connected by rail to the Llynvi Valley collieries and thus took away Porthcawl's trade. Although an article in the 1905 Railway Magazine implies that the dock was still functioning, it seems to have closed in 1898. It was filled in to provide space for the new esplanade. In 1916 a new passenger station was opened on the site of the old dock lines, at which time Porthcawl was described as having become ....'a watering place of renown from a port of small importance'.

PORT TALBOT and ABERAVON (owned; formerly Port Talbot Railway)

At the beginning of the C19th, Aberavon was a minor creek giving access to small coasters. Trade in copper and tin ores, and coal, was conducted at wharves along the River Avon, the copper works and tinplate works being connected to the quays by tramroads. Trade flourished but the river was both shallow and winding, and larger vessels required by the increasing trade could not use it. A group of entrepreneurs led by the major local landowner (C.R.M.Talbot), and including the owners of the copper smelting works at nearby Cwmavon, formed the Aberavon Harbour Co (later called the Port Talbot Dock Co) in 1834. A navigable cut was made to connect the copper works to the widened, and deepened, river and in 1837 Aberavon Dock was opened which, it was claimed, had the largest entrance lock then on the Bristol Channel. Talbot became chairman of the SWR in 1852 (later a director of the GWR) and had interests in the Shrewsbury & Chester Rly before it became part of the GW. In 1865, the entrance lock at Aberavon was lengthened and the breakwater extended to give more protection to shipping in the approaches to the dock, but by this time Swansea had become the world's centre for copper smelting, and the Cwmavon works near Port Talbot went into liquidation soon afterwards. In consequence, trade at Port Talbot dock slowed down. Even so, some coal began to be exported in 1870, and there was a regular service of steamers especially to Bristol.

The construction of a railway to link the Rhondda valley directly with Swansea had been first mooted in the 1830's, but it was not until 1882 that the Rhondda & Swansea Bay Rly was authorised. The plan originally had Briton Ferry dock as the terminus, but Swansea was made the ultimate destination after businessmen from that town got involved. The first part of the line (between Pontrhydyfen and Aberavon) was opened for traffic in 1885 and fed shipment coal into Port Talbot from collieries along the line. The completion of the Rhondda Tunnel in 1890 enabled the R&SB Rly to bring coal from south east Wales to Port Talbot dock. The RSB reached Briton Ferry and its dock in 1893, and traffic to the Prince of Wales Dock at Swansea started in 1895.

Trade through Port Talbot picked up even more after colliery proprietors in the Ogmore and Garw valleys formed the Port Talbot Railway and Dock Co in 1894 by which to export their coal. The PTR (the last independent railway company of the C19th) acquired the old docks and proceeded to enlarge and modernise them with a new lock and a breakwater to provide an enclosed water area of 24 acres, comprising the Old dock and New dock and other wharves. A new Armstrong Whitworth coal hoist with lifting capacity of 19 tons was erected in 1895; it had a height of lift of 37 ft. The PTR bought the 122-ton *Emily Charlotte* screw tug in 1896 for the opening of the new dock (she was sold by the GWR in 1933). In later years, the lock entrance proved to be rather on the small side for large vessels, although improvements were made in 1914.

The PTR obtained powers in 1896 to link its system with the old South Wales Mineral Rly. This originally-BG line incorporated in 1853 ran from Briton Ferry to Glyncorrwg with an intermediate branch to Tonmawr. It was at Tonmawr that the PTR made its junction in 1898. The SWMR included a 1½ mile cable-operated incline at the Briton Ferry end. This could be avoided by the new connexion, and a consequence was that most of the coal conveyed by the SWMR that formerly went to Briton Ferry dock was diverted to Port Talbot. The double-track PTR opened throughout in 1897-8 and was 35 miles long, joining the GW in the east at at Pont-y-rhyll (where it tapped the Blaengarw coalfield), Kenfig Hill and Pyle.

It was found that coal could be carried to Port Talbot from the central and western Glamorgan coalfield along the new PTRly for 3d to 7d less per ton than to Cardiff and Swansea. The latter port in particular suffered a reduction in traffic owing to the new railway. Another immediate consequence of this new competition for the export coal trade was the decline and ultimate closure of Porthcawl dock. In 1898 the total dock area was 89 acres with over 1½ miles of quays and some small area of sheds. Port Talbot was granted independent status as a port in 1904. In 1906 the Port Talbot Steel Co was formed at the docks to take advantage of the new facilities.

The GW took over working of the PTR (but not the docks) in 1908, at which time the annual trade of the port was some half-a-million tons. Swindon manufactured breakdown vans, J12 rail wagons and other vehicles for the PTR before WWI (see *GWR Goods Wagons*). The bankrupt SWMR also came under the control of the PTR and hence GWR in 1908; its incline was closed in 1910. The old junctions at Briton Ferry between the SWMR (1853) and the RSB (1893) were later swept away in the Briton Ferry alterations of 1935. Coal exports increased at Port Talbot to 2.5 million tons in 1916, a new 900 ft long wharf having been built in 1914 equipped with four 2-ton hydraulic cranes and one 15-tonner for general cargo (including tinplate). Between the end of WWI and the Grouping, Baldwin's opened a new iron and steel works at Margam on the eastern side the dock.

The PTR, the SWMR and the Port Talbot docks all came over to the GW at the grouping in 1922 at which time E. Lowther, General Manager of the PTR became Chief Goods Manager of the enlarged GWR (and later Chief Docks Manager). The year 1923 saw traffic peak through Port Talbot at over three million tons, nearly all of which was coal. In 1924, there were eight modern coal hoists at Port Talbot, four with lifting capacities of 30 tons gross, and Port Talbot Dock had the honour of tipping the first Pole 20-ton wagons in August 1924.

At Port Talbot there were, in addition to the usual type of coal hoist, three belt conveyors for coal, two at New dock and one at Old dock. Two had been erected in 1911 by Spencers and Co Ltd of Melksham and a third new one was introduced in 1925. Here the coal wagon was not hoisted to a high level, but was tilted at ground level into a hopper which fed an endless belt about 3 ft wide (two of the three

conveyors could handle 20-ton wagons). The height to which the belt raised the coal was adjustable and, having taken it to the necessary height above the hatchway of the ship, it fell off the belt down a chute into the hold. Belt conveyors were later installed at Newport, and at the Roath Dock in Cardiff in 1931. While the speed with which coal could be loaded with belts was quite high, the efficiency was reduced by the pauses required for trimming the coal within ship holds. Although belt conveyors were used a lot by the NER, they were not generally suitable for Welsh coal owing to the wide range in lump size. They also required considerably more room to lay out; belts were best for small coal of which there was in fact a large traffic at Port Talbot. Belt conveyors had been installed by the GWR at Fowey in 1909 for bulk loading of china clay.

The 1936 edition of GWR Docks stated that there were seven coal hoists still in use at Port Talbot (one less than in 1932), all of which could raise wagons 70 ft into the air; only two of the three coal conveyors remained in use, both elevating coal up to 60 ft above the quayside. On the general cargo side, there were 18 hydraulic cranes (up to 15 tons capacity), one 5-ton mobile steam crane and a 12 ton hand crane. There was a single transit shed, having a 3,400 sq ft floor area.

At Port Talbot, as at many other places in the coalfield, finely broken coal and coal dust was made into 'patent fuel' briquettes by combining with tar. Crown Patent Fuel works, Atlas Coke & Patent Fuel works and British Briquettes Ltd had factories around the dock at various times. Packages of patent fuel intended for export were loaded on to the last company's own flat wagons and run from the factory to the quayside where the whole wagon (acting rather like a pallet) was craned down into the holds of ships, unloaded and returned back to the rails on the dockside.

The Port Talbot Steel Co's works, Baldwin's Iron & Steelworks, and the Ffrwdwyllt Tinplate works were all located around the dock estate. Iron ore was imported in large quantities for the blast furnaces. Originally the iron ore was unloaded by means of cranes and buckets but in 1926, as part of its modernisation plan, the GW installed transporter grabs which lifted the ore from the hold of a ship and transported it in the air, over the railway tracks on the Baldwin Wharf, directly to storage bins at the steelworks. Each grab load was about 3-4 tons. Ore imports became ever-more important with the expansion of the steelworks at Port Talbot, particularly after WWII.

In preparation for the D-Day landings in Normandy in 1944, Port Talbot was one of a number of 'oil ports' from where the liberating armies were supplied.

BRITON FERRY (owned; formerly Vale of Neath Rly); NEATH (served)

Copper and lead smelting had taken place around Neath in the C17[th] and this figured prominently in trade at the riverside wharves in later years, in addition to the usual 'market goods', timber and building materials. In the 1860's coal was by far the greatest material exported at the river wharves (100,000 tons/annum) with iron bars a weak second

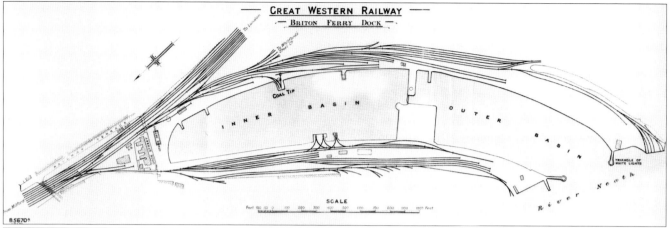

Left - The three tips on the south-eastern side of Briton Ferry dock photographed in the early 1920's. There were four tips on the other side of the dock, but they were progressively taken out of use. The shelving sides to the dock meant that all were built out on wooden jetties. All the tips were originally served by wagon turntables, but the three shown had in-and-out tracks forming triangles installed by the turn of the C19th/20th. Loaded wagons arrived from the top of the picture on the line closer to the water, and empties passed away on the outer track to the right. The picture was taken from the end of the dock looking towards the outer basin and the entrance from the River Neath in the far distance. [GWR]

(about 7,000 tons/annum). Biggest imports were copper ore (roughly 30,000 tons /annum), pig iron and iron ore (about 20,000 tons of each/annum). However, little refined copper seems to have been exported. At different times in the C19th efforts were made to deepen the channel to wharves on the River Neath serving various works. Even as late as 1913 it was proposed that the river should be 'dockised' with locks at Briton Ferry which would create facilities for the largest ships afloat, but like many previous schemes for which Acts had actually been obtained by the Neath Harbour Commissioners, it came to nothing.

The Act authorising the construction of the standard gauge Vale of Neath Rly was obtained in 1849. It was surveyed by Brunel and had fine timber viaducts at Dare and Gamlyn, similar to those in Cornwall. The aim of the line was to tap the rich coal fields between Merthyr and Neath (some 22 miles) and, via running powers over the SWR, reach Swansea. As well as gaining access to coal shipping staithes on the River Neath, a new dock at Briton Ferry was to be built. The VofN Rly started its shipment coal traffic in 1851 from the North dock at Swansea as soon as the SWR had erected coal stages there, but there had to be transhipment of coal between gauges at Neath. Later, in 1863, when the Swansea Harbour Trust permitted the VofN to manage its 'harbour railway', a new mixed gauge route into Swansea docks was built. Merthyr had been reached by the VofN in 1853 and the Dowlais Iron works and other companies joined up to the railway so as to be able to ship their products at Briton Ferry and Swansea, in addition to the existing outlets at Cardiff.

Authorisation for the wet dock at the mouth of the River Neath was obtained in 1851, much of the capital coming not only from the VofN Rly, but also the SWR and the Swansea Vale Rly. The dock was about 1600 ft long by 400 ft wide (15 acres) with a 50 ft wide entrance basin and opened in 1861. Unusually, there was a *single* gate to the inner dock with a buoyancy chamber (designed by Sir Marc Brunel). Along much of the dock, the sides were simple sloping banks, rather than stone quays of which there was only a 432 ft run. On this limited quayage there were various cargo-handling facilities. For the coal traffic, three Armstrong hydraulic coal hoists were erected on short jetties sticking out over the sloping banks of the dockside. The hoists could handle wagons of 20 ton gross weight (ie tare plus load), which could be raised up to 40 ft in the air. Craneage at Briton Ferry dock consisted of two, 1½-ton capacity, hydraulic cranes. Water depth was 25/17 ft spring/ neap tides. Within a few months of the opening of the dock at Briton Ferry, coal exports doubled.

Before the opening of the dock, the VofN Rly had its eye on the new packet port of Neyland (New Milford) which, it was believed at the time, would come to rival Liverpool as a major trans-Atlantic steamer port. The VofN Rly agreed to share with the SWR the cost of doubling the Carmarthen-New Milford Pier stretch of line, so that it could send bunkers and shipment coal right through, which it began to do after 1858.

The BG South Wales Mineral Rly subsequently used

Briton Ferry dock for coal exports. The SWMR was opened in stages between 1860-2, linking Briton Ferry with Glyncorrwg, and there was an intermediate branch to Tonmawr. It had been promoted by local coalowners who had pits in the Corrwg valley and was leased to the Glyncorrwg Coal Co. At the Briton Ferry end, the SWMR had the undesirable feature of a 1½ mile cable-operated incline which limited the capacity of the line (but see below). The VofN Rly was acquired by the GWR in 1865 and Briton Ferry Dock in 1873.

Briton Ferry Dock was also the original destination of the 29-mile long Rhondda & Swansea Bay Rly, which was incorporated in 1882 as one of a number of railways promoted to provide alternative routes and docks for coal from the Rhondda which could by-pass Cardiff docks, which at the time were clogged with traffic. It ran from Treherbert through the 2-mile long Rhondda tunnel that was eventually completed in 1890. Its junction for Briton Ferry dock was at Baglan Burrows, opened in 1893. In the following year the R&SBR reached Swansea, via its unique opening bridge over the River Neath (built on a skewed curve).

In 1898 the Port Talbot Railway & Dock Co linked its system with the South Wales Mineral Rly at Tonmawr. The cable-operated incline at the Briton Ferry end of the SWMR could now be avoided by the new connexion, and a consequence was that most of the coal that formerly went to Briton Ferry dock was diverted to Port Talbot. However, the Briton Ferry Steel Co had established a new works at the docks in 1895 that to an extent compensated for the loss of traffic to Port Talbot.

The town quay at Neath was 200 ft long with a depth at quayside of 12 ft at high water (ordinary spring tides). For many years, the Main Colliery Co had wharves down river, about a mile from Briton Ferry Dock. They had a water frontage of 1500 ft and were improved after WWI. There were eight tipping stages, so arranged that three tips could be put to work simultaneously on the same vessel. At spring tides, ships of 1800 tons with a draught of 17 ft could easily be dealt with, but at other times only smaller vessels could be berthed. Tonnage of all goods handled at the Neath riverside wharves declined as the years went by, although the quantity of tinplate grew in the late C19[th] as works began to be established around the town. Nevertheless, Neath as a shipping venue decayed because larger ships could not get up river, and because nearby Swansea offered better service with regular sailings of ocean-going ships carrying goods directly to the export destinations without double handling from small vessels.

To counter the threat of the Barry Rly expanding westwards, the GW acquired control of the R&SBR in 1906 (and of both the PTR and SWMR in 1908), and of course took them all over completely at the Grouping. The steelworks in the environs of Briton Ferry dock was enlarged between the wars but, according to Appleby's GWR Docks, only one hydraulic coal tip for 12-ton wagons remained at Briton Ferry in 1936 (there had been three working in 1932). Shell-Mex and BP had, however, by then

Swansea Harbour Trust.

THE DOCKS consist of the Prince of Wales Dock, the North Dock, and the South Dock ; each equipped with modern appliances for the rapid loading and unloading of vessels.

THE ENTRANCE CHANNEL to the Harbour is lighted by means of Gas Buoys.

THE LOCK to the Prince of Wales Dock has a depth of water over the outer cill at Ordinary Spring Tides of 32 feet, and at Ordinary Neap Tides of 24 feet. The length of the Lock is 500 feet.

THE ENTRANCE to the North Dock Basin has a depth of water at Ordinary Spring Tides of 32 feet, and at Ordinary Neap Tides of 24 feet.

THE LOCK to the South Dock is 370 feet in length, and has over the outer cill 34 feet of water at Ordinary Spring Tides, and 26 feet at Ordinary Neap Tides.

THE NEW KING'S DOCK, capable of accommodating the largest vessels afloat, is in course of construction.

THE QUAYS are 19,000 feet in length

THE WAREHOUSES contain a floor area of 283,000 square feet.

THE RAILWAYS OF THE TRUST have direct connections with the Great Western, London and North Western, Midland, and Rhondda and Swansea Bay Railways.

There are 26 COAL TIPS, and 80 HYDRAULIC, STEAM and HAND CRANES.

SWANSEA is the centre of the Anthracite Coal district.

There are more PATENT FUEL WORKS in Swansea than at any other port in the Kingdom , and the Fuel is held in high repute in Continental and other markets.

There is a LARGE AREA OF LAND available for Fuel Works, Creosote Works, Saw Mills and other commercial purposes.

LINES OF STEAMERS run between Swansea and the following ports, viz. :— New York, Baltimore, Philadelphia, Singapore, Hong Kong, Yokohama, Nagasaki, Hiogo, Java ports, Rio de Janeiro, Santos, Rosario, Montevideo, Beunos Ayres, Ports in Chili and Peru, St. Petersburg, Hamburg, Amsterdam, Rotterdam, Antwerp, Treport, Rouen, Nantes, Bordeaux, Oporto, Lisbon, Setubal, Barcelona, Genoa, Leghorn, Venice, Trieste, Fiume, ports in Greece, Constantinople and other Turkish ports, Galatz, Ibrail, Odessa, Batoum, Alexandria, etc.

Within the Harbour are NINE GRAVING DOCKS

Extensive provisions has been made for the FISH TRADE, both in the Tidal Harbour and in the South Dock. The Swansea Fleet now numbers about thirty Steam Trawlers, in addition to Liners and Smacks.

PILOTAGE —The Trustees are the Pilotage Authority Pilotage is non-compulsory, both inward and outwards.

RATES AND CHARGES are moderate.

A Reed FOG HORN SIGNAL has recently been erected on the Mumbles Head, giving three blasts of about two seconds' duration every two minutes.

The Mumbles Lighthouse Signal Station is now worked by Lloyd's. Vessels calling for orders can communicate with their Owners without lowering a boat—good and sheltered free anchorage being found under the Mumbles Head at any tate of the tide. For information on any point connected with the Port and Harbour, apply to—

WILLIAM LAW,
General Manager.

Registered Address for Telegrams—" LAW, SWANSEA "

Swansea Harbour Trust advertisement.

established importing and distribution depots in the dock. Even so, the dock closed for all other traffic in 1940. After WWII many warships were broken up at the dock, that eventually closed in 1959.

SWANSEA (owned; formerly Swansea Harbour Trust)

Numerous works for the smelting of copper, lead and zinc, and manufacture of iron and tinplate were established in the Swansea valley area in the C18[th] owing to the presence of coal, limestone and iron ore. Many wharves along the River Tawe served these industries, and one or two were connected by tramroads to nearby mines.

Non-ferrous metal ores were brought to Swansea for smelting from North Wales and from the mines in the Tamar valley (shipped from Calstock quay, for example) and the returning sailing vessels went home with coal. The shipping places were sanctioned by the Corporation of Swansea which levied dues (similar to the royal charters and privileges along the Thames in London). Despite all the local industry, some of the civic leaders wanted Swansea to develop as a fashionable seaside resort and it was not until 1791 that The Swansea Harbour Trust was created to look

King's dock, Swansea. One of a set of two fixed (nos 1 and 5) and three moveable (nos 2-4) hydraulic coal hoists designed by Messrs Taunatt, Walker & Co of Leeds, newly constructed (1909-11) by the GWR on land rented from the SHT. They were operated at a water pressure of about 725 lbs/square inch supplied from the SHT pumping stations ('power stations'). The wagon roads ran on a gantry 18ft above quay level, and spanned a cart road and three rail tracks, leaving the quay free for traffic. Wagons could be raised a further 42 ft to give a maximum tip height of 60 ft above quay level. This moveable hoist shows the traverser operated by the running-in-and-out 'monkey'. [GWR]

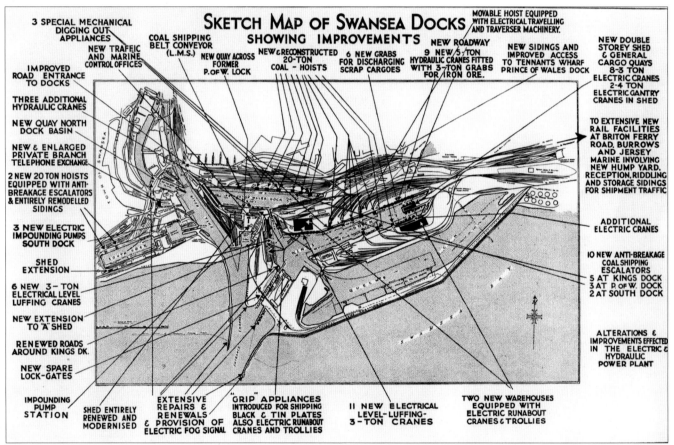

after and improve shipping facilities. Things moved along in 1800 when the Swansea Canal to Ystradgynlais was opened (later to be leased, and then taken over, by the GWR in 1872), and Tennant's canal of 1810-20 brought goods from the Neath valley to a basin on the eastern side of the Tawe at Fabian's Bay. The region around Swansea contained the largest deposits of anthracite coal in Europe. Anthracite ('stone coal') began to be used for smelting in 1830's, and was also exported, particularly at first to France for domestic use.

Although Swansea did eventually have important commercial docks by the end of the C19th capable of accommodating the biggest steamers afloat, its rise was surprisingly slow in comparison to the other South Wales ports. The offer of finance from Liverpool speculators to build, much earlier in the century, a dock and a railway which followed a route essentially the same as the much later Rhondda & Swansea Bay Railway, was spurned by the Corporation. Between 1810-40 shipping activity rose by about 5% at Newport, Cardiff and Llanelly, and after wet

One of the Taunatt, Walker fixed hoists of the 1909-11 set at King's dock. There were two cranes per hoist: a 3-ton crane (this side) used to collect up screenings (small coal riddled through bars in the shoot and/or spilt on the deck of the ship) in a bucket to be transferred back into the two Evans & Bevan of Neath wagons on the screening road; and a 6-ton crane to raise and lower an anti-breakage box that would sometimes be placed at the bottom of the shoot from which the first loads of coal would be lowered into an empty ship to build up a cushion for the rest of the load. The wagon on the right is labelled G A C, i.e. Gwendraeth Anthracite Collieries & Co Ltd of Swansea. [GWR]

docks were opened at these places, activity rose by 13%, but at Swansea it continued to languish at just over 1%. Collieries local to Swansea began to send coal to Llanelly's New Dock for shipment after 1834. In addition to not having a wet dock, the bar at the river mouth meant that at low tide cargo from ocean-going ships had expensively to be transferred overside into lighters and barges for delivery to the quays and the smelters. Clearly Swansea was losing out.

A wet dock was eventually formed from a navigable waterway cut to bypass a bend in the Tawe in 1836-42. It was provided with a half-tide basin equipped with locks at both ends. The arrival of the South Wales Rly in 1852 caused the navigable cut to be improved and renamed the North Dock. The SWR soon opened a branch from Hafod Jct between Landore and High St (near the goods depot at Brewery Wharf) which ran down to the public quay on the western side of the new dock where coal tips were erected. It was at this time that the VofN Rly began its coal traffic to Swansea, shipping out coal at the SWR tips despite having to change gauge at Neath. The floating harbour was 162 ft long by 56 ft wide having 22 acres of water of depth 22 ft (this included the so-called Duke of Beaufort's dock which was a basin on the east side of the river, opposite the town quay). The Act of 1847 by which the North dock came into being specified the dock dues to be charged: 2d per ton for cargoes from UK ports and up to 2/6d per ton for cargoes from any port to the east of the Cape of Good Hope or westwards of Cape Horn.

While the North Dock was clearly an improvement on what had gone before, it had narrow quays. There was a need for new docks with broad quays, linked to the railways. A group of private investors (the Swansea Dock Co) chose an area on the western side of the river as the site of the future South Dock. During construction in 1856/7 of this 13-acre dock with a 5½ acre basin, the Harbour Trust successfully negotiated to buy out the Swansea Dock Co. Then the SHT got the SWR and VofN Rly to guarantee to pay the interest on the Trustees' borrowings to build the 'Swansea Harbour Rly' of 1859 which extended the BG North Dock branch to the new South Dock. Along with the Victoria Dock in London, the South dock at Swansea was one of the first in the world to be fitted out with Armstrong

hydraulic equipment for lock gates, its swing bridge, coal wagon hoists, capstans and cranes.

To avoid the break of gauge at Neath, the VofN arranged to enter Swansea over a new mixed gauge route 7¾-miles long (the Swansea & Neath Rly of 1863 alongside the Jersey Marine coastline) which additionally bypassed the steep gradient at Skewen on the broad gauge SWR mainline. In anticipation of the arrival of the new line, the SHT leased the Swansea Harbour Rly and 1,000ft of wharf to the VofN Rly from 1862. The new line ran to Wind St Jct between the North and South docks, the lines of the harbour railway having been made mixed gauge by the VofN under its lease (broad gauge remained until 1872 in this part of the GW system). The new line enabled Aberdare and Merthyr coal to be shipped directly, and connected Swansea with the "narrow gauge outside world"; it also deprived the SWR/GWR its share of haulage revenue over the old route into Swansea. After opening of the new mixed gauge route, trade at the port rapidly developed, particularly VofN coal exports.

Another railway had access to the tracks at the North and South docks: this was the private Swansea Vale Rly which had its origins in tramroads built to bring Graigola coal to Swansea along the east bank of the Tawe. Much later it was extended northwards through Pontardawe to Brynamman (1862), and a branch bridged the Tawe to reach the North dock and Harbour Rly. There had been a scheme whereby the SWR was to purchase the Swansea Vale Rly but, as elsewhere in South Wales, the SWR seemed more concerned about completing the mainline line westwards than realising the traffic potential of the valley railways. This later let in the Midland Rly to the region, the MR leasing the Swansea Vale in 1874 and taking it over in 1876. The Midland reached its isolated acquisition from Hereford via the Neath & Brecon Rly at Ynys-y-Geinon Jct. The MR shipped coal from hoists at Swansea, the tips later being taken over by the LMS after the GWR bought up the SHT after the grouping.

In the period after 1861, the Llanelly Railway & Dock Co obtained various Acts enabling it and its subsidiary companies to extend lines into the Gower peninsular and to Carmarthen and Swansea (some new lines, others via running powers). The subsidiary Swansea & Carmarthen Rly came in from the west and connected with the South Dock, the line opening for mineral traffic in 1865. Later (1873) the S&C was taken over by the LNWR to which it was connected over the Central Wales line from Craven Arms via Llandovery and Llandeilo. Its terminal station was Swansea Victoria adjacent to the South Dock.

By 1879, the North and South docks had between them 10,000 ft of quayage, the whole of which was traversed by the 6¾ -mile long harbour railway which joined up with the GW, LNW and Midland Rlys all of which leased different parts from the Swansea Harbour Trustees. From 1865, the GW controlled the SWR, VofN Rly and Swansea & Neath Rly.

Trade through the port and the prosperity of the town grew quickly after the opening of the South Dock. There was also a dramatic change thereafter, not so much in the number of ships using the port but in their registered tonnage: in 1851, 3616 ships of 269,454 tons passed through but, in 1879, 5745 ships of 761,708 tons. This pattern continued: in 1903 for example, it would be 4730 ships of 2,041,181 registered tons. This came about because of the replacement of sail by steam and the ever-increasing size of steamers. These vessels were not only larger but also more costly to purchase than sailing ships, and hence required more deeply-dredged entrance channels and bigger docks with much better facilities for rapid loading and discharge. Between 1853 and 1863, comprehensive dredging obtained an extra 4 ft in the main channel at Swansea. Nevertheless it was not unknown for large steamers to have to ride at anchor off the Mumbles for the spring tides that would allow them to get in. Thus despite all the expenditure on dock facilities at Swansea, eventually neither of the two existing docks were able to meet the requirements of shippers.

In 1872 therefore, James Abernethy (who designed some of Birkenhead's docks) was asked to prepare plans for a grand new dock on the east side of the Tawe at Port Tennant and Fabian's Bay. The 27½ acre 'East dock' (soon named the Prince of Wales Dock), was opened in 1881, financial assistance having been given to the SHT by the GW for its construction. The contractor was the firm of

Walker's who were constructing the Severn Tunnel for the GWR. Only after the opening of the Prince of Wales dock was Swansea able to compete on something like equal terms with the other main ports in South Wales, at all of which newer and larger docks had been built on a regular basis for some years before. Between 1884 and 1890 the export trade of Swansea doubled in value, in which tinplate and copper figured prominently.

The rapidly expanding trade in tinplate for canning, in addition to the traditional trades connected with lead smelting, the extraction of silver and zinc, iron and steel, etc contributed greatly to the wealth of Swansea and its port at the end of the C19[th]. Chemical by-products became important: it was discovered in the 1860's how to produce sulphuric acid from copper waste, and this acid was required by the tinplate industry (the ready availability of sulphuric acid led to the location of the Mond nickel-refining works at Clydach nearby). Many factories were built on the dock estate itself, including the Kings Dock tinplate works The first shipment of tinplate direct to the USA took place in 1879; before that time the transatlantic trade was handled through Liverpool, coastal shipping taking the plates there from South Wales. Only about 1300 tons were exported in 1880, yet 30,000 tons in 1881, with 100,000-odd tons of tinplates in 1885 and nearly 280,000 tons in 1895! The USA levied a punitive import duty (the McKinley Tariff) which reduced trade from all the South Wales tinplate-exporting ports, but new markets were found in Russia and the Far East which compensated. The tinplate works around Swansea and Llanelly had almost a world monopoly until the USA entered the field at end of the C19[th]. Three-quarters of all tinplate produced in Great Britain was manufactured within 12 miles of Swansea.

New industries established themselves on or near the dock estate (Mond Nickel Co, Weaver's flour mill and grain warehouses of 1892 at the North dock; the factories of Graigola Merthyr Fuel Works and Rose Fuel Works making briquettes; tin stampers; creosote works etc) and a fishing fleet became established at the South Dock in 1903 when the Castle Steam Trawling Co moved to Swansea from Milford Haven. Between 1877 and 1884 there was a 185% increase in the tonnage of steamers using the port, and an increase of 60% for all types of ship; the national average was 26%. Weaver's opened a second flour mill in 1898, the multi-storey reinforced concrete framed building being the first of its type in Britain.

All this traffic required more quayage and a small extension to the Prince of Wales Dock was opened in 1898 which provided an extra 2000ft of quay around an extra 4 ¾ acres of water. This was important for the new Rhondda & Swansea Bay Rly which had been given independent access to the port by the SHT in 1895, and given the use of two coal tipping appliances on the northern side of the PoW dock extension when it opened (the third new coal hoist at that site was leased to the GWR, which already rented 1500 ft of quay in the PoW dock proper on which five coal hoists and general cargo hydraulic cranes had been erected together with associated wagon storage sidings). The R&SB

had its Swansea Riverside terminus at the side of the PoW dock from which its first train ran in 1895. In 1897 the company acquired old wharves on the east side of the North Dock for a goods depot for merchandise coming in by sea for dispatch to the Midlands. The coaling arrangements at the PoW extension were cramped at the rearranged tips where special arrangements, involving overlapping mooring, had to be made so that three large steamers could be coaled simultaneously. The rest of the quayage in the extension was equipped with moveable hydraulic cranes for general cargo.

As well as constructing the new dock, the Harbour Trust improved the old docks too: a new deeper entrance was given to the South dock in 1896 (to the cost of which the GW and LNW contributed) and the North dock had a new 30 ft deep lock in 1902, so that ships no longer got stuck at neap tides.

The growth of trade through Swansea up to WWI is illustrated by the following figures:

Year	Imports (tons)	Exports (tons)
1870	481,000	1,040,000
1881	623,000	1,342,000
1890	700,000	2,270,000
1900	845,000	3,260,000
1913	1,100,000	7,230,000

Given that the new docks at Port Talbot were opened in 1904 and took a lot of Swansea's potential coal exports, the above figures are impressive. Of the 1913 export figure, coal and coke amounted to 4 ½ million tons and briquettes to one million tons; tinplates and galvanised sheets amounted to over half a million tons, and a great quantity of copper and silver ores, pig iron and castings, timber and pitwood, grain and general cargo were imported. There were some 500 works and collieries within a radius of 20 miles. New markets were found for anthracite in San Francisco before WWI (and in Canada after). Anthracite was popular for domestic stoves in Northern Europe, particularly France, but the most important customers in France took small grades of anthracite for production of briquettes, with factories at Rouen and Caen.

In 1901 the SHT had applied to Parliament to build a new dock that would more than double the accommodation at Swansea. The resulting King's Dock was opened in 1909. There were 67½ acres of water area of depth about 30ft, and the new dock was connected to the PoW dock by a 70 ft wide channel, which had been the old sea lock. The new sea lock was 875 ft long by 90 ft wide with water depth above the outer cill of 40/32 ft spring/neap tides, and could be divided into separate 500 ft and 375 ft compartments, vessels entering being protected by an extended western pier and a new breakwater. There were over two miles of quays for general cargo (with associated transit sheds and handling equipment) and over ½ mile of quays devoted to coal shipment. Much of the transit cargo was tinplate which

arrived by rail from the mills in flat wooden boxes weighing between 1-2 cwts. Other cargo handled through the sheds was galvanised steel sheets and (ungalvanised) 'black plate'. Quantities of exported sheet metal at Swansea were known to reach over 600,000 tons in some years. The King's dock transit sheds were two-storied, the upper floors being used for foodstuffs and general cargo imports. By this time there were nine graving docks within the dock estate.

Under the 1901 Act authorising the construction of the King's dock, the RSB had the option of renting 475 ft of frontage which it did in 1910 and erected coal tips along the dock side. The GW also erected a quintet of three fixed (Nos 1,2 and 5) and two moveable (Nos 3 and 4) hydraulic coal hoists at the 1,000 ft of frontage that it leased alongside the King's dock. On land rented behind the tips, extensive sidings were laid down for full and empty wagons. The SHT also put in extensive sidings for the storage of loaded wagons awaiting shipment. Each tip was designed to cope with loaded wagons of 32-ton gross weight (ie 20-ton load) and each was equipped with 16 ft long Pooley automatic wagon weighbridges. The two moveable hoists had a range of 500 ft, and the rails on which they ran were of very heavy section (327 lb/yard), supplied by the Port Talbot Steel Co. Incoming wagons arrived at 18 ft above quay level; wagons could be tipped at any point between this height and 60 ft above the quay. The high arrival lines, which approached the hoists on overbridges, meant that three rail tracks and a cart road on the quay were left free for other traffic while tipping was in progress. Two of the hoists were erected on reinforced concrete jetties extending 50 ft out into the dock, thus enabling a greater number of vessels to be loaded or bunkered simultaneously. The set of 18 ft diameter wagon turntables were supplied by Ransomes & Rapier of Ipswich. The hoists ran off the SHT hydraulic mains. Early in their life, the tips proved their rapid loading abilities, over 6,600 tons of coal being loaded in a day. In addition to employing anti-breakage boxes at the end of chute extensions during the early stages of loading to avoid break-up of the coal, the tipping mechanism of these hoists had two fulcra whereby the drop from wagon to chute was practically eliminated, thus also helping to avoid breakage.

The capacity of wagon weighbridges around the dock was: a 25 tonner at the RSB Burrows sidings and another at the GW hoist at the PoW dock extension; at the King's dock, ten at 35 tons each; at the North dock, four at 20 tons each; at the PoW dock (i) the GW had six at 20 tons, one at 15, one at 8 tons; and (ii) the RSB two at 8 tons; and at the South dock there were six 20 tonners.

A further big dock (the Queen's dock) was then proposed before WWI. It was the last and biggest of the docks at Swansea, being over twice the size of the King's dock. So big a venture was the new dock, and its cost so high, that the Swansea Harbour Trustees sought and obtained the financial backing of Swansea Corporation, the loan to be repaid over a 10-year period after opening. The dock opened for traffic during the war (its official opening was 1920), but unfortunately the submarine threat during WWI reduced traffic and revenue at Swansea almost to nil, and the Trust was unable to repay the loan. Other ports around the UK were also affected to a greater or lesser degree by the lack of traffic in WWI, but those owned and controlled by railways received compensation, because the government took control of railways at the outset of war and promised to pay the 1913 'standard revenue'. The Swansea Harbour Trust was a private concern and despite appeals to Parliament was not baled out. Consequently, immediately after WWI, the Corporation took 'friendly action' against the Trust which went into receivership. The SHT invited the GWR to take over Swansea Docks which became vested officially in the GWR in 1923, after the GW had already taken over the other South Wales docks by virtue of the Grouping. Owing to the shortage of coastal vessels immediately after WWI, double the amount of anthracite was sent off by rail from West Wales in 1919 as compared with pre-war days.

The SHT owned four tugs: *Beaufort(I)* (1898) also used for tending buoys; the 148-ton *Trusty* (1913); the 147-ton *Swansea* (1918); and *Amy(I)* a small Blackwall tug of 1901 bought by the SHT in 1920. The *Don Frederico* (1909) was a bucket dredger built in 1909 for the Buenos Ayres & Pacific Rly Co and bought by the SHT in 1920. All were bought by the GW, but the *Beaufort* was sold to the Llanelly Harbour Trustees in 1925, (scrapped by them in 1931); and *Amy(I)* was sold off in 1933. The 119-ton *Beaufort(II)* and *Amy(II)* were built as replacements. There were dredgers operating at Swansea, and the *Abertawe* -- a dredger built for Swansea in 1947 -- had the distinction of being the final ship to be constructed for the GWR. The SHT owned tank shunting locos which the GW took over. Powlesland & Mason, a firm of shipping agents at Swansea and local agents for the GWR, were contracted by the SHT to supply additional dock locos; these were also taken over at that time by the GW which terminated the contract.

The Swansea docks when taken over by the GWR had a collective deep water area of 282 acres with an average depth of water of 21-29 ft. There were over 6 miles of quays and 17 acres of sheds (six transit sheds at the King's dock having a total floor area of 480,000 sq ft; seven at the Prince of Wales with 226,000 sq ft; five at the South dock with 79,000 sq ft and also the 26,000 sq ft Fish Market there; and one shed at the Riverside Wharf having 8,500 sq ft). The largest lock was 825 ft long by 90 ft wide; in addition there were three other smaller locks. There were 27 coal hoists, of which the seven in the King's dock were capable of tipping 20-ton wagons; the remaining 20 could handle only 12-ton wagons (nine in the Prince of Wales dock; five in the North dock; and six in the South dock).

In taking over the SHT, the GWR became the owner of the lighthouse on the outer of the two islets at Mumbles Head. The original lighthouse with coal fires in braziers dated from 1794; soon after an oil lantern was installed which lasted until 1905 when a compressed air and paraffin vapour lamp was put in. The 'occulted' signal was one short and one long flash every 20 seconds. In 1934 the GW decided to alter the illumination to electricity after which keepers were no longer required. The word 'telegraphs' was lettered boldly across the outside of the base of the lighthouse. This was a service to ships in the days when not all had wireless: messages received from ship owners were relayed by the lighthouse keeper to ships waiting in Mumbles roads for sailing orders. Flags were used by day and lamp at night in Morse code

The new Queen's dock never did have coal hoists, because an important development took place just after WWI which was probably just as well in the circumstances. The Anglo-Persian Oil Co (later BP) was looking for a UK site to refine imported crude oil. National Oil Refineries Ltd were to run the site. Swansea was chosen, the refinery (called by the made-up name 'Llandarcy' after the name (Darcy) of the founder of the oil company and 'llan' Welsh for church) being located at Skewen some three miles east of Queen's dock. The refinery was served by rail off the Jersey Marine-Lonlas Jct loop line. The whole of the south frontage of the new Queen's Dock was devoted to crude oil importing and refined petroleum exporting. Traffic started after the refinery came into operation in 1922 and soon contributed over one million tons to the port's business, rising to over two million tons per annum by the mid-1920's. Vessels of the British Tanker Co carried oil from Abadan in the Persian Gulf which was converted into petrol, lubricating oils, scents and dyes, drugs etc. With the refinery on its doorstep, it was easy to provide facilities for oil bunkering of steamers at a jetty near the entrance to the lock of King's Dock; vessels did not have to enter the dock, and could be quickly handled at almost any state of the tide.

As part of the modernisation plan for Swansea, and with a view to encouraging diversified trade, the GW developed the 680 ft long by 141 ft wide mole, that jutted out into the King's dock, into two general cargo berths in 1928. A large new 352 ft by 75 ft two-storey warehouse with 4-ton gantry cranes was built on the site. Eight semi-portal 3-ton electric level-luffing cranes were provided, four on each side of the quay. A feature of general trade through Swansea between the wars was that many cargo lines operated from the port. The vessels employed by such companies were larger than could be accommodated in neighbouring ports so trade tended to gravitate to Swansea to the exclusion of Llanelly, Burry Port, Briton Ferry and Neath. Coal shipment too was made more efficient: old hoists were refurbished to take the new 20-ton Pole wagons and new hoists erected; and the layout of coal storage yards were improved. Before WWI, coal shipments at Swansea were 4.5 million tons; in 1925 it was still at the 3 million ton level.

There was a wider scheme to rationalise the running lines of all the former independent companies operating around Swansea. Before the amalgamation, the RSB and GWR (ex VofN) had parallel sets of lines from Briton Ferry to Court Sart, and again from Dynevor Jct to the RSB terminus. After the Grouping all the RSB passenger traffic was put on to GW lines (in stages between 1933-6) and the RSB lines made mineral-only (the stations being closed). This enabled the extensive Burrows hump marshalling yards to be remodelled and enlarged to accommodate 1782 wagons (a 60 % increase), and these sidings together with the old RSB double track between Briton Ferry Road station and the Swansea docks, were handed over for the exclusive use of the Docks Department for its traffic.

The North dock was closed to commercial traffic in 1928, being too small for modern shipping, but the 2½ acre (now tidal) basin remained. According to the 1936 edition of GWR Docks there were 4 dry docks at Swansea (all privately-owned): the Castle fishing fleet belonging to Consolidated Fisheries owned the 370 ft by 60 ft graving dock off the South dock; there was a 455 ft by 60 ft dry dock off the Prince of Wales dock; and Palmer's operated the large 560 ft by 75 ft graving dock as well as a repairing jetty that could berth ships up to 760 ft long. In comparison with the equipment when the GW took over the SHT in 1923, there was one more coal hoist in the King's Dock making eight in all (all capable of lifting wagons 60ft; a Vickers-Armstrong travelling hoist had been built at the Tennant Canal Laybye in 1934); two fewer in both the Prince of Wales and South docks (leaving seven and four, respectively, all rising to 50 ft) but there was by then a coal conveyor belt operating in the Prince of Wales dock. All five hoists had been removed from the closed North dock, of course. There were four 'bucket escalator' anti-coal-breakage appliances at Swansea. The distribution of cranes was as follows:

Hydraulic: 24 GW cranes at the King's dock (70 tons biggest capacity) and six more privately owned (2 tons); 32 in the Prince of Wales dock (12 tons and all GW-owned); seven GW cranes in the South dock and one private (all 1½-ton capacity).
Electric: 28 GW cranes at the King's dock (3 tons) and 5 private (2 tons); four privately-owned at the South dock (2 tons). There was also a private 1½-ton electric crane at the Riverside Wharf.

After Milford Haven, Swansea was the next most important trawler port and many fish vans (S6 from 1912, and S12 of 1925, in the GW Wagon Diagram book) were assigned to Swansea when built and had written instructions that they should be returned to the South Dock (see *GWR Goods Wagons*). In the 1920's over 15,000 tons of fish/year were landed at Swansea South Dock by the Castle Steam Trawling Co (owned by Consolidated Fisheries Ltd of Grimsby). In 1947, the weekly loading of fish wagons at Swansea was 120. There was an ice factory, fish curing equipment and a factory off the Queen's dock where fish offal was manufactured into fish meal for poultry food. The LNWR (LMS) carried fish away from Swansea as well as the GWR: its trains for the north would run to Llandeilo to attach vans from Milford Haven before proceeding along the central Wales route.

In July 1940 the King's dock at Swansea suffered one of the early air attacks on Great Britain. A single German plane probing the air defences strafed the quay, killed a number of workers and damaged the railway tracks. Swansea suffered severely from bombing, particularly in the heavy raids of February 1941.

LLANELLY, BURRY PORT, KIDWELLY, PEMBREY, and CARMARTHEN (some served; some owned)

The town of Carmarthen is situated on a small hill on the west bank of the River Towy and is some 10 miles from the sea. Long before the railway arrived in 1852, the river was navigable quite far upstream and there was a commercial quay at Carmarthen. Brunel kept the main line of the SWR on level ground to the south and established a station (the later Carmarthen Jct) near the east bank of the Towy. As the river was navigable, (in 1851 steam packets sailed twice a week to Bristol), the railway had to be carried on a bridge having two spans each 50 ft clear at the centre. This 1853 bridge was replaced in 1908 by a bascule opening bridge, even though trade through Carmarthen quay had been falling away for years owing to silting up of the river and the consequent difficulties of vessels getting up to the quay. Trade diminished fairly rapidly after WWI.

The south-east corner of Carmarthenshire was rich in anthracite coal which had been dug out from surface pits since the C16[th] and exported by sea to Ireland, and across the Bristol Channel. Approaches to the Gwendraeth estuary were however very dangerous owing to the shifting Cefn Sidan sands, compounded by shipwrecks. Furthermore, navigation on the Gwendraeth and Lougher river estuaries has always been hazardous, so few sites were ideal for commercial harbours. Nevertheless, when anthracite pits in the vicinity began to be worked, Kidwelly harbour was employed for exporting the coal. Coal from further inland was got down to the sea by Kymer's canal which had been cut up the valley from the old Kidwelly harbour in 1766 to serve pits in the lower reaches of the Gwendraeth; (such 'canals' were really short sections of waterway without locks and lock gates, which became navigable at high tide). Twenty thousand tons of coal per annum were being exported from around the Burry estuary in coastal and near-continental shipping as early as 1770.

East along the coast, at Llanelly, smelting of metal had begun in the early C18[th] and the Carmarthenshire Railway of 1802 (a 16-mile long horse-drawn tramway) was projected to bring limestone, for both agricultural use and as a flux in iron smelting, from quarries at Castell-y-Garreg to the dock there that dated from 1795, and was called the 'Carmarthenshire' dock. Pemberton's coal dock (1803) and Copper Works dock (1805) were soon in operation too. All were really tidal basins with stone-built loading points and timber staging for coal tips on to which the tramroads ran. The Copper Works Dock was also called Nevill's Dock after the name of the owners of the works (who were a colliery/smelting empire with extensive tramroads and railways feeding the port). The dock, built to import copper ore from Cornwall, was converted into a proper wet dock with lock gates in 1825. When copper smelting went into decline in the 1840's, this dock with its 396 ft of quayage, became the main Llanelly dock handling coal.

In 1813 the Kidwelly & Llanelly Canal & Tramroad Co was created to construct a canal and tramroads to

A 1920's view of the New Dock (GW Dock) at Llanelly taken from the entrance gates. In 1880 there were eight coal hoists in all, four on either side, but only two left by 1906. Hydraulic cranes on the quay at the top left. [Amgueddfa Cymru National Museum of Wales]

connect collieries in the Gwendraeth Valley with the towns of Kidwelly and Llanelly. These tramroads, built a few years later, ran down to Kymer's canal. In 1825, the Pembrey Harbour Company was formed to improve the existing (1819) harbour at Pembrey (a tidal creek) and to build more tramroads to connect with the Kidwelly & Llanelly company's lines. Silting of Pembrey Harbour and its approaches restricted the size of vessels able to enter the port to about 100 tons, so local industrialists concerned with the growing coal export trade formed a new company in 1825 to construct a larger and better-located 'New Pembrey Harbour' (later called 'Burry Port'). Burry Port outer harbour was completed in 1836 and the connecting East (wet) dock in 1840 with four coal tips (for details of the West dock, see later). Because of the opening of Burry Port dock, the K&LlC&TCo's canal from Kidwelly in fact terminated there and never reached Llanelly. By the mid-C19[th], nearly all the coal traffic from the Gwendraeth Valley was being exported from Burry Port, as silting at Kidwelly severely limited shipping activities there. Industry was attracted to Burry Port because of the dock facilities, so that copper and lead smelting, iron and steel, and tinplate works were set up in the vicinity in Victorian times. Near Pembrey too, a dynamite and explosives factory was built in the 1880's and efforts were made to revive trade through Pembrey. The dock was never connected by rail and it seems that the harbour was abandoned in the early 1900's owing to silting.

Soon after Burry Port had obtained its 1825 Act for a dock, the Llanelly Railway & Dock Co came into being in 1828 as a 2½ mile horse-drawn tramway to exploit the Llangennech and other coal reserves and transport the coal to a new floating harbour at Machynys Pool (later to be called 'Llanelly New Dock'). The Llanelly Rly & Dock Co is sometimes said to have been the first combined dock and railway enterprise in the world, but it was preceded by three years by the Duffryn, Llynvi & Porthcawl Dock & Rly company (see Porthcawl). The Llanelly New dock was opened in 1834 just before the Burry Port dock was completed. There were coal shipping staithes both within the wet dock at Llanelly and outside (these latter being tidal, of course). Rivalry between Burry Port and Llanelly docks features strongly in the development of shipping activities in this area and both docks were equally afflicted by the problems of navigation on the Gwendraeth and Lougher estuaries

Coal exports from Llanelly rose from 70,000 tons/year in the 1820's to 212,000 tons/year in the 1840's since Llangennech coal was the favourite for steamships in the days before steam coal from south east Wales had become famous and in high demand. In fact Llanelly was the first port in Wales to ship coal to distant places such as India, the Red Sea, Africa and South America for bunkering steamers belonging to the Peninsular Line, the Orient Line, East India Line and so on. Soon after the Llanelly New Dock was opened, the owners of the Cwm Amman colliery also began to send coal by rail to Llanelly instead of to Swansea as it considered the Llanelly dock authorities to be much more up to date. It was a warning shot across the bows of the Swansea Harbour Trust to get its act together and improve facilities there. Nevertheless, it was difficult to encourage shipowners to use Llanelly and even when they did, they would demand higher freight charges which cut coalowners' profits. In 1833, the Nevill collieries were quoting 7/3d per ton for coal shipped from the quay, but 9/9d per ton for coal shipped from lighters in the outer harbour which was as far as larger vessels could reach. As at so many other places, the lock gate entrance at Llanelly later proved rather narrow for newer and bigger vessels.

By 1845, exports of coal from Llanelly had been surpassed by those from Cardiff and Newport, and tonnage stagnated thereafter. Bituminous coal extraction in the Llanelly area was replaced in later years by anthracite coal from the northern periphery of the Carmarthenshire coalfield, but by that time most coal from the area was being shipped from the more-easily-accessed ports at Swansea and Briton Ferry.

The LR&DC came into new ownership in 1835. The new proprietors were expansionist and obtained permission to construct a steam-locomotive railway westwards to Llandilo,
eventually reached in 1857. By leasing the independent Vale of Towy line beyond Llandilo, the LR&DC reached Llandovery. The first cargo of anthracite from Pontardulais (on the line to Llandilo) was shipped from the Llanelly New dock in 1839. The company also bought a steam paddle tug *PT Hercules* for the dock in 1837 which was also used on a service between Llanelly and Bristol, but it had to be sold in 1845 after it was established that the company had exceeded its statuary powers.

Prospects for generating sufficient income in order to modernise the facilities at Llanelly were not good and in 1857 the Llanelly Rly & Dock Co attempted to sell the dock to the Burry Harbour Commissioners, but the offer was declined. The LD&RC decided to concentrate on its railway interests rather than its dock and in 1867 constructed a branch line eastwards from Pontardulais to Swansea (Victoria) which gave access to the superior accommodation at South dock, Swansea, for export of the anthracite it carried from pits along its line. Soon afterwards the LNWR reached Llandovery and persuaded the LR&DC to give it running powers into Swansea: this the LR&DC later regretted as the LNWR took much of its traffic. Eventually, in 1873, an agreement was reached for the GWR to administer the financially-troubled LR&DC and this was followed by a formal Act in 1889 by which the company was divided between the GWR and LNWR. The subsidiary Swansea and Carmarthen Rly (Llandilo line) went to the LNW, and the GWR took over the New Dock at Llanelly together with all the locos and rolling stock. The New Dock then began to be called the 'Great Western' or 'GWR' dock. When opened by the LR&DC there were four coal tips built on short jetties extending out in to the water over the sloping banks of that side of the dock; a proper wharf for general cargo was on the other side of the dock where the railway had its terminus. Later, the four tips were reduced to two in order to accommodate larger vessels. The LNWR began to work goods and mineral traffic to Llanelly docks in 1875.

Over at Burry Port, the dock, canal and tramroad companies amalgamated in 1866 to form the Burry Port and Gwendraeth Valley Rly (not to be confused with the Gwendraeth Valley Rly which was an entirely different concern running from Kidwelly to Mynydd-y-Garreg). The canal and tramways were abandoned and converted into a steam-hauled railway. Plans for a second basin (the West dock) at Burry Port had been prepared in the 1840's and the West dock had in fact been built by the 1860's, but had not been opened for traffic as the demand had not grown as expected. Later, with the working of new seams of anthracite, trade increased so much so that the BP&GVR brought the West dock into use in 1888; (but it was closed again 13 years later, see below). Then, in 1891, the old defunct tramroads from Pembrey to Llanelly were converted into a standard gauge railway and added to the BP&GV Rly system; the new lines made a junction at Sandy Gate with the Llanelly and Mynydd Mawr Rly (see below). Although the BP&GVR had a branch to Kidwelly Quay (the original terminus of the canal and tramroad), Kidwelly's natural hinterland was now connected to Burry Port and thereafter trade at Kidwelly declined sharply as ships became bigger and could not get into the harbour. Kidwelly closed in the 1930's, even though still rail-connected. In 1885 total imports to Burry Port were over 20,000 tons of which 75% was copper ore; total exports were nearly 80,000 tons of which 90% was coal. Other imports included pig iron, iron ore, timber, limestone, bricks and fertiliser; other exports included copper, bricks, lead products, and tinplate.

The Carmarthenshire Rly (the horse-drawn tramway of 1802) had fallen into decay and the company went into liquidation in 1844. The Burry Harbour Commissioners bought the Carmarthenshire Rly tidal dock at Llanelly and erected some coal tips, but the Commissioners had little revenue with which to develop facilities and it became a marginal facility for the port as a whole. Even so, it was listed after the Grouping in GW publicity as a working rail-connected dock. The important development, however, was that in 1875 the trackbed of the old Carmarthenshire Rly was bought by a new railway (the Llanelly & Mynnyd Mawr) who relaid it for steam locomotives and began to bring down anthracite for export. Contractors and operators of the LMM were John Waddell & Sons of Edinburgh. The firm had been a contractor on the conversion of the Kidwelly & Llanelly Canal into the BP&GV railway in 1867-69, and the firm returned to the region in 1880 to construct the LMM. After completion, Waddell's worked the line under contract and eventually owned it. As part of the development of the area, Waddell's opened Great Mountain Colliery near Cross Hands in 1887 and others in the Tumble area. Waddell's had secured an agreement in 1882 with the Burry Harbour Commissioners to have access to their pier where the LMM built a wagon coal tip. The tip was tidal but the Commissioners undertook to maintain a safe berth with a reasonable depth of water. Unfortunately the Commissioners were strapped for money, and dredging (done on a shoestring) was unsatisfactory. It was a Catch-22 situation: revenue from the port was not big enough to give

A close-up of the nearer of the two tips in the other picture taken at an earlier date. Wooden jetty sticking out from sloping sides. Timber framework of hoist. Crane attached to bucket sitting on jetty at rail level. On the other side of the dock the quay is also wooden framed and has a travelling steam crane. [GWR]

them adequate funds to improve things, and earnings from the docks could only increase when improvements had been made. This gave rise to a dispute with Waddell's that was not resolved until just before the Grouping.

In the second half of the C19[th] coast trade between Llanelly and Liverpool was more important than with Bristol. Timber imports grew in Victorian times as local supplies ran out. To the historical exports of copper ingots, copper sheets, lead ingots and so on, tinplates appeared, the production of which eventually replaced copper smelting at Llanelly and around Burry Port. By 1880 there were 31 tinplate works in the town, some three-quarters of the production being exported to the USA. To cope with the trade, the Burry Harbour Commissioners decided in 1895 to build a new dock (called the Llanelly North Dock upon its opening in 1903) on the site of the reservoir in which water was stored for scouring the navigable channel into the port. A large amount of money had to be borrowed from the Bank of England. The nine-acre dock, 1000 ft long by 400 ft wide, was opened in 1903 with 24/16ft water depth at spring/neap tides. Hydraulic power was employed throughout for a swing bridge carrying the railway, the 53 ft wide lock gates,

capstans, winches, coal hoists and cranes. There were three coal stages on the western side of the dock, only two of which were fitted with Armstrong Whitworth hydraulic hoists. On the eastern side, the berths were equipped with hydraulic and steam cranes for general cargo, and also a warehouse for cargo requiring storage. A 1911 pamphlet states that there was a 20 ton wagon weighbridge on both sides of the dock, that on the south side having a slightly smaller plate than the other. There were some 7 miles of sidings and connecting lines to the LMM, BPGVR and GWR. The long-standing dispute, mentioned above, with the LMM over mud at the coal tip berth and the channel leading to it, was exacerbated after the new North dock was built, as it blocked the scouring stream. When the North Dock was opened, the Llanelly Harbour Trust (the name taken by the Burry Harbour Commissioners in 1903), gave the LMM exclusive rights to No 1 hydraulic hoist in the North dock as an interim settlement of the dispute, and the tidal coal stage was abandoned. But by then the LMM exported more coal from Swansea (118,000 tons) than from Llanelly (55,000 tons).

The most active dock at Llanelly was the privately-owned Nevill's Copperworks dock that not only was linked by extensive industrial tramways (and later railways) to local copper smelters and collieries, but was also connected to the other railways in the region. In the early days, copper ore required a bonded store since it bore a substantial import duty upon which manufacturers could obtain a drawback of duty when manufactured copper goods were exported. The Nevill dock and associated warehouses served a wide range of local manufacturing in the iron, steel and tinplate trades and there was regular cargo liner traffic to and from the Clyde, Mersey, Bristol and London. Ships in this trade had used the Copper Works Dock in sailing days and carried on into steamer times in preference to the other docks. Nevill's made improvements in the facilities at its dock (hydraulic power for lock gates and craneage), but non-ferrous smelting began to decline and production of coal from the Nevill collieries was on the wane, so in 1894 Nevill's offered the dock to the Burry Harbour commissioners. The offer was declined. As the C20th progressed, more and more cargo-carrying ocean liners began to use Swansea. In consequence cargoes of tinplate and steel, formerly sent from Llanelly to the Mersey for transhipment, could now more easily be sent directly. Trade at Nevill's dock declined even further and the dock was offered to the GWR. Once again, the offer was refused. Nevertheless, when the Copper Works Dock closed in 1945, it was still making a profit and paying a dividend, unlike the Llanelly Harbour Trust's North Dock on which so much money had been spent. In the inter-war years, the annual levels of trade at Nevill's Dock & Rly Co were: 120,000-odd tons of seaborne goods and 250,000-odd tons carried by rail. A new trade started in 1932 at Nevill's dock with the importation of large quantities of gas coal from Ayr and Troon; in earlier times Llanelly had sent coal to the Clyde!

At the turn of the C19th/20th, the threat of competition from a rival new (North) dock at Llanelly having the latest facilities spurred the BP&GVR (who owned the Burry Port Dock) to modernise. It closed the short-lived West dock permanently in 1901, and concentrated on the old East dock. There, between 1900-4, it installed hydraulic equipment including two new hoists (but only capable of lifting wagons 15ft into the air). Together with new steel lock gates in 1908, all this put Burry Port Dock on a par with Llanelly. Burry Port could accommodate vessels up to 1800 tons. For occasional general cargo, there were one-ton capacity hydraulic cranes attached to the coal hoists and a 2½ ton capacity steam crane was available.

The viability of Llanelly as a port was in already doubt by the time the North dock was opened, since (i) tinplate exports to the USA stopped after the crippling McKinley tariff was imposed on imported tinplate; (ii) a lot of the export coal from the Amman Valley was siphoned off to the docks at Swansea on the opening of the LNWR direct line from Pontardulais; and (iii) approaches to the port, already difficult for small vessels, were even worse for newer, larger vessels. Prospects for the New Dock were equally precarious. The absence of trade in WWI, and lack of government help (not being a railway-owned dock) put the

Llanelly Harbour Trust into heavy debt. Just before WWI, 110 vessels/month had called at Llanelly, but the port saw only 10 or 20 vessels/month, or even none at all, during the war.

Similar trends were to be found at Burry Port where, although the revamped dock was not really adequate, copper smelters and new businesses were attracted immediately after opening, and trade through the harbour increased. But, like the adjacent ports, it experienced trading difficulties at the beginning of the C20th. Copper smelting was in decline and the last imports of copper ore were landed in 1911. Then, in 1912-14, the harbour experienced a build-up of sand and the port was kept open only with difficulty. Traffic declined markedly: in 1913 only 182 vessels loading 97,000 tons of coal and anthracite paid dock dues, compared with 954 vessels loading 211,000 tons at Llanelly in the same year. During WWI exports and imports of coal and other trades fell dramatically, and Burry Port saw only 2 or 3 vessels/month (or none) arrive and depart. While freight rates went up during WWI and so the earnings of ships went up, the income of the port did not. In 1918, only 52 vessels docked with 30,000 tons of coal shipped. In the immediate post-WWI boom, an incredible 475 ships docked in 1920, but then only 141 vessels in 1921. During the boom there was a shortage of ships, and people believed that coal exports would return to prewar levels, so local shipowners invested in new shipping, but it came to nought and the new vessels were soon laid up.

Matters were not in a happy state at the time of the Grouping. The navigational problems that had made Kidwelly Harbour go into decline after the opening of Burry Port, and after the formation of the BP&GV Rly, together with the increasing size of ships, eventually had their effect on the harbours at Burry Port and Pembrey too. The little harbour at Pembrey had become so silted that it had been abandoned long before, and Kidwelly harbour fell into disuse in the 1920's. In the 1924 *List of Collieries on or connected with the Great Western Railway* the complicated dock ownership and facilities at Llanelly and Burry Port was explained as follows:

'...........The docks of the port are the Great Western Railway Dock, the North Dock, the Copper Works dock, and the Carmarthenshire Dock.

The GWR Dock is 600 ft long by 200 ft wide, the width at entrance being 30 ft and is equipped with coal tips each having a lifting capacity of 20 tons gross. There is also a River wharf 300 ft long outside the dock where vessels load and discharge aground.

The North Dock, owned by the Llanelly Harbour Trust, is about 1000 ft long by 400 ft wide, with a lock entrance 53 ft wide. One side of the dock is devoted to the shipment of coal; the other to imports and general exports. The dock is in direct railway communication with the main line of the GWR, which runs close alongside. The coal tips are capable of dealing with wagons of 20 tons gross weight.

The Copper Works Dock is 680 ft long and 110 ft wide with

an entrance 31 ft wide. The dock is equipped with coal shipping appliances, and hydraulic, fixed and travelling cranes.

The Carmarthenshire Dock is tidal and has a depth of water of 19ft at high water spring tides.

The Great Western dock at Burry Port is 392 ft long and 153 ft wide (1¼ acres), with an entrance width of 45 ft. The 478 ft of quays are equipped with hydraulic cranes and coal shipment hoists. The water depth is 21 ft (High Water Ordinary Spring Tide) and 14 ft (High Water Ordinary Neap Tide). There is also a tidal harbour 15 acres in extent with a 221 ft entrance, having cranes for discharging ballast.........'

So much Carmarthenshire coal was being taken to Swansea with its better facilities and shipping connexions that the GW indicated after the Grouping that its dock at Llanelly (the old New dock) would become merely a tidal harbour and would eventually cease to operate altogether; there was a tidal wharf used by Richard Thomas & Co for iron and steel in the New Dock channel which would be affected. The GW declined an offer to buy Nevill's dock and the GW closed its dock at Llanelly in 1927.

After WWI things picked up somewhat at Llanelly's North dock. In 1923, for example, about 700,000 tons of coal were exported from the two coal tips on the North Dock (the LMM was carrying over 400,000 tons of coal a year to Llanelly just before absorption by the GWR), and tinplate production and exports were robust with the growth of the international canning industry. But by 1926 (the year of the General Strike) there was a low of 99,000 tons of coal exports, which were back at the level of 1835. At Burry Port, too, the coal trade declined after the Grouping, only 59 ships calling in 1926 taking off 24,000 tons of coal. The coal shipping equipment remained as before, ie two hydraulic lifts capable of merely 15 ft elevation. There were brief spells of prosperity for Llanelly North dock in the inter-war years, interspersed with more periods of not much happening. Ships did arrive with timber, but they had to leave in ballast to ship coal at other South Wales ports. The Cymric Fuel Works and the Reliance Fuel Works ran briquette factories on the dock estate in 1930's, and the Harbour Trust had some income from small businesses established on the dock estate between the wars, but it still was in deep debt to the Bank of England. Exports fluctuated between highs of 80,000 tons/annum to lows of 20,000 tons/annum. Coal shipments were suspended during 1940-42 and there was a sharp decline in import cargo. In 1943 only 966 tons of coal were shipped at Burry Port and that was effectively the end of the place as a commercial dock and it closed. Earnings from ancillary industries, brokerage, and employment at Llanelly suffered greatly. Some government supplies did come through (130,000 tons of iron and steel; and 11,000 tons of steel scrap, all stored on the Trust's dock estate). Llanelly was one of a number of 'oil ports' from where the liberating armies were supplied after the D-Day landings in Normandy in 1944 and 157,000 tons of petrol

were handled. A significant factor at Llanelly and Burry Port during WWII was that dredging was suspended, making access to the docks even more difficult.

A feature of operation at Llanelly and Burry Port was that coal shipping and general cargo work at the docks was dealt with by contractors. Both docks were too small to be improved, and with the decline of both the local coal and steel industries, things began to run down quickly after WWII. Eventually, the Llanelly Trustees could no longer afford to maintain the port and the dock closed in 1951.

PEMBROKE DOCK (served)

The Admiralty had been building ships in West Wales from the time of the Napoleonic Wars. Originally the dockyard had been on the north side of Milford Haven, but in 1814 the Admiralty moved these activities to Paterchurch on the south side, which was known as 'Pembroke Dock' thereafter. Pembroke Dock did not get a railway until 1864 (the Pembroke & Tenby). The SWR terminus at Neyland (New Milford) on the northern shores of the Haven had been reached earlier, in 1856, and some traffic for the town of Pembroke was taken by regular ferry and lighter across the River Cleddau from New Milford to Hobbs Point.

The standard gauge P&T Rly was extended to Whitland on the SWR main line in 1866, and thence to Carmarthen. The P&T was built at the time when it was firmly believed that the natural harbour at Milford Haven would come to rival Liverpool and the Mersey as a transatlantic port (see New Milford). Until the narrowing of the broad gauge in South Wales in 1872, the P&T wooed, and was wooed by, other 'narrow' gauge lines with a view to opening up through routes, but after 1872 there were good relations with the GW and through trains were run. The P&T was taken over by the GW in 1897.

It would seem logical that the Dockyard should have wanted to become connected with the railway to bring in supplies but, as at Devonport, the Admiralty was not keen on the prospect of commercial shipping cluttering up the waters. For that reason it had prevented the P&T building a short branch to the ferry wharf at Hobbs Point where it had been originally intended to build the terminus of the railway. In response, the P&T saw no reason why it should build a line to the dockyard. Eventually, however, agreement was reached on both matters and in 1870/1 the ½-mile goods branch to Hobbs Point wharf was built and the tracks from Pembroke Dock passenger station were extended to the dockyard. The extension to the dockyard had severe gradients and many level crossings where it passed through the town of Pembroke. The wharf at Hobbs Point was equipped with a series of sidings and wagon turntables, together with a steam crane and tip for coal and culm. It was never a commercial success as the water was not deep enough and the Admiralty (again!) objected to building a pier out into deeper water.

The Royal Dockyard employed about 3000 people in Victorian times and it brought traffic to the P&T in terms of supplies of coal, ships stores, iron and steel plate, munitions and so on. At first the P&T were responsible for

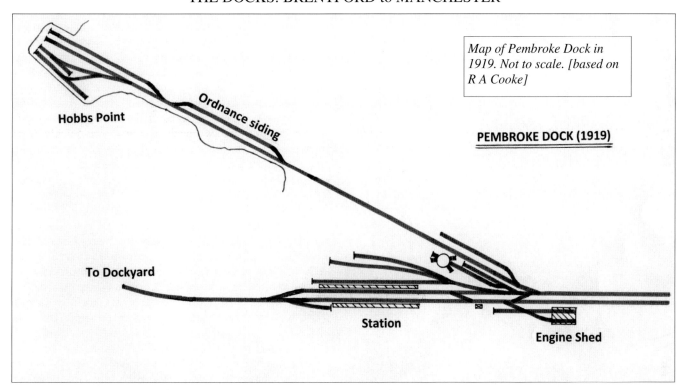

Map of Pembroke Dock in 1919. Not to scale. [based on R A Cooke]

PEMBROKE DOCK (1919)

Hobbs Point

Ordnance siding

To Dockyard

Station

Engine Shed

maintenance of the tracks within the dockyard, as well as the approach lines, but in 1891 the Admiralty bought the dock railway and took control. The Royal Dockyard at Pembroke continued to build ships, and even submarines, in WWI but its last ship was launched in 1922 (the *Oleander*, a Royal Fleet Auxiliary tanker). Some ships would be sent to Devonport for fitting out. The sudden closing of the dockyard in 1926 caused local unemployment but the difficulties were alleviated somewhat when Pembroke Dock became an RAF seaplane/flying boat base in 1930.

NEW MILFORD (NEYLAND) (owned; ex-SWR)

Brunel had concluded in his planning of the South Wales Rly in the 1840's that the best place for the western terminus of the line that would provide a port for rail-connected services to Ireland would be the natural harbour at Fishguard (nearby Abermawr was also considered). When the GW leased the SWR in 1846, it was on the understanding that the line would run to Fishguard. Owing to problems in Ireland in 1849, the SWR realised that the costs of a line to Fishguard would not be recouped. The GW, initially uncompromising that the line must go to Fishguard, eventually agreed in 1851 that somewhere on the shores of the natural harbour of Milford Haven would be the port of embarkation for boats to Ireland. The site chosen was Neyland, on the other side of the Haven from the Admiralty Dockyard at Pembroke. At a special meeting of the South Wales Railway shareholders in 1853, it was agreed to submit a Bill for constructing and maintaining a pier at Neyland that was to be reached through Haverfordwest from Carmarthen.

A factor that played a role in the choice of the natural harbour of Milford Haven was that it could be entered by the largest vessels at all states of the tide and it was firmly believed in the 1840's and 1850's that it would become a great port for ocean steamers and probably for fast transatlantic mail and passenger services as well, and rival, if not surpass, the then premier transatlantic port of Liverpool. This hope led to the promotion of the Manchester & Milford Haven Rly in 1846. The intention was to make a railway from the town of Milford Haven to Crewe from which Manchester would be reached, and it was hoped that much of the goods traffic from the north of England, then exported from Liverpool, would go instead by train to West Wales, and from there by ship. But the scheme was too ambitious for the times (1846 was the year of the 'railway mania' in which no less than 272 Acts relating to new railways were passed!) and little happened. In the years following, much of the northern area to be served by the proposed M&MHR became occupied by small companies that eventually became part of either the Cambrian Rlys or the LNWR. Interest was reawakened, however when the SWR was opened as far as Carmarthen and Haverfordwest in 1854. This made possible the opening of the local Carmarthen & Cardigan Railway whose line penetrated into the proposed territory of the M&MHR. The promoters of this dormant railway now had another go, and a new company called the Manchester & Milford Railway was formed in 1860 to construct a line from Llanidloes on the Lanidloes & Newtown Rly to Pencader on the Carmarthen & Cardigan Rly. In 1865 another Act enabled the M&MR to get to Aberystwyth. For various complicated reasons (including the crazy situation that both the M&MR and the Mid-Wales Railway had independently acquired construction rights over the same piece of ground between Llanidloes and Penpontbren!), the M&MR failed and by the

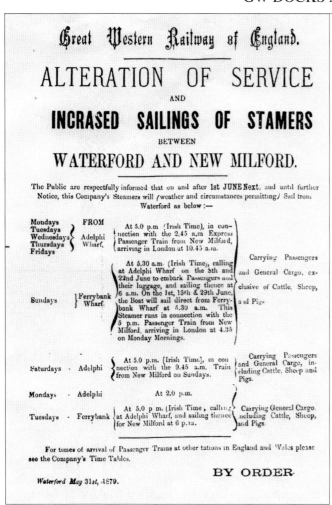

Great Western Railway of England.

ALTERATION OF SERVICE

AND

INCRASED SAILINGS OF STAMERS

BETWEEN

WATERFORD AND NEW MILFORD.

The Public are respectfully informed that on and after 1st JUNE Next, and until further Notice, this Company's Steamers will (weather and circumstances permitting) Sail from Waterford as below :—

Mondays Tuesdays Wednesdays Thursdays Fridays	FROM Adelphi Wharf,	At 5.0 p.m (Irish Time), in connection with the 2.45 a.m Express Passenger Train from New Milford, arriving in London at 10.45 a.m.	Carrying Passengers and General Cargo, exclusive of Cattle, Sheep, and Pigs
Sundays	Ferrybank Wharf	At 5.30 a.m. (Irish Time), calling at Adelphi Wharf on the 8th and 22nd June to embark Passengers and their luggage, and sailing thence at 6 a.m. On the 1st, 15th & 29th June, the Boat will sail direct from Ferrybank Wharf at 6.30 a.m. This Steamer runs in connection with the 5 p.m Passenger Train from New Milford, arriving in London at 4.35 on Monday Mornings.	
Saturdays - Adelphi		At 5.0 p.m. (Irish Time), in connection with the 9.45 a.m. Train from New Milford on Sundays.	Carrying Passengers and General Cargo, including Cattle, Sheep and Pigs.
Mondays - Adelphi		At 2.0 p.m.	
Tuesdays - Ferrybank		At 5.0 p m. (Irish Time, calling at Adelphi Wharf, and sailing thence for New Milford at 6 p.m.	Carrying General Cargo, including Cattle, Sheep, and Pigs.

For times of arrival of Passenger Trains at other stations in England and Wales please see the Company's Time Tables.

BY ORDER.

Waterford May 31st, 1879.

early 1880's was in receivership. The GW wanted to buy the line, but was opposed by the Cambrian Rlys. Eventually the GW leased the line for 999 years in 1905. Details of its history may be found in a series of three articles in the 1916 *Railway Magazine*.

The last (single-line) section of the original South Wales Railway from Haverfordwest to the pier at Neyland was opened in April 1856. Because the station and pier at Neyland formed the only railway-connected harbour facilities on the Milford Haven natural harbour at the time (the Pembroke and Tenby Rly did not open until 1864) and because 'Milford Haven' was better-known than Neyland, the station and pier at Neyland were named 'New Milford' – 'New' because Milford proper was what is now known as the town of Milford Haven, seven miles or so westwards along the coast. When, in 1863, that town was joined by rail to the SWR at Johnston by the independent Milford Jct Rly, its station was named 'Old Milford'. When the port of embarkation for the Irish boats was moved to Fishguard in 1906, New Milford station reverted to Neyland, and Old Milford became Milford Haven.

Soon after the SWR line to Neyland was opened, negotiations were concluded with the Vale of Neath Railway, who helped pay for the laying of a second line of rails from Carmarthen so that the VofN could bring trains of coal for shipment and bunkers. Doubling was completed in 1857. (There was a break of gauge, of course, at Neath and it was not until 1863 that the VofN was extended into Swansea docks when the harbour lines there were made mixed gauge). An extensive coal trade with Ireland developed at Milford and other South Wales ports.

As soon as the SWR reached Neyland in 1856,

Top - *Poster advertising increased sailings of steamers between Waterford and New Milford as from 1st June 1879. There were two wharves at Waterford, the Adelphi wharf and Ferrybank wharf (above the Adelphi on the River Suir). Note the somewhat creative spelling! [D J Hyde]*

Left - *Adelphi Wharf at Waterford at the end of the C19th.*

New Milford (Neyland) station and pier soon after conversion of the gauge in South Wales in 1872. Departure platform on curve at right. Arrival platform under shed in centre. There are numerous 4-wheeled coaches. A variety of cattle trucks are alongside the open-air lairs, and loads of sawn timber are carried on single and double bolster wagons (J8 Macaw; J9 Mite) at the left centre. Coal tip at top left is fed by track from wagon turntable. Tips are also on the pontoon that was connected to the land by the wooden bridge seen behind the tall disc and crossbar signal. There is a coal hulk anchored out in the haven.

arrangements were made with the London firm of Ford & Jackson (who owned the Milford Haven & Waterford Steamship Co and operated an Irish packet service) to run a twice-weekly steamship service for passengers and goods between Neyland and Waterford (114 miles). The iron-hulled single screw steamer *City of Paris* (built 1850) was employed on the new Ford & Jackson service. Traffic had increased so much within one year of operation that in 1857 a second steamer, the *Griffin*, became necessary, and also a service to Cork was begun with the *PS Pacific*. What later became the City of Cork Steam Packet Co had originally been called the St George Packet Co, and it was from this firm that the 700-ton *PS Sirius* was chartered in 1838 by the rivals to Brunel's *PS Great Western* project, in order to be the first steamship to sail across the Atlantic. Sailing from Cork, four days before the *Great Western* left Bristol, the

Sirius arrived in New York only 12 hours ahead of the Brunel ship.

The pier constructed by the SWR at Neyland/New Milford consisted of a timber viaduct with pontoon 150 ft in length, and beam of 42 ft, loaded to draw 7 ft with a depth alongside at low water of 16 ft, connected with the shore by a landing bridge. The wrought iron pontoon, aligned by wooden dolphins (bundles of piles), was moored by chain cables. The original pier was soon lengthened to 500 ft by the addition of pontoons that had been used to float out the spans of the Brunel Saltash Bridge during its construction. The pier was parallel to the shoreline, and formed a 'T' with the bridge connecting it to the land. Placing the jetty offshore was necessary to give adequate depth of water at the moorings at all states of the tide. Ships could moor on both sides of the floating pier. The connecting bridge had a

Left - PS Malakhoff beached for repairs probably at New Milford [STEAM Swindon]

Opposite page - The Irish services cargo boat SS Great Western (II) dating from 1902. Further images of steamers normally sailing from New Milford/Fishguard will be found under Weymouth. [STEAM Swindon]

rail track running from turntables in the goods yard, and at its end was a wooden-framed hydraulic wagon lift that enabled wagons to be lowered to turntabled tracks on the pontoon. There was a power station for the wagon lift, which also provided power for cranes, shunting capstans and so on around the whole area. Wagon movement on the bridge was by rope and capstan, and on the pier by hand (pinch bar) or possibly by means of a hydraulic capstan from up on the bridge and rope via reels and pulleys down on to the pier.

On the shore, behind the pier, were a couple of small jetties with coal tips used for bunkering. Wagons were capstanned to the tips, having been swung at right angles from turntables on the siding running along the shore. Wagons were tipped using a wooden frame and coal fell down a sloping chute to the boats below. The wagon tips at New Milford were typical of such arrangement at all ports where the boats were below the track level. Also on the foreshore, further along from the coal tips, were two fish jetties with a wooden platform between them where large stocks of fish boxes could be stored. In 1884, a peak of 19,000 tons of mackerel were sent all over the country by train from New Milford. At the end of the C19th, considerable quantities of boxed mackerel, which had been brought from Norway to the port of Fenit near Tralee in Ireland, were taken by special Irish train the 156 miles to Waterford. Thence they arrived by ship at New Milford for onward shipment all over the country. At the end of May when the mackerel were plentiful and prices low, it did not pay to send them fresh-packed in ice to New Milford, so instead they were salted on the pier at Fenit and shipped to New York via Liverpool.

The operation of the vessels on the Irish runs was not the responsibility of the SWR and GWR even though the boats ran in connexion with timetabled trains because railway companies were not permitted to own and operate steamers. However, that prohibition in the Railway Act was repealed in 1862 and eventually, in 1871, the GW obtained

Parliamentary powers to operate steam vessels from New Milford to Waterford and Cork in Ireland and also from Weymouth to the Channel Islands, St Malo and Cherbourg. Whereas the Channel Islands traffic was left in the hands of an independent shipping company for many years, the GW made use of the Act straight away for its Irish traffic. In 1872 the railway bought out the ships of Ford & Jackson then on the Irish service as a going concern for £45,500. There were four: the 1851-built 400 ton *PS Malakhoff* (ex-Antwerp Steam Navigation Co's *Baron Osy*, which had been in Government service in the Crimea – hence the later name – and was kept by the GWR until broken up in 1884); 790 ton *PS Vulture* built in 1864 by J Aitken of Glasgow (bought by Ford & Jackson in 1870 and scrapped by the GW 1886); and the 490 ton *PS South of Ireland* and *PS Great Western (I)*, sister ships both built by Wm Simmons of Renfrew in 1867. The *Vulture* was Ford & Jackson's standby vessel for emergencies, necessary since the Irish service was a mail contract. The history of the GW's Marine Department dates from this time. The GW Marine Workshops, eventually employing 200-odd staff, developed over the years from Ford & Jackson's much smaller repair facilities. Both the Waterford and Cork routes began to be operated by the GW but, after only a year, it was arranged that the City of Cork Steam Packet Co. should take over the sailings to Cork to connect with the trains. GW staff were put in place at Waterford for the first time and movements of staff are occasionally recorded in the *GWR Magazine*; in 1890, for example, W Power, Goods Superintendent at Gloucester succeeded W J Bussell as District Superintendent at Waterford.

As soon as it had taken over the Waterford services, the GW placed orders for two new paddle steamers, the 914 ton sister ships *PS Limerick (I)* and *PS Milford* both of which appeared in 1873. The *Limerick (I)* was wrecked when fairly new, because in 1874 a second *Limerick (II)* appeared along with a third sister ship *PS Waterford (I)*.

Trade on the Irish route increased rapidly after the GW

began operating ships. The English market was opened up to Southern Irish farmers and traffic in cattle became very important, the more so as more and more wasteland in Ireland was turned into pasture. Port facilities were improved (when the route was first opened, passengers and pigs were disembarked by barge at New Milford, and the cattle and horses encouraged to swim ashore!) and in 1880 yet another new vessel was used on the service, the 927-ton *PS Pembroke*. A serious accident to the *Pembroke's* compound oscillating paddle engine in 1895 meant she had to return to Lairds, her builders. There it was decided to convert her to twin-screw propulsion in which form she lasted until 1925 (see Weymouth).

In 1878 the *PS South of Ireland* and *PS Great Western (I)* were transferred to Weymouth for another attempt at operating a Cherbourg route: there had been an unsuccessful operation in 1858-9. *South of Ireland* was wrecked off Dorset in 1883 and *Great Western (I)* returned to New Milford in 1885 when the second Cherbourg service was taken off. It was employed thereafter as a spare vessel before being sold in 1891 to MacBrayne's for West Highland services.

The 1881 Paddington audit of facilities at New Milford stated that

"The disadvantage of conveying livestock by the daily service is recognised and the unpleasant smells have necessitated the closing of the ships hatches before the cattle are put aboard. The cattle have therefore to be shipped at the last moment and sometimes this leads to rough treatment that is annoying to passengers. The cattle occupy space that could be better used for our increasing traffic in perishables. On being loaded at Neyland [sic] the passengers leave the pontoon to cross the line of livestock to gain access to the gangway. Each person on being questioned thought the steamer service should take everything on offer. Traffic in livestock is increasing with an additional £4,900 in 1880 compared with 1879. Traffic in horses accounted for £1,400 of the increase".

Tugs employed at New Milford included the 109-ton *PS Palmerston* (built 1864 on the Isle of Dogs) bought in 1883 from the Dover Harbour Board and the 103 ton *PS Thames (II)* introduced in 1886. Both had 'grasshopper' steam engines, i.e. the fulcrum of the beam was at one end, rather than the more common arrangement in the middle. [The *Thames (I)* was one of three 1868-built ships employed on the LNWR Monk's Ferry across the Mersey. The ferry ceased after Birkenhead Woodside GW station opened in 1878, after which the rest of the GW could be reached via Chester. The LNWR kept two of the boats and sold the third, *Thames (I)* to the GW in 1879. It was sold on to the LTSR for the Tilbury Gravesend Ferry in 1882]. In the GWR magazine of 1890, the South Wales Hotel at New Milford was advertising itself to travellers to and from Ireland: 'steamers leave New Milford for Waterford about 2.0 am and arrive from Waterford about 1.30 am and the Hotel is open at these times for the convenience of Passengers arriving and departing by the Steamers and trains'. At the turn of the C19th/20th, the first long-distance train of importance to arrive at Paddington in the morning was the Irish Boat Train, which came in at 9.55am carrying passengers who had left Waterford at 7.45 the previous evening.

The *PS Milford* of 1873 was broken up in 1901 after storm damage; she had cost £41,342 4s 10d and her scrap value was £2,649 12s 0d. The *Limerick (II)* was also sold for scrapping in 1902. In that year, two 1339-ton twin-screw vessels called the *TSS Great Western (II)* and the *TSS Great Southern* (built by Laird Bros) were introduced; each was capable of accommodating 500 head of fat cattle. The *PS Waterford (I)* of 1874 was then relegated to cargo and cattle

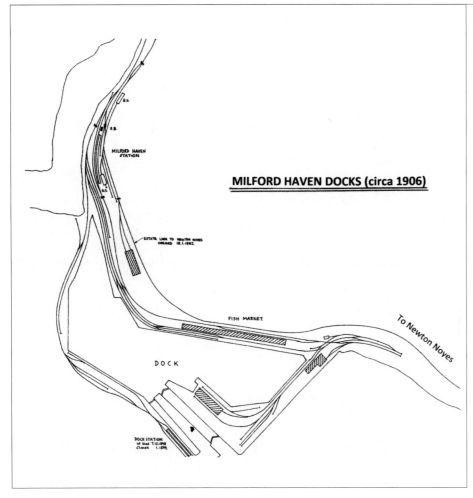

MILFORD HAVEN DOCKS (circa 1906)

jetties for the Fishing Co to rent, in return for which the Fishing Co agreed to send and receive goods by routes favourable to the GW. The official opening of the market was late in 1908. Built partly on land and partly on the old fish jetties, catches in barrels were craned in groups of six in open-topped boxes from fishing boats to the 100 ft long x 57 ft wide market by four 30-cwt cranes (there had been two at the fish jetties before rebuilding). A new ice factory was built just across Westfield Pill at Barnlake, there being no room on the Neyland side. The GWR were keen to foster the fish traffic which used the facilities at Neyland and which brought in revenue for a port abandoned as far as passenger traffic was concerned. In 1914, for example, wet fish of value £41,828 was landed and sold through the market. Even so, after WWI the much smaller market at Neyland could not compete with that at Old Milford/Milford Haven and the Neyland market closed in 1919 and was demolished in the 1920's, the boats transferring to Milford Haven. The ice factory, however, continued working until 1935 supplying boats from Milford Haven.

traffic only, and lasted until 1905 when she was scrapped: she was the last paddle steamer operated by the GWR on a major route

As explained in the section on Fishguard, the Fishguard & Rosslare Rly & Harbours Co was formed in 1893 to build new docks at Rosslare and Fishguard, and to put in appropriate rail connexions, which would provide the shortest sea route between Ireland and Great Britain. This was done in the expectation that with new fast steamers on the service, transatlantic passengers and mails landed at Queenstown (Cobh) would be brought to London in far quicker time than the existing route via Dublin and Holyhead. Better still, liners homeward bound for Liverpool could perhaps be persuaded to call at Fishguard instead of Cohb. The new route opened in 1906 and thereafter Irish services ceased at New Milford, which reverted to its 'proper' name of Neyland.

The future of not only the town but of the small fishing fleet at New Milford/Neyland was in doubt after the move to Fishguard. The private docks at Milford Haven just along the coast had opened in 1888 and a large fleet of steam trawlers, much bigger than that at Neyland, had had been established. Nevertheless, development of fishing at Neyland was thought to offer a future and the Neyland Steam Trawling & Fishing Co was formed in 1906. The GWR agreed to build a new covered fish market at the fish

MILFORD HAVEN (called OLD MILFORD by the railway between 1863-1906) (served)

A local landowner had built a small port at Milford Haven in 1790 and in the Napoleonic Wars the Navy began to build warships there. But in 1814 the Admiralty moved these activities to Pembroke Dock and thereafter Milford Haven fell into a state of desuetude. Its overtures to the SWR to be the Irish packet port instead of nearby Neyland ('New Milford') seven miles or so along the coast were spurned, and it had to wait until 1863 when construction of a private railway by 'Old Milford' businessmen linked it to the mainline at Johnston. The connexion to the SWR renewed dreams that docks at Milford Haven could capture the transatlantic liner trade (recalling the old idea of the Manchester-Milford Rly) but problems with contractors delayed the opening of the docks until 1888. One or two liners called soon after the dock opened, but the ships could not berth and had to be serviced by tender and the idea came to nothing. One particular vessel that called was the Anchor Line's *City of Rome* in 1890 bringing Barnum and his circus from the USA. The 162 passengers who had elected to travel by rail to Paddington were taken off by tender (the GW's *Gael* that was the summer relief steamer at New Milford that year----see Weymouth). They were landed at

Top - *A view across Milford Haven dock.*
Coal wagons on quay for bunkering
trawlers by shovelling down off quay or
by use of travelling steam crane. Wagons
belonging to North's Navigation, Rock,
Parkend, and Fernhill Merthyr collieries.
North's Rock colliery that produced
anthracite was near Glyn Neath and was
owned by Amalgamated Anthracite
Collieries Ltd. [Amgueddfa Cymru
National Museum of Wales]

Centre - *Trawlers berthed further along*
the same quay as in the picture above.
The building with a tall central section
that is on the right in the picture above,
is on the extreme left in this image.

Bottom - *The south quay in 1926*
showing the herring curing sheds behind
which is the low-water landing stage on
the haven. GW Mica refrigerated meat
vans (white-painted with red lettering)
and a GW Bloater fish van. Wooden coal
wagons for firing up the boilers for the
machinery are from Glyncorrwg colliery
and newly-built GW Pole 20-ton steel
wagons are to the right.

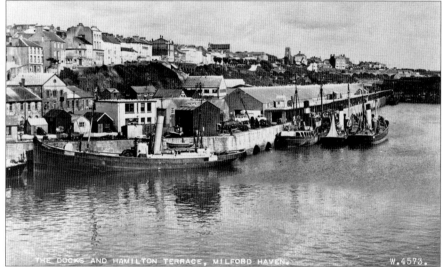

8.30 pm at the Milford Haven docks' basin where their luggage was examined in the adjacent warehouse and thence to the special train which departed at 10.20 pm, arriving at Paddington at 4.41 am the next morning.

The tracks alongside the quays were installed and owned by the private Milford Haven Railway & Dock Co, the system making an end-on junction with the GWR through exchange sidings situated on an extension of the line from the passenger station. The dock company's own shunting locos took over at the exchange sidings. The MHR&DCo also built a line, about two miles long, round to Noyes Point, opened in 1882, which served ship repairers, a fish meal factory and later a government depot.

Although the grand aspirations of becoming a transatlantic port did not materialise, Milford Haven docks did prosper as a fishing port using steam trawlers, and became the principal fishing port on the GWR. The dock had 23 acres of water having an average depth of 34/24 (later 28) ft at spring/neap tides. There were about 1¼ miles of quays, 28 acres of quay area and over a third of an acre of covered accommodation. The lock was 548 ft long by 70 ft

wide.

In 1890, 10,000 tons fish/year were being landed. The total grew rapidly to 40,000 tons/year just before WWI, was 51,000 tons/year in 1931, and remained at about 40,000 tons/year until WWII. The pamphlet 'Milford Haven – where the Fish comes from' remarked "To look at the port

Fishguard Harbour station and sidings during construction in 1906. Completed open-air cattle lairage in centre. Contractor's railway lines on right with travelling steam cranes and spoil wagons. The GW put its own tracks in this location, but later this area would eventually have roofed-over cattle lairs. [A G Atkins collection]

and to survey its manifold activities one would never suppose that the docks were only opened in 1888, when the first vessel to enter was the *Sybil*, a steam trawler of 127 tons. It speaks much for the energy, foresight and business acumen of the shipowners and dealers, and for the hearty co-operation of the dock and railway companies". In 1946 a record catch of 60,000 tons was landed. For comparison, in the 1930's 10,000 tons/year were landed at Swansea (South Dock – Consolidated Fisheries Ltd) and 6,000 tons/year at Cardiff (West Dock - Neale and West). In 1947, the weekly loading of fish wagons was 250 wagons at Milford Haven and 120 at Swansea. In the West Country 12 fish wagons/ week were required at Penzance (fish from Newlyn) and a few more wagons again for traffic from St Ives (meeting the main line at St Erth); from Looe at Liskeard; from Kingsbridge at Brent; and from Brixham at Churston.

When the dock opened at Old Milford there was no market or other facilities at the port and the first catches were sent direct to Billingsgate by rail, but the fish was so good that a few enterprising merchants established themselves at Milford Haven, and by WWI there were well over 100 dealers on the docks. Milford Haven had over 100 steam trawlers landing their catches. The total fleet tonnage was about 30,000 tons. In 1911, the GW conveyed 100,000 tons of coal for these ships, and since the trawlers remained steamers into the 1950's, bunkers coal of this magnitude continued right through to nationalisation. Two electric coal conveyors, each capable of dealing with 200 tons/hour of

shipment coal, were installed in the 1920's. The supplies of fish were regular and during the height of the season the daily loadings frequently amounted to over five hundred tons of various kinds, hake being the speciality. More than half the deep-sea fish landed in UK from the southern and western Irish fishing grounds, and nearly all the fish from the Portuguese and Moroccan coasts, came to Milford Haven. From early in April until the end of October, herring and mackerel were landed. Milford Haven herring rivalled in quality the older-established East Coast catches so much so that buyers from all parts of the country came to Milford. Of the 106,640 cwts landed in one year in the 1920's 77,120 cwts were sent to the long-established East coast herring parts for curing. Other fish, mainly sea ling and herring were also salted at Milford Haven for the continental export trade.

Even the heaviest catches could be unloaded, sold, cleaned, packed and despatched in a few hours. The trawler fish market was 1150 ft long and 66 ft wide, and railway lines and platforms ran the whole length so that the traffic could be rapidly loaded into fish wagons. The separate herring and mackerel market was 200 ft long by 35 ft wide, adjoining a low-water stage outside the dock proper. There were two ice factories, 40,000 tons of ice being used annually. Over 1500 workers were employed on the docks with more than 1200 fishermen always at sea in Milford boats. To support the fishing industry, all the ancillary trades existed at Milford Haven: box, rope and net making concerns, ships chandlers and a large graving dock.

Fishguard Harbour soon after opening (the contractor's railway lines are still in place on the extreme left). Two of the new steam turbine vessels are present, one moored to buoys in the harbour and one berthed at the passenger station. A wide variety of wagons is in the yard. The dead-end siding on the left is used for carriages. [Postcard]

Sales of fish at Milford Haven commenced at 8am and as each lot was sold the buyer fixed his own label to it, after which the fish was prepared, packed and addressed. Then the employees of the dock company trollied the boxes to the fish vans, under the supervision of the railway checkers, who recorded the name and address on each package. (In later years, the Fish Traders Association at Milford Haven owned a number of Lister electric trolleys – like those used by the GW in its own large good depots – to aid handling). From about 1pm consignment notes from the fish merchants were distributed to the clerks engaged in waybilling. The GW 'Travel Office' collated all the information, performing the same functions as the staff in ordinary goods depots.

Traffic was sent as far north as Glasgow, as far west as Penzance and, crossing the Channel, as far east as Paris. By regular fish trains all the important towns and fish markets of Great Britain were reached in time for the fish to be marketed and sold to the public the next morning after despatch from Milford Haven. In the 1920's the first regular fish train left the Great Western station for Carmarthen at 3.15pm (there were 10.0 am and noon departures for urgent needs in South Wales, and in Southampton and Plymouth, respectively). The 3.15pm train took the LNWR/LMS central Wales line through Llandilo, often joining the fish train from Swansea South dock, and served places in the

north of England and in Scotland. At 3.50pm another train was despatched with fish for South Wales, Bristol and the West of England, Birmingham and the Midlands. This was followed at 5.10pm by a train running direct to Paddington (calling at Swindon and Reading), which was reached at 1.45am, supplying not only London's needs but also the Midland Division of the LMS and the southern and north-eastern areas of the LNER. It also conveyed considerable quantities of fish for Dieppe, Boulogne, Ostend and Paris.

In GW literature, it was advised that rates and other information could be obtained not only from the private Milford Docks Co itself but also from the GW District Goods Manager at Swansea. It was also listed that Milford had three transit sheds of 24,000 sq ft floor area and that (in 1932) electric conveyors for shipment of coal, each capable of dealing with 200 tons/hour, had been installed.

FISHGUARD (owned jointly with the GSWR of Ireland)

In 1844 Brunel had planned the South Wales Rly to run the 162 miles from Standish (Gloucester) to the natural harbour at Fishguard, where its deep water could accommodate the biggest ships. It was to be reached by a 'branch railway' beyond Carmarthen to the North Pembrokeshire coast, and it was contemplated that a service of steamers should run to Wexford.

FISHGUARD HARBOUR.

Fishguard Harbour is situated in South Cardigan Bay on the Pembrokeshire coast.

The high lands on three sides of the Harbour shelter it from the south, east, and west, and to protect it from the north a substantial breakwater 2,000 feet long has been constructed. There is sufficient depth of water in all parts of the Harbour to accommodate in perfect safety vessels of the largest draught at all states of the tide, and excellent anchorage on a soft rockless bottom is afforded.

Owing to the exceptional climatic conditions Fishguard Harbour is more free from fog than any other port on the coast.

The tidal currents do not exceed three-quarters of a knot.

The Harbour Works, in addition to the breakwater alluded to above, include :—

Electric cranes, capable of dealing with loads up to 5 tons, are available for lifting mails, cargo, etc., direct from the steamer to the quay or train or direct from the train or quay to the steamer. A 21-ton stationary electric crane is also available. This crane is capable of lifting a laden coal wagon in a cradle and tipping coal direct into steamer or lighter. Special low rates will be quoted for the carriage of coal from the steam coal pits, the proximity of which renders Fishguard a suitable port for bunkering purposes.

The accommodation for dealing with cattle traffic is exceptionally good, including a slaughterhouse and 65 commodious pens capable of holding many hundred head of cattle at one time. A special gallery runs along the whole length of the quay wall underneath the passenger stage, and this is so constructed that cattle can be loaded upon any part of it from any gangway of a vessel in whatever position it may be moored, or from any number of gangways at the same time. The cattle pass from the gallery direct to the pens by means of a subway independently of all other traffic. The G.W.R. Company will afford facilities for the through booking of every description of Merchandise traffic to and from all parts, *via* the Port of Fishguard.

FISHGUARD HARBOUR—continued.

The following notes summarise the great potentialities of the new and extensive Harbour of Fishguard :—

Sheltered position.
Freedom from fog.
Accessibility at all states of the tide.
Depth of water and safe anchorage.
Large area of accommodation for vessels.
Extensive quay space and siding accommodation.
Exceptional facilities for dealing with all descriptions of traffic.
Adaptability for bunkering purposes.
Within easy reach of all parts.

NEW ROUTE TO IRELAND.

Fishguard Harbour is only 54 nautical miles from the Harbour of Rosslare, in Ireland, and the new turbine steamers built specially for the new service, with an estimated speed of 22½ knots, reduce the time of the journey to well under three hours.

The new steamers excel those of any other channel service in equipment and speed, and are specially adapted for the conveyance of perishable goods, commodious refrigerating chambers being provided.

IRELAND.

There are through bookings between all important cities and towns in Ireland and the principal stations on the Great Western Railway and lines in connection therewith, *via* **FISHGUARD** and **THE GREAT WESTERN RAILWAY COMPANY'S STEAMERS** and the Steamers of the City of Cork Steamship Company, or *via* Liverpool and the Steamers of the City of Dublin Steamship Company, Belfast Steamship Company, etc.

The Company's route, *via* Fishguard, is the shortest and most convenient to and from places in the Midlands, the **EAST** and **SOUTH OF ENGLAND AND WALES**, and all places in Central and Southern Ireland.

The Steamers are fitted with every modern appliance for the accommodation of all classes of traffic, including live stock, provisions, dairy produce, etc., and the special through services ensure quick transit of perishables and Live Stock, to which special attention is given.

All that was required at Fishguard was the protection of a breakwater to complete the shelter given by hills on the three sides of the bay. Unfortunately, on the southern shores where it would be best to build a harbour, the hills rose sheer out of the water to a height of over 300 ft and were formed of hard and tough quartzite rock. Construction of the harbour was going to be costly, on top of the cost of a breakwater. In 1848 plans were drawn up for a harbour at nearby Abermawr instead and work on the line was started (see later). However, the Irish famine prevented connecting rail developments on the Irish side and also cast doubt on the financial prospects of the line. Thus, instead of Fishguard, Neyland on the natural harbour of Milford Haven became the port of embarkation for boats to Ireland. The place was renamed 'New Milford' by the SWR and services to Ireland sailed from there up until the early 1900's (see New Milford).

Joseph Rowland and John Cartland, businessmen from Birmingham, saw the potential of a sea route between Fishguard and Rosslare as, at 54 nautical miles across St George's Channel, it would be shorter than any other, particularly Dublin-Holyhead. In 1893 they obtained an Act to form the Fishguard Bay Rly & Pier Co, intending to use the independent North Pembrokeshire & Fishguard Rly (a union of the Rosebush & Fishguard, and Maenclochog, railways) to access the port, and later hoping to join up with the LNWR at Swansea. They financed the completion of the North Pembrokeshire Rly, and went into partnership with the Waterford and Wexford Rly and the Rosslare Harbour Commission at which time the name of the company was changed to the Fishguard & Rosslare Railway & Harbours Co. At this juncture the GWR and the Great Southern & Western Rly in Ireland woke up to the threat of competition to their existing sea routes, and subscribed to Rowland's and Cartland's scheme. Soon they took it over but before that happened, the Fishguard & Rosslare Co purchased late in 1896 the 29-year old secondhand *SS Voltaic* (580 gross tons) that was placed on a service from

WATERFORD AND SOUTH OF IRELAND.

Through rates are in operation for Merchandise between Waterford and the South of Ireland and the principal stations on the Great Western Railway, as well as the principal stations on other English Railways, *Via* **FISHGUARD.**

At Adelphi Wharf, Waterford, the Company's establishment comprises wharfage and warehouse accommodation, loose boxes for horses, cattle lairs, and every facility for carrying on a general goods and live stock traffic.

CORK.

Through rates are in operation for merchandise traffic between Cork and all the principal stations on the Great Western Railway, as well as the principal stations on other English Railways,

Via **FISHGUARD.**

The traffic is conveyed *via* Great Southern and Western Railway, Rosslare and Fishguard, also by the City of Cork Steam Packet Company's Steamers between Cork and Fishguard under arrangements with the Great Western Railway. There is ample accommodation at the Packet Company's Penrose Quay, Cork, for dealing with all descriptions of traffic, including live stock. There is also a cartage establishment, and "Carted" rates between Cork and English stations include cartage at the former place.

DUBLIN.

Through rates are in operation for merchandise traffic between Dublin and Great Western stations

Via **FISHGUARD,** or

via Liverpool, or *via* Chester and Holyhead, and traffic charged at "Carted" rates is carted free by the Company's teams within the usual limits in Dublin.

BELFAST AND NORTH OF IRELAND.

Through rates are in operation for merchandise traffic between Belfast and the North of Ireland and stations on the Great Western Railway

Via **LIVERPOOL AND BELFAST STEAMSHIP COMPANY,**

and traffic charged at "Carted" rates is collected and delivered free within the usual limits.

The Company's Traffic Manager in Ireland is Mr. E. J O'B. Croker, 5, Lower Sackville Street, Dublin; and the following are Agents, from whom full information can be obtained :—

BELFAST AND LONDONDERRY—
Belfast Steamship Company, Donegal Quay, Belfast, and Queen's Quay, Londonderry.
MR W.E WILLIAMS. G.W.R. DONEGAL QUAY

DUBLIN DISTRICT AND NORTH OF IRELAND
Mr. ~~W. E. Williams~~, 5, Lower Sackville Street, Dublin.
E.J. O'B CROKER

CORK DISTRICT—
Mr. A. G. Dodd, 98, Patrick Street, Cork.

KILKENNY—
Mr. W J Francis, Rose Inn Street, Kilkenny.

LIMERICK—
Mr. J A. O'Kelly, 123, George Street, Limerick.

WATERFORD AND ROSSLARE DISTRICTS—
Mr. A. W Perks, Adelphi Wharf, Waterford. CITY BUSINESS
- W BEDDOES " " " (DISTRICT

ROSSLARE—
Mr. M. Costello, G.W Agent, Rosslare Harbour.

WEXFORD—
Mr. R. O'Toole, 10, Commercial Quay, Wexford.

Wexford to Bristol via Rosslare. The route was short-lived as it was unprofitable and the vessel was sold in 1899.

Over two million tons of rock were dynamited from the surrounding hills at Fishguard to form the level ground required for the quays and all the associated buildings and track. Most of the large pieces of rock went to form the breakwater (eventually 3000 ft long). The difficulties of construction were no less than 50 years previously; the nearest GW station was Letterston and all equipment had to be taken by road to the site. When completed there were 275 acres of water, having a depth of 34/20 ft spring/neap tides, and nearly 1800 ft of quayage. Construction included station buildings, six miles of sidings, cattle-pens, stabling, offices, a GW Marine Department depot and an electric generating station for machinery and lighting. The *Porteur No 5* vessel was bought for the works in 1899. At Rosslare a jetty over 1000 ft long was connected to the mainland by a rail bridge (strangely with no roadway, something not corrected until 1965, so that road vehicles had to be taken to and from the

ships on flat rail wagons). In addition to the new connecting railways from Rosslare to the GSWR Waterford and Cork mainline, a new cross-town railway in Cork was built to speed up fish and vegetable traffic for the British market; the cross-town railway was partly paid for by the government (in London, of course, before Partition).

Although the North Pembrokeshire & Fishguard Rly (taken over by the GW in 1899) provided, on the face of it, a ready-made rail route to Fishguard, the gradients on this single line were steep and there was a general speed restriction of 25 mph, dropping to 10 mph at certain points including the final descent at 1 in 50 from Letterston to the town station of Fishguard & Goodwick ('w' not pronounced). Indeed, the steepest gradient anywhere on the GW system over which passenger trains ran was on this line at 1 in 27 between Llanycefn and Maenclochog. Consequently a new double line for the running of corridor boat trains was opened in 1906 from Clarbeston Rd (6½ miles west of Clynderwen on the line to Haverfordwest and

Left - Irish dairy produce and eggs being unloaded by one of the 5-ton travelling cranes at Fishguard in 1919. The support rail for these cranes ran along, and was part of, the construction of the platform awning. [GWR]

***Opposite page** - Number 4 platform at Fishguard in 1919 with boxes of Irish dairy produce marked 'CWS Tralee Depot' being loaded into open wagons. Boxes are craned from ship on flat plates with rings at the corners, seen on the luggage trolleys. Tarpaulins for putting over sheet supporters on open wagons are folded up and further along the platform. Note signals. [GWR]*

New Milford), to Letterston Junction (2 miles north of Letterston station on the North Pembrokeshire line). A mile of the new line near Clarbeston Rd was laid on partially-formed banks and in cuttings that were commenced by Brunel and abandoned in 1851. The 64 chains of track from Fishguard & Goodwick station to the harbour was owned by the joint GW/GSW company.

The new Fishguard-Rosslare sea route was opened in August 1906, the rebuilt *SS Pembroke* making the first ceremonial sailing (see New Milford). For the new service, three turbine steamers TrSS (triple screw steamer) *St George, St David (I)* and *St Patrick (I)* were built in 1906 by the John Brown shipyard in Glasgow, and a fourth sister ship the *TrSS St Andrew (I)* was brought into service in 1908. All were owned by the Fishguard & Rosslare Co. Their livery was, for all practical purposes, the same as the

GWR fleet. A telegraph station was opened on the cliffs above Fishguard, wireless signals from which could be received 500 miles out into the Atlantic. The new turbine steamers were all built with Marconi wireless (then in its infancy). They were capable of speeds of 22½ knots and crossed St George's Channel in about three hours. At that time it was believed that to operate a day and night daily service, four vessels were really required: two to maintain the actual service, one to be an emergency standby and one being laid off for refitting. Even so, standby vessels were sometimes transferred to Weymouth and vice versa. (In the event, the GW found that three of the more modern turbine steamers were sufficient to maintain the Irish Service so the *St George* was sold in 1913 to the Canadian Pacific Rly to operate the Digby-St John route in New Brunswick; she had to be towed across the Atlantic owing to lack of bunker

space). The night sailing from Fishguard was at 2.15am, the boat train having left Paddington at 8.0 pm the previous evening; connecting Irish trains ran from Rosslare to Wexford, Waterford and Dublin (arrive 10.45 am), and to Cork (arrive 10.03 am). The daytime sailing from Fishguard was at 2.15 pm with similarly-timed connecting trains (8.0 am from Paddington etc). The night crossing from Rosslare was at 11.45 pm and the daytime sailing at 12.30 pm, the connecting train arriving at Paddington at 9.0 pm. [Until 1914, time at Rosslare was 25 minutes later than London].

After the opening of the new services, New Milford was forsaken by the GWR and the company's Marine Department was transferred to Fishguard. The GW route to Waterford, which became mainly for goods and livestock after the Rosslare route was opened, also began to sail from Fishguard, as did the service to Cork, run by the independent City of Cork Steam Packet Company. Its vessel at this time was the *SS Iniscarra*. New steamers had been constructed for the Waterford service. The *SS Great Southern* (owned by the GSWR) and *SS Great Western (II)* (owned by the GWR) both dated from 1902 and were powered by triple expansion reciprocating engines. Since the new Irish services were a joint responsibility, the

Weymouth-Channel Islands services became the principal GWR-only shipping route.

At the tail-end of the C19th, transatlantic liners called at Cobh in Southern Ireland (named Queenstown from Victoria's visit in 1847 until Partition) on their way to and from the principal transatlantic port of Liverpool. Passengers and mails from inbound vessels were taken to Dublin by the GSWR, thence by boat to Holyhead and onwards to London by the LNWR. This traffic grew in importance, and the GW realised that with fast new steamers from Rosslare to Fishguard, passengers and mail could be got to London from Cobh a good three or more hours quicker than via Dublin and Holyhead. (The GW sea routes into New Milford could not achieve any such saving). Furthermore, if the Atlantic steamers could be persuaded when inward bound to Liverpool to call at Fishguard instead of Queenstown, the journey time to London would be reduced even more. Fishguard was 2902 miles from New York, 55 miles nearer than Plymouth and 115 miles nearer than Liverpool. The investment in Fishguard by the GW was aimed as much at transatlantic liners as at the Irish traffic.

Getting London-bound passengers and mails more quickly to destination by disembarking at a port on the

Just delivered from the John Brown Shipyard in Glasgow, the new triple screw turbine steamers St David(I) (on left) and St Patrick(I) in June 1906. Following a severe fire in 1929, St Patrick(I) was condemned. The St David(I) followed in 1932. [GWR].

western side of the country, to be taken onwards by train, had been happening for years at Plymouth. The LNWR had already invited the White Star Line to put passengers and mails ashore at Holyhead to proceed to London by train; the GWR now tempted the rival Cunard Line to call at Fishguard that was reached many hours earlier than Holyhead. [Ernest Cunard was elected a director of the GW in 1907; earlier that year the Churchward unnamed 4-6-0 no 98 had been named *Vanguard*, but at the year's end was re-named *Ernest Cunard*]. Booth Line steamers from Portugal and South America were the first ocean liners to call at Fishguard (*Lanfranc* in 1908), and on 30th August 1909 the two-year old 32,000-ton Cunard liner *Mauretania* (holder of the Blue Riband for 20 years) made her first in-bound call at Fishguard. As at Plymouth, tenders were required to take off passengers, their baggage, mails, bullion and specie (coinage), and goods. The *Smeaton* and *Sir Francis Drake (II)* from Plymouth, and the *Great Western (II)* Irish cargo boat, were employed for this prestigious occasion. A record journey time from New York to London was established, the three special, luxurious ocean expresses arriving in London even before the *Mauretania* had sailed into the Mersey. Thereafter liners began to call regularly: the first Blue Funnel liner for Australia left Fishguard in 1910 and liners from Boston called (the Cunard *Franconia* in 1911 dropped anchor at 5 am and the special left at 6.40 am, arriving in Paddington at 11.28 am).

The GW advertised '4½ hour boat trains to Paddington' from Fishguard, and plans had been in hand from 1904 to reduce these times by the construction of the Swansea Extension lines that bypassed the congested lines around Swansea. Two-thirds had been opened by 1913 from Skewen west of Neath to Llangennech (Llandilo Jct) west of Llanelly. The easternmost end of the Swansea Extension Lines used running powers over the Rhondda & Swansea Bay Rly between Cardonnel Jct and Court Sart that crossed the River Neath on a swing bridge. Brunel had planned that the SWR should have crossed the River Neath by a high level bridge at Briton Ferry but he was thwarted by the Neath Harbour Commissioners and this, of course, is why Swansea ended up being served by a branch line from Landore.

A general view of the Irish quays and the passenger station at Fishguard harbour in August 1928. The cattle pens that were originally in the open are now roofed over and additional pens have been added where the railway lines of the harbour contractors once ran. The long harbour mole is in the distance. Tugs and lighters moored within the harbour. Nearer ships at the quay belong to the City of Cork Steam Packet Co; the further vessel belongs to the GW. [LGRP].

Other improvements at Fishguard were begun, such as the construction of an eastern breakwater in 1909. Furthermore, plans were made in 1911 to construct an ocean quay on the northern breakwater which could take alongside the biggest liners at all states of the tide, and the necessary dredging to a depth of 38 ft at low water was started. This covered an area big enough for the ships to enter and leave bow first, swinging round within the harbour. Plans were also made to realign the railway track up from the harbour on easier gradients. So keen was the GW to encourage the transatlantic traffic and to keep it running smoothly, that during a railwaymen's strike of 1911, the army was brought in to the port. Again, an extension of the Irish quay towards the northern breakwater was begun to provide a berth at which GW steamers could be laid up for repairs. This work was interrupted in 1917 when the site was taken over for an anti-submarine seaplane station where a collapsible hanger was erected. Larger accommodation for an airship followed later. The berth for ship repairs was completed by 1921. The GW Marine Dept Charge Code for the Fishguard workshops was 23A.

An average of 14,000 passengers and 55,000 bags of mail were handled at Fishguard annually up to WWI. However, all the development of the port for transatlantic and other ocean-going liners was in vain because, in 1919,

Cunard moved its base from Liverpool to Southampton, partly to shorten the rail journey to London but perhaps more to pick up the traffic of the former German transatlantic shipping lines that no longer functioned. White Star had already moved to Southampton in 1911. Southampton thus displaced Liverpool as the principal passenger port after WWI and the calls by liners at Fishguard ceased.

The final part of the Swansea Avoiding lines from Morlais Junction to Pembrey was never built. Even so, that part which was built did remove congestion on the GW main line around Swansea and avoided banking of trains on the notorious Cockett bank which rose at 1 in 50 going west, and 1 in 53/50 going east, to reach the highest point on the whole of the South Wales Rly. The vac-fitted C-code express goods trains from Fishguard were routed over the extension lines. A marshalling yard holding 1000 wagons was built at Felin Fran to serve the virgin coal fields that the lines opened up in the Clydach, Cwmgorse and Egel valleys. The lines also provided an easier route for existing traffic from the Amman valley to those Swansea docks on the eastern side.

There was an extensive GW staff in Ireland and vigorous canvassing went on to encourage people to send via the GW route. In a booklet entitled *Instructions*

The 1900-ton SS St Patrick(II) built in 1930 as a relief ship for both Fishguard and Weymouth was bombed and sunk when crossing from Rosslare to Fishguard in June 1941. [A G Atkins collection]

Relating to Irish Traffic published in 1910, the GW emphasised to its mainland staff that communications from agents in Ireland should have prompt attention; that persons in their neighbourhood who were receiving or sending perishable and livestock by other routes should be encouraged to send by the GWR; and that ... 'Station Agents should look out for horse dealers journeying to Ireland, and not only canvas for their traffic, but also notify the Company's Irish Agent by wire, so that he may look out for them ...'.

The principal traffic passing from the South and West of Ireland to Britain before WWI was ales and porter; bacon and hams; casein; condensed milk; butter and cheese; eggs; ferns; fruit; fish (including shellfish for Dieppe); hay; lard; livestock; manure in bags; moss peat; motor cars; oats; parcels; potatoes; live and dead poultry; rabbits; salt; provisions; timber; whiskey; wool, etc. And from Britain to Ireland parcels; agricultural implements; bicycles; biscuits; boots; china; drapery; drugs; earthenware; fish; fruit; furniture; galvanized sheet iron; grain and flour; groceries; hardware; hats; hosiery; iron; leather; machinery; matches; motor cars; paper; skins; copper sulphate; tea; timber; tinplate; wines and spirits; woollen goods.

Through rates were in operation between stations in Ireland and the principal stations on the Great Western system and other lines in Great Britain. The standard classification of goods (see *GW Goods Services*) did not apply to Ireland and the ritual for working the Irish Rate Books was arcane. 'Returned empties' from Britain to Ireland such as poultry hampers provided by the railway for dead game from Ireland, had to be sent back to the GW Agent at the Adelphi Wharf in Waterford via Fishguard and

Opposite top - Inside the cattle pens at Fishguard in April 1926 with the Ministry of Agriculture's vet (J N Slinn's father) inspecting Irish cattle. [GWR]

Opposite bottom - Irish horses being unloaded from ship to the under-quay gallery which led to the Fishguard lairage, in September 1922. [GWR].

The 1700-ton Great Western(III) in BR days. Built by Cammell, Laird & Co in 1933.

direct steamer, or to the GW Agent at Belfast, via Liverpool. When containers were introduced, only small open containers (H and SL types), conveying traffic in classes 1-10 (old A, B and C) could be sent to Irish ports. The volume of perishable traffic arriving at Rosslare harbour for shipment to Fishguard, that had travelled over 100 miles by passenger train within Ireland, had grown so greatly by the early 1920's that delays in transhipment were being experienced. The problem was overcome by an early use of pallets (then called 'false bottoms' or 'flats'). In addition to speeding up transfer to ship, the damage consequent on handling was reduced considerably, consignments not being handled from the time they were placed on a train in Ireland to their arrival at Fishguard. Electric platform trucks were introduced for the first time on the GW at Fishguard (and Jersey) in 1922.

Fishguard was a properly-designed 'railway port' where the railway was the port authority. Facilities were quite extensive and included covered platforms for goods traffic between steamer and wagons. There were electric cranes capable of dealing with loads up to 5 tons direct from the steamer to the quay or train and vice versa. There was also a 21-ton crane available for furniture vans, railway carriages and wagons, boilers and other heavy articles. This crane was also used to lift coal wagons and tip them into barges for the supply of bunker coal to the steamers. Goods traffic to and from Ireland more-or-less balanced at 20-30,000 tons per annum in each direction in the inter-war

period; 11,000 parcels came from, and 6,000 went to, Ireland every year.

The cattle business was especially important and at Fishguard there was a slaughter-house and 65 pens capable of holding many hundred head of cattle at one time. Between 1913 and 1937, numbers of cattle shipped from Ireland were never less than 90,000 per year and often near 200,000; in 1931 277,000 head of cattle, mostly Aberdeen Angus and Shorthorn were shipped (and this in a year when an outbreak of foot-and-mouth disease in West Wales caused the diversion of animals to Cardiff Docks for a period). Cattle were landed at Fishguard on a special gallery that ran along the entire length of the quay wall underneath the passenger stage, so that passengers saw nothing of the animals. After quarantining for 10 hours, they were despatched in special trains to the various large cattle centres such as Norwich or Bristol, and thence to abattoirs. Special Train Control arrangements existed in order to secure the most rapid journey time for the trains to their destinations. Although conveyed at goods rates, livestock such as this received a better service than ordinary goods trains, as they travelled in trains having 'C' class head codes. In the 1927 annual GW report on its goods activities, improvements in livestock accommodation at Wexford are listed.

Greyhounds also travelled from Ireland in fairly large numbers (some 2,000 in 1927) but apart from ample van room and plenty of straw, no special arrangements were

Outside-framed 0-6-0PT shunting at Fishguard Quay. A number of lime-washed cattle wagons (MEX) in the sidings.

made. Although Irish traffic predominated at Fishguard, many coasters plied between the port and Cork, Liverpool, Bristol, Plymouth, Southampton, London, Newport and Cardiff.

When the LSWR gave up its Plymouth ocean liner operation in 1910 (see Plymouth), the GW bought its tender *Atalanta* and used it at Fishguard. Vessel *GW No 1* was a 95 ft long flush-decked lighter built in 1906 for Fishguard, and *GW No 182* was an 18 ft motor launch also dating from 1906. An additional cattle-and-cargo ship, the *TSS Waterford (II)*, was supplied for the Waterford service in 1912. She was similar to the 1902-built *Great Western (II)* and *Great Southern* but was distinguished as being the only GW vessel ever to have quadruple expansion steam engines.

In 1914, E. J. O'B. Croker, the GW Irish Traffic Manager at Waterford since 1903, retired and was succeeded by F.W.Tyler. On the outbreak of WWI, all the GW steamers on the Irish services, together with their captains and crews, were requisitioned by the Admiralty, but the need for the *Great Western (II)* and *Great Southern* was cancelled when they were en route to Cork to report for duty. With the *Waterford (II)* and *Pembroke*, they put on a limited service to and from Waterford; it was suspended 5-

17th August 1914 and the sailings thereafter were limited to 3 a week. The three turbine vessels on the Rosslare service were converted into cross-channel hospital ships/ambulance transports having 200 hospital cases per ship. Assistance for the Rosslare service was provided initially by the LNWR's *SS Rathmore* but she was replaced within days by *SS Duke of Connaught* ¾ belonging to the LNWR/L&Y Joint Committee. The timetables had to be altered as the *Duke of Connaught* was slower than the GW turbine ships. When she returned to the Fleetwood-Belfast service, the GCR loaned the *Dewsbury* and the L&Y the cargo boat *Mersey*.

The *Pembroke* was transferred to Weymouth in 1915, (and the *Great Southern* briefly in 1916), to help that route keep going, as Weymouth's big ships had also been taken over by the Admiralty. The *St George* also came back from Canada for war service. After 1916, aliens were forbidden to travel to and from Ireland via Fishguard and Rosslare/ Waterford/Cork, and also between Bristol and Cork, owing to worries about 'fifth columnists'; the same applied between the Channel Islands and Weymouth, The only approved ports through which aliens could travel were London, Folkestone, Falmouth, Holyhead, Birkenhead/ Liverpool, and Southampton.

Between them, the Rosslare turbine steamers *St Andrew (I)*, *St David (I)* and *St Patrick (I)* carried a total of 380,000 sick and wounded by the war's end. *St Patrick (I)*, for example, made 759 passages across the channel, steaming a total distance of 73,693 miles, carrying 125,000 sick and wounded. At the signing of the Armistice, the vessels were converted to troopships and used in the demobilisation from France.

Instead of returning to Canada after the war, the *St George* was sold in 1919 to the GER for Harwich services. The three GW turbine steamers returned to their old Rosslare route, *St Andrew (I)* being the last to be decommissioned at the end of 1919. In 1922-23, the Fishguard-Rosslare service was interrupted for over a year by the civil war in Ireland, and the GW ships were not in full use. In the summer of 1923, *St Andrew (I)* was chartered to the Isle of Man Steam Packet Co to run between Liverpool and Douglas. The *St David (I)* was re-engined in 1925, and the *St Patrick (I)* also in 1926 in order to reduce the cost of fuel and running. In the 1920's the number of cars wishing to take the Irish crossing increased, and vessels were adapted to take more road vehicles. After WWI, it was found that a nightly boat in each direction was sufficient to meet the demands of the traffic. In 1925 the capacity of the lairage at Fishguard was increased from 1060 animals to 1660. At this time the City of Cork Steam Packet Co sailed three times a week (on Tues, Thurs and Sat) to Waterford using the 1627-ton *Killarney* dating from 1893; the GWR sailed on the other days (Mon, Wed and Fri). The Irish service in the 1930's comprised a once-daily night sailing to Rosslare (plus in the summer some daytime extra sailings) and bi-weekly sailings to Waterford (from Fishguard on Mondays and Fridays; from Waterford on Tuesdays and Saturdays).

Following a severe fire on board at Fishguard in 1929, *St Patrick (I)* was condemned and a new boat of the same name, *St Patrick (II)*, was built by the John Brown shipyard on the Clyde to replace her in 1930. However, *St Patrick (I)'s* Brown-Curtis single reduction geared turbines of 1926 were saved and transferred to the *St Andrew (I)* in 1930. *St Patrick (II)* was a 1900-ton, 913 passenger vessel having 216 first, and 116 third, berths. She was intended as a relief ship for both the Irish and Channel Islands routes, and in the late 1930's, *St Patrick (II)* sailed regularly from Weymouth during the summer and relieved or assisted the *St Andrew (II)* and *St David (II)* in the winter at Fishguard.

Two new oil-fired boats, similar to *St Patrick (II)* but 800 tons larger were launched in 1932 for the Fishguard service. They were capable of speeds of 21 knots and took the names of the old *St Andrew* and *St David*. Those, in consequence, were renamed, the *St Andrew (I)* becoming the *Fishguard* for a short period before being sold for scrap in 1933; similarly the *St David (I)* became the *Rosslare* in 1932 before also being sold to John Cashmore at Newport for scrapping. The new ships were designed to carry cargo and motorcars as well as passengers. They were constructed by Cammell-Laird, were twin screw turbine driven, with single reduction gearing, instead of the triple screw direct drive

turbines of the older ships. Both had four Babcock & Wilcox water tube boilers operating at 230 psi. The *St David (II)* and the *Isle of Sark* (built for the Southern Rly at the same time) were among the first ships to be built according to the recommendations of the International Convention for the Safety of Life at Sea.

The 1912-vintage *Waterford* had been sold off to a Philippines company in 1924, but the 1902-vintage *Great Western (II)* and *Great Southern* continued to sail up until the early 1930's, the *Great Western (II)* spending the summers of 1921 onwards at Weymouth to help bring over Channel Islands produce. *Great Western (II)* was succeeded by a new ship of the same name in 1933 (when *Great Western (II)* became *GWR No 20* for a few months before being sold for scrap; the *Great Southern* followed for scrap in 1934). While the 1700 ton *Great Western (III)* did carry passengers, she was principally a cargo and cattle carrier for the Fishguard-Waterford night service, and was GW-owned. She had three ventilated holds for cargo and could accommodate 666 cattle, and had special stalls that could take 35 horses. Among other boats at Fishguard at that time were *GW No 183*, a 28 ft motor launch in 1930. Later she was transferred to Weymouth. *Pen Cw (II)* was a third motor launch (40 ft long) built for Fishguard, in 1938. (*Pen Cw (I)* had been a 168 ton paddle steamer tug built for the GW in 1912 by Eltringham's of South Shields which worked at Fishguard and was sold in 1927; Pen Cw was the name of rocks near the harbour at Fishguard). The 95-ton *Sir John Wright* was a single screw 95-ton tug that worked at Fishguard from 1921-1938.

After the independence of the Irish Free State in 1922, export and import customs duties applied, all the paperwork for which the GW, as Port Authority, was responsible. According to Leslie King, it was an invoicer's nightmare! The GW undertook to perform all customs clearances and similar tasks, and to this end the customs facilities at Fishguard were expanded in 1925. Matters were complicated by various disputes between the countries at different times and that since the bulk of imports from Eire were perishable duty was, in theory, to be paid on clearance of the goods without which the goods could not be sent on. Problems were overcome by the GW acting for all the separate traders as a go-between with Customs, guaranteeing quick clearance. In the 1930's the GW dealt with £1 million in duties per year employing over 30 clerical staff for the task. The fees received for this work were determined by the RCH (a graduated scale based on weight with a maximum of 6s for one consignment; and a separate scale for livestock at the rate of 1d per horse, with a minimum of 4s and a maximum of 7/6d for any number of horses in one consignment).

On the outbreak of war in 1939, *St Andrew (II)* (H C Bond captain) and *St David (II)* (C Joy, then B H Mendus, captains) together with their crews were requisitioned by the War Office. They were converted into hospital ships (nos 24 and 27 respectively) each having 267 beds, 58 medical staff and 93 crew. Both took part in the Dunkirk evacuation. The *Great Western (III)* remained to operate the Waterford service. *St Patrick (II)* was requisitioned for a troop transport in September 1939 and sailed between Avonmouth and France until October when she came to the Rosslare route. In June 1941, *St Patrick (II)* was bombed off Strumble Head as she approached Fishguard, broke in two and sank with the loss of 29 lives; there were 66 survivors. Stewardess Mary Owen was awarded the George Medal and Lloyd's War Medal for her bravery in saving the life of an injured passenger whom she supported in the water for two hours without lifejackets. *St Patrick (II)* was replaced by the SR's *Hantonia,* but the service was suspended for the duration in January 1942. The *Innisfallen* belonging to the British & Irish Steam Packet Co (formerly the City of Cork Steam Packet Co) was sunk in the Mersey when off her regular route. Both the *St Andrew (II)* and *St David (II)* went to Malta in 1943. *St David (II)* was sunk in 1944, 25 miles south of the Anzio beach head where *St Andrew (II)* was also damaged. The Waterford service was temporarily suspended in April 1944, when *Great Western (III)* was requisitioned for cross Channel trooping during that D-Day summer, after which she returned to GW service. Shots for "Western Approaches", a Ministry of Information film, were taken at Fishguard in 1944. Captain Read, GWR Harbour Master and Marine Assistant, and his staff assisted the Crown Film Unit producers. The launch *Pen Cw(II)* and one of the quarter boats of the *Great Western (III)* appear in the film. Eventually the damaged *St Andrew (II)* returned, was repaired at Birkenhead and re-opened the post-war Irish service in 1946.

Replacement vessels for the sunken *St David (II)* and *St Patrick (II)* were ordered after WWII. The new *St David (III)* and *St Patrick (III)* were 3400 ton sister ships which, however, differed internally since *St David (III)* was a night boat for Fishguard while *St Patrick (III)* - despite her name - was a day boat for Weymouth. *St David (III)* was the first to be delivered from Cammell-Laird at Birkenhead and was running out of Fishguard in July 1947. She spent September 1947 at Weymouth. *St Patrick (III)* finished her trials in January 1948, so was not handed over until after nationalisation. Since, technically, she belonged to the Fishguard & Rosslare Docks & Harbour Co (which was not nationalised) she continued in the old GWR colours and flew the GW house flag.

ABERDOVEY (owned; formerly Cambrian Railways)

The port at Aberdovey served parts of three Welsh counties: south Merioneth; north Cardiganshire; and western Montgomeryshire (which was otherwise landlocked) by means of an up-river wharf at Derwenlas near Machynlleth. The harbour originally was privately owned but in 1865 was acquired by the Cambrian Railways. Oak bark and timber, farm produce and both lead and copper ores from Llanidloes were exported from Aberdovey and, until major improvements were made to Aberystwyth harbour in the late 1830's, timber cargoes from North America were unloaded at Aberdovey to be rafted under tow to Aberystwyth. But the backbone of trade in Aberdovey's heyday centred on the slate products of Abergynolwyn, Corris and elsewhere in south Merioneth. Slate underpinned maritime activity, even when it was in decline at the end of the C19[th]. Imports were timber, grain and limestone (burned in local kilns to spread upon the acid soils of the district).

The Aberystwith & Welch [sic] Coast Rly arrived in Aberdovey in 1863-4; a year later it became part of the new Cambrian Rlys. The A&WCRly was promoted on the basis that the harbours at Aberystwyth and Aberdovey would become busy ferry stations for Ireland, particularly for passengers and goods from the English Midlands who, despite the difficult terrain of mid-Wales, would arrive on railways along the valleys of the Severn, and Dovey or Mawddach. The line from Morben (Dovey Jct) ran behind the town of Aberdovey on its way to Arthog and Barmouth, and a short branch was constructed along the top of the beach and out on to the quay. Until the Dovey river bridge at Morben had been built, and the coast line completed, the Cambrian operated a ferry service across the Dovey estuary from Aberdovey to Ynyslas (Borth) from 1867-69, worked by the small wooden paddle tug *Lady Elizabeth.*

Grand plans proposed by Thomas Savin the railway contractor on behalf of the Cambrian Rlys to improve the existing harbour at Aberdovey and to introduce steamer services, came to nothing owing to local disputes about navigation and the hostility of the local sailing vessels interests who felt that Savin's plans were aimed at creating opportunities for new railway company steamers rather than benefiting the long-established Aberdovey sailing fleet. Nevertheless, the arrival of the railway did prompt the construction of the Talyllyn Rly from quarries at Brynyreglwys down to Towyn Wharf, where the 2 ft 4 ins gauge trams were run directly on to standard gauge railway wagons to be brought to Aberdovey dock for shipment (see *GWR Goods Wagons*). Steamers did eventually appear on the coastal trade and *Telephone* (succeeded by *Dora*) of the Aberdovey and Barmouth Steamship Co plied between Liverpool and the northern ports of Cardigan Bay right up to WWI. Schooners continued to dominate the slate trade, however, because the railways could not compete in terms of freight rates. In truth the shipping rates were so low as to make them barely profitable.

Around 1880 the whole country was in a deep economic depression and slates were stockpiled on the quays awaiting shipment. In an effort to bring traffic on to their lines and revive the hoped-for Irish trade, the Cambrian Rlys commenced new harbour works at Aberdovey in 1883, including extensive cattle pens at Sands sidings. This time, the new harbour facilities were welcomed locally since Aberdovey's sailing fleet was diminishing year by year. In 1883 the Waterford & Aberdovey Steam Shipping Co began operating two passenger steamers *Cambria* and *Liverpool* both of about 250 tons. These vessels delivered pigs, sheep and cattle from Ireland (Arklow, Rosslare, Waterford, Wexford and Wicklow, but not Dublin) several times a month. In 1889 the Cambrian itself was authorised to run steamers up and down the coast between Aberdovey, Aberystwyth, Portmadoc and Pwllheli, and also to Ireland. To operate these services it bought up the Waterford &

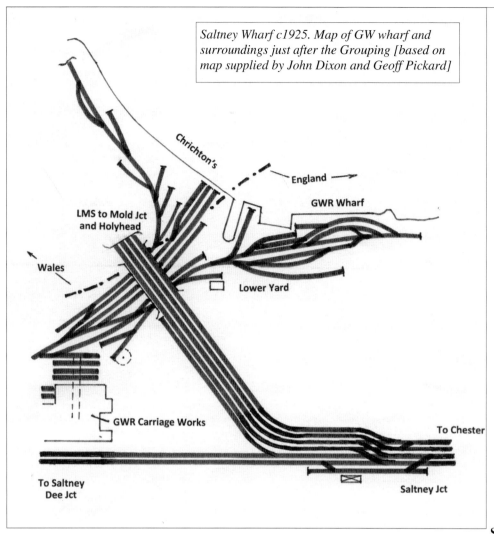

Saltney Wharf c1925. Map of GW wharf and surroundings just after the Grouping [based on map supplied by John Dixon and Geoff Pickard]

the wharf and pier at Aberdovey to herself, so much so had shipping declined. She steamed out of Aberdovey for the last time in the winter of 1916; she was torpedoed off the Mull of Galloway in the spring of 1917.

When the GW took over the harbour at the Grouping, the prosperity of Aberdovey already depended on summer tourists. Nevertheless, small as it was, and as insignificant as it became, Aberdovey remained one of the ports owned by the GW right through to nationalisation. The last trade of any significance occurred in 1927 with the import of cement that was taken away by rail for the construction of dams to form reservoirs in mid-Wales; this was a repeat of the same exercise performed in 1863, when cement was imported at Aberdovey and taken to the Llanfyllin branch for water reservoirs being built at Lake Vyrnwy to supply Liverpool with water.

SALTNEY (owned; ex-Shrewsbury & Chester Rly)

Aberdovey shipping company. Thus the Irish service envisaged 30 years previously in the A&WCRly prospectus came into being. However, passenger traffic to and from Ireland did not materialise and, threatened with a rate war by the LNWR (Holyhead service) and the GWR (New Milford service), the Cambrian gave up and withdrew from shipping services. The Cambrian Rlys used Aberdovey as a landing place for its materials, and a creosoting plant for imported sleepers was set up at Sawmill siding.

The Cambrian's Harbour Accounts of 1882 for Aberdovey states that the system of loading slates by hand at the new jetty was 'behind the times' and that more stevedores should be employed, particularly since sailing ships could find themselves weatherbound at Aberdovey for weeks owing to the long bar at the entrance to the port, and a day saved in loading might allow a vessel to make her passage. Brittle slates did, however, have to be carefully stowed so as not to work loose and be damaged at sea.

There was a steam flour mill at Arduwy and wheat (much of it originating from South Australia) was brought by sea from Liverpool for grinding. But this was gone in 1920. In the early years of the C20th, the Cambrian Rlys shipping records show that the coaster *Dora* virtually had

Despite problems of silting and difficulties of navigation on the Dee, Chester's river outlet at Saltney wharf was busy with traffic long before the arrival of the railway, particularly with goods for North Wales which was difficult to reach by road owing to the mountainous terrain. The Shrewsbury & Chester Rly opened in 1846 and a line from South Dee Jct (between Ruabon and Chester) was taken to Saltney Wharf. Rail freight to and from the wharf commenced a year or so later (the harbourmaster was in charge of goods at the wharf itself and at Saltney station). A low water wharf was completed about the same time to complement the original quay, giving a total quayage of some 587 ft.

After the rail connexion was made, North Wales traffic from the Chester area 'reversed direction' to bypass all the problems of navigation on the Dee that limited the size of vessels that could use Saltney Wharf. Instead of going out by ship, goods from the Chester area passed by rail over the Chester & Birkenhead Rly (opened in 1844) to Merseyside ports where cargo was transferred to coasters sailing to Wales. Despite the extra transhipment, the economics were presumably favourable. Even after the opening of the Chester and Holyhead Rly, low-rated goods traffic was

A view of the wharf from the bank of the River Dee showing the jib of one of the large cranes facing out of the picture; a second large crane is at the extreme left. [J Dixon and R Pickard collections]

G. W. RY. WHARF. SALTNEY.

carried this way well into the C20th. Much of the early traffic brought by rail to Saltney Wharf to be shipped out originated at collieries and ironworks around Brymbo and Minera on the Wheatsheaf branch. Imports to Saltney came in small sailing ships bringing iron ore from Barrow, a few returning with coal, and corn for Cobden's mill in Wrexham.

In the competition between different railway companies at that time, Huish of the LNWR was bullying the Birkenhead, Lancashire & Cheshire Jct Rly (the later Birkenhead Rly) to make timetabled train connexions so awkward for both the Chester & Birkenhead Rly, and the Shrewsbury & Chester Rly, that none of their traffic could get through to Liverpool and Manchester via Warrington. In response, the S&CRly chartered a steamer to tow boats with its goods traffic from Saltney to and from the Mersey. In fact the BL&CJRly exchanged far more traffic with the S&C than with the LNWR, and its craven action in fear of the LNWR led to the S&C obtaining compulsory running powers over the BL&CJRly in 1851, which were ultimately inherited by the GWR when the S&C Rly and S&B Rly asked to be taken over by the GW in 1854.

The GW's earliest steamers were inherited from the S&CRly. They were the two wooden paddle tugs *PT Cymro* (70 tons) and *PT Test* whose duties were towing at Saltney Wharf The *Derby* was brought secondhand in 1880 to replace the 54-year old *Cymro*, and the 56 ton *Manxman* of 1891 was purchased by the GWR in 1894 to replace the 40-year old *Test*.

Silting up and difficulties of navigation remained, however, and the wharf at Saltney was falling out of use in the years leading up to WWI. In 1912 the GW withdrew its tug from river. The wharf sidings were counted as part of

the Lower yard of the extensive GW marshalling yards at Saltney and had been useful for wagon storage; but after 1925, extra siding accommodation was provided at the Saltney Middle and Upper yards, and the wharf branch fell into disuse.

According to a 1929 re[port by the GW Chester Division civil engineer, the Dee Conservancy Board proposed improvements to navigation by dredging but it was unable to obtain funding.

BIRKENHEAD/LIVERPOOL (served)

In 1801 the population of Birkenhead was about 100 when the population of Liverpool across the River Mersey was nearly 80,000. Liverpool on the northern side of the river had its first wet dock in 1715 and had grown as a port because of the easily navigable rivers, turnpikes and later canal connexions to Manchester and the surrounding manufacturing towns of Lancashire.

At the beginning of the C19th, although there was some industrial activity on the Wirral, Liverpool continued to grow inexorably while Birkenhead slumbered. However exporters and importers were not happy, on two counts, with the state of affairs at Liverpool docks. By the 1820's there were not enough berths for the number of ships wanting to dock; and secondly, the way of calculating dock charges was considered to be unreasonable, in particular 'town dues' which Liverpool Corporation pocketed. Shippers and merchants based outside Liverpool (particularly those in Manchester) objected since they obtained no benefit to what was, in essence, a rates subsidy. Town dues would be one of the reasons behind the GWR's backing the proposal to set up the Mersey Docks and Harbour Board, and to the eventual proposal for a Manchester Ship Canal. Given the

BIRKENHEAD.

The Company have large Goods and Mineral Stations and extensive warehouse accommodation for Grain and General Merchandise. Their trucks run alongside the Steamers' berths, Dock Warehouses, and Oil Distributing Depôts; and Goods, Coal and Minerals, etc., are transhipped direct.

The Company's Stations are particularly convenient for dealing with the extensive meat traffic, being close to the foreign animals wharf at which cattle are landed, and connected by rail with the Lairages, where the animals are slaughtered and loaded.

The China, Japan, Java, India and South Africa Steamers load at the Morpeth, Egerton and Wallasey Docks, and at the Great Float, near to the Company's Warehouses, and every facility exists for carrying from all parts of the Kingdom in connection with these Steamers.

Collection and delivery can also be made by barge to and from any of the Birkenhead and Liverpool Docks.

Special facilities exist for dealing with **COAL** traffic at the Great Float, where four hoists and six flat tips are provided.

The Company's Stations and Receiving Offices are:—

MORPETH DOCK (for Shipment Traffic).

CATHCART STREET STATION AND WHARF.

CANNING STREET (for Town Traffic).

ARGYLE STREET.

WOODSIDE (Inquiry Office and Passenger Station).

ABBEY STREET,
JACKSON STREET,
TUNNEL ROAD,
BLACKPOOL STREET, } For Coal and Mineral Traffic.

Goods should be addressed and consigned " per Great Western Railway."

LIVERPOOL.

The Company have Stations and Receiving Offices at:—

CARRIER'S DOCK,   DUKE'S DOCK,

MANCHESTER DOCK,   STANLEY DOCK,

11, JAMES STREET, and 3, RANELAGH STREET,

and other authorised Receiving Offices in all parts of the City. The Company's carts collect and deliver Merchandise in all parts of Liverpool.

The Company also collect and deliver Merchandise by barge direct from and to all the Mersey Docks and Harbour Board's Docks, on both the Liverpool and Birkenhead sides of the Mersey, thus ensuring prompt despatch of shipping traffic in both directions. The Company also undertake the shipping of Coal in any quantities at the tips of the Mersey Docks and Harbour Board.

Through Rates are in force by the Great Western Railway Route to and from London, Birmingham and South Staffordshire, the South and West of England, Channel Islands, Severn Ports, and North and South Wales.

ISLE OF MAN.

There are through booking arrangements between the G.W.R. System and the Isle of Man (via Liverpool and the Isle of Man Steam Packet Company's Steamers), for General Merchandise.

discontent with Liverpool, plans for docks at Birkenhead were first mooted in 1828 in which William Laird was a prime mover (he had moved his boilermaking and shipbuilding firm across to Birkenhead from Liverpool in 1824). In fact, Birkenhead was on the more sheltered, and deeper-channelled, side of the river and was a better place to have docks than Liverpool, but (at least before the arrival of the railway) could not be reached so easily from the Lancashire manufacturing areas.

The 1828 proposal for a dock at Birkenhead came to nothing, but a second scheme was put forward in the 1840's for which Parliamentary approval was granted and financial backing gained. The docks were based upon deepening and walling-in the large marshy inlet known as Wallasey Pool between Woodside and Seacombe, off which wet-docks would be located with entrance locks and basins from the Mersey. In 1847 the first two Birkenhead docks (Egerton and Morpeth) were opened. Crucial in their development was the active involvement of the Chester & Birkenhead Rly (opened in 1840), and the Birkenhead, Lancashire &

Cheshire Jct Rly (incorporated in 1846) which ran from Chester to Walton Jct (Warrington) and thence by running powers over the Grand Jct Rly to Manchester. Furthermore, connexions with other new railways gave additional routes to Birkenhead from (a) the North Wales coalfields and ironworks around Wrexham and Brymbo (North Wales Mineral Rly of 1846 into Chester with a connexion to Saltney Wharf over the Chester & Holyhead Rly); (b) Coalbrookdale and other Salop towns (Shrewsbury & Chester Rly, opened 1848); and (c) the Midlands manufacturing areas (Shrewsbury & Birmingham Rly, opened 1849). It was hoped that all these places to the south would look to Birkenhead as their 'export' docks and connexion with all these lines did eventually secure Birkenhead's importance in rail-borne goods docks traffic. But first the antagonism of the recently-formed LNWR to the other railway companies serving Shrewsbury had to be overcome.

The LNWR had been formed in 1846 from the Liverpool & Manchester, the Grand Jct, the Manchester &

Birmingham and the London & Birmingham railways. It controlled access to Liverpool docks and now controlled the BL&CJct's connexion at Warrington that gave access to Manchester. Under Huish as General Manager, the LNWR was predatory to neighbouring small railways. In the north, it bullied the BL&CJct (which had taken over the C&B in 1847) not only to block traffic between Manchester and the rival port of Birkenhead, but also to block traffic coming from the S&B and S&C. Around Wolverhampton the LNWR also did its best to prevent S&B traffic from reaching Birmingham. In desperation, the two Chester companies sought the help of the GWR. Eventually in 1854, with the agreement of the two companies and the support of the Birkenhead Dock Commissioners (but with the LNW, Chester & Holyhead and BL&CJct railways opposing) Parliament approved the GW's taking over the S&C and S&B. This gave the GW access to Birkenhead via inherited S&C running powers from Chester over the BLCJct Rly. This was a direct challenge to the LNWR for traffic between the Midlands and Merseyside. Matters were complicated by the fact that the LNWR had already obtained running powers over the BL&CJct Rly in 1850. Relations between the GW and LNW did, however, improve in the years following and in 1860 it was agreed that the BL&CJct Rly (which had changed its name to the Birkenhead Rly in 1859) should be run jointly by the GW and LNW; the line remained a separate company until nationalisation in 1948. The act stipulated that Birkenhead and Liverpool dock rates should be made the same, and thereafter the way was open for Birkenhead docks to develop fully.

While all these events were taking place on the railways that would serve Birkenhead, construction of the docks there was in a mess, owing to financial and political shenanigans. The quality of construction was not too good and Thomas Brassey the well-known railway contractor (a local man) was not able to complete the dock works with the funds available. Debts grew, loans could not be repaid and eventually in 1855 the Birkenhead Trustees got Liverpool to take over Birkenhead Docks. Actual dock trade at Birkenhead at this time was less than 2% of the total trade of the Mersey, despite the fact that problems continued with lack of dock accommodation in Liverpool. Birkenhead's desuetude resulted mainly from its poor dock facilities and from well-judged rate reductions by Liverpool to keep its volume of business. The little freight that there was at Birkenhead comprised imports of guano (bird droppings used for fertiliser) and timber, and exports of Welsh coal and other goods coming up from the south. Despite the small number of ships using Birkenhead, the availability of land led to much industrial development on the Dock estate. For example, in addition to Lairds, other ship-repairing yards were established on the waterfront. There were also brick and lime works etc. Brassey's 'Canada Works', which was originally set up in 1853 to build and supply equipment for the Grand Trunk Railway in Canada (precursor of the Canadian National Rly), were producing railways for all over the world and in 1857 used a number of the dock warehouses to construct the first trans-Atlantic telegraph

The new GWR office at Hood St, Liverpool, when opened in 1911. This was the GW's central goods and parcels depot in Liverpool from where traffic was barged over to Birkenhead (later taken through the Birkenhead Tunnel). [Rly Magazine]

The office of the GW Agent in Belfast. [D J Hyde collection]

cable that would be laid by Brunel's *SS Great Eastern*.

The BL&CJct Rly and others had invested enormous sums (about £1 million) in harbour construction at Birkenhead on which they were seeing little return. There was a suspicion that the Liverpool Trustees were avoiding completion of Birkenhead docks in favour of further

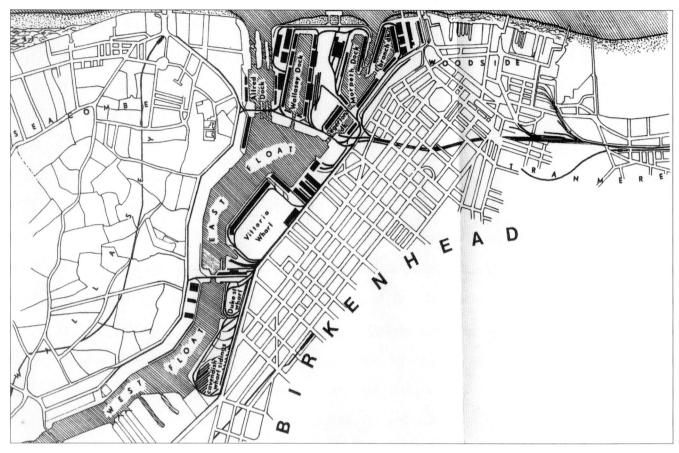

Map of Birkenhead docks for 1910. [Mersey Maritime Museum]

construction at Liverpool itself. The BL&CJct Rly, the Manchester Chamber of Commerce and the Manchester Commercial Association were fed up with the problems at Birkenhead and Liverpool, with its rival factions and exorbitant rates. This led to a country-wide Parliamentary investigation of dock charges. Manchester interests, supported by the GWR, induced Parliament to pass the Mersey Conservancy Bill in 1858 by which the Liverpool docks, the Birkenhead docks, and the bodies responsible for the buoying, pilotage and dredging of the Mersey, were merged into one public trust (the Mersey Docks & Harbour Board). Part of the scheme setting up the MD&HB was an obligation to complete the docks at Birkenhead and very large sums were invested, around £5 million, causing much acrimony among Board members, some of whom regarded the Birkenhead construction as a 'bottomless pit'. [The new Dock Board did little, in the event, to meet the Manchester objections to the payment of excessive 'monopolistic' rates and in 1883 a Bill to construct a ship canal from the Mersey to Manchester was promoted, the canal being opened throughout in 1894]. Birkenhead Corporation had difficulty in getting the MD&HB to complete works on its side of the river so that proposals for new facilities on the Birkenhead side that would not come under the control of the MD&HB were encouraged. The Tranmere foreshore (part of which was occupied by the Laird shipyards) seemed an ideal anchorage for large vessels and the GWR prepared a scheme

in 1892 for a dock capable of taking Atlantic liners, as well as general cargo ships. It was claimed that despite the longer rail journey, passengers would arrive in London earlier by the GW from Birkenhead than from Liverpool by the LNWR. The scheme was, of course, opposed and the GW withdrew its Parliamentary Bill on the understanding that the MD&HB would itself provide the facilities. What the Board then did was to buy up the land to frustrate any similar ideas in the future!

When the Wallasey 'Great Float' dock at Birkenhead was finally fully opened in 1860, a number of the quays were in a very poor state and entrance was still via the Morpeth and Egerton Docks rather than the planned big separate locks. It was difficult to persuade shipowners to use Birkenhead, even though ships entering the Great Float were granted a free indemnity against any responsibility for damage if the gates or walls gave way! Birkenhead's early experience proved that the existence of a brand-new, up-to-date, railway-connected dock did not guarantee the arrival of ships, because there also had to be present all the agents, merchants, bankers, brokers, factors and so on necessary to transact shipping business; they were across the Mersey in Liverpool and actively opposed development of rival docks having lower charges.

Nevertheless, a long-lasting major feature of the Birkenhead docks was that railways along the quays were planned integrally with construction of docks and

Imported meat carcases in a GW insulated container on a GW motor lorry at Birkenhead in July 1931. About to be loaded on t2o an old G9 Serpent C (holes along side raves), recently converted to carry containers from its original use of conveying agricultural machines or horse-drawn furniture vans. The container (No. E 572) was built in June 1930. Will be conveyed to Smithfield Market in London. [GWR]

warehouses. This enabled loading and unloading to be carried out in one operation and contrasted strongly with Liverpool where there was far less space for tracks in the crowded confines of the docks. Thus the practice of carting goods from the Liverpool & Manchester Rly terminus goods depot into the docks continued for most of the Victorian period (125,000 tons carted by the LNWR alone in 1851). Furthermore the sizes of the individual docks at Liverpool were soon too small to handle the biggest sailing vessels and also incapable of berthing the ever-bigger steamships in which world trade was being performed. Ultimately these facts gave Birkenhead its opportunity against Liverpool, particularly in the quick handling of perishable goods such as fresh meat, flour and fruit from quayside direct to wagon. Birkenhead Docks blossomed after the Northern Lock Entrances were opened in 1866. The docks were equipped with the latest hydraulic cargo handling equipment, coal tips and so on. There was a widespread hydraulic capstan and reel system for moving wagons over the quays. The first major shipping firm to show interest in Birkenhead was the

Cunard Steamship Company, whose owners had suffered substantial losses through vessels being detained in the Mersey awaiting berths at Liverpool.

The dates of opening, size and main use, of the different docks at Birkenhead, were as follows:

Morpeth (nearly 12 acres, 1847) and *Morpeth Branch* dock including lock (4 acres, 1870, being the closed-off former Woodside Basin with access to the Mersey) having a combined quayage of a mile-and-a-half, used almost exclusively by ships in South African, Indian, China and Dutch East Indian trades;

Egerton (about 4 acres, 1847, with 700 yds of quays for general cargo); enlarged 1890.

Great Float (111 acres, 1851-60)----later split into East Float with one basin and West Float with two basins. The water area of East Float was 59 acres with two miles of quays, used by grain ships, and steamship companies trading with China, India, Burma and South Africa and having one fixed hydraulic coal hoist for bunkering and six hydraulic coal tips for flats or barges). The water area of West Float was 52 acres with 2 ½ miles of quays, used by vessels coaling (one moveable and two fixed coal hoists) or undergoing repairs; and also for petroleum and general traffic (a special 87-ton crane was located there).

Low Water basin (nearly 13 acres, 1863; converted in 1877/8 into Wallasey wet dock having 1500 yards of quays used for general cargo and grain ships).

Alfred Dock (nearly 9 acres, 1866, originally part of the Float, 611 yards of quays, principally used as a 'vestibule dock' for vessels proceeding to and from the Great Float and adjoining docks, but also used for some cargo handling); enlarged 1895 and 1903.

Inner and Outer Northern Entrances, 1866.

Canal dock at Corn Warehouse, East Float 1869.

GWR basin, Morpeth dock 1869 (filled in during 1920's rebuilding)

Vittoria (over 11 acres, 1909---the Vittoria Wharf was originally part of the East Float---with 1200 yards of quays used mainly by steamers engaged in the Far Eastern trade and also some general cargo);

Bidston (nearly 11acres, 1933, additional quays for general cargo).

There were also three graving docks with a total floor length of 2430 feet.

Before taking over the joint running of the Birkenhead Rly with the LNWR in 1860, the GW had inherited the S&C running powers to Birkenhead over the BLCJct Rly and in 1854 it had taken over a large area of reclaimed land (the South Reserve) between Morpeth Dock and the Low Water Basin (the later Wallasey Dock) on which to house a goods depot for its town and shipment traffic. Reclamation came from tipping the enormous amount of earth excavated in digging out the new docks. The site was close to the Woodside Ferry landing stage. The GW opened a small depot in 1859, and in 1869 a fully-equipped goods station was brought into use which then remained in substantially the same form until the opening of the Mersey Tunnel in the 1920's. There were, of course, goods facilities at Birkenhead from BL&CJct/BR days and from the time after the Birkenhead Rly became jointly managed by the GWR and LNWR. The latter company rented the old Cathcart St depot for its goods offices and yard; traffic increased so much that in 1873 the LNW had to open a large new goods depot at Egerton dock. The old Birkenhead Rly Canning St shed eventually became the GW town goods depot. All mileage and coal traffic was, however, handled at joint yards in Birkenhead, as was all goods traffic at wayside stations on the Birkenhead Rly. In the 1870's there were

joint mileage yards in Birkenhead at Abbey St, Jackson St and Old Chester Rd (also called Tunnel Rd yard); an additional mileage yard was opened in 1881 at Blackpool St and yet another in 1913 at Hinderton Rd (when the Abbey and Tunnel yards closed). Only in Birkenhead and Chester did each of the joint companies maintain its own goods depots: Morpeth had to be large as it handled all the GW traffic from Liverpool as well as Birkenhead (unlike the GW, the LNW had no need to cater for Liverpool traffic on the Birkenhead side, of course, but Chester was important for the LNW as a transfer centre). In competing directly with the LNWR for Birmingham, Bristol and London goods traffic from Liverpool, the GW had to run an efficient cross-Mersey operation.

All Liverpool and Birkenhead goods traffic passing to and from the Great Western system went through Morpeth Dock goods depot (except for coal and other mileage traffic mentioned above). Until the opening of the Mersey Tunnel, all GW traffic to and from Liverpool was taken across the Mersey from or to Morpeth, either by railway cartage vehicles on the ferries, or by barge. Distinction ought to be made between goods to and from ships in the docks, and local goods, although local traffic for Liverpool and traffic for the Liverpool docks might find itself all carried together across the Mersey. There were through booking arrangements for general merchandise between the GWR and the Isle of Man via Liverpool (the Isle of Man Steam Packet Co). By the turn of the C19[th]/20th, the GW had depots on the Liverpool shore at Carriers' dock (also called the Langton, or North, dock); Duke's dock (the original BC&LJct depot); and Manchester dock, the latter near the Pier Head in Liverpool being the Joint Birkenhead Rly goods receiving, covered boatage and cartage depot. Manchester dock had started life as a tidal basin for Mersey Flats belonging to the Mersey & Irwell Navigation Co, and later the Shropshire Union Canal Co (a subsidiary of the LNWR), but came to be used by railway companies, part being leased to the C&B in 1860; it was not rail-connected. The Manchester dock site was the GW's first depot on the Liverpool side. After 1872, the GW/LNWR and LNWR/SU canal jointly occupied the whole of the north side and three berths at the east end, with the GW alone occupying the three remaining berths at the east end and the whole of the south side. A new warehouse was built soon after. Local and shipment traffic was handled by all the depots, dependent on destination and customer requirement. In lots of 10 tons and upwards, shipment traffic could be barged direct from Birkenhead alongside ships in any of the Liverpool docks. Morpeth goods depot included a large water basin under the roof of the main building (the 'GWR Branch Dock' of 1869 connected to the Morpeth dock) where barges were loaded and unloaded into railway wagons. Mersey flats and Leeds & Liverpool Canal boats were also berthed there. The GW had expected to generate lots of traffic from coasters using

Opposite page - Grain being craned by grab through the removable roof hatch of the 20-ton convertible hopper grain van no 42243 to Diagram V20 at Birkenhead docks, before being worked to Cobden Flour Mills at Wrexham. Unloading was through a bottom hopper controlled by the handwheel near the brake v-hanger) or by suction pipe through the hatch. The vans, introduced in 1927, could be converted into vans for ordinary merchandise having a flat floor by swinging down the interior hopper ends. [GWR]

the Low Water Basin at Birkenhead with its direct access to the Mersey, but early problems with silting up were never solved, so in 1877 the MD&HB converted the Low Water Basin into the enclosed Wallasey Dock.

The shunter's trucks employed at Morpeth yard were different from the standard GW design, in that shunters rode in the wagon that was fitted with waist-high hand rails and a pillar hand brake. The first batch of this type was built in 1897 and more followed in 1909. Earlier shunting trucks of standard GWR design sent to Birkenhead had been returned to Swindon as 'unsuitable'. Why this particular design was preferred at Morpeth is not known.

Although the Manchester dock depot in Liverpool belonged to the Birkenhead Joint Rly, it almost entirely handled GW traffic. It was badly damaged by fire in 1890 and was rebuilt the next year. Just before WWI, the GW opened a number of additional depots in Liverpool, the naming of which is confusing since different names were used at different times for what were the same places. In 1911 it adapted existing premises Hood St/Tryon St near the Liverpool markets 'for use as a goods and passenger depot'; the depot was called Hood St. In the same year the GW took over buildings at Chaloner St/Norfolk St to convert to a goods depot that eventually opened in 1914; this was known as Chaloner St South End depot. That year too saw another depot open along the riverfront on the Liverpool side at Lightbody St (which had warehousing and a timber stacking yard, and was linked to the Leeds & Liverpool Canal). This depot was called Stanley Dock station. After its opening, the GW gave up premises belonging to the Manchester Ship Canal at Stanley dock which it had been using. Similarly in 1914 it stopped using MSC premises at the Carriers dock and opened a new depot in a nearby location (the Langton & North docks station), at which a new waterside depot with a new service of flats and barges was opened. This depot became more important in later years as it was convenient for the new down-river ocean docks at Liverpool. There were also GW passenger and parcels receiving offices in the city of Liverpool at Ranelagh St, and at James St (the BL&CJct's old office, where the GW District Goods Manager's office was located).. Boatage services, and cross-Mersey lighterage, remained integral with the operation of the Morpeth depot until the 1920's. Indeed it was customary that a vessel berthed at one of the Birkenhead quays would unload part of its cargo into lighters moored alongside, for landing elsewhere in the docks or taken along the navigations and canals. This speeded up ship turn-around times at a single berth. Grain was often dealt with in this way and it is surprising, perhaps, to discover that much of the grain exported from New York came as ballast in passenger ships. Except for the very early days of the BL&CJctRly, the Birkenhead Rly contracted barging to the SU Canal Co.

Railways other than the GWR and LNWR had yards in the Birkenhead docks estate. The Cheshire Lines Committee opened a warehouse in 1871, and additional yards in 1892; and the Manchester, Sheffield & Lincolnshire Rly (GCRly after 1905) opened a depot in 1896. The GCR's route up the middle of the Wirral, having bridged the Dee at Hawarden, gave an alternative route that, many years later in 1933, made the Bidston Dock development at Birkenhead easier to accomplish. While the railway companies controlled operations within the environs of their own goods depots, the connecting tracks over the dock estate to their own main lines were under MD&HB management and operated under various bye-laws. All companies with premises on the dock estate were permitted to use their own (or hired) shunting locos on the dock 'mainlines' (in Birkenhead docks, unlike Liverpool, the MD&HB operated none of its own locos except for permanent way work). Shunting contractors were a feature of Birkenhead docks and firms that had once hired out horses, later hired locomotives. Firms delivering or removing goods from the actual quayside berths were exempt from the tolls charged to those who used the dock railway system just as a means of getting to their factories and works from the main lines. At the end of the C19[th] there were nearly 40 miles of track on the Birkenhead dock estate; the length had grown to nearly 50 miles by WWI after the construction of large flour mills. The numerous road/rail bridges, which opened for the passage of ships, were bottlenecks for road and railway traffic alike, as they were in other docks elsewhere.

After WWI the GW Morpeth goods depot was dealing with an average of 1,700 tons of goods daily, representing over 400 railway wagon loads; of the total, perhaps 1,000 tons of traffic would have come over from Liverpool, involving 300 road vehicles being passed over by ferries. The amount of barged traffic from Liverpool had declined considerably by that time (delays in locking in and out on both sides of the tidal river prevented lighters running to a timetable), so much so that the SU Canal Co gave up its carrier business in 1921. Just before, and just after, WWI the GW put in some improvements to cope with the increased traffic through Morpeth: the shed loading platform was extended and additional sidings installed in 1914, along with a crane road and new delivery office; and in 1922 an outside covered goods platform adjoining the shed was provided with improved rail connexions with the dock lines. But the prospect of the new road tunnel encouraged the GW to rent more land from the MD&HB and completely remodel the layout of the Morpeth depot, maximising the number of sidings, cart roads, sheds etc. The GW branch dock for lighters and barges inside the main building at Morpeth was filled in, allowing more goods platforms under one roof. Similarly, on the Liverpool side, the GW Traffic Committee had decided in 1920 that it was no longer necessary to continue with the goods depot at Hood St and the site was sold (but confusingly a new depot was opened at Hood St in 1941 to maintain GW services after most of the other GW depots on the Liverpool side had been bombed out). The GW concentrated its facilities at Manchester Basin, the company giving up other accommodation previously rented from the MD&HB, and taking over a large shed vacated by the LNWR. At the Manchester Basin some activities were joint with the LNWR (through the Birkenhead Rly), and some were solely GW. Manchester dock was later filled in with spoil from the new Mersey Tunnel in 1930 and the GW depot there was renamed the Pier Head depot. Despite refusing any barged traffic for loading/unloading at the quays after 1921, the facility to barge large loads direct to and from shipside was nevertheless maintained by the GW for some years afterwards.

Remodelling work was finally finished at the GWR Morpeth depot in 1933, by which time all the wagon turntables of the old shed and yard at Morpeth were eliminated. Compared with the former capacity of about 540 trucks, the new scheme had room for nearly 850 trucks, of which over 280 were accessible to road vehicles, as against 174 originally. After the opening of the Mersey Tunnel, most goods was taken to and from Liverpool by motor lorry. The rearrangements included additional 'holding, marshalling, reception and in-position' sidings out in the yard. Road layout was much improved, to avoid the bottlenecks caused by the original main approach road having to share the same dock bridges that carried the tracks serving the depot. Up-to-date depot facilities were installed, including a 30-ton electric goliath travelling gantry crane spanning three sidings and adjacent cart roads outside the shed. Improved weighing facilities were made available, such as a 35-ton truck weighbridge. Ten electric capstans and about 40 reels were installed at suitable points for internal yard shunting. An extra-wide cartway faced the outwards platforms of the depot with the intention of later installing equipment for 'demountable body' cartage working which had just then been installed at South Lambeth goods depot. However it was never put in since demountable bodies for motor lorries fell out of favour after the 'mechanical horse' had been shown to be so versatile.

On the Liverpool side, GW goods traffic (except coal and livestock) totalled some 225,000 tons annually just before and after WWI. Of that, about 150,000 tons was forwarded (nearly all general merchandise) and 75,000 tons received (of which 10,000-odd tons was minerals). In GW literature, it was advised that information on rates, shipment of coal, and other information could be obtained not only from the MD&HB itself but also from the GW District Goods Manager at Liverpool.

Cargoes through Birkenhead

By the middle-end of the C19th imports and exports on the Mersey had both grown and changed: manufactured engineering goods, machinery, chemicals, railway equipment etc in addition to cotton goods ----and coal and salt --- were exported from the Mersey; and wool now came in ever-increasing quantities from Australia and South Africa, meat from the Argentine and New Zealand, wheat from Canada, Australia and Argentina, fruit from the Mediterranean, South Africa and Brazil, tea and rice from India and China, palm oil from Africa, jute and linseed from India, cotton from Brazil, etc. Huge quantities of finished manufactured goods from the Midlands passed through Birkenhead. Much of the Mersey's Far Eastern and South American trade was concentrated there, with shipping lines such as Brocklebank, Bibby, Holt, Clan, and the Pacific

Steam Navigation Co, all having assigned berths. Just before WWI, for every 1000 tons of grain, oil, meat and general goods imported into Birkenhead, about 3000 tons of locomotives, rolling stock, Lancashire cotton goods, artificial manures and general merchandise were exported.

Birkenhead was a natural outlet for coal from the North Wales coalfield around Wrexham but it is surprising, perhaps, to realise that the export of *South Wales* coal contributed significantly to the early growth of Birkenhead as a port. The rail connexion to the south was completed in 1856 by the opening of the Newport, Abergavenny & Hereford Rly, and enabled Birkenhead to provide a service of South Wales bunker coal for the numerous steamships berthing in the Mersey. Six hydraulic hoists were installed in 1861 at Vittoria Creek on the south side of the Great Float which were capable of lifting 8-ton wagons 20 feet above the quay. Stevedoring companies/coal agents were charged 3d/ton for use of the hoists. Birkenhead also loaded colliers with bunker coal for distribution to the coaling stations across the world. Cargo coal was also shipped as part loads or ballast, frequently on ships returning to Ireland. As newer ships became taller, the hoists at Birkenhead had to be improved so as to be able to lift wagons higher to clear the sides of the vessels. New hoists were constructed from 1890, including a moveable hoist at Duke Street capable of lifting a loaded coal wagon 50 feet into the air that obviated moving the ship to line up different holds at a stationary hoist.

Transport of South Wales coal to Birkenhead was a regular earner for not only the GW but also the LNWR with its lines from Merthyr and Tredegar to Abergavenny and the north. The extent of the traffic is indicated by the number of coal trains timetabled into Birkenhead. In 1865 there were four GW and one LNW as well as three GW coal trains from North Wales. The number of coal trains continued to increase up to the end of the C19th with seven GW and ten LNW from South Wales as well as eight GW trains from the Wrexham area. In addition there were seven coal trains to 'run if required' (RR in the Service Timetable) and, of course, all the trains of returned empty wagons. In 1886, Birkenhead exported nearly 2 million tons of coal, of which over half was carried by the GW. Owing to the need for cheap coal for other purposes, coal was also *imported* into Birkenhead by coastal shipping. In 1885, for example, six coal trains (and six more 'RR') were timetable to leave the port for inland destinations. Although railways were integral with the design of Birkenhead Docks, there was inadequate siding and marshalling accommodation for the increasing number of coal wagons, and congestion problems remained until the 1890's. The problem was caused, in part, by the fact that all the different types of goods handled in the port were brought in on common railtracks, in contrast to the dedicated coal ports in South Wales where extensive storage sidings were provided not only in the dock area but also along the main lines leading to the docks.

While the demand for large quantities of South Wales bunkers coal continued well into the C20th, the amount of rail-hauled coal into Birkenhead fell off rapidly after Rea's (a major Merseyside coal handling and lighterage company) began shipping coal by coastal vessels from the Bristol Channel in the 1890's. The railways could not compete with the firm's charge of 4/- per ton to move coal from South Wales to Merseyside. Also, by this time, many coaling stations in the Pacific were being supplied with coal from Australia rather than by collier from Britain. Even so, coal exports from Birkenhead remained high right up to the 1930s at over 500,000 tons/annum, most now from North Wales and Shropshire. In 1931, for example, a total of 625,000 tons of coal from all sources were exported, about half of which was shipped to Ireland. There were, in the 1920's still 16 timetabled coal trains (five GW and eleven LMS) scheduled into Birkenhead. Coal traffic in 1922-23 represented 80% of the total tonnage handled by the GWR at Birkenhead, and 33% of all goods trains. Many ships that unloaded at Liverpool were sent the two miles across the Mersey to Birkenhead for loading and bunkering. The imbalance in full and empty wagon movements between the two ports, particularly between the wars, caused many traffic working problems.

As in South Wales, complaints were made that tipping from too great a height broke up the coal into smaller lumps and some 'anti-breakage boxes' were installed at Birkenhead. In the 1924 edition of *List of Collieries on or connected with the Great Western Railway* it was stated that there were (a) in the West Float, one movable hydraulic hoist and two fixed hydraulic hoists; and (b) in the East Float, one fixed hydraulic hoist and three hydraulic tips for barge loading (for 20-ton gross weight end-door wagon loads). By 1932, while facilities in the East Float had not altered, one of the fixed hoists in the West Float had been

removed to be replaced by a 500-ton/hour electric belt conveyor that could handle 12-ton end-door, or 20-ton bottom door, wagons; the remaining fixed hoist could handle 22¼ ton gross weight end-door wagons. Two belt conveyors of 200 tons/hour and 500 tons/hour capacity respectively were installed in 1925 and 1931 at the South Vittoria Wharf on the East Float. The Brocklebank Line's *SS Malakand* took on 2,415 tons of bunkers coal in 14 hours using the latter conveyor. As coal traffic declined, the coal appliances at Birkenhead began to be used for the export of sand, fluorspar and crushed gravel and other minerals, when not required for coal.

Birkenhead also specialised in the handling of bulky cargoes and heavy lifts. An 87 ton steam crane was available at the Cavendish Wharf on the south of the West Float. Unusual loads came to Birkenhead because the Liverpool Overhead Railway (built 1893-6) made access into the Liverpool docks difficult. One Liverpool firm of crane manufacturers (Dunlop, Bell and Co) had to take its cranes by rail via Warrington to Birkenhead for export. While Liverpool is only two miles from Birkenhead as the crow flies, the shortest journey round the Mersey is some 40 miles. In pre-Grouping days, wagon-loads of traffic for Liverpool docks originating on the GW, and articles of exceptional dimensions or weight best kept on rail vehicles right up to shipside, were sent from GWR territory over the Cheshire Lines Committee route via Helsby to access Liverpool docks. Vehicles of all shapes and sizes passed through Birkenhead: locomotives from Beyer Peacock in Manchester and the Vulcan (old Tayleur's) Foundry at Newton-le-Willows, trucks from Alvis and so on. In addition to carrying exceptional loads to the quays for export, the dock railway lines were busy with local traffic between the heavy engineering works located on the Great Float, eg Thomas Brassey's, and ships boilers from Lairds steelworks on Beaufort Rd to their shipbuilding yards on the river. Laird Bros merged with Cammell & Co (steel plate makers of Sheffield) at the end of the C19th to form the Cammell-Laird shipbuilding company. Its 76-acre yard at Tranmere had two wet docks (15 acres and nearly 3 acres), two graving docks with a total length of 1,600 feet, and related equipment including a 150-ton crane.

In 1873 the Liverpool Oil Storage Company Limited built large concrete casements at the West Float for storing lubricating oil, fuel oil and petrol and in 1885 bulk storage tanks were constructed with pipes connecting directly to berths on the West Float. Four years later the Anglo-American Oil Company set up works at the end of the West Float for the blending of different grades of oil. Before WWI, thousands of gallons of various oils were dispatched in tank wagons or in barrels all over the country. By 1924 oil storage tanks with a total capacity of 39,000 tons had been erected and the demand for oil as bunker fuel for ships was increasing. At the West Float there was land for timber stacking and a number of saw-mills and woodwork factories grew up nearby, although most of the wood was moved on to be worked elsewhere, or was in the form of pit props for collieries. In comparison with the timber imported at Liverpool's Canada and Brunswick Docks, the Birkenhead trade was of minor importance.

The two principal imports into Birkenhead were grain and cattle. After the repeal of the Corn Laws in 1846, imports of grain from the Continent and ports around the Black Sea, rose quickly. New corn warehouses having a capacity of over 30,000 tons were built on the Great Float and trade grew so rapidly warehouses and transit sheds over the dock estate were pressed into service. In those days, the new warehouses stored imported grain prior to its onward transport by railway to inland mills in Birmingham and the Midlands, where it was converted into flour for bread making. Towards the end of the C19[th], the millers realised that it would be cheaper to have the mills at the coast, and only have to pay for transport around the country of the less bulky flour without husks etc. In 1893 Buchanans erected a flour mill at Birkenhead which was quickly followed by others, including Vernons mill in 1898 and the massive Ranks and Spillers mills in 1912 and 1914. As at other ports served by the GW, all were located on the quayside permitting direct discharge of the grain ships that, by this time, came from North and South America, Australia, India and Europe. At its peak between the wars, Merseyside was the second-largest flour milling centre in the world--- only Minneapolis in the USA being larger.   The mills of Merseyside could produce 1710 sacks/hour each weighing 10 quarters or 280 lbs. In 1926, some 700,000 tons of wheat were turned into over four million sacks of flour.   Another 400,000 tons of wheat were distributed from Merseyside for milling elsewhere. As sidelines, the milling firms moved into the production of animal feedstuffs using residues from milling, lower quality grain, and molasses. The oil cake product was transported by rail to country stations for local distribution.

Grain was carried in sacks at first: the Swindon wagon notebook said that 60 sacks of wheat were to be reckoned as 6 tons 12 cwt, and 60 of barley as 5 tons 7 cwt. The GW built a limited number of grain hopper wagons, starting with an experimental 20-ton convertible van in 1905 (diagram V10). For details of others, see *GWR Goods Wagons*. For grain traffic from Birkenhead to Cobden's Flour Mills in Wrexham, the GW built in 1927 a dozen new convertible wooden 20-ton vans with hopper floor and roof doors (diagram V27). They were converted to bulk cement wagons in the early 1930's but at the outbreak of WWII were reconverted back to grain wagons. All the grain vehicles were loaded through the roof with crane and grab. While some unloading of grain ships took place in this way, grain elevators/suction pipes were most often used to transfer grain to the dockside flour mills.

The second major import trade of the Birkenhead docks was livestock.   Irish cattle had been transported live from Ireland to ports on the British west coast since the C16[th] but in the late 1870's, the countries of North and South America began rearing sheep and cattle. These countries (and Australia and New Zealand later) could easily produce far more meat than they could consume, and the development of fast reliable steamships enabled the excess to be exported to feed the rapidly growing population of Victorian Britain; (the population doubled between 1800 and 1850 and doubled again by 1900). Since steamers with reliable refrigeration were yet to come, these animals had to be transported live over very long distances. The first cargo of 273 live cattle from the Americas was imported into Birkenhead in 1874.

Imported cattle fell into two categories, namely 'fat cattle' ready for immediate slaughter and 'store cattle' which required fattening before slaughter (or were imported for breeding purposes). Traditionally, in Britain, cattle had been slaughtered locally where the meat was going to be eaten, and many home-reared cattle used to be taken by train to towns from the countryside. This practice continued with imported cattle, regular trains being timetabled from Birkenhead to cattle markets all over the country, as well as trains of fresh meat or chilled meat slaughtered on the dock premises.

Originally, as at other British ports, foreign animals were landed at any convenient berth before being sold off to farmers or driven off to slaughter. There was always the danger of disease being brought into the country and spread by the importation of live cattle, and in 1860 a contagious bovine pleuro-pneumonia outbreak wiped out 187,000 cattle in Britain. In the two decades that followed, the country was swept by series of epidemics that decimated the cattle and sheep populations.   The government eventually realised that the only effective method of control was to slaughter infected herds and to restrict the import of foreign animals to prevent the re-introduction of disease. The Contagious Diseases (Animals) Act of 1878 made the import of animals from foreign countries illegal, unless it was carried out at a licensed isolated quay where the animals could be examined and quarantined or slaughtered. (Irish cattle did not fall under these regulations because, of course, all of Ireland was part of the UK until after WWI, and Irish animals continued to be landed wherever convenient). The Act laid down regulations for the disposal of cargoes found to be infected on arrival, along with procedures for the treatment of carcasses, slaughter-house by-products, fodder and manure. Nothing could be moved off a Foreign Animals Wharf without the permission of a Government Inspector. Since the movement of imported store cattle by rail could itself spread disease, this led to the requirement for cattle wagons (GW telegraph code Mex) to be disinfected before and after use. The Cardiff Bute docks had a Foreign Animal Wharf at its Roath basin; the cattle wharves at Bristol's Cumberland basin dealt mainly with Irish cattle.

The MD&HB built a huge complex of lairages, slaughterhouses, chill-rooms and meat-stores from 1878 onwards around Morpeth (Woodside) and Wallasey Docks to form the Birkenhead Foreign Animals Quay. The trade grew so quickly that warehouses at Wallasey and Morpeth Docks were converted into accommodation for cattle and sheep. The lairages covered nearly 100,000 square yards and provided accommodation for some 6,000 head of cattle and 16,000 of sheep. The slaughter houses could deal with 3,400 cattle and 3,000 sheep per day.

The importance of the foreign animal trade to Birkenhead may be judged from the fact that during the year 1876 only some 7,788 cattle, 14,452 sheep and 44 pigs had been landed in the whole Customs Port of Liverpool from abroad: in 1897, in contrast, 281,740 cattle and 286,611 sheep were landed in Birkenhead alone. The Birkenhead

MANCHESTER.

GOODS DEPÔT .. LIVERPOOL ROAD STATION.
RECEIVING OFFICE FOR GOODS .. No. 6, GEORGE STREET.

The Company have accommodation for dealing with all descriptions of Traffic, they also have **EXTENSIVE WAREHOUSES** and their own teams for collecting and delivering Merchandise in all parts of the City and Suburbs.

Through rates are in operation by the **GREAT WESTERN** route between **MANCHESTER** and **MANCHESTER DOCKS** and all parts of the Great Western Railway and lines beyond, including :—

LONDON. BIRMINGHAM.
SOUTH STAFFORDSHIRE.
SOUTH AND WEST OF ENGLAND.
SEVERN PORTS. SOUTH WALES.
SOUTH OF IRELAND. &C. &C. &C.
(For full list, see pages 54, &c.)

and excellent services of Express trains ensure prompt and expeditious transit to and from those Districts.

Inquiries and orders for the collection and delivery of Goods should be addressed to :—

Mr. J. W. MAY, Great Western Railway, LIVERPOOL ROAD STATION.

Information in regard to Goods Rates and arrangements may also be obtained from :—

Mr. R. A. STRADLING, District Goods Manager, 2, BROWN STREET.

TELEPHONE NUMBERS :—

GOODS AGENT'S OFFICE	746a Central.
DISTRICT GOODS MANAGER'S OFFICE ...	3882 City.
GEORGE STREET (No. 6) RECEIVING OFFICE	746 City.

Goods should be addressed and consigned " per Great Western Railway."

SCOTLAND.

There are through booking arrangements for all descriptions of traffic between the G.W.R. system and the Railways in Scotland. The G.W.R. route will be found a most convenient one to and from the South of England, Southampton, the Channel Islands, West of England, South Wales, Severn Ports, Birmingham, South Staffordshire and Shropshire. There is an efficient service of trains which ensures traffic between places served by the Great Western Railway and towns in Scotland being worked through in an expeditious manner.

The Company's Principal Agent for Scotland is :—

Mr. R. RICHARD,

34, Renfield Street,

GLASGOW.

WARRINGTON.

At **BANK QUAY STATION**, which is conveniently situated for the Town business, the Company have accommodation for general traffic and its teams perform the service of collection and delivery.

The Company have rail access to the principal Works and Private Sidings in the vicinity, also to the Warrington Lay-bye of the Manchester Ship Canal, the trucks being worked direct to vessels and to the Warehouses and Wharves adjoining.

The Company's representative is Mr. J Quine, whose address is 42, Sankey Street.

Goods should be addressed and consigned " per Great Western Railway."

lairages saw 40-50% of Britain's total trade in American cattle and sheep pass through them each year. The American trade peaked between June and November and was worth from £5 to £10 million annually. The slaughter of so many animals in one place led to the establishment of firms to utilise the by-products, meat in the animal being only some 85% of its value, the rest being in terms of hide and skin, entrails and other products. For the twenty or so years of its peak period of activity, Birkenhead was dealing with 500,000 animals per year. British Leather in Tranmere took hides, Birkenhead Oleo Company took fat for candle and chemical manufacture, and Thomson Brothers took bones for their gelatine and glue works on Tranmere Pool. Around forty other small firms existed at one time or another in the Dock estate using the blood, intestines and bones. The railways distributed the products of these firms around the country. Several thousand people, one way or the other, were employed at the lairages or in subsidiary activities.

The live animal trade fell off in the late 1890's when the development of reliable refrigeration made it possible to bring in frozen carcasses from far away without spoilage. It was far more economical to butcher an animal abroad and transport only the saleable cuts of meat to Britain. It also removed the distress to animals of a sea journey of several weeks and the need to feed them. Furthermore the solidly-frozen meat could be handled pretty roughly, whereas fresh or chilled meat required care, otherwise bruising and damage resulted. Liverpool came to specialise in frozen meat at Alexandra Dock and Albert Dock. Birkenhead dealt mostly in fresh meat and chilled meat (meat that had been hung in refrigerated rooms for at least 12 hours (often longer) after butchering at the quayside).

In the earliest days fresh meat was packed in railway hampers for distribution or, later, carcasses were sewn up in canvas or sacking; both types were transported in sheeted open wagons. By the end of the C19[th], the GWR catered for the different types of meat by having different types of flush-sided Mica meat van. Fresh meat was hung from hooks in the roofs of meat vans so that the carcases did not touch in order to minimise damage.

Later, in the 1930's, in response to road competition, refrigerated containers were introduced by the GW for meat traffic. Live cattle from the docks travelled in GW Mex wagons, in the W-index of wagon diagrams.

All meat and cattle trains were run as quickly as possible, in the one case because of needing to keep the meat fresh and in the other to minimise the stops laid down by regulation for watering and feeding the animals en route. In 1885, GW meat trains left Birkenhead at 4.15 pm and 6.0 pm, passing Chester Cutting at 5.5 and 6.25pm respectively, with consignments for all parts of the country but especially for London, Birmingham and South Wales. In later years 'The Meat' was the nickname of the 3.55pm 'C'-headcode vacuum-fitted express goods train from Birkenhead to Acton (due 11.00pm) and then to Smithfield. Imported meat generated far more rail traffic than home-reared beef: in 1903, some 70,000 tons of foreign meat was carried annually by the GWR and LNWR together from Birkenhead which was over ten times the tonnage of Scottish beef taken from Aberdeen by rail.

Use of the Birkenhead lairages fell off as the amount of refrigerated meat increased, and the Wallasey lairage was closed in 1910. The same happened elsewhere, the foreign animal wharves in Deptford in London (intended for animals from the Continent, dating from 1871 and connected to the LBSCR), closing just before WWI. However, a massive outbreak of foot-and-mouth disease in Ireland in 1912 changed matters. Because of the risk of introducing the disease into Britain, Irish cattle were now specially brought under the Foreign Animals Act regulations, and Birkenhead, Bristol and Glasgow designated as quarantine and slaughter centres. Since there were no quarantine facilities on the Liverpool side of the Mersey where Irish cattle were usually landed, Woodside took over and the Wallasey lairages were reopened. Thereafter, about a million animals were imported into them each year, just as long as it remained economical (particularly throughout WWI) to ship live animals from Ireland.

The lairages remained profitable up to the mid-1920's, but by 1930 they were losing money and once again, the Wallasey/Alfred Dock warehouses were returned to general goods traffic. In the event, after bomb damage in 1940, some of those sheds had to be returned yet again to the Cattle Wharf to maintain capacity. The Woodside facilities were still functioning at nationalisation and remained in operation until the early 1980's, but the number of animals passing through from Ireland fell right away.

There was much bomb damage during WW II. In January 1941, GW shunter Norman Tunna removed burning incendiaries from a wagon at Birkenhead containing 250 lb bombs, his bravery being acknowledged by the award of the George Cross. In 1941 the James St offices and part of the roof of the adjoining warehouse were bombed with incendiaries and destroyed by fire. The Lightbody St (Stanley dock) goods warehouse, offices and timber stacking yard were likewise destroyed and, at the Pier Head, the goods warehouse and two dock offices were severely damaged. To maintain GW facilities in Liverpool, a new

depot was opened in Hood St in 1941 (recall that there was a GW Hood St depot between 1911 and 1920). As soon as the Allies went on to the offensive in North Africa in 1941-2, much of the materiel for the campaign was shipped from Birkenhead. As many as six ordnance trains arrived daily, many over the GW from government factories at Harlescott and Nesscliff in Salop. Later, ammunition arrived from the USA, one ship of which required up to perhaps 300 wagons to clear. The great increase in traffic caused congestion on the dock railway and on the lines leading to it from the south. The problem was eased somewhat by putting in a connexion in 1942 between the joint line at Mickle Trafford, on the Warrington line out of Chester, and the adjoining CLC tracks from which the LNER (GC) route to Bidston could be reached.

ELLESMERE PORT (Manchester Ship Canal) (served)

Ellesmere Port, on the Birkenhead side of the Mersey, was where the Shropshire Union (SU) Canal entered the river and was therefore a 'canal dock' of seven acres in extent. The town of Ellesmere itself was due south of Wrexham on the later Cambrian Rlys line between Oswestry and Whitchurch, and the canal served Ellesmere, Ruabon, Oswestry etc. The Ellesmere and the Montgomery canals linked three rivers (the Severn, Dee and Mersey),and brought together the woollen and farming districts of Montgomeryshire, the coalmines and ironworks of Denbighshire, and the industrial areas of the north of England. Ellesmere Port was the most important ore-importing dock in the country in the early C19th, with considerable quantities being taken to the Midlands by water. Other traffic handled included cement, grain, flour, dyes, timber, machinery, tinplate, oil and petrol. The canal was leased by the LNWR in 1851 and bought outright in 1857. Because the region served by the SU canal was all in the territory of rivals (Cambrian Rlys and the GWR) in which it had no lines of its own, the LNWR worked the SU to the full, and improved handling facilities at the Ellesmere dock. At that time no railway passed near Ellesmere Port, traffic from Birkenhead to Manchester having to go down to Chester and then up through Warrington on the Birkenhead, Lancashire & Cheshire Jct Rly, later to be part of the Birkenhead Rly which itself was taken over jointly by the GW and LNWR in 1860. The journey between Birkenhead and Manchester was shortened by some 11miles when the Hooton-Helsby branch was opened in 1863; this line relieved the considerable congestion that had built up at Chester for traffic from northern areas to Birkenhead and it encouraged the transport of Lancashire coal. A station (called Whitby Locks until 1870) was opened at Ellesmere Port but there was no connexion with the canal docks. This seems odd given that the LNWR owned the SU canal, but there were complications in that the Trent & Mersey Canal (owned by the Midland Rly) competed for the same ore traffic as the SU canal, and also the LNWR itself competed for ore traffic through Garston dock on the Liverpool side of the river, the traffic being taken onwards by rail. Eventually the SU built an 'unofficial' horse-drawn tramway in 1870 to join the canal dock to the railway station and this remained in use until the Manchester Ship Canal (MSC) arrived at Ellesmere Port in 1891.

The building of the MSC had come about because of shippers' dissatisfaction with dues charged at Liverpool, particularly the 'town' dues for which only those resident in Liverpool gained any benefit (see Birkenhead). During the construction of the MSC, a line was built from the Hooton-Helsby branch over the SU canal to supply the workings, and after completion the line was bought by the SU company to replace the horse-drawn tramway. The MSC got to the River Weaver also in 1891 and a temporary port was established there for importing timber and grain, and exporting salt. The Birkenhead Rly built a 6-mile long branch from Ellesmere Port to the temporary dock and, during the period in which the MSC was being finished, carried a substantial amount of general goods traffic to and from Manchester. Afterwards, the branch was removed.

The MSC was opened throughout in 1894 and new opportunities were presented to Ellesmere Port since large ocean-going ships could now berth at the rail-connected quay on which the canal company ran its own locos. With a depth of water of 28 ft alongside the 1200 ft long wharf (later 2400 ft), vessels up to 14,000 tons could be berthed. A few industries had already become established around the dock and the number increased after the opening of the MSC (grain warehousing, galvanising and corrugated iron works, flour mills). The population of Ellesmere Port nearly doubled early in the C20th. The SU canal had been the largest employer in the area, but by the end of WWI its losses forced the LNWR to close it for goods traffic (it remained open as a waterway). Much of the canal freight transferred to rail. The SU canal docks were then leased to the MSC.

One of the MSC's developments after WWI was to install coal bunkering tips at Ellesmere Port (which was only 25 miles from the heart of the North Wales coalfield and somewhat closer than Birkenhead) but while they continued in use for many years, the move to oil-fired ships limited their potential. A major development immediately before the Grouping was the opening of an oil installation at Stanlow on the MSC and this brought new traffic to Ellesmere Port and the Birkenhead Rly. Facilities grew in the inter-war period, and expanded even more in WWII with a new Shell oil refinery and the Mollington Wervin Aviation Fuel Depot.

In GW literature, it was advised that information on rates, shipment of coal, and other information about Ellesmere Port could be obtained not only from the Manchester Ship Canal Co itself but also from the GW District Goods Manager at Manchester.

WARRINGTON (Manchester Ship Canal) (served)

Warrington was served by six railways before the Grouping but the GW was the first railway company to open a town office there in 1909 at 42 Sankey St, where J Quine was the representative. The GW maintained a goods depot at Bank Quay station and performed its own C&D cartage work. In addition to having rail access to the principal factories and private sidings in the vicinity, the GW had rail access to the Warrington lay-by of the Manchester Ship canal. Rail vehicles could be worked direct to vessels and to the adjoining warehouses and wharves.

MANCHESTER (SHIP CANAL DOCKS) (served)

The Manchester Ship Canal was built owing to dissatisfaction by traders with the operations of the port of Liverpool, particularly the imposition of 'town dues' (see section on Birkenhead). The 36-mile long canal was opened throughout in 1894. Long before that, however, the GW had running powers to Manchester from Walton Old Jct (at Warrington on the Birkenhead Rly, GW&LNW Jt) over the LNWR via Newton-le-Willows. In fact, from as early as 1850 the LNW had been providing facilities for the Birkenhead, Lancashire & Cheshire Jct Rly at (i) Manchester (Victoria) for passenger traffic; and (ii) Liverpool Road and Ordsall Lane in Manchester for goods traffic and warehousing. An alternative route to Manchester via Timperley and the Manchester, South Jct & Altrincham Rly for which the GW had running powers was later abandoned after the formation of the Birkenhead Rly in 1860.

Consideration was given by the GW to opening its own goods depot in Manchester but by the late 1870's it was decided that it was better to stick with the existing arrangement of employing the LNWR as agents and concentrating goods and clerical work at the Liverpool Rd depot where the GW continued to employ its own staff and to provide its own cartage service. There was also a GW Receiving Office for goods at 6 George St in Manchester. GW goods trains to and from Manchester with northern traffic were marshalled at Chester (Saltney) and could be hauled either by GW or LNWR locos (GW engines used part of Patricroft loco depot which was designated as a sub-shed of Chester). Such arrangements continued until the country-wide elimination of 'penetration rosters' in 1943 after when LMS locos took all goods trains since they could proceed onwards from Manchester whereas GW locos could not.

The L&Y and LNWR accessed the Manchester Ship Canal dock estate from the north and the Cheshire Lines Committee from the south. The GWR route to the docks was reached by a branch from Eccles. Through goods rates applied for the GW route between Manchester and Manchester Docks and all parts of the GW system and beyond, including to Ireland.

There were seven terminal docks when opened, along with three dry docks. Ships up to about 8,000 tons could transit the canal, the dimensions of locks being 535 ft by 64 ft. As the years went by various firms set up business on the dock estate, and the adjacent Trafford Park industrial estate became the largest in Europe. The MSC had its own railway that served the dock estate and Trafford Park.

If an incoming vessel called at Birkenhead en route to Manchester, it would be unusual for freight destined for somewhere on the GW system to be taken through to Manchester; similarly for outwards traffic. But if the vessel sailed directly to and from Manchester, the rail/ship-side connexion had to be made at Manchester Ship Canal docks. In this way, full or part wagon loads of goods to and from the GW could be taken by rail to Manchester Ship Canal docks, on the instructions of shippers for particular steamers, via the Birkenhead Rly and running powers.

Bibliography & References

In addition to numerous documents and pamphlets published by the GWR, the following books have been consulted:

A Glance Back at Lydney Docks by Neil Parkhouse. Lydney: Black Dwarf Publications, 2001.

A History of the Railways of the Forest of Dean by H W Paar. Part One: *The Severn & Wye Railway*; Part Two *The Great Western Railway in Dean* Newton Abbot: David & Charles 1st editions 1963 and 1965 respectively; 2nd editions 1973 and 1971 respectively.

A History of Truro by Viv and Bob Acton (vol 2) Landfall Publications 2002.

An Illustrated History of Cardiff Docks (3 vols) by J Hutton Silver Link press 2008/9.

A Real Little Seaport: the Port of Aberdyfi and its people 1565-1920 by Lloyd Lewis. Caernarfon: Gwasg Pantycelyn 1996.

A Regional History of the Railways of Great Britain, vol 12 South Wales by D S M Barrie David & Charles, 1980.

Birkenhead's Docks & Railways by K.McCarron and D.Marks. Liverpool University/Merseyside Maritime Museum Research Papers 1997.

Branch Lines around Plymouth by V Mitchell and K Smith. Middleton Press 1997.

Bridgwater Docks and the River Parrett (1st ed) by Brian Murless. Somerset County Library, 1983.

Bristol City Docks Remembered 1900 – 1973 by E J Farr, A T G Bower and R M Parsons. Bristol: The Bristol Shiplovers Society, 1986.

British Railways in the Great War by E A Pratt. 1921.

British Railways Pre-Grouping Atlas and Gazeteer (5th ed) by W Philip Conolly. Ian Allan.

Cardiff's Vanished Docklands by B Lee. Sutton Publishing 2006.

Chepstow Ships by G.E.Farr Chepstow: The Chepstow Society and the Newport and Monmouthshire Branch of the Historical Association, 1954.

Cornwall; Branches and Byways by J Vaughan. Oxford Publishing Co, 2002.

Cornwall (British Railways Past and Present) by D. Mitchell. Ian Allan, 1974.

Cornwall's Maritime Heritage by A Kittridge Truro: Twelveheads Press, 2003.

Devon Harbours by V.C.Boyle and D.Payne. London: Christopher Johnson, 1952.

Docks & Ports: 1 Southampton by D L Williams London: Ian Allan, 1984.

Docks, Railways & the Movement of Goods papers presented at Research Day School. Liverpool University/ Merseyside Maritime Museum Research Papers 1994.

Dunball Village Works and Wharf by G Body and R Gallop. Fuducia Press, 2001.

Dunkirk and the Great Western by Ashley Brown. London: GWR. (undated).

Felix Pole:His Book Town & Country Press, 1968.

Gloucester Docks by H.Conway-Jones. Gloucester: Alan Sutton & Gloucester County Library.

GWR Goods Wagons by A G Atkins, W Beard, D J Hyde and R Tourret. (originally in two vols, the combined) David & Charles, 1975/6; enlarged new edition in one vol, pub by Tourret Publishing 1998; reprinted by Ian Allan, 2013.

GWR Goods Services (various volumes) by Tony Atkins and David Hyde. Wild Swan, 2000 and subsequent dates.

Industrial Archaeology of Wales by D Morgan Rees. David & Charles 1975.

Isle of Portland Railways by B L Jackson. Oakwood Press 1999.

London's Docks by J Pudney. London: Thames & Hudson, 1976.

Merchant Fleets: Britain's Railway Steamers: Western and Southern Companies by D Haws. Hereford: TCL Publications, 1993.

Modern Railway Administration (2 vols) London: Gresham Publishing Co Ltd (1925).

Newton Abbot to Plymouth including Totnes Quay by V Mitchell and K Smith. Midhurst, W.Sussex: Middleton Press 2001.

Neyland – A Great Western Outpost by Richard Parker. KRB Publications, 2002.

150 Years of Southampton Docks by Bert Moody. Southampton: Kingfisher Railway Productions 1988.

Old Docks by Nancy Ritchie-Noakes. Shire Publications Ltd 1987.

Our Home Railways by W. J. Gordon. Fredk Warne, 1910.

Plymouth's Railways in the 1930's by R Leitch. Peterborough: RCTS 2002

Ports of the Exe Estuary 1660-1860 by E A G Clark. University of Exeter Press 1960/68.

Railway and Other Steamers by C L D Duckworth and G E Langmuir 1st edition Glasgow 1948; 2nd edition Prescot, Lancs: T Stephenson & Sons Ltd, 1968.

Railway and Seaport Freight and Movement by G. Bulkley. London: Crosby Lockwood 1930.

Railways of Cardiff by L. Waters. London: Ian Allan, 1995.

Reflections on the Portishead Branch by M Vincent. Oxford Publishing Co, 1983.

St Ives Port & Harbour by Bret Guthrie. St Ives Printing &Publishing Co, 1994.

Somerset Harbours by Grahame Farr. Christopher Johnson, 1954.

Teignmouth: A Maritime History by H J Trump. Chichester: Phillimore & Co Ltd. 2nd ed 1986.

The Avonmouth Story by Ethel Thomas. Dursley Glos: F.Bailey & Son and Derek Archer, 1977.

The Birkenhead Railway by T.B.Maund. Sawtry, Hunts: RCTS, 2000.

The Branch Lines of Cornwall by L Reade. Redruth: Atlantic Publishing, 1983.

The Bridport Branch by B.L.Jackson and M.J.Tattershall. Oxford Publishing Co, 1976.

The Brixham Branch by C.R.Potts. Oakwood Press, 1986.

The Exeter Canal by K.R.Clew. Phillimore, 1984.

The Fall & Rise of Birkenhead Docks by K.McCarron. Liverpool University/Merseyside Maritime Museum Research Papers 1998.

The Glamorganshire and Aberdare Canals vols 1 and 2 by S. Rowson and I.L.Wright. Whitney: Black Dwarf Publications 2004.

The Gloucester & Sharpness Canal by H. Conway-Jones. Stroud: Tempus Publishing, 1999.

The GWR in West Cornwall by A Bennett. Runpast Publishing 1988.

The Industrial and Maritime History of Llanelli and Burry Port 1750-2000 by R S Craig, R Prothero Jones and M V Symons. Carmarthen: Carmarthenshire County Council, 2005.

The Kingsbridge Branch by K.Williams and D.Reynolds. Oxford Publishing Co, 1977.

The Great Western Rly in Mid Cornwall by A Bennett. Kingfisher Rly Productions, 1988.

The Maritime Heritage of Dyfed by D Jenkins, J G Jenkins and S Evans. Cardiff: National Museum of Wales, 1982.

The New Maritime History of Devon (vol II) edited by M.Duffy et al. London: Conway Maritime Press, 1994.

The Oxford Companion to British Railway History J. Simmons and G.Biddle (eds) Oxford University Press, 1997.

The Ocean Railway by Stephen Fox. London: Harper Collins, 2003.

The Parrett Navigation by G Body and R Gallop. Fiducia Press, 2002.

The Pembroke & Tenby Railway by M.R.C.Price. Oakwood Press, 1986.

The Port of Chepstow by Ivor Waters. Chepstow, Gwent: The Chepstow Society, 1977.

The Ports and Harbours of Cornwall by R.Pearse. St Austell: H.E.Warne 1963

The Ports of the Bristol Channel (1893) anon. The London Printing and Engraving Co, 1893.

The Rhondda Valles by E D Lewis. Pheonix House, 1959.

The Story of Cornwall's Railways by A Fairclough. Truro: Tor Mark Press, 1970.

The Taff Vale Lines to Penarth by E.Mountford and N.Sprinks. Oakwood Press, 1993.

The Town of Chepstow by Ivor Waters Part I: Riverside. Chepstow: The Chepstow Society, 1972.

The West Cornwall Rly: Truro to Penzance by S C Jenkins and R C Langley. Oakwood Press, 2002.

The West Somerset Railway by C.R.Clinker. Exmoor Press, 1980.

The Weymouth Harbour and Tramway by G.Beale. Wild Swan, 2001.

Timetable for Victory (The British Railways War History) by Evan John. London: The British Railways Press Office, 1947.

Twixt Rail & Sea by W.G.Chapman: H.N. Appleby Ltd, 1927 (reprinted by Patrick Stephens Ltd, 1971).

War Reports of the General Manager to the Board of Directors 1914-1919 GWR, 1920.

Welsh Ports of the Great Western Railway by P Bennett and D Jenkins. National Museum of Wales, 1994.